THE SEABOARD PARISH

Page 10.

THE SEABOARD PARISH

A Sequel to "Annals of a Quiet Neighbourhood"

By GEORGE MACDONALD, LL.D.

GEORGE ROUTLEDGE AND SONS
NEW YORK: 416 BROOME STREET
1873

THE SEABOARD PARISH

A Sequel to "Annals of a Quiet Neighbourhood"

BY GEORGE MACDONALD, LL.D.

AUTHOR OF "ROBERT FALCONER," "RANALD BANNERMAN," "AT THE BACK OF THE NORTH WIND," ETC.

NEW YORK:
GEORGE ROUTLEDGE & SONS.
LONDON:
ALEXANDER STRAHAN & COMPANY.
1873.

TO

JAMES POWELL, Esq.

HIS GRATEFUL AND LOVING

SON-IN-LAW

DEDICATES THIS BOOK

CHAPTER I.

HOMILETIC.

EAR FRIENDS,—I am beginning a new book like an old sermon; but, as you know, I have been so accustomed to preach all my life, that whatever I say or write will more or less take the shape of a sermon; and if you had not by this time learned at least to bear with my oddities, you would not have wanted any more of my teaching. And indeed, I did not think you would want any more. I thought I had bidden you farewell. But I am seated once again at my writing-table, to write for you—with a strange feeling, however, that I am in the heart of some curious, rather awful acoustic contrivance, by means of which the words which I have a habit of whispering over to myself as I write them, are heard aloud by multitudes of people whom I cannot see or hear. I will favour the fancy that, by a sense of your presence, I may speak the more truly, as man to man.

But let me, for a moment, suppose that I am your grandfather, and that you have all come to beg for a story; and that, therefore, as usually happens in such cases, I am sitting with a puzzled face, indicating a more puzzled mind. I know that there are a great many stories in the holes and corners of my brain; indeed, here is one, there is one, peeping out at me like a rabbit; but alas! like a rabbit, showing me almost at the same instant the tail-end of it, and vanishing with a contemptuous *thud* of its hind feet on the ground. For I must have suitable regard to the desires of my children. It is a fine thing to be able to give people what they want, if at the same time you can give them what you want. To give people what they want, would sometimes be to give them only dirt and poison. To give them what you want, might be to set before them something of which they could not eat a mouthful. What both you and I want, I am willing to think, is a dish of good wholesome venison. Now I suppose my children around me are neither young enough nor old enough to care about a fairy tale. So that will not do. What they want is, I believe, something that I know about—that has happened to myself. Well, I confess, that is the kind of thing I like best to hear anybody talk to me about. Let any one tell me something that has happened to himself, especially if he will give me a peep into how his heart took it, as it sat in its own little room with the closed door, and that person will, so telling, absorb my attention: he has something true and genuine and valuable to communicate. They are mostly old people that can do so. Not that young people have nothing happen to them, but that only when they grow old, are they able to see things right, to disentangle confusions, and judge righteous judgment. Things which at the time appeared insignificant or wearisome, then give out the light that was in them, show their own truth, interest, and influence : they are far enough off to be seen. It is not when we are nearest to anything that we know best what it is. How I should like to write a story for old people ! The young are always having stories written for them. Why should not the old people come in for a share ? A story without a young person in it at all ! Nobody under fifty admitted ! It could hardly be a fairy tale, could it ? Or a love story either ? I am not so sure about that. The worst of it would be, however, that hardly a young person would read it. Now we old people would not like that. We can read young people's books, and enjoy them : they would not try to read old men's books or old women's books; they would be so sure of their being dry. My dear old brothers and sisters, we know better, do we not ? We have nice old jokes, with no end of fun in them ; only they cannot see the fun. We have strange tales, that we know to be true, and which look more and more marvellous every time we turn them over again; only somehow they do not belong to the ways of this year—I was going to say *week*,—and so the young people generally do not care to hear them. I have had one pale-faced boy, to be sure, who would sit at his mother's feet, and listen for hours to what took place before he was born. To him his mother's wedding-gown was as old as Eve's coat of skins. But then he was young enough not yet to have had a chance of losing the childhood common to the young and the old. Ah! I should like to write for you, old men, old women, to help you to read the past, to help you to look for the future. Now is your salvation nearer than when you believed; for, however your souls may be at peace, however your quietness and confidence may give you strength, in the decay of your earthly tabernacle, in the shortening of its cords, in the weakening of its stakes, in the rents through which you see the stars, you have yet your share in the cry of the creation after the sonship. But the one thing I should keep saying to you, my companions in old age, would be, "Friends, let us not grow old." Old age is but a mask; let us not call the mask the face. Is the acorn old, because its cup dries and drops it from its hold—because its skin has grown brown and cracks in the earth? Then only is a man growing old when he ceases to have sympathy with the young. That is a sign that his heart has begun to wither. And that is a dreadful kind of old age. The heart needs never be old. Indeed it should always be growing younger. Some of us feel younger, do we not, than when we were nine or ten? It is not necessary to be able to play at leap-frog to enjoy the game. There are young creatures whose turn it is, and perhaps whose duty it would be, to play at leap-frog—if there was any necessity for putting the matter in that light; and for us, we have the privilege, or if we will not accept the privilege, then I say we have the duty, of enjoying their leap-frog. But if we must withdraw in a measure from sociable relations with our fellows, let it be as the wise creatures that creep aside and wrap themselves up and lay themselves by, that their wings may grow and put on the lovely hues of their coming resurrection. Such a withdrawing is in the name of youth. And while it is pleasant—no one knows how pleasant except him who experiences it—to sit apart and see the drama of life going on around him, while his feelings are calm and free, his vision clear, and his judgment righteous, the old man must ever be ready, should the sweep of action catch him in its skirts, to get on his tottering old legs, and go with brave heart to do the work of a true man, none the less true that his hands tremble, and that he would gladly return to his chimney-corner. If he is never thus called out, let him examine himself, lest he should be falling into the number of those that say, "I go, sir," and go not; who are content with thinking beautiful things in an Atlantis, Oceana, Arcadia, or what it may be, but put not forth one of their fingers to work a salvation in the earth. Better than such is the man who, using just weights and a true balance, sells good flour, and never has a thought of his own.

I have been talking—to my reader is it? or to my supposed group of grandchildren? I remember—to my companions in old age. It is time I returned to the company who are hearing my whispers at the other side of the great thundering gallery. I take leave of my old friends with one word: We have yet a work to do, my friends; but a work we shall never do aright after ceasing to understand the new generation. We are not the men, neither shall wisdom die with us. The Lord hath not forsaken his people because the young ones do not think just as the old ones choose. The Lord has something fresh to tell them, and is getting them ready to receive his message. When we are out of sympathy with the young, then I think our work in this world is over. It might end more honourably.

Now, readers in general, I have had time to consider what to tell you about, and how to begin. My story will be rather about my family than myself now. I was, as it were, a little withdrawn, even by the time of which I am about to write. I had settled into a gray-haired, quite elderly, yet active man—young still, in fact, to what I am now. But even then, though my faith had grown stronger, life had grown sadder, and needed all my stronger faith; for the vanishing of beloved faces, and the trials of them that are dear, will make even those that look for a better country both for themselves and their friends, sad, though it will be with a preponderance of the first meaning of the word *sad*, which was *settled, thoughtful.*

I am again seated in the little octagonal room, which I have made my study because I like it best. It is rather a shame, for my books cover over every foot of the old oak panelling. But they make the room all the pleasanter to the eye, and after I am gone, there is the old oak, none the worse, for any one who prefers it to books.

I intend to use as the central portion of my present narrative the history of a year during part of which I took charge of a friend's parish, while my brother-in-law, Thomas Weir, who was and is still my curate, took the entire charge of Marshmallows. What led to this will soon appear. I will try to be minute enough in my narrative to make my story interesting, although it will cost me suffering to recall some of the incidents I have to narrate.

CHAPTER II.

CONSTANCE'S BIRTHDAY.

AS it from observation of nature in its association with human nature, or from artistic feeling alone, that Shakspere so often represents Nature's mood as in harmony with the mood of the principal actors in his drama? I know I have so often found Nature's mood in harmony with my own, even when she had nothing to do with forming mine, that in looking back I have wondered at the fact. There may, however, be some self-deception about it. At all events, on the morning of my Constance's eighteenth birthday, a lovely October day with a golden east, clouds of golden foliage about the ways, and an air that seemed filled with the ether of an *aurum potabile*, there came yet an occasional blast of wind, which, without being absolutely cold, smelt of winter, and made one draw one's shoulders together with the sense of an unfriendly presence. I do not think Constance felt it at

all, however, as she stood on the steps in her riding-habit, waiting till the horses made their appearance. It had somehow grown into a custom with us that each of the children, as his or her birthday came round, should be king or queen for that day, and, subject to the veto of father and mother, should have everything his or her own way. Let me say for them, however, that in the matter of choosing the dinner, which of course was included in the royal prerogative, I came to see that it was almost invariably the favourite dishes of others of the family that were chosen, and not those especially agreeable to the royal palate. Members of families where children have not been taught from their earliest years that the great privilege of possession is the right to bestow, may regard this as an improbable assertion; but others will know that it might well enough be true, even if I did not say that so it was. But there was always the choice of some individual treat, which was determined solely by the preference of the individual in authority. Constance had chosen "a long ride with papa."

I suppose a parent may sometimes be right when he speaks with admiration of his own children. The probability of his being correct is to be determined by the amount of capacity he has for admiring other people's children. However this may be in my own case, I venture to assert that Constance did look very lovely that morning. She was fresh as the young day: we were early people—breakfast and prayers were over, and it was nine o'clock as she stood on the steps and I approached her from the lawn.

"Oh, papa! isn't it jolly?" she said, merrily.

"Very jolly indeed, my dear," I answered, delighted to hear the word from the lips of my gentle daughter. She very seldom used a slang word, and when she did, she used it like a lady. Shall I tell you what she was like? Ah! you could not see her as I saw her that morning if I did. I will, however, try to give you a general idea, just in order that you and I should not be picturing to ourselves two very different persons while I speak of her.

She was rather little, and so slight that she looked tall. I have often observed that the impression of height is an affair of proportion, and has nothing to do with feet and inches. She was rather fair in complexion, with her mother's blue eyes, and her mother's long dark wavy hair. She was generally playful, and took greater liberties with me than any of the others; only with her liberties, as with her slang, she knew instinctively when, where, and how much. For on the borders of her playfulness there seemed ever to hang a fringe of thoughtfulness, as if she felt that the present moment owed all its sparkle and brilliance to the eternal sunlight. And the appearance was not in the least a deceptive one. The eternal was not far from her—none the farther that she enjoyed life like a bird, that her laugh was merry, that her heart was careless, and that her voice rang through the house—a sweet soprano voice—singing snatches of songs—now a street tune she had caught from a London organ, now an air from Handel or Mozart—or that she would sometimes tease her elder sister about her solemn and anxious looks; for Wynnie, the eldest, had to suffer for her grandmother's sins against her daughter, and came into the world with a troubled little heart, that was soon compelled to flee for refuge to the rock that was higher than she. Ah! my Constance! But God was good to you, and to us in you.

"Where shall we go, Connie?" I said, and the same moment the sound of the horses' hoofs reached us.

"Would it be too far to go to Addicehead?" she returned.

"It is a long ride," I answered.

"Too much for the pony?"

"Oh dear, no. Not at all. I was thinking of you, not of the pony."

"I'm quite as able to ride as the pony is to carry me, papa. And I want to get something for Wynnie. Do let us go."

"Very well, my dear," I said, and raised her to the saddle—if I may say *raised,* for no bird ever hopped more lightly from one twig to another than she sprung from the ground on her pony's back.

In a moment I was beside her, and away we rode.

The shadows were still long, the dew still pearly on the spiders' webs, as we trotted out of our own grounds into a lane that led away towards the high road. Our horses were fresh and the air was exciting; so we turned from the hard road into the first suitable field, and had a gallop to begin with. Constance was a good horsewoman, for she had been used to the saddle longer than she could remember. She was now riding a tall well-bred pony, with plenty of life—rather too much, I sometimes thought, when I was out with Wynnie; but I never thought so when I was with Constance. Another field or two sufficiently quieted both animals—I did not want to have all our time taken up with their frolics—and then we began to talk.

"You are getting quite a woman, now, Connie, my dear," I said.

"Quite an old grannie, papa," she answered.

"Old enough to think about what's coming next," I said gravely.

"Oh, papa! And you are always telling us that we must not think about the morrow, or even the next hour. But, then, that's in the pulpit," she added, with a sly look up at me from under the drooping feather of her pretty hat.

"You know very well what I mean, you puss," I answered. "And I don't say one thing in the pulpit and another out of it."

She was at my horse's shoulder with a bound, as if Spry, her pony, had been of one mind and one piece with her. She was afraid she had offended me. She looked up into mine with as anxious a face as ever I saw upon Wynnie.

"Oh, thank you, papa!" she said, when I smiled. "I thought I had been rude. I didn't mean it. Indeed I didn't. But I do wish you would make it a little plainer to me. I do think about things sometimes, though you would hardly believe it."

"What do you want made plainer, my child?" I asked.

"When we're to think, and when we're not to think," she answered.

I remember all of this conversation because of what came so soon after.

"If the known duty of to-morrow depends on the work of to-day," I answered—"if it cannot be done right except you think about it, and lay your plans for it, then that thought is to-day's business, not to-morrow's."

"Dear papa, some of your explanations are more difficult than the things themselves. May I be as impertinent as I like on my birthday?" she asked suddenly, again looking up in my face.

We were walking now, and she had a hold of my horse's mane, so as to keep her pony close up.

"Yes, my dear, as impertinent as you like—not an atom more, mind."

"Well, papa, I sometimes wish you wouldn't explain things so much. I seem to understand you all the time you are preaching, but when I try the text afterwards by myself, I can't make anything of it, and I 've forgotten every word you said about it."

"Perhaps that is because you have no right to under stand it."

"I thought all Protestants had a right to understand every word of the Bible," she returned.

"If they can," I rejoined. "But, last Sunday, for instance, I did not expect anybody there to understand a certain bit of my sermon, except your mamma and Thomas Weir."

"How funny! What part of it was that?"

"Oh! I'm not going to tell you. You have no right to understand it. But most likely you thought you understood it perfectly, and it appeared to you, in consequence, very commonplace."

"In consequence of what?"

"In consequence of your thinking you understood it."

"Oh, papa dear! you're getting worse and worse. It's not often I ask you anything—and on my birthday too! It is really too bad of you to bewilder my poor little brains in this way."

"I will try to make you see what I mean, my pet. No talk about an idea that you never had in your head at all, can make you have that idea. If you had never seen a horse, no description even, not to say no amount of remark, would bring the figure of a horse before your mind. Much more is this the case with truths that belong to the convictions and feelings of the heart. Suppose a man had never in his life asked God for anything, or thanked God for anything, would his opinion as to what David meant in one of his worshipping psalms be worth much? The whole thing would be beyond him. If you have never known what it is to have care of any kind upon you, you cannot understand what our Lord means when he tells us to take no thought for the morrow."

"But indeed, papa, I am very full of care sometimes, though not perhaps about to-morrow precisely. But, that does not matter, does it?"

"Certainly not. Tell me what you are full of care about, my child, and perhaps I can help you."

"You often say, papa, that half the misery in this world comes from idleness, and that you do not believe that in a world where God is at work every day, Sundays not excepted, it could have been intended that women any more than men should have nothing to do. Now what am I to do? What have I been sent into the world for? I don't see it; and I feel very useless and wrong sometimes."

"I do not think there is very much to complain of you in that respect, Connie. You, and your sister as well, help me very much in my parish. You take much off your mother's hands too. And you do a good deal for the poor. You teach your younger brothers and sister, and meantime you are learning yourselves."

"Yes, but that 's not work."

"It is work. And it is the work that is given you to do at present. And you would do it much better if you were to look at it in that light. Not that I have anything to complain of."

"But I don't want to stop at home and lead an easy, comfortable life, when there are so many to help everywhere in the world."

"Is there anything better in doing something where God has not placed you, than in doing it where he has placed you?"

"No, papa. But my sisters are quite enough for all you have for us to do at home. Is nobody ever to go away to find the work meant for her? You won't think, dear papa, that I want to get away from home, will you?"

"No, my dear. I believe that you are really thinking about duty. And now comes the moment for considering the passage to which you began by referring:—What God may hereafter require of you, you must not give yourself the least trouble about. Everything he gives you to do, you must do as well as ever you can, and that is the best possible preparation for what he may want you to do next. If people would but do what they have to do, they would always find themselves ready for what came next. And I do not believe that those who follow this rule are ever left floundering on the sea-deserted sands of inaction, unable to find water enough to swim in."

"Thank you, dear papa. That's a little sermon all to myself, and I think I shall understand it even when I think about it afterwards. Now let's have a trot."

"There is one thing more I ought to speak about though, Connie. It is not your moral nature alone you ought to cultivate. You ought to make yourself as worth God's making as you possibly can. Now I am a little doubtful whether you keep up your studies at all."

She shrugged her pretty shoulders playfully, looking up in my face again.

"I don't like dry things, papa."

"Nobody does."

"Nobody!" she exclaimed. "How do the grammars and history-books come to be written then?"

In talking to me, somehow, the child always put on

a more childish tone than when she talked to any one else. I am certain there was no affectation in it, though. Indeed, how could she be affected with her fault-finding old father?

"No. Those books are exceedingly interesting to the people that make them. Dry things are just things that you do not know enough about to care for them. And all you learn at school is next to nothing to what you have to learn."

"What must I do, then?" she asked with a sigh. "Must I go all over my French Grammar again? Oh dear! I do hate it so."

"If you will tell me something you like, Connie, instead of something you don't like, I may be able to give you advice.—Is there nothing you are fond of?" I continued, finding that she remained silent.

"I don't know anything in particular—that is, I don't know anything in the way of school-work that I really liked. I don't mean that I didn't try to do what I had to do, for I did. There was just one thing I liked—the poetry we had to learn once a week. But I suppose gentlemen count that silly—don't they?"

"On the contrary, my dear, I would make that liking of yours the foundation of all your work. Besides, I think poetry the grandest thing God has given us—though perhaps you and I might not quite agree about what poetry was poetry enough to be counted an especial gift of God. Now, what poetry do you like best?"

'Mrs Hemans's, I think, papa."

"Well—very well—to begin with. 'There is,' as Mr

Carlyle said to a friend of mine—'There is a thin vein of true poetry in Mrs Hemans.' But it is time you had done with thin things, however good they may be. Most people never get beyond spoon-meat—in this world, at least, and they expect nothing else in the world to come. I must take you in hand myself, and see what I can do for you. It is wretched to see capable enough creatures, all for want of a little guidance, bursting with admiration of what owes its principal charm to novelty of form, gained at the cost of expression and sense. Not that that applies to Mrs Hemans. She is simple enough, only diluted to a degree. But I hold that whatever mental food you take should be just a little too strong for you. That implies trouble, necessitates growth, and involves delight."

"I shan't mind how difficult it is if you help me, papa. But it is anything but satisfactory to go groping on without knowing what you are about."

I ought to have mentioned that Constance had been at school for two years, and had only been home a month that very day, in order to account for my knowing so little about her tastes and habits of mind. We went on talking a little more in the same way, and if I were writing for young people only, I should be tempted to go on a little farther with the account of what we said to each other; for it might help some of them to see that the thing they like best should, circumstances and conscience permitting, be made the centre from which they start to learn; that they should go on enlarging their knowledge all round from that one point at which

God intended them to begin. But at length we fell into a silence, a very happy one on my part; for I was more than delighted to find that this one too of my children was following after the truth—wanting to do what was right, namely, to obey the word of the Lord, whether openly spoken to all, or to herself in the voice of her own conscience and the light of that understanding which is the candle of the Lord. I had often said to myself in past years, when I had found myself in the company of young ladies who announced their opinions —probably of no deeper origin than the prejudices of their nurses—as if these distinguished them from all the world besides; who were profound upon fashion and ignorant of grace; who had not a notion whether a dress was beautiful, but only whether it was of the newest cut —I had often said to myself: "What shall I do if my daughters come to talk and think like that—if thinking it can be called?" but being confident that instruction for which the mind is not prepared only lies in a rotting heap, producing all kinds of mental evils, correspondent to the results of successive loads of food which the system cannot assimilate, my hope had been to rouse wise questions in the minds of my children, in place of overwhelming their digestions with what could be of no instruction or edification without the foregoing appetite. Now my Constance had begun to ask me questions, and it made me very happy. We had thus come a long way nearer to each other; for however near the affection of human animals may bring them, there are abysses between soul and soul—the souls even of father and daughter—over which they must pass to meet. And I do not believe that any two human beings alive know yet what it is to love as love is in the glorious will of the Father of lights.

I linger on with my talk, for I shrink from what I must relate.

We were going at a gentle trot, silent, along a woodland path—a brown, soft, shady road, nearly five miles from home, our horses scattering about the withered leaves that lay thick upon it. A good deal of underwood and a few large trees had been lately cleared from the place. There were many piles of faggots about, and a great log lying here and there along the side of the path. One of these, when a tree, had been struck by lightning, and had stood till the frosts and rains had bared it of its bark. Now it lay white as a skeleton by the side of the path, and was, I think, the cause of what followed. All at once my daughter's pony sprang to the other side of the road, shying sideways; unsettled her so, I presume; then rearing and plunging, threw her from the saddle across one of the logs of which I have spoken. I was by her side in a moment. To my horror she lay motionless. Her eyes were closed, and when I took her up in my arms she did not open them. I laid her on the moss, and got some water and sprinkled her face. Then she revived a little, but seemed in much pain, and all at once went off into another faint. I was in terrible perplexity.

Presently a man who, having been cutting faggots at a little distance, had seen the pony careering through the wood, came up and asked what he could do to help me. I told him to take my horse, whose bridle I had thrown over the latch of a gate, and ride to Oldcastle Hall, and ask Mrs Walton to come with the carriage as quickly as possible. "Tell her," I said, "that her daughter has had a fall from her pony, and is rather shaken. Ride as hard as you can go."

The man was off in a moment; and there I sat watching my poor child, for what seemed to me a dreadfully long time before the carriage arrived. She had come to herself quite, but complained of much pain in her back; and, to my distress, I found that she could not move herself enough to make the least change in her position. She evidently tried to keep up as well as she could; but her face expressed great suffering: it was dreadfully pale, and looked worn with a month's illness. All my fear was for her spine.

At length I caught sight of the carriage coming through the wood as fast as the road would allow, with the woodman on the box directing the coachman. It drew up, and my wife got out. She was as pale as Constance, but quiet and firm, her features composed almost to determination. I had never seen her look like that before. She asked no questions: there was time enough for that afterwards. She had brought plenty of cushions and pillows, and we did all we could to make an easy couch for the poor girl; but she moaned dreadfully as we lifted her into the carriage. We did our best to keep her from being shaken; but those few miles were the longest journey I ever made in my life.

When we reached home at length, we found that Ethel,

or, as we commonly called her, using the other end of her name, Wynnie—for she was named after her mother—had got a room on the ground-floor—usually given to visitors—ready for her sister; and we were glad indeed not to have to carry her up the stairs. Before my wife left, she had sent the groom off to Addicehead for both physician and surgeon. A young man who had settled at Marshmallows as general practitioner a year or two before, was waiting for us when we arrived. He helped us to lay her upon a mattress in the position in which she felt the least pain. But why should I linger over the sorrowful detail? All agreed that the poor child's spine was seriously injured, and that probably years of suffering were before her. Everything was done that could be done; but she was not moved from that room for nine months, during which, though her pain certainly grew less by degrees, her want of power to move herself remained almost the same.

When I had left her at last a little composed, with her mother seated by her bedside, I called my other two daughters—Wynnie, the eldest, and Dorothy, the youngest, whom I found seated on the floor outside, one on each side of the door weeping—into my study, and said to them :—"My darlings, this is very sad; but you must remember that it is God's will; and as you would both try to bear it cheerfully if it had fallen to your lot to bear, you must try to be cheerful even when it is your sister's part to endure."

"O papa! poor Connie!" cried Dora, and burst into fresh tears.

Wynnie said nothing, but knelt down by my knee, and laid her cheek upon it.

"Shall I tell you what Constance said to me just before I left the room?" I asked.

"Please do, papa."

"She whispered, 'You must try to bear it, all of you, as well as you can. I don't mind it very much, only for you.' So, you see, if you want to make her comfortable, you must not look gloomy and troubled. Sick people like to see cheerful faces about them; and I am sure Connie will not suffer nearly so much if she finds that she does not make the household gloomy."

This I had learned from being ill myself once or twice since my marriage. My wife never came near me with a gloomy face, and I had found that it was quite possible to be sympathetic with those of my flock who were ill, without putting on a long face when I went to see them. Of course, I do not mean that I could, or that it was desirable that I should, look cheerful when any were in great pain or mental distress. But in ordinary conditions of illness a cheerful countenance is as a message of *all's well*, which may surely be carried into a sick chamber by the man who believes that the heart of a loving Father is at the centre of things, that he is light all about the darkness, and that he will not only bring good out of evil at last, but will be with the sufferer all the time, making endurance possible, and pain tolerable. There are a thousand alleviations that people do not often think of, coming from God himself. Would you not say, for instance, that time must pass very slowly in pain? But have you never observed, or has no one ever made the remark to you, how strangely fast, even in severe pain, the time passes after all?

"We will do all we can, will we not," I went on, "to make her as comfortable as possible? You, Dora, must attend to your little brothers, that your mother may not have too much to think about now that she will have Connie to nurse."

They could not say much, but they both kissed me, and went away leaving me to understand clearly enough that they had quite understood me. I then returned to the sick chamber, where I found that the poor child had fallen asleep.

My wife and I watched by her bed-side on alternate nights, until the pain had so far subsided, and the fever was so far reduced, that we could allow Wynnie to take a share in the office. We could not think of giving her over to the care of any but one of ourselves during the night. Her chief suffering came from its being necessary that she should keep nearly one position on her back because of her spine, while the external bruise and the swelling of the muscles were in consequence so painful, that it needed all that mechanical contrivance could do to render the position endurable. But these outward conditions were greatly ameliorated before many days were over.

This is a dreary beginning of my story, is it not? But sickness of all kinds is such a common thing in the world, that it is well sometimes to let our minds rest upon it, lest it should take us altogether at unawares, either in ourselves or our friends, when it comes. If it were not a good thing in the end, surely it would not be; and perhaps before I have done my readers will not be sorry that my tale began so gloomily. The sickness in Judæa eighteen hundred and thirty-five years ago, or thereabouts, has no small part in the story of him who came to put all things under our feet. Praise be to him for evermore!

It soon became evident to me that that room was like a new and more sacred heart to the house. At first it radiated gloom to the remotest corners; but soon rays of light began to appear mingling with the gloom. I could see that bits of news were carried from it to the servants in the kitchen, in the garden, in the stable, and over the way to the home-farm. Even in the village, and everywhere over the parish, I was received more kindly and listened to more willingly, because of the trouble I and my family were in; while in the house, although we had never been anything else than a loving family, it was easy to discover that we all drew more closely together in consequence of our common anxiety. Previous to this, it had been no unusual thing to see Wynnie and Dora impatient with each other; for Dora was none the less a wild, somewhat lawless child, that she was a profoundly affectionate one. She rather resembled her cousin Judy, in fact—whom she called Aunt Judy, and with whom she was naturally a great favourite. Wynnie, on the other hand, was sedate, and rather severe—more severe, I must in justice say, with herself than with any one else. I had sometimes wished, it is true, that her mother, in regard to the younger children, were more like her; but there I was wrong. For one of the great goods that come of having two parents, is that the one balances and rectifies the motions of the other. No one is good but God. No one holds the truth, or can hold it, in one and the same thought, but God. Our human life is often, at best, but an oscillation between the extremes which together make the truth; and it is not a bad thing in a family, that the pendulums of father and mother should differ in movement so far, that when the one is at one extremity of the swing, the other should be at the other, so that they meet only in the point of *indifference*, in the middle; that the predominant tendency of the one should not be the predominant tendency of the other. I was a very strict disciplinarian — too much so, perhaps, sometimes: Ethelwyn, on the other hand, was too much inclined, I thought, to excuse everything. I was law, she was grace. But grace often yielded to law, and law sometimes yielded to grace. Yet she represented the higher; for in the ultimate triumph of grace, in the glad performance of the command from love of what is commanded, the law is fulfilled: the law is a schoolmaster to bring us to Christ. I must say this for myself, however, that, although obedience was the one thing I enforced, believing it the one thing upon which all family economy primarily depends, yet my object always was to set my children free from my law as soon as possible; in a word, to help them to become, as soon as it might be, a law unto themselves. Then they would need no more of mine. Then I would go entirely over to the mother's higher side, and become to them, as much as in me lay, no longer law and truth, but grace and truth. But to return to my children—it was soon evident not only that Wynnie had grown more indulgent to Dora's vagaries, but that Dora was more submissive to Wynnie, while the younger children began to obey their eldest sister with a willing obedience, keeping down their effervescence within doors, and letting it off only out of doors, or in the out-houses.

When Constance began to recover a little, then the sacredness of that chamber began to show itself more powerfully, radiating on all sides a yet stronger influence of peace and goodwill. It was like a fountain of gentle light, quieting and bringing more or less into tune all that came within the circle of its sweetness. This brings me to speak again of my lovely child. For surely a father may speak thus of a child of God. He cannot regard his child as his even as a book he has written may be his. A man's child is his because God has said to him, "Take this child and nurse it for me." She is God's making; God's marvellous invention, to be tended and cared for, and ministered unto as one of his precious things; a young angel, let me say, who needs the air of this lower world to make her wings grow. And while he regards her thus, he will see all other children in the same light, and will not dare to set up his own against others of God's brood with the new-budding wings. The universal heart of truth will thus rectify, while it intensifies, the individual feeling towards one's own; and the man who is most free from poor partisanship in regard to his own family, will feel the most individual tenderness for the lovely human creatures whom God has given into his own especial care and responsibility. Show me the man who is tender, reverential, gracious towards the children of other men, and I will show you the man who will love and tend his own best, to whose heart his own will flee for their first refuge after God, when they catch sight of the cloud in the wind.

CHAPTER III.

THE SICK CHAMBER.

N the course of a month there was a good deal more of light in the smile with which my darling greeted me when I entered her room in the morning. Her pain was greatly gone, but the power of moving her limbs had not yet even begun to show itself.

One day she received me with a still happier smile than I had yet seen upon her face, put out her thin white hand, took mine and kissed it, and said, "Papa," with a lingering on the last syllable.

"What is it, my pet?" I asked.

"I am so happy!"

"What makes you so happy?" I asked again.

"I don't know," she answered; "I haven't thought about it yet. But everything looks so pleasant round me. Is it nearly winter yet, papa? I've forgotten all about how the time has been going."

"It is almost winter, my dear. There is hardly a leaf left on the trees—just two or three disconsolate yellow ones that want to get away down to the rest. They go fluttering and fluttering and trying to break away, but they can't.

"That is just as I felt a little while ago. I wanted to die and get away, papa; for I thought I should never be well again, and I should be in everybody's way.—I am afraid I shall not get well, after all," she added, and the light clouded on her sweet face.

"Well, my darling, we are in God's hands. We shall never get tired of you, and you must not get tired of us. Would you get tired of nursing me, if I were ill?"

"O papa!" And the tears began to gather in her eyes.

"Then you must think we are not able to love so well as you."

"I know what you mean. I did not think of it that way. I will never think so about it again. I was only thinking how useless I was."

"There you are quite mistaken, my dear. No living creature ever was useless. You've got plenty to do there."

"But what have I got to do? I don't feel able for anything," she said; and again the tears came in her eyes, as if I had been telling her to get up and she could not.

"A great deal of our work," I answered, "we do without knowing what it is. But I'll tell you what you have got to do: you have got to believe in God, and in everybody in this house."

"I do, I do. But that is easy to do," she returned.

"And do you think that the work God gives us to do is never easy? Jesus says his yoke is easy, his burden is light. People sometimes refuse to do God's work just because it is easy. This is, sometimes, because they cannot believe that easy work is his work; but there may be a very bad pride in it: it may be because they think that there is little or no honour to be got in that way; and therefore they despise it. Some again accept it with half a heart, and do it with half a hand. But, however easy any work may be, it cannot be well done without taking thought about it. And such people, instead of taking thought about their work, generally take thought about the morrow, in which no work can be done any more than in yesterday. The Holy Present!—I think I must make one more sermon about it—although you, Connie," I said, meaning it for a little joke, "do think that I have said too much about it already."

"Papa, papa! do forgive me. This is a judgment on me for talking to you as I did that dreadful morning. But I was so happy that I was impertinent."

"You silly darling!" I said. "A judgment! God be angry with you for that! Even if it had been anything wrong, which it was not, do you think God has no patience? No, Connie. I will tell you what seems to me much more likely. You wanted something to do; and so God gave you something to do."

"Lying in bed and doing nothing!"

"Yes. Just lying in bed, and doing his will."

"If I could but feel that I was doing his will!"

"When you do it, then you will feel you are doing it."

"I know you are coming to something, papa. Please make haste, for my back is getting so bad."

"I 've tired you, my pet. It was very thoughtless of me. I will tell you the rest another time," I said rising.

"No, no. It will make me much worse not to hear it all now."

"Well, I will tell you. Be still, my darling, I won't be long.—In the time of the old sacrifices, when God so kindly told his ignorant children to do something for him in that way, poor people were told to bring, not a bullock or a sheep, for that was more than they could get, but a pair of turtle-doves, or two young pigeons. But now, as Crashaw the poet says, 'Ourselves become our own best sacrifice.' God wanted to teach people to offer themselves. Now, you are poor, my pet, and you cannot offer yourself in great things done for your fellow-men, which was the way Jesus did. But you must remember that the two young pigeons of the poor were just as acceptable to God as the fat bullock of the rich. Therefore you must say to God something like this:—'O heavenly Father, I have nothing to offer thee but my patience. I will bear thy will, and so offer my will a burnt-offering unto thine. I will be as useless as thou pleasest.' Depend upon it, my darling, in the midst of all the science about the world and its ways, and all the ignorance of God and his greatness, the man or woman who can thus say, *Thy will be done*, with the true heart of giving up, is nearer the secret of things than the geologist and theologian. And now, my darling, be quiet in God's name."

She held up her mouth to kiss me, but did not speak, and I left her, and sent Dora to sit with her.

In the evening, when I went into her room again, having been out in my parish all the morning, I began to unload my budget of small events. Indeed, we all came in like pelicans with stuffed pouches to empty them in her room, as if she had been the only young one we had, and we must cram her with news. Or, rather, she was like the queen of the commonwealth sending out her messages into all parts, and receiving messages in return. I might call her the brain of the house; but I have used similes enough for a while.

After I had done talking, she said—

"And you have been to the school too, papa?"

"Yes. I go to the school almost every day. I fancy in such a school as ours the young people get more good than they do in church. You know I had made a great change in the Sunday-school just before you came home."

"I heard of that, papa. You won't let any of the little ones go to school on the Sunday."

"No. It is too much for them. And having made this change, I feel the necessity of being in the school myself nearly every day, that I may do something direct for the little ones."

"And you'll have to take me up soon, as you promised, you know, papa—just before Sprite threw me."

"As soon as you like, my dear, after you are able to read again."

"Oh, you must begin before that, please.—You could spare time to read a little to me, couldn't you?" she said, doubtfully, as if she feared she was asking too much.

"Certainly, my dear; and I will begin to think about it at once."

It was in part the result of this wish of my child's that it became the custom to gather in her room on Sunday evenings. She was quite unable for any kind of work such as she would have had me commence with her, but I used to take something to read to her every now and then, and always after our early tea on Sundays.

What a thing it is to have one to speak and think about and try to find out and understand, who is always and altogether and perfectly good! Such a centre that is for all our thoughts and words and actions and imaginations? It is, indeed, blessed to be human beings, with Jesus Christ for the centre of humanity.

In the papers wherein I am about to record the chief events of the following years of my life, I shall give a short account of what passed at some of these assemblies in my child's room, in the hope that it may give my friends something, if not new, yet fresh to think about. For God has so made us that every one who thinks at all, thinks in a way that must be more or less fresh to every one else who thinks, if he only have the gift of setting forth his thoughts so that we can see what they are.

I hope my readers will not be alarmed at this, and suppose that I am about to inflict long sermons upon them. I am not. I do hope, as I say, to teach them something; but those whom I succeed in so teaching will share in the delight it will give me to write about what I love most.

As far as I can remember, I will tell how this Sunday-evening class began. I was sitting by Constance's bed. The fire was burning brightly, and the twilight had deepened so nearly into night that it was reflected back from the window, for the curtains had not yet been drawn. There was no light in the room but that of the fire.

Now Constance was in the way of asking often what kind of day or night it was, for there never was a girl more a child of nature than she. Her heart seemed to respond at once to any and every mood of the world around her. To her the condition of air, earth, and sky was news, and news of poetic interest too. "What is it like?" she would often say, without any more definite shaping of the question. This same evening she said,—

"What is it like, papa?"

"It is growing dark," I answered, "as you can see. It is a still evening, and what they call a black frost. The trees are standing as still as if they were carved out of stone, and would snap off everywhere if the wind were to blow. The ground is dark, and as hard as if it were of cast iron. A gloomy night rather, my dear. It looks as if there were something upon its mind that made it sullenly thoughtful; but the stars are coming out one after another overhead, and the sky will be all awake soon. A strange thing the life that goes on all night, is it not? The life of owlets, and mice, and beasts of prey, and bats, and stars," I said, with no very categorical arrangement, "and dreams, and flowers that don't go to sleep like the rest, but send out their scent all night long. Only those are gone now. There are no scents abroad, not even of the earth in such a frost as this."

"Don't you think it looks sometimes, papa, as if God turned his back on the world, or went farther away from it for a while?"

"Tell me a little more what you mean, Connie."

"Well, this night now, this dark, frozen, lifeless night, which you have been describing to me, isn't like God at all—is it?"

"No, it is not. I see what you mean now."

"It is just as if he had gone away and said, 'Now you shall see what you can do without me.'"

"Something like that. But do you know that English people—at least I think so—enjoy the changeful weather of their country much more upon the whole than those who have fine weather constantly? You see it is not enough to satisfy God's goodness that he should give us all things richly to enjoy, but he must make us able to enjoy them as richly as he gives them. He has to consider not only the gift, but the receiver of the gift. He has to make us able to take the gift and make it our own, as well as to give us the gift. In fact, it is not real giving, with the full, that is, the divine, meaning of giving, without it. He has to give us to the gift as well as give the gift to us. Now for this, a break, an interruption is good, is invaluable, for then we begin to think about the thing, and do something in the matter ourselves. The wonder of God's teaching is that, in great part, he makes us not merely learn, but teach ourselves, and that is far grander than if he only made our minds as he makes our bodies."

"I think I understand you, papa. For since I have been ill, you would wonder, if you could see into me, how even what you tell me about the world out of doors gives me more pleasure than I think I ever had when I could go about it just as I liked."

"It wouldn't do that, though, you know, if you hadn't had the other first. The pleasure you have comes as much from your memory as from my news."

"I see that, papa."

"Now can you tell me anything in history that confirms what I have been saying?"

"I don't know anything about history, papa. The only thing that comes into my head is what you were saying yourself the other day about Milton's blindness."

"Ah, yes. I had not thought of that. Do you know, I do believe that God wanted a grand poem from that man, and therefore blinded him that he might be able to write it. But he had first trained him up to the point —given him thirty years in which he had not to provide the bread of a single day, only to learn and think; then set him to teach boys; then placed him at Cromwell's side, in the midst of the tumultuous movement of public affairs, into which the late student entered with all his heart and soul; and then last of all he cast the veil of a divine darkness over him, sent him into a chamber far more retired than that in which he laboured at Cambridge, and set him like the nightingale to sing darkling. The blackness about him was just the great canvas which God gave him to cover with forms of light and music. Deep wells of memory burst upwards from below; the windows of heaven were opened from above; from both rushed the deluge of song which flooded his soul, and which he has poured out in a great river to us."

"It was rather hard for poor Milton, though, wasn't it, papa?"

"Wait till he says so, my dear. We are sometimes too ready with our sympathy, and think things a great deal worse than those do who have to undergo them. Who would not be glad to be struck with *such* blindness as Milton's?"

"Those that do not care about his poetry, papa," answered Constance, with a deprecatory smile.

"Well said, my Connie. And to such it never can come. But, if it please God, you shall love Milton before you are about again. You can't love one you know nothing about."

"I have tried to read him a little."

"Yes, I daresay. You might as well talk of not liking a man whose face you had never seen, because you did not approve of the back of his coat. But you and Milton together have led me away from a far grander instance of what we had been talking about. Are you tired, darling?"

"Not the least, papa. You don't mind what I said about Milton?"

"Not at all, my dear. I like your honesty. But I should mind very much if you thought, with your ignorance of Milton, that your judgment of him was more likely to be right than mine, with my knowledge of him."

"O papa! I am only sorry that I am not capable of appreciating him."

"There you are wrong again. I think you are quite capable of appreciating him. But you cannot appreciate what you have never seen. You think of him as dry, and think you ought to be able to like dry things. Now he is not dry, and you ought not to be able to like dry things. You have a figure before you in your fancy, which is dry, and which you call Milton. But it is no more Milton than your dull-faced Dutch doll, which you called after her, was your merry Aunt Judy. But here comes your mamma; and I haven't said what I wanted to say yet."

"But surely, husband, you can say it all the same," said my wife. "I will go away if you can't."

"I can say it all the better, my love. Come and sit down here beside me. I was trying to show Connie"——

"You did show me, papa."

"Well I was showing Connie that a gift has sometimes to be taken away again before we can know what it is worth, and so receive it right."

Ethelwyn sighed. She was always more open to the mournful than the glad. Her heart had been dreadfully wrung in her youth.

"And I was going on to give her the greatest instance of it in human history. As long as our Lord was with his disciples, they could not see him right: he was too near them. Too much light, too many words, too much revelation, blinds or stupifies. The Lord had been with them long enough. They loved him dearly, and yet often forgot his words almost as soon as he said them. He could not get it into them, for instance, that he had not come to be a king. Whatever he said, they shaped it over again after their own fancy; and their minds were so full of their own worldly notions of grandeur and command, that they could not receive into their souls the gift of God present before their eyes. Therefore he was taken away, that his Spirit, which was more himself than his bodily presence, might come into them—that they might receive the gift of God into their innermost being. After he had gone out of their sight, and they might look all around and down in the grave and up in the air, and not see him anywhere—when they thought they had lost him, he began to come to them again from the other side—from the inside. They found that the image of him which his presence with them had printed in light upon their souls, began to revive in the dark of his absence; and not that only, but that in looking at it without the overwhelming of his bodily presence, lines and forms and meanings began to dawn out of it which they had never seen before. And his words came back to them, no longer as they had received them, but as he meant them. The spirit of Christ filling their hearts and giving them new power, made them remember, by making them able to understand, all that he had said to them. They were then always saying to each other, 'You remember how;' whereas before, they had been always staring at each other with astonishment and something very near incredulity, while he spoke to them. So that after he had gone away, he was really nearer to them than he had been before. The meaning of anything is more than its visible presence. There is a soul in everything, and that soul is the meaning of it. The soul of the world and all its beauty has come nearer to you, my dear, just because you are separated from it for a time."

"Thank you, dear papa. I do like to get a little sermon all to myself now and then. That is another good of being ill."

"You don't mean me to have a share in it, then, Connie, do you?" said my wife, smiling at her daughter's pleasure.

"Oh, mamma! I should have thought you knew all papa had got to say by this time. I daresay he has given you a thousand sermons all to yourself."

"Then you suppose, Connie, that I came into the world with just a boxful of sermons, and after I had taken them all out there were no more. I should be sorry to think I should not have a good many new things to say by this time next year."

"Well, papa, I wish I could be sure of knowing more when next year comes."

"Most people do learn, whether they will or not. But the kind of learning is very different in the two cases."

"But I want to ask you one question, papa: do you think that we should not know Jesus better now if he were to come and let us see him—as he came to the disciples so long, long ago? I wish it were not so long ago."

"As to the time, it makes no difference whether it was last year or two thousand years ago. The whole question is how much we understand, and understanding, obey him. And I do not think we should be any nearer that if he came amongst us bodily again. If we should, he would come. I believe we should be further off it."

"Do you think, then," said Connie, in an almost despairing tone, as if I were the prophet of great evil, "that we shall never, never, never see him?"

"That is *quite* another thing, my Connie. That is the heart of my hopes by day and my dreams by night. To behold the face of Jesus seems to me the one thing to be desired. I do not know that it is to be prayed for; but I think it will be given us as the great bounty of God, so soon as ever we are capable of it. That sight of the face of Jesus is, I think, what is meant by his glorious appearing, but it will come as a consequence of his spirit in us, not as a cause of that spirit in us. The pure in heart shall see God. The seeing of him will be the sign that we are like him, for only by being like him can we see him as he is. All the time that he was with them, the disciples never saw him as he was. You must understand a man before you can see and read his face aright; and as the disciples did not understand our Lord's heart, they could neither see nor read his face aright. But when we shall be fit to look that man in the face, God only knows."

"Then do you think, papa, that we, who have never seen him, could know him better than the disciples? I don't mean, of course, better than they knew him after he was taken away from them, but better than they knew him while he was still with them?"

"Certainly I do, my dear."

"Oh, papa! Is it possible? Why don't we all then?"

"Because we won't take the trouble; that is the reason."

"Oh, what a grand thing to think! That would be worth living—worth being ill for. But how? how? Can't you help me? Mayn't one human being help another?"

"It is the highest duty one human being owes to another. But whoever wants to learn must pray, and think, and, above all, obey—that is simply, do what Jesus says."

There followed a little silence, and I could hear my child sobbing. And the tears stood in my wife's eyes—tears of gladness to hear her daughter's sobs.

"I will try, papa," Constance said at last. "But you *will* help me?"

"That I will, my love. I will help you in the best way I know; by trying to tell you what I have heard and learned about him—heard and learned of the Father, I hope and trust. It is coming near to the time when he was born;—but I have spoken quite as long as you are able to bear to-night."

"No, no, papa. Do go on."

"No, my dear; no more to-night. That would be to offend against the very truth I have been trying to set forth to you. But next Sunday—you have plenty to think about till then—I will talk to you about the baby Jesus; and perhaps I may find something more to help you by that time, besides what I have got to say now."

"But," said my wife, "don't you think, Connie, this is too good to keep all to ourselves? Don't you think we ought to have Wynnie and Dora in?"

"Yes, yes, mamma. Do let us have them in. And Harry and Charlie too."

"I fear they are rather young yet," I said. "Perhaps it might do them harm."

"It would be all the better for us to have them anyhow," said Ethelwyn smiling.

"How do you mean, my dear?"

"Because you will say things more simply if you have them by you. Besides, you always say such things to children as delight grown people, though they could never get them out of you."

It was a wife's speech, reader. Forgive me for writing it.

"Well," I said, "I don't mind them coming in, but I don't promise to say anything directly to them. And you must let them go away the moment they wish it."

"Certainly," answered my wife; and so the matter was arranged.

CHAPTER IV

A SUNDAY EVENING.

HEN I went in to see Constance the next Sunday morning before going to church, I knew by her face that she was expecting the evening. I took care to get into no conversation with her during the day, that she might be quite fresh. In the evening, when I went into her room again with my bible in my hand, I found all our little company assembled. There was a glorious fire, for it was very cold, and the little ones were seated on the rug before it, one on each side of their mother; Wynnie sat by the further side of the bed, for she always avoided any place or thing she thought another might like; and Dora sat by the further chimney-corner, leaving the space between the fire and my chair open that I might see and share the glow.

"The wind is very high, papa," said Constance, as I seated myself beside her.

"Yes, my dear. It has been blowing all day, and since sundown it has blown harder. Do you like the wind, Connie?"

"I am afraid I do like it. When it roars like that in the chimneys, and shakes the windows with a great rush as if it *would* get into the house and tear us to pieces, and then goes moaning away into the woods, and grumbles about in them till it grows savage again, and rushes up at us with fresh fury, I am afraid I delight in it. I feel so safe in the very jaws of danger."

"Why, you are quite poetic, Connie!" said Wynnie.

"Don't laugh at me, Wynnie. Mind I 'm an invalid, and I can't bear to be laughed at," returned Connie, half laughing herself, and a little more than a quarter crying.

Wynnie rose and kissed her, whispered something to her which made her laugh outright, and then sat down again.

"But tell me, Connie," I said, "why you are *afraid* you enjoy hearing the wind about the house."

"Because it must be so dreadful for those that are out in it."

"Perhaps not quite so bad as we think. You must not suppose that God has forgotten them, or cares less for them than for you because they are out in the wind."

"But if we thought like that, papa," said Wynnie, "shouldn't we come to feel that their sufferings were none of our business?"

"If our benevolence rests on the belief that God is less loving than we, it will come to a bad end somehow before long, Wynnie."

"Of course, I could not think that," she returned.

"Then your kindness would be such that you dared not, in God's name, think hopefully for those you could not help, lest you should, believing in his kindness, cease to help those whom you could help! Either God intended that there should be poverty and suffering, or he did not. If he did not intend it—for similar reasons to those for which he allows all sorts of evils—then there is nothing between but that we should sell everything that we have and give it away to the poor."

"Then why don't we?" said Wynnie, looking truth itself in my face.

"Because that is not God's way, and we should do no end of harm by so doing. We should make so many more of those who will not help themselves, who will not be set free from themselves by rising above themselves. We are not to gratify our own benevolence at the expense of its object—not to save our own souls as we fancy, by putting other souls into more danger than God meant for them."

"It sounds hard doctrine from your lips, papa," said Wynnie.

"Many things will look hard in so many words, which yet will be found kindness itself, when they are interpreted by a higher theory. If the one thing is to let people have everything they want, then of course every one ought to be rich. I have no doubt such a man as we were reading of in the papers the other day, who saw his servant girl drown without making the least effort to save her, and then bemoaned the loss of her labour for the coming harvest, thinking himself ill used in her death, would hug his own selfishness on hearing my words, and say, 'All right, parson! Every man for himself! I made my own money, and they may make theirs!' *You* know that is not exactly the way I should think or act with regard to my neighbour. But if it were only that I have seen such noble characters cast in the mould of poverty, I should be compelled to regard poverty as one of God's powers in the world for raising the children of the kingdom, and to believe that it was not because it could not be helped that our Lord said, 'The poor ye have always with you.' But what I wanted to say was, that there can be no reason why Connie should not enjoy what God has given her, although he has not thought fit to give as much to everybody; and, above all, that we shall not help those right whom God gives us to help, if we do not believe that God is caring for every one of them as much as he is caring for every one of us. There was once a baby born in a stable, because his poor mother could get no room in a decent house. Where she lay, I can hardly think. They must have made a bed of hay and straw for her in the stall, for we know the baby's cradle was the manger. Had God forsaken them? or would they not have been more *comfortable*, if that was the main thing, somewhere else? Ah! if the disciples, who were being born about the same time of fisher-fathers and cottage-mothers, to get ready for him to call and teach by the time he should be thirty years of age—if they had only been old enough, and had known that he was coming—would they not have got everything ready for him? They would have clubbed their little savings together, and worked day and night, and some rich women would have helped them, and they would have dressed the baby in fine linen, and got him the richest room their money would get, and they would have made the gold that the wise men brought into a crown for his little head, and would have burnt the frankincense before him. And so our little manger-baby would have been taken away from us. No more the stable-born Saviour—no more the poor Son of God born for us all, as strong, as noble, as loving, as worshipful, as beautiful as he was poor! And we should not have learned that God does not care for money; that if he does not give more of it, it is not that it is scarce with him, or that he is unkind, but that he does not value it himself. And if he sent his own Son to be not merely brought up in the house of the carpenter of a little village, but to be born in the stable of a village inn, we need not suppose, because a man sleeps under a hay-stack, and is put in prison for it next day, that God does not care for him."

"But why did Jesus come so poor, papa?"

"That he might be just a human baby; that he might not be distinguished by this or by that accident of birth; that he might have nothing but a mother's love to welcome him, and so belong to everybody; that from the first he might show that the kingdom of God and the favour of God lie not in these external things at all—that the poorest little one, born in the meanest dwelling, or in none at all, is as much God's own and

God's care as if he came in a royal chamber with colour and shine all about him. Had Jesus come amongst the rich, riches would have been more worshipped than ever. See how so many that count themselves good Christians honour possession and family and social rank, and I doubt hardly get rid of them when they are all swept away from them. The furthest most of such reach is to count Jesus an exception, and therefore not despise him. See how, even in the services of the church, as they call them, they will accumulate gorgeousness and cost. Had I my way, though I will never seek to rouse men's thoughts about such external things, I would never have any vessel used in the eucharist but wooden platters and wooden cups."

"But are we not to serve him with our best?" said my wife.

"Yes, with our very hearts and souls, with our wills, with our absolute being. But all external things should be in harmony with the spirit of his revelation. And if God chose that his son should visit the earth in homely fashion, in homely fashion likewise should be everything that enforces and commemorates that revelation. All church-forms should be on the other side from show and expense. Let the money go to build decent houses for God's poor, not to give them his holy bread and wine out of silver and gold and precious stones—stealing from the significance of the *content* by the meretricious grandeur of the *continent*. I would send all the church-plate to fight the devil with his own weapons in our overcrowded cities, and in our villages where the husbandmen are housed like swine, by giving them room to be clean, and decent air from heaven to breathe. When the people find the clergy thus in earnest, they will follow them fast enough, and the money will come in like salt and oil upon the sacrifice. I would there were a few of our dignitaries that could think grandly about things, even as Jesus thought—even as God thought when he sent him. There are many of them willing to stand any amount of persecution about trifles: the same enthusiasm directed by high thoughts about the kingdom of heaven as within men and not around them, would redeem a vast region from that indifference which comes of judging the gospel of God by the church of Christ with its phylacteries and hems."

"There is one thing," said Wynnie, after a pause, "that I have often thought about—why it was necessary for Jesus to come as a baby: he could not do anything for so long."

"First, I would answer, Wynnie, that if you would tell me why it is necessary for all of us to come as babies, it would be less necessary for me to tell you why *he* came so: whatever was human must be his. But I would say next, Are you sure that he could not do anything for so long? Does a baby do nothing? Ask mamma there. Is it for nothing that the mother lifts up such heartfuls of thanks to God for the baby on her knee? Is it nothing that the baby opens such fountains of love in almost all the hearts around? Ah! you do not think how much every baby has to do with the saving of the world—the saving of it from selfishness, and folly, and greed. And for Jesus, was he not going to establish the reign of love in the earth? How could he do better than begin from babyhood? He had to lay hold of the heart of the world: how could he do better than begin with his mother's—the best one in it. Through his mother's love first, he grew into the world. It was first by the door of all the holy relations of the family that he entered the human world, laying hold of mother, father, brothers, sisters, all his friends; then by the door of labour, for he took his share of his father's work; then, when he was thirty years of age, by the door of teaching—by kind deeds, and sufferings, and through all by obedience unto the death. You must not think little of the grand thirty years wherein he got ready for the chief work to follow. You must not think that while he was thus preparing for his public ministrations, he was not all the time saving the world, even by that which he was in the midst of it, ever laying hold of it more and more. These were things not so easy to tell. And you must remember that our records are very scanty. It is a small biography we have of a man who became—to say nothing more—the Man of the world—the Son of Man. No doubt it is enough, or God would have told us more; but surely we are not to suppose that there was nothing significant, nothing of saving power in that which we are not told. Charlie, wouldn't you have liked to see the little baby Jesus?"

"Yes, that I would. I would have given him my white rabbit with the pink eyes."

"That is what the great painter Titian must have

thought, Charlie ; for he has painted him playing with a white rabbit,—not such a pretty one as yours."

"I would have carried him about all day," said Dora, "as little Henny Parsons does her baby-brother."

"Did he have any brother or sister to carry him about, papa?" asked Harry.

"No, my boy ; for he was the eldest. But you may be pretty sure he carried about his brothers and sisters that came after him."

"Wouldn't he take care of them, just!" said Charlie.

"I wish I had been one of them," said Constance.

"You are one of them, my Connie. Now he is so great and so strong that he can carry father and mother and all of us in his bosom."

Then we sung a child's hymn in praise of the God of little children, and the little ones went to bed. Constance was tired now, and we left her with Wynnie. We too went early to bed.

About midnight my wife and I awoke together—at least neither knew which waked the other. The wind was still raving about the house, with lulls between its charges.

"There's a child crying!" said my wife, starting up.

I sat up too, and listened.

"There is some creature," I granted.

"It is an infant," insisted my wife. "It can't be either of the boys."

I was out of bed in a moment, and my wife the same instant. We hurried on some of our clothes, going to the windows and listening as we did so. We seemed to hear the wailing through the loudest of the wind, and in the lulls were sure of it. But it grew fainter as we listened. The night was pitch dark. I got a lantern, and hurried out. I went round the house till I came under our bed-room windows, and there listened. I heard it, but not so clearly as before. I set out as well as I could judge in the direction of the sound. I could find nothing. My lantern lighted only a few yards around me, and the wind was so strong that it blew through every chink, and threatened momently to blow it out. My wife was by my side before I knew she was coming.

"My dear!" I said, "it is not fit for you to be out."

"It is as fit for me as for a child, anyhow," she answered. "Do listen."

It was certainly no time for expostulation. All the mother was awake in Ethelwyn's bosom. It would have been cruelty to make her go in, though she was indeed ill fitted to encounter such a night-wind.

Another wail reached us. It seemed to come from a thicket at one corner of the lawn. We hurried thither. Again a cry, and we knew we were much nearer to it. Searching and searching we went.

"There it is!" Ethelwyn almost screamed, as the feeble light of the lantern fell on a dark bundle of something under a bush. She caught at it. It gave another pitiful wail—the poor baby of some tramp, rolled up in a dirty, ragged shawl, and tied round with a bit of string, as if it had been a parcel of clouts. She set off running with it to the house, and I followed, much fearing she would miss her way in the dark, and fall. I could hardly get up with her, so eager was she to save the child. She darted up to her own room, where the fire was not yet out.

"Run to the kitchen, Harry, and get some hot water. Take the two jugs there—you can empty them in the sink: you won't know where to find anything. There will be plenty in the boiler."

By the time I returned with the hot water, she had taken off the child's covering, and was sitting with it, wrapped in a blanket, before the fire. The little thing was cold as a stone, and now silent and motionless. We had found it just in time. Ethelwyn ordered me about as if I had been a nursemaid. I poured the hot water into a foot-bath.

"Some cold water, Harry. You would boil the child."

"You made me throw away the cold water," I said, laughing.

"There's some in the bottles," she returned. "Make haste."

I did try to make haste, but I could not be quick enough to satisfy Ethelwyn.

"The child will be dead," she cried, "before we get it in the water."

She had its rags off in a moment—there was very little to remove after the shawl. How white the little thing was, though dreadfully neglected! It was a girl—not more than a few weeks old, we agreed. Her little heart was still beating feebly; and as she was a well-made, apparently healthy infant, we had every hope of recovering her. And we were not disappointed. She began to move her little legs and arms with short, convulsive motions.

"Do you know where the dairy is, Harry?" asked my wife, with no great compliment to my bumps of locality, which I had always flattered myself were beyond the average in development.

"I think I do," I answered.

"Could you tell which was this night's milk now?"

"There will be less cream on it," I answered.

"Bring a little of that and some more hot water. I've got some sugar here. I wish we had a bottle."

I executed her commands faithfully. By the time I returned the child was lying on her lap, clean and dry—a fine baby I thought. Ethelwyn went on talking to her, and praising her as if she had not only been the finest specimen of mortality in the world, but her own child to boot. She got her to take a few spoonfuls of milk and water, and then the little thing fell fast asleep.

Ethelwyn's nursing days were not so far gone by that she did not know where her baby's-clothes were. She gave me the child, and going to a wardrobe in the room, brought out some night-things, and put them on. I could not understand in the least why the sleeping darling must be indued with little chemise, and flannel, and nightgown, and I do not know what all, requiring a world of nice care, and a hundred turnings to and fro, now on its little stomach, now on its back, now sitting up, now lying down, when it would have slept just as well, and I venture to think much more comfortably, if laid in soft blankets and well covered over. But I had never ventured to interfere with any of my own children, devoutly believing up to this moment, though in a dim unquestioning way, that there must be some hidden feminine wisdom in the whole process; and now that I had begun to question it I found that my opportunity had long gone by, if I had ever had one. And after all there may be some reason for it, though I confess I do strongly suspect that all these matters are so wonderfully complicated in order that the girl left in the woman may have her heart's content of playing with her doll; just as the woman hid in the girl expends no end of lovely affection upon the dull stupidity of wooden cheeks and a body of sawdust. But it was a delight to my heart to see how Ethelwyn could not be satisfied without treating the foundling in precisely the same fashion as one of her own. And if this was a necessary preparation for what should follow, I would be the very last to complain of it.

We went to bed again, and the forsaken child of some half-animal mother, now perhaps asleep in some filthy lodging for tramps, lay in my Ethelwyn's bosom. I loved her the more for it; though, I confess, it would have been very painful to me had she shown it possible for her to treat the baby otherwise, especially after what we had been talking about that same evening.

So we had another child in the house, and nobody knew anything about it but ourselves two. The household had never been disturbed by all the going and coming. After everything had been done for her, we had a good laugh over the whole matter. Then Ethelwyn fell a-crying.

"Pray for the poor thing, Harry," she sobbed, "before you come to bed."

I knelt down, and said—

"O Lord our Father, this is as much thy child and as certainly sent to us as if she had been born of us. Help us to keep the child for thee. Take thou care of thy own, and teach us what to do with her, and how to order our ways towards her."

Then I said to Ethelwyn—

"We will not say one word more about it to-night. You must try to go to sleep. I dare say the little thing will sleep till the morning, and I am sure I shall if she does. Good-night, my love. You are a true mother. Mind you go to sleep."

"I am half asleep already, Harry. Good-night," she returned.

I know nothing more about anything till I woke in the morning, except that I had a dream, which I have not made up my mind yet whether I shall tell or not. We slept soundly—God's baby and all.

CHAPTER V.

MY DREAM.

 THINK I will tell the dream I had. I cannot well account for the beginning of it: the end will appear sufficiently explicable to those who are quite satisfied that they get rid of the mystery of a thing when they can associate it with something else with which they are familiar. Such do not care to see that the thing with which they associate it may be as mysterious as the other. For although use too often destroys marvel, it cannot destroy the marvellous. The origin of our thoughts is just as wonderful as the origin of our dreams.

In my dream I found myself in a pleasant field full of daisies and white clover. The sun was setting. The wind was going one way, and the shadows another. I felt rather tired, I neither knew nor thought why. With an old man's prudence, I would not sit down upon the grass, but looked about for a more suitable seat. Then

I saw, for often in our dreams there is an immediate response to our wishes, a long, rather narrow stone lying a few yards from me. I wondered how it could have come there, for there were no mountains or rocks near: the field was part of a level country. Carelessly, I sat down upon it astride, and watched the setting of the sun. Somehow I fancied that his light was more sorrowful than the light of the setting sun should be, and I began to feel very heavy at the heart. No sooner had the last brilliant spark of his light vanished, than I felt the stone under me begin to move. With the inactivity of a dreamer, however, I did not care to rise, but wondered only what would come next. My seat, after several strange tumbling motions, seemed to rise into the air a little way, and then I found that I was astride of a gaunt, bony horse—a skeleton horse almost, only he had a gray skin on him. He began, apparently with pain, as if his joints were all but too stiff to move, to go forward in the direction in which he found himself. I kept my seat. Indeed, I never thought of dismounting. I was going on to meet what might come. Slowly, feebly, trembling at every step, the strange steed went, and as he went his joints seemed to become less stiff, and he went a little faster. All at once I found that the pleasant field had vanished, and that we were on the borders of a moor. Straight forward the horse carried me, and the moor grew very rough, and he went stumbling dreadfully, but always recovering himself. Every moment it seemed as if he would fall to rise no more, but as often he found fresh footing. At length the surface became a little smoother, and he began a horrible canter which lasted till he reached a low, broken wall, over which he half walked, half fell into what was plainly an ancient neglected churchyard. The mounds were low and covered with rank grass. In some parts, hollows had taken the place of mounds. Gravestones lay in every position except the level or the upright, and broken masses of monuments were scattered about. My horse bore me into the midst of it, and there, slow and stiff as he had risen, he lay down again. Once more I was astride of a long narrow stone. And now I found that it was an ancient gravestone which I knew well in a certain Sussex churchyard, the top of it carved into the rough resemblance of a human skeleton—that of a man, tradition said, who had been killed by a serpent that came out of a bottomless pool in the next field. How long I sat there I do not know; but at last I saw the faint gray light of morning begin to appear in front of me. The horse of death had carried me eastward. The dawn grew over the top of a hill that here rose against the horizon. But it was a wild dreary dawn—a blot of gray first, which then stretched into long lines of dreary yellow and gray, looking more like a blasted and withered sunset than a fresh sunrise. And well it suited that waste, wide, deserted churchyard, if churchyard I ought to call it where no church was to be seen—only a vast hideous square of graves. Before me I noticed especially one old grave, the flat stone of which had broken in two and sunk in the middle. While I sat with my eyes fixed on this stone, it began to move; the crack in the middle closed, then widened again as the two halves of the stone were lifted up, and flung outward, like the two halves of a folding door. From the grave rose a little child, smiling such perfect contentment as if he had just come from kissing his mother. His little arms had flung the stones apart, and as he stood on the edge of the grave next to me, they remained outspread from the action for a moment, as if blessing the sleeping people. Then he came towards me with the same smile, and took my hand. I rose, and he led me away over another broken wall towards the hill that lay before us. And as we went the sun came nearer, the pale yellow bars flushed into orange and rosy red, till at length the edges of the clouds were swept with an agony of golden light, which even my dreamy eyes could not endure, and I awoke weeping for joy.

This waking woke my wife, who said in some alarm—

"What is the matter, husband?"

So I told her my dream, and how in my sleep my gladness had overcome me.

"It was this little darling that set you dreaming so," she said, and turning, put the baby in my arms.

CHAPTER VI.

THE NEW BABY.

WILL not attempt to describe the astonishment of the members of our household, each in succession, as the news of the child spread. Charlie was heard shouting across the stable-yard to his brother—

"Harry, Harry! Mamma has got a new baby. Isn't it jolly?"

"Where did she get it?" cried Harry in return.

"In the parsley-bed, I suppose," answered Charlie, and was nearer right than usual; for the information on which his conclusion was founded had no doubt been imparted as belonging to the history of the human race.

But my reader can easily imagine the utter bewilderment of those of the family whose knowledge of human affairs would not allow of their curiosity being so easily satisfied as that of the boys. In them was exemplified that confusion of the intellectual being which is produced by the witness of incontestable truth to a thing incredible—in which case the probability always is, that the incredibility results from something in the mind of the hearer falsely associated with and disturbing the true perception of the thing to which witness is borne.

Nor was the astonishment confined to the family, for it spread over the parish that Mrs Walton had got another baby. And so, indeed, she had. And seldom has baby met with a more hearty welcome than this baby met with from every one of our family. They hugged it first, and then asked questions. And that, I say, is the right way of receiving every good gift of God. Ask what questions you will, but when you see that the gift is a good one, make sure that you take it. There is plenty of time for you to ask questions afterwards. Then the better you love the gift, the more ready you will be to ask, and the more fearless in asking.

The truth, however, soon became known. And then, strange to relate, we began to receive visits of condolence. Oh! that poor baby! how it was frowned upon, and how it had heads shaken over it, just because it was not Ethelwyn's baby! It could not help that, poor darling!

"Of course, you'll give information to the police," said, I am sorry to say, one of my brethren in the neighbourhood, who had the misfortune to be a magistrate as well.

"Why?" I asked.

"Why! That they may discover the parents, to be sure."

"Wouldn't it be as hard a matter to prove the parentage, as it would be easy to suspect it?" I asked. "And just think what it would be to give the baby to a woman who not only did not want her, but who was not her mother. If her own mother came to claim her now, I don't say I would refuse her, but I should think twice about giving her up after she had once abandoned her for a whole night in the open air. In fact, I don't want the parents."

"But you don't want the child."

"How do you know that?" I returned—rather rudely, I am afraid, for I am easily annoyed at anything that seems to me heartless—about children especially.

"Oh! of course, if you want to have an orphan asylum of your own, no one has a right to interfere. But you ought to consider other people."

"That is just what I thought I was doing," I answered; but he went on without heeding my reply—

"We shall all be having babies left at our doors, and some of us are not so fond of them as you are. Remember, you are your brother's keeper."

"And my sister's too," I answered. "And if the question lies between keeping a big, burly brother like you, and a tiny, wee sister like that, I venture to choose for myself."

"She ought to go to the workhouse," said the magistrate—a friendly, good-natured man enough in ordinary—and rising, he took his hat and departed.

This man had no children. So he was—or was not, so much to blame. Which? *I* say the latter.

Some of Ethelwyn's friends were no less positive about her duty in the affair. I happened to go into the drawing-room during the visit of one of them—Miss Bowdler.

"But, my dear Mrs Walton," she was saying, "you 'll be having all the tramps in England leaving their babies at your door."

"The better for the babies," interposed I, laughing.

"But you don't think of your wife, Mr Walton."

"Don't I? I thought I did," I returned, drily.

"Depend upon it, you 'll repent it."

"I hope I shall never repent of anything but what is bad."

"Ah! but, really! it 's not a thing to be made game of."

"Certainly not. The baby shall be treated with all due respect in this house."

"What a provoking man you are! You know what I mean well enough."

"As well as I choose to know—certainly," I answered.

This lady was one of my oldest parishioners, and took liberties for which she had no other justification, except indeed an unhesitating belief in the superior rectitude of whatever came into her own head can be counted as one. When she was gone, my wife turned to me with a half-comic, half-anxious look, and said—

"But it would be rather alarming, Harry, if this were to get abroad, and we couldn't go out at the door in the morning without being in danger of stepping on a baby on the door-step."

"You might as well have said, when you were going to be married, 'If God should send me twenty children, what ever should I do?' He who sent us this one can surely prevent any more from coming than he wants to come. All that we have to think of is to do right—not the consequences of doing right. But leaving all that aside, you must not suppose that wandering mothers have not even the attachment of animals to their offspring. There are not so many that are willing to part with their babies as all that would come to. If you believe that God sent this one, that is enough for the present. If he should send another, we should know by that that we had to take it in."

My wife said the baby was a beauty. I could see that she was a plump, well-to-do baby; and being by nature no particular lover of babies as babies—that is, feeling none of the inclination of mothers and nurses and elder sisters to eat them, or rather, perhaps, loving more for what I believed than what I saw—that was all I could pretend to discover. But even the aforementioned elderly parishioner was compelled to allow before three months were over that little Theodora—for we turned the name of my youngest daughter upside down for her—"was a proper child." To none, however, did she seem to bring so much delight as to our dear Constance. Oftener than not, when I went into her room, I found the sleepy useless little thing lying beside her on the bed, and her staring at it with such loving eyes! How it began, I do not know, but it came at last to be called Connie's Dora, or Miss Connie's baby, all over the house, and nothing pleased Connie better. Not till she saw this did her old nurse take quite kindly to the infant; for she regarded her as an interloper, who had no right to the tenderness which was lavished upon her. But she had no sooner given in than the baby began to grow dear to her as well as to the rest. In fact, the house was ere long full of nurses. The staff included every one but myself, who only occasionally, at the entreaty of some one or other of the younger ones, took her in my arms.

But before she was three months old, anxious thoughts began to intrude, all centring round the question in what manner the child was to be brought up. Certainly there was time enough to think of this, as Ethelwyn constantly reminded me; but what made me anxious was that I could not discover the principle that ought to guide me. Now no one can tell how soon a principle in such a case will begin, even unconsciously, to operate; and the danger was that the moment when it ought to begin to operate would be long past before the principle was discovered, except I did what I could now to find it out. I had again and again to remind myself that there was no cause for anxiety; for that I might certainly claim the enlightenment which all who want to do right are sure to receive; but still I continued uneasy just from feeling a vacancy where a principle ought to have been.

CHAPTER VII.

ANOTHER SUNDAY EVENING.

URING all this time Connie made no very perceptible progress—in the recovery of her bodily powers, I mean, for her heart and mind advanced remarkably. We held our Sunday evening assemblies in her room pretty regularly, my occasional absence in the exercise of my duties alone interfering with them. In connexion with one of these I will show how I came at length to make up my mind as to what I would endeavour to keep before me as my object in the training of little Theodora, always remembering that my preparation might be used for a very different end from what I purposed. If my intention was right, the fact that it might be turned aside would not trouble me.

We had spoken a good deal together about the infancy and childhood of Jesus, about the shepherds, and the wise men, and the star in the east, and the children of Bethlehem. I encouraged the thoughts of all the children to rest and brood upon the fragments that are given us, and, believing that the imagination is one of the most powerful of all the faculties for aiding the growth of the truth in the mind, I would ask them questions as to what they thought he might have said or done in ordinary family occurrences, thus giving a reality in their minds to this part of his history, and trying to rouse in them a habit of referring their conduct to the standard of his. If we do not thus employ our imagination on sacred things, his example can be of no use to us except in exactly corresponding circumstances—and when can such occur from one end to another of our lives? The very effort to think how he would have done, is a wonderful purifier of the conscience, and, even if the conclusion arrived at should not be correct from lack of sufficient knowledge of his character and principles, it will be better than any that can be arrived at without this inquiry. Besides, the asking of such questions gave me good opportunity, through the answers they returned, of seeing what their notions of Jesus and of duty were, and thus of discovering how to help the dawn of the light in their growing minds. Nor let any one fear that such employment of the divine gift of imagination will lead to foolish vagaries and useless inventions: while the object is to discover the right way—the truth—there is little danger of that. Besides, there I was to help hereby in the actual training of their imaginations to truth and wisdom. To aid in this, I told them some of the stories that were circulated about him in the early centuries of the church, but which the church has rejected as of no authority; and I showed them how some of them could not be true, because they were so unlike those words and actions which we had the best of reasons for receiving as true; and how one or two of them might be true—though, considering the company in which we found them, we could say nothing for certain concerning them. And such wise things as those children said sometimes! It is marvellous how children can reach the heart of the truth at once. Their utterances are sometimes entirely concordant with the results arrived at through years of thought by the earnest mind—results which no mind would ever arrive at save by virtue of the child-like in it.

Well, then, upon this evening I read to them the story of the boy Jesus in the temple. Then I sought to make the story more real to them by dwelling a little on the growing fears of his parents as they went from group to group of their friends, tracing back the road towards Jerusalem, and asking every fresh company they knew if they had seen their boy, till at length they were in great trouble when they could not find him even in Jerusalem. Then came the delight of his mother when she did find him at last, and his answer to what she said. Now, while I thus lingered over the simple story, my children had put many questions to me about Jesus being a boy, and not seeming to know things which, if he was God, he must have known, they thought. To some of these I had just to reply, that I did not understand myself, and therefore could not teach them; to others, that I could explain them, but that they were not yet, some of them, old enough to receive and understand my explanation: while others I did my best to answer as simply as I could. But at this point we arrived at a question put by Wynnie, to answer which aright I considered of the greatest importance. Wynnie said,—

"That is just one of the things about Jesus that have always troubled me, papa."

"What is, my dear?" I said; for although I thought I knew well enough what she meant, I wished her to set it forth in her own words, both for her own sake, and the sake of the others, who would probably understand the difficulty much better if she presented it herself.

"I mean that he spoke to his mother——"

"Why don't you say *mamma*, Wynnie?" said Charlie. "she was his own mamma, wasn't she, papa?"

"Yes, my dear; but don't you know that the shoemaker's children down in the village always call their mamma *mother?*"

"Yes; but they are shoemaker's children."

"Well, Jesus was one of that class of people. He was the son of a carpenter. He called his mamma *mother*. But, Charlie, *mother* is the more beautiful word of the two, by a great deal, I think. *Lady* is a very pretty word; but *woman* is a very beautiful word. Just so with *mamma* and *mother*. *Mamma* is pretty, but *mother* is beautiful."

"Why don't we always say *mother* then?"

"Just because it is the most beautiful, and so we

keep it for Sundays—that is, for the more solemn times of life. We don't want it to get common to us with too much use. We may think it as much as we like; thinking does not spoil it; but saying spoils many things, and especially beautiful words. Now we must let Wynnie finish what she was saying."

"I was saying, papa, that I can't help feeling as if—I know it can't be true—but I feel as if Jesus spoke unkindly to his mother when he said that to her."

I looked at the page and read the words, "How is it that ye sought me? wist ye not that I must be about my Father's business?" And I sat silent for a while.

"Why don't you peak, papa?" said Harry.

"I am sitting wondering at myself, Harry, I said. "Long after I was your age, Wynnie, I remember quite well that those words troubled me as they now trouble you. But when I read them over now, they seemed to me so lovely that I could hardly read them aloud. I can recall the fact that they troubled me, but the mode of the fact I scarcely can recall. I can hardly see now wherein lay the hurt or offence the words gave me. And why is that? Simply because I understand them now, and I did not understand them then. I took them as uttered with a tone of reproof: now I hear them as uttered with a tone of loving surprise. But really I cannot feel sure what it was that I did not like. And I am confident it is so with a great many things that we reject. We reject them simply because we do not understand them. Therefore, indeed, we cannot with truth be said to reject them at all. It is some false appearance that we reject. Some of the grandest things in the whole realm of truth look repellent to us, and we turn away from them, simply because we are not—to use a familiar phrase—we are not up to them. They appear to us, therefore, to be what they are not. Instruction sounds to the proud man like reproof; illumination comes on the vain man like scorn; the manifestation of a higher condition of motive and action than his own, falls on the self-esteeming like condemnation; but it is consciousness and conscience working together that produce this impression; the result is from the man himself, not from the higher source. From the truth comes the power, but the shape it assumes to the man is from the man himself."

"You are quite beyond me now, papa," said Wynnie.

"Well, my dear," I answered, "I will return to the words of the boy Jesus, instead of talking more about them, and when I have shown you what they mean, I think you will allow that that feeling you have about them is all and altogether an illusion."

"There is one thing first," said Connie, "that I want to understand. You said the words of Jesus rather indicated surprise. But how could he be surprised at anything? If he was God, he must have known everything."

"He tells us himself that he did not know everything. He says once that even *he* did not know one thing—only the Father knew it."

"But how could that be if he was God?"

"My dear, that is one of the things that it seems to

me impossible I should understand. Certainly I think his trial as a man would not have been perfect had he known everything. He, too, had to live by faith in the Father. And remember that for the Divine Sonship on earth perfect knowledge was not necessary, only perfect confidence, absolute obedience, utter holiness. There is a great tendency in our sinful natures to put knowledge and power on a level with goodness. It was one of the lessons of our Lord's life that they are not so; that the one grand thing in humanity is faith in God; that the highest in God is his truth, his goodness, his rightness. But if Jesus was a real man, and no mere appearance of a man, is it any wonder that, with a heart full to the brim of the love of God, he should be for a moment surprised that his mother, whom he loved so dearly, the best human being he knew, should not have taken it as a matter of course that if he was not with her, he must be doing something his Father wanted him to do? For this is just what his answer means. To turn it into the ordinary speech of our day, it is just this: 'Why did you look for me! Didn't you know that I must of course be doing something my Father had given me to do?' Just think of the quiet sweetness of confidence in this. And think what a life his must have been up to that twelfth year of his, that such an expostulation with his mother was justified. It must have had reference to a good many things that had passed before then, which ought to have been sufficient to make Mary conclude that her missing boy must be about God's business somewhere. If her heart had been as full of God and God's business as his, she would not have been in the least uneasy about him. And here is the lesson of his whole life: it was all his Father's business. The boy's mind and hands were full of it. The man's mind and hands were full of it. And the risen conqueror was full of it still. For the Father's business is everything, and includes all work that is worth doing. We may say in a full grand sense that there is nothing but the Father and his business."

"But we have so many things to do that are not his business," said Wynnie, with a sigh of oppression.

"Not one, my darling. If anything is not his business, you not only have not to do it, but you ought not to do it. Your words come from the want of spiritual sight. We cannot see the truth in common things—the will of God in little every-day affairs, and that is how they become so irksome to us. Show a beautiful picture, one full of quiet imagination and deep thought, to a common-minded man: he will pass it by with some slight remark, thinking it very ordinary and commonplace. That is because he is commonplace. Because our minds are so commonplace, have so little of the divine imagination in them, therefore we do not recognize the spiritual meaning and worth, we do not perceive the beautiful will of God, in the things required of us, though they are full of it. But if we *do* them we shall thus make acquaintance with them, and come to see what is in them. The roughest kernel amongst them has a tree of life in its heart."

"I wish he would tell me something to do," said Charlie. "Wouldn't I do it!"

I made no reply, but waited for an opportunity which I was pretty sure was at hand, while I carried the matter a little further.

"But look here, Wynnie; listen to this," I said: "'And he went down with them, and came to Nazareth, and was subject unto them.' Was that not doing his Father's business too? Was it not doing the business of his Father in heaven to honour his father and his mother, though he knew that his days would not be long in that land? Did not his whole teaching, his whole doing, rest on the relation of the Son to the Father, and surely it was doing his Father's business then to obey his parents—to serve them, to be subject to them. It is true that the business God gives a man to do may be said to be the peculiar walk in life into which he is led, but that is only as distinguishing it from another man's peculiar business. God gives us all our business, and the business which is common to humanity is more peculiarly God's business than that which is one man's and not another's—because it lies nearer the root, and is essential. It does not matter whether a man is a farmer or a physician, but it greatly matters whether he is a good son, a good husband, and so on. O my children!" I said, "if the world could but be brought to believe—the world did I say?—if the best men in the world could only see, as God sees it, that service is in itself the noblest exercise of human powers; if they could see that God is the hardest worker of all, and that his nobility are those who do the most service, surely it would alter the whole aspect of the church.

Menial offices, for instance, would soon cease to be talked of with that contempt which shows that there is no true recognition of the fact that the same principle runs through the highest duty and the lowest—that the lowest work which God gives a man to do must be in its nature noble, as certainly noble as the highest. This would destroy condescension, which is the rudeness, yes, impertinence, of the higher, as it would destroy insolence, which is the rudeness of the lower. He who recognized the dignity of his own lower office, would thereby recognize the superiority of the higher office, and would be the last either to envy or degrade it. He would see in it his own—only higher, only better, and revere it. But I am afraid I have wearied you, my children."

"Oh, no, papa!" said the elder ones, while the little ones gaped and said nothing.

"I know I am in danger of doing so when I come to speak upon this subject: it has such a hold of my heart and mind!—Now, Charlie, my boy, go to bed."

But Charlie was very comfortable before the fire, on the rug, and did not want to go. First one shoulder went up, and then the other, and the corners of his mouth went down, as if to keep the balance true. He did not move to go. I gave him a few moments to recover himself, but as the black frost still endured, I thought it was time to hold up a mirror to him. When he was a very little boy, he was much in the habit of getting out of temper, and then as now, he made a face that was hideous to behold; and to cure him of this, I used to make him carry a little mirror about his neck, that the means might be always at hand of showing himself to him: it was a sort of artificial conscience which, by enabling him to see the picture of his own condition, which the face always is, was not unfrequently operative in rousing his real conscience, and making him ashamed of himself. But now the mirror I wanted to hold up to him was a past mood, in the light of which the present would show what it was.

"Charlie," I said, "a little while ago you were wishing that God would give you something to do. And now when he does, you refuse at once, without even thinking about it."

"How do you know that God wants me to go to bed?" said Charlie, with something of surly impertinence, which I did not meet with reproof at once because there was some sense along with the impudence.

"I know that God wants you to do what I tell you, and to do it pleasantly. Do you think the boy Jesus would have put on such a face as that—I wish I had the little mirror to show it to you—when his mother told him it was time to go to bed?"

And now Charlie began to look ashamed. I left the truth to work in him, because I saw it was working. Had I not seen that, I should have compelled him to go at once, that he might learn the majesty of law. But now that his own better self, the self enlightened of the light that lighteneth every man that cometh into the world, was working, time might well be afforded it to work its perfect work. I went on talking to the others. In the space of not more than one minute, he rose and came to me, looking both good and ashamed, and held up his face to kiss me, saying, "Good-night, papa." I bade him good-night, and kissed him more tenderly than usual, that he might know that it was all right between us. I required no formal apology, no begging of my pardon, as some parents think right. It seemed enough to me that his heart was turned. It is a terrible thing to run the risk of changing humility into humiliation. Humiliation is one of the proudest conditions in the human world. When he felt that it would be a relief to say more explicitly, "Father, I have sinned," then let him say it; but not till then. To compel manifestation is one surest way to check feeling.

My readers must not judge it silly to record a boy's unwillingness to go to bed. It is precisely the same kind of disobedience that some of them are guilty of themselves, and that in things not one whit more important than this, only those things happen to be *their* wish at the moment and not Charley's, and so gain their superiority.

CHAPTER VIII

THEODORA'S DOOM.

RY not to get weary, respected reader, of so much of what I am afraid most people will call tiresome preaching. But I know if you get anything practicable out of it, you will not be so soon tired of it. I promise you more story by and by. Only an old man, like an old horse, must be allowed to take very much his own way—go his own pace, I should have said. I am afraid there must be a little more of a similar sort in this chapter.

On the Monday morning I set out to visit one or two people whom the severity of the weather had kept from church on the Sunday. The last severe frost, as it turned out, of the season, was possessing the earth. The sun was low in the wintry sky, and what seemed a very cold mist up in the air hid him from the earth. I was walking along a path in a field close by a hedge. A tree had been cut down, and lay upon the grass. A short distance from it lay its own figure marked out in hoar-frost. There alone was there any hoar-frost on the field; the rest was all of the loveliest tenderest green. I will not say the figure was such an exact resemblance as a photograph would have been; still it was an indubitable likeness. It appeared to the hasty glance that not a branch, not a knot of the upper side of the tree at least was left unrepresented in shining and glittering whiteness upon the green grass. It was very pretty, and, I confess, at first very puzzling. I walked on, meditating on the phenomenon, till at length I found out its cause. The hoar-frost had been all over the field in the morning. The sun had been shining for a time, and had melted the frost away, except where he could only cast a shadow. As he rose and rose, the shadow of the tree had shortened and come nearer and nearer to its original, growing more and more like as it came nearer, while the frost kept disappearing as the shadow withdrew its protection. When the shadow extended only to a little way from the tree, the clouds came and covered the sun, and there were no more shadows, only one great one of the clouds. Then the frost shone out in the shape of the vanished shadow. It lay at a little distance from the tree, because the tree having been only partially lopped, some great stumps of boughs held it up from the ground, and thus, when the sun was low, his light had shone a little way through beneath, as well as over the trunk.

My reader needs not be afraid; I am not going to "moralise this spectacle with a thousand similes." I only tell it him as a very pretty phenomenon. But I confess I walked on moralizing it. Any new thing in nature—I mean new in regard to my knowledge, of course —always made me happy; and I was full of the quiet pleasure it had given me and of the thoughts it had brought me, when, as I was getting over a stile, whom should I see in the next field, coming along the footpath, but the lady who had made herself so disagreeable about Theodora? The sight was rather a discord in my feeling at that moment; perhaps it would have been so at any moment. But I prepared myself to meet her in the strength of the good humour which nature had just bestowed upon me. For I fear the failing will go with me to the grave that I am very ready to be annoyed, even to the loss of my temper, at the urgings of ignoble prudence.

"Good morning, Miss Bowdler," I said.

"Good morning, Mr Walton," she returned. "I am afraid you thought me impertinent the other week; but you know by this time it is only my way."

"As such I take it," I answered, with a smile.

She did not seem quite satisfied that I did not defend her from her own accusation; but as it was a just one, I could not do so. Therefore she went on to repeat the offence by way of justification.

"It was all for Mrs Walton's sake. You ought to consider her, Mr Walton. She has quite enough to do with that dear Connie, who is likely to be an invalid all her days—too much to take the trouble of a beggar's brat as well."

"Has Mrs Walton been complaining to you about it, Miss Bowdler?" I asked.

"Oh, dear, no!" she answered. "She is far too good to complain of anything. That's just why her friends must look after her a bit, Mr Walton."

"Then I beg you won't speak disrespectfully of my little Theodora."

"Oh, dear me! no. Not at all. I don't speak disrespectfully of her."

"Even amongst the class of which she comes, 'a beggar's brat' would be regarded as bad language."

"I beg your pardon, I'm sure, Mr Walton! If you *will* take offence"——

"I do take offence. And you know there is One who has given especial warning against offending the little ones."

Miss Bowdler walked away in high displeasure—let me hope in conviction of sin as well. She did not appear in church for the next two Sundays. Then she came again. But she called very seldom at the Hall after this, and I believe my wife was not sorry.

Now, whether it came in any way from what that lady had said as to my wife's trouble with Constance and Theodora together, I can hardly tell; but before I had reached home I had at last got a glimpse of something like the right way, as it appeared to me, of bringing up Theodora. When I went into the house I looked for my wife to have a talk with her about it; but, indeed, it seemed always necessary to find her every time I got home. I found her in Connie's room, as I had expected. Now although we were never in the habit of making mysteries of things in which there was no mystery, and talked openly before our children, and the more openly the older they grew, yet there were times when we wanted to have our talks quite alone, especially when we had not made up our minds about something. So I asked Ethelwyn to walk out with me.

"I 'm afraid I can't just this moment, husband," she answered. She was in the way of using that form of address, for she said it meant everything without saying it aloud. "I can't just this moment, for there is no one at liberty to stay with Connie."

"Oh, never mind me, mamma," said Connie, cheerfully. "Theodora will take care of me," and she looked fondly at the child, who was lying by her side fast asleep.

"There!" I said. And both looked up surprised, for neither knew what I meant. "I will tell you afterwards," I said, laughing. "Come along, Ethel."

"You can ring the bell, you know, Connie, if you should want anything, or your baby should wake up and be troublesome. You won't want me long, will you, husband?"

"I 'm not sure about that. You must tell Susan to watch for the bell."

Susan was the old nurse.

Ethel put on her hooded cloak, and we went out together. I took her across to the field where I had seen the hoary shadow. The sun had not shone out, and I hoped it would be there to gladden her dear eyes as it had gladdened mine; but it was gone. The warmth of the sun, without its direct rays, had melted it away, as sacred influences will sometimes do with other shadows, without the mind knowing any more than the grass how the shadow departed. There, reader! I have got a bit of a moral in about it before you knew what I was doing. But I was sorry my wife could see it only through my eyes and words. Then I told her about Miss Bowdler, and what she had said. Ethel was very angry at her impertinence in speaking so to me. That was a wife's feeling, you know, and perhaps excusable in the first impression of the thing.

"She seems to think," she said, "that she was sent into the world to keep other people right instead of herself. I am very glad you set her down, as the maids say."

"Oh, I don't think there's much harm in her," I returned, which was easy generosity, seeing my wife was taking my part. "Indeed, I am not sure that we are not both considerably indebted to her; for it was after I met her that a thought came into my head as to how we ought to do with Theodora."

"Still troubling yourself about that, husband?"

"The longer the difficulty lasts, the more necessary is it that it should be met," I answered. "Our measures must begin *sometime*, and when, who can tell? We ought to have them in our heads, or they will never begin at all."

"Well, I confess they are rather of a general nature at present,—belonging to humanity rather than the individual, as you would say—consisting chiefly in washing, dressing, feeding, and apostrophe, varied with lullabying.

But our hearts are a better place for our measures than our heads, aren't they?"

"Certainly; I walk corrected. Only there's no fear about your heart. I'm not quite so sure about your head."

"Thank you, husband. But with you for a head it doesn't matter, does it?"

"I don't know that. People should always strengthen the weaker part, for no chain is stronger than its weakest link; no fortification stronger than its most assailable point. But seriously, wife, I trust your head nearly, though not quite, as much as your heart. Now to go to business. There's one thing we have both made up our minds about—that there is to be no concealment with the child. God's fact must be known by her. It would be cruel to keep the truth from her, even if it were not sure to come upon her with a terrible shock some day. She must know from the first, by hearing it talked of—not by solemn and private communication—that she came out of the shrubbery. That's settled, is it not?"

"Certainly. I see that to be the right way," responded Ethelwyn.

"Now, are we bound to bring her up exactly as our own, or are we not?"

"We are bound to do as well for her as for our own."

"Assuredly. But if we brought her up just as our own, would that, the facts being as they are, be to do as well for her as for our own?"

"I doubt it; for other people would not choose to receive her as we have done."

"That is true. She would be continually reminded of her origin. Not that that in itself would be any evil; but as they would do it by excluding or neglecting her, or, still worse, by taking liberties with her, it would be a great pain. But keeping that out of view, would it be good for herself, knowing what she will know, to be thus brought up? Would it not be kinder to bring her up in a way that would make it easier for her to relieve the gratitude which I trust she will feel—not for our sakes—I hope we are above doing anything for the sake of the gratitude which will be given for it, and which is so often far beyond the worth of the thing done ——"

"Alas! the gratitude of men
Hath oftener left me mourning,"

said Ethel.

"Ah! you understand that now, my Ethel!"

"Yes, thank you, I do."

"But we must wish for gratitude for others' sake, though we may be willing to go without it for our own. Indeed, gratitude is often just as painful as Wordsworth there represents it. It makes us so ashamed; makes us think how much more we *might* have done; how lovely a thing it is to give in return for such common gifts as ours; how needy the man or woman must be in whom a trifle awakes so much emotion."

"Yes; but we must not in justice think that it is merely that our little doing seems great to them: it is the kindness shown them therein, for which, often, they are more grateful than for the gift, though they can't show the difference in their thanks."

"And, indeed, are not aware of it themselves, though it is so. And yet, the same remarks hold good about the kindness as about the gift. But to return to Theodora. If we put her in a way of life that would be recognizant of whence she came, and how she had been brought thence, might it not be better for her? Would it not be building on the truth? Would she not be happier for it?"

"You are putting general propositions, while all the time you have something particular and definite in your own mind; and that is not fair to my place in the conference," said Ethel. "In fact, you think you are trying to approach me wisely, in order to persuade, I will not say *wheedle*, me into something. It 's a good thing you have the harmlessness of the dove, Harry, for you've got the other thing."

"Well, then, I will be as plain as ever I can be, only premising that what you call the cunning of the serpent——"

"Wisdom, Harry, not cunning."

"Is only that I like to give my arguments before my proposition. But here it is—bare and defenceless, only —let me warn you—with a whole battery behind it: it is, to bring up little Theodora as a servant to Constance."

My wife laughed.

"Well," she said, "for one who says so much about not thinking of the morrow, you do look rather far forward."

"Not with any anxiety, however, if only I know that I am doing right."

"But just think: the child is about three months old."

"Well; Connie will be none the worse that she is being trained for her. I don't say that she is to commence her duties at once."

"But Connie may be at the head of a house of her own long before that."

"The training won't be lost to the child though. But I much fear, my love, that Connie will never be herself again. There is no sign of it. And Turner does not give much hope."

"Oh! Harry, Harry, don't say so. I can't bear it. To think of the darling child lying like that all her life!"

"It is sad, indeed; but no such awful misfortune surely, Ethel. Haven't you seen, as well as I, that the growth of that child's nature since her accident has been marvellous? Ten times rather would I have her lying there such as she is, than have her well and strong and silly, with her bonnets inside instead of outside her head."

"Yes, but she needn't have been like that. Wynnie never will."

"Well, but God does all things not only well, but best, absolutely best. But just think what it would be in any circumstances to have a maid that had begun to wait upon her from the first days that she was able to toddle after something to fetch it for her."

"Won't it be like making a slave of her?"

"Won't it be like giving her a divine freedom from the first? The lack of service is the ruin of humanity."

"But we can't train her then like one of our own."

"Why not? Could we not give her all the love and all the teaching?"

"Because it would not be fair to give her the education of a lady, and then make a servant of her."

"You forget that the service would be part of her training from the first; and she would know no change of position in it. When we tell her that she was found in the shrubbery, we will add that we think God sent her to take care of Constance. I do not believe myself that you can have perfect service except from a lady. Do not forget the *true* notion of service as the essence of Christianity, yea, of divinity. It is not education that unfits for service: it is the want of it."

"Well, I know that the reading girls I have had, have, as a rule, served me worse than the rest."

"Would you have called one of those girls educated? Or even if they had been educated, as any of them might well have been, better than nine-tenths of the girls that go to boarding-schools, you must remember that they had never been taught service—the highest accomplishment of all. To that everything aids, when any true feeling of it is there. But for service of this high sort, the education must begin with the beginning of the dawn of will. How often have you wished that you had servants who would believe in you, and serve you with the same truth with which you regarded them! The servants born in a man's house in the old times were more like his children than his servants. Here is a chance for you, as it were of a servant born in your own house. Connie loves the child: the child will love Connie, and find her delight in serving her like a little cherub. Not one of the maids to whom you have referred had ever been taught to think service other than an unavoidable necessity, the end of life being to serve yourself, not to serve others; and hence most of them would escape from it by any marriage almost that they had a chance of making. I don't say all servants are like that; but I do think that most of them are. I know very well that most mistresses are as much to blame for this result as the servants are; but we are not talking about them. Servants now-a-days despise work, and yet are forced to do it—a most degrading condition to be in. But they would not be in any better condition if delivered from the work. The lady who despises work is in as bad a condition as they are. The only way to set them free is to get them to regard service not only as their duty, but as therefore honourable, and besides and beyond this, in its own nature divine. In America, the very name of servant is repudiated as inconsistent with human dignity. There is *no* dignity but of service. How different the whole notion of training is now from what it was in the middle ages! Service was honourable then. No doubt we have made progress as a whole, but in some things we have degenerated sadly. The first thing taught then was how to serve. No man could rise to the honour of knighthood without service. A nobleman's son even had to wait on his father, or to go into the family of another nobleman, and wait upon him as a page, standing behind his chair at dinner. This was an honour. No notion of degradation was in it. It was a necessary step to higher honour. And what was the next higher honour? To be set free from service? No. To serve in the harder service of the field; to be a squire to some noble knight; to tend his horse, to clean his armour, to see that every rivet was sound, every buckle true, every strap strong; to ride behind him and carry his spear, and if more than one attacked him, to rush to his aid. This service was the more honourable because it was harder, and was the next step to higher honour yet. And what was this higher honour? That of knighthood. Wherein did this knighthood consist? The very word means simply *service.* And for what was the knight thus waited upon by his squire? That he might be free to do as he pleased? No, but that he might be free to be the servant of all. By being a squire first, the servant of one, he learned to rise to the higher rank, that of servant of all. His horse was tended, his armour observed, his sword and spear and shield held to his hand, that he might have no trouble looking after himself, but might be free, strong, unwearied, to shoot like an arrow to the rescue of any and every one who needed his ready aid. There was a grand heart of Christianity in that old chivalry, notwithstanding all its abuses, which must be no more laid to its charge than the burning of Jews and heretics to Christianity. It was the lack of it, not the presence of it, that occasioned the abuses that coexisted with it. Train our Theodora as a holy child-servant, and there will be no need to restrain any impulse of wise affection from pouring itself forth upon her. My firm belief is, that we should then love and honour her far more than if we made her just like one of our own."

"But what if she should turn out utterly unfit for it?"

"Ah! then would come an obstacle. But it will not come till that discovery is made."

"But if we should be going wrong all the time?"

"Now there comes the kind of care that never troubles me, and which I so strongly object to. It won't hurt her anyhow. And we ought always to act upon the ideal; it is the only safe ground of action. When that which contradicts and resists, and would ruin our ideal, opposes us, then we must take measures; but not till then can we take measures, or know what measures it may be necessary to take. But the ideal itself is the only thing worth striving after. Remember what our Lord himself said: 'Be ye therefore perfect, even as your Father which is in heaven is perfect.'"

"Well, I will think about it, Harry. There is time enough."

"Plenty. No time only not to think about it. The more you think about it the better. If a thing be a good thing, the more you think about it the better it will look; for its real nature will go on coming out and showing itself. I cannot doubt that you will soon see how good it is."

We then went home. It was only two days after that my wife said to me—

"I am more than reconciled to your plan, husband. It seems to me delightful."

When we re-entered Connie's room, we found that her baby had just waked, and she had managed to get one arm under her, and was trying to comfort her, for she was crying.

CHAPTER IX.

A SPRING CHAPTER.

MORE especially now in my old age, I find myself "to a lingering motion bound." I would, if I might, tell a tale day by day, hour by hour, following the movement of the year in its sweet change of seasons. This may not be, but I will indulge myself now so far as to call this a spring chapter, and so pass to the summer, when my reader will see why I have called my story "The Seaboard Parish."

I was out one day amongst my people, and I found two precious things: one, a lovely little fact, the other a lovely little primrose. This was a pinched, dwarfish thing, for the spring was but a baby herself, and so could not mother more than a brave-hearted weakling. The frost lay all about it under the hedge, but its rough leaves kept it just warm enough, and hardly. Now, I should never have pulled the little darling; it would have seemed a kind of small sacrilege committed on the church of nature, seeing she had but this one; only with my sickly cub at home, I felt justified in ravening like a beast of prey. I even went so far in my greed as to dig up the little plant with my fingers, and bear it, leaves and all, with a lump of earth about it to keep it alive, home to my little woman—a present from the outside world which she loved so much. And as I went there dawned upon me the recollection of a little mirror in which, if I could find it, she would see it still more lovely than in a direct looking at itself. So I set myself to find it; for it lay in fragments in the drawers and cabinets of my memory. And before I got home I had found all the pieces and put them together; and then it was a lovely little sonnet which a friend of mine had written and allowed me to see many years before. I was in the way of writing verses myself; but I should have been proud to have written this one. I never could have done that. Yet, as far as I knew, it had never seen the light through the windows of print. It was with some difficulty that I got it all right; but I thought I had succeeded very nearly, if not absolutely, and I said it over and over, till I was sure I should not spoil its music or its meaning by halting in the delivery of it.

"Look here, my Connie, what I have brought you," I said.

She held out her two white, half-transparent hands, took it as if it had been a human baby, and looked at it lovingly till the tears came in her eyes. She would have made a tender picture, as she then lay, with her two hands up, holding the little beauty before her eyes. Then I said what I have already written about the mirror, and repeated the sonnet to her. Here it is, and my readers will owe me gratitude for it. My friend had found the snowdrop in February, and in frost. Indeed he told me that there was a tolerable sprinkling of snow upon the ground :—

"I know not what among the grass thou art,
Thy nature nor thy substance, fairest flower,
Nor what to other eyes thou hast of power
To send thine image through them to the heart;
But when I push the frosty leaves apart,
And see thee hiding in thy wintry bower,
Thou growest up within me from that hour,
And through the snow I with the spring depart.

"I have no words. But fragrant is the breath,
Pale Beauty, of thy second life within.
There is a wind that cometh for thy death,
But thou a life immortal dost begin,
Where, in one soul, which is thy heaven, shall dwell
Thy spirit, beautiful Unspeakable!"

"Will you say it again, papa?" said Connie; "I do not quite understand it."

"I will, my dear. But I will do something better as well. I will go and write it out for you, as soon as I have given you something else that I have brought."

"Thank you, papa. And please write it in your best Sunday hand, that I may read it quite easily."

I promised, and repeated the poem.

"I understand it a little better," she said; "but the meaning is just like the primrose itself, hidden up in its green leaves. When you give it me in writing, I will push them apart and find it. Now, tell me what else you have brought me."

I was greatly pleased with the resemblance the child saw between the plant and the sonnet; but I did not say anything in praise; I only expressed satisfaction. Before I began my story, Wynnie came in and sat down with us.

"I have been to see Miss Aylmer, this morning," I said. "She feels the loss of her mother very much, poor thing."

"How old was she, papa?" asked Connie.

"She was over ninety, my dear; but she had forgotten how much herself, and her daughter could not be sure about it. She was a peculiar old lady, you know. She once reproved me for inadvertently putting my hat on the tablecloth. 'Mr Shafton,' she said, 'was one of the old school; he would never have done that. I don't know what the world is coming to.'"

My two girls laughed at the idea of their papa being reproved for bad manners.

"What did you say, papa?" they asked.

"I begged her pardon, and lifted it instantly. 'Oh, it's all right now, my dear,' she said, 'when you've taken it up again. But I like good manners, though I live in a cottage now.'"

"Had she seen better days, then?" asked Wynnie.

"She was a farmer's daughter, and a farmer's widow. I suppose the chief difference in her mode of life was that she lived in a cottage instead of a good-sized farm-house."

"But what is the story you have to tell us?"

"I'm coming to that when you have done with your questions."

"We have done, papa.

"After talking a while, during which she went bustling a little about the cottage, in order to hide her feelings, as I thought, for she has a good deal of her mother's sense of dignity about her,—but I want your mother to hear the story. Run and fetch her, Wynnie."

"Oh, do make haste, Wynnie," said Connie.

When Ethelwyn came, I went on.

"Miss Aylmer was bustling a little about the cottage, putting things to rights. All at once she gave a cry of surprise, and said, 'Here it is at last!' She had taken up a stuff dress of her mother's, and was holding it in one hand, while with the other she drew from the pocket—what do you think?"

Various guesses were hazarded.

"No, no—nothing like it. I know you *could* never guess. Therefore it would not be fair to keep you trying. A great iron horseshoe. The old woman of ninety years, had in the pocket of the dress that she was wearing at the very moment when she died, for her death was sudden, an iron horseshoe."

"What did it mean? Could her daughter explain it?"

"That she proceeded at once to do. 'Do you remember, sir,' she said, 'how that horseshoe used to hang on a nail over the chimney-piece?' 'I do remember having observed it there,' I answered; for once when I took notice of it, I said to your mother, laughing, "I hope you are not afraid of witches, Mrs Aylmer?" And she looked a little offended, and assured me to the contrary.' 'Well,' her daughter went on, 'about three months ago, I missed it. My mother would not tell me anything about it. And here it is! I can hardly think she can have carried it about all that time without me finding it out, but I don't know. Here it is anyhow. Perhaps when she felt death drawing nearer, she took it from somewhere where she had hidden it, and put it in her pocket. If I had found it in time, I would have put it in her coffin?' 'But why?' I asked. 'Do tell me the story about it, if you know it.' 'I know it quite well, for she told me all about it once. It is the shoe of a favourite mare of my father's—one he used to ride when he went courting my mother. My grandfather did not like to have a young man coming about the house, and so he came after the old folks were gone to bed. But he had a long way to come, and he rode that mare. She had to go over some stones to get to the stable, and my mother used to spread straw there, for it was under the window of my grandfather's room, that her shoes mightn't make a noise and wake him. And that's one of the shoes,' she said, holding it up to me. 'When the mare died, my mother begged my father for the one off her near fore-foot, where she had so often stood and patted her neck when my father was mounted to ride home again.'"

"But it was very naughty of her, wasn't it," said Wynnie, "to do that without her father's knowledge?"

"I don't say it was right, my dear. But in looking at what is wrong, we ought to look for the beginning of the wrong; and possibly we might find that in this case farther back. If, for instance, a father isn't a father, we must not be too hard in blaming the child for not being a child. The father's part has to come first and teach the child's part. Now, if I might guess from what I know of the old lady, in whom probably it was much softened, her father was very possibly a hard, unreasoning, and unreasonable man—such that it scarcely ever came into the daughter's head that she had anything else to do with regard to him than beware of the consequences of letting him know that she had a lover. The whole thing, I allow, was wrong; but I suspect the father was first to blame, and far more to blame than the daughter. And that is the more likely from the high character of the old dame, and the romantic way in which she clung to the memory of the courtship. A true heart only does not grow old. And I have, therefore, no doubt that the marriage was a happy one. Besides, I daresay, it was very much the custom of the country where they were, and that makes some difference."

"Well, I'm sure, papa, you wouldn't like any of us to go and do like that," said Wynnie.

"Assuredly not, my dear," I answered, laughing. "Nor have I any fear of it. But shall I tell you what I think would be one of the chief things to trouble me if you did?"

"If you like, papa. But it sounds rather dreadful to hear such an *if*," said Wynnie.

"It would be to think how much I had failed of being such a father to you as I ought to be, and as I wished to be, if it should prove at all possible for you to do such a thing."

"It's too dreadful to talk about, papa," said Wynnie; and the subject was dropped.

She was a strange child, this Wynnie of ours. Whereas most people are in danger of thinking themselves in the right, or insisting that they are whether they think so or not, she was always thinking herself in the wrong. Nay more, she always expected to find herself in the wrong. If the perpetrator of any mischief was inquired after, she always looked into her own bosom to see whether she could not with justice aver that she was the doer of the deed. I believe she felt at that moment as if she had been deceiving me already, and deserved to be driven out of the house. This came of an over-sensitiveness, accompanied by a general dissatisfaction with herself, which was not upheld by a sufficient faith in the divine sympathy, or sufficient confidence of final purification. She never spared herself; and if she was a little severe on the younger ones sometimes, no one was yet more indulgent to them. She would eat all their hard crusts for them, always give them the best and take the worst for herself. If there was any part in the dish that she was helping that she thought nobody would like, she invariably assigned it to her own share. It looked like a determined self-mortification sometimes; but that was not it. She did not care for her own comfort enough to feel it any mortification; though I observed that when her mother or I helped her to anything nice, she ate it with as much relish as the youngest of the party. And her sweet smile was always ready to meet the least kindness that was offered her. Her obedience was perfect, and had been so for very many years, as far as we could see. Indeed, not since she was the merest child had there been any contest between us. Now, of course, there was no demand of obedience: she was simply the best earthly friend that her father and mother had. It often caused me some passing anxiety to think that her temperament, as well as her devotion to her home, might cause her great suffering some day; but when those thoughts came, I just gave her to God to take care of. Her mother sometimes said to her that she would make an excellent wife for a poor man. She would brighten up greatly at this, taking it for a compliment of the best sort. And she did not forget it, as the sequel will show. She would choose to sit with one candle lit when there were two on the table, wasting her eyes to save the candles. "Which will you have for dinner to-day, papa, roast beef or boiled?" she asked me once, when her mother was too unwell to attend to the housekeeping. And when I replied that I would have whichever she liked best—"The boiled beef lasts longest, I think," she said. Yet she was not only as liberal and kind as any to the poor, but she was, which is rarer, and perhaps more important for the final formation of a character, carefully just to every one with whom she had any dealings. Her sense of law was very strong. Law with her was something absolute, and not to be questioned. In her childhood there was one lady to whom for years she showed a decided aversion, and we could not understand it, for it was the most inoffensive Miss Boulderstone. When she was nearly grown up, one of us happening to allude to the fact, she volunteered an explanation. Miss Boulderstone had happened to call one day when Wynnie, then between three and four, was in disgrace—*in the corner*, in fact. Miss Boulderstone interceded for her; and this was the whole front of her offending.

"I *was* so angry!" she said. "'As if my papa did not know best when I ought to come out of the corner!' I said to myself. And I couldn't bear her for ever so long after that."

Miss Boulderstone, however, though not very interesting, was quite a favourite before she died. She left Wynnie—for she and her brother were the last of their race—a death's-head watch, which had been in the family she did not know how long. I think it is as old as Queen Elizabeth's time. I took it to London to a skilful man, and had it as well repaired as its age would admit of; and it has gone ever since, though not with the greatest accuracy; for what could be expected of an old death's-head, the most transitory thing in creation? Wynnie wears it to this day, and wouldn't part with it for the best watch in the world.

I tell the reader all this about my daughter that he may be the more able to understand what will follow in due time. He will think that as yet my story has been nothing but promises. Let him only hope that I will fulfil them, and I shall be content.

Mr Boulderstone did not long outlive his sister. Though the old couple, for they were rather old before they died, if indeed, they were not born old, which I strongly suspect, being the last of a decaying family that had not left the land on which they were born for a great many generations—though the old people had not, of what the French call sentiments, one between them, they were yet capable of a stronger and, I had almost said, more romantic attachment, than many couples who have married from love; for the lady's sole trouble in dying was what her brother *would* do without her; and from the day of her death, he grew more and more dull and seemingly stupid. Nothing gave him any pleasure but having Wynnie to dinner with him. I knew that it must be very dull for her, but she went often, and I never heard her complain of it, though she certainly did looked fagged —not *bored*, observe, but fagged—showing that she had been exerting herself to meet the difficulties of the situation. When the good man died, we found that he had left all his money in my hands, in trust for the poor of the parish, to be applied in any way I thought best. This involved me in much perplexity, for nothing is more difficult than to make money useful to the poor. But I was very glad of it, notwithstanding.

My own means were not so large as my readers may think. The property my wife brought me was much encumbered. With the help of her private fortune, and the income of several years, (not my income from the church, it may be as well to say), I succeeded in clearing off the encumbrances. But even then there remained much to be done, if I would be the good steward that was not to be ashamed at his Lord's coming. First of all there were many cottages to be built for the labourers on the estate. If the farmers would not, or could not, help, I must do it; for to provide decent dwellings for them, was clearly one of the divine conditions in the righteous tenure of property, whatever the human might be; for it was not for myself alone, or for myself chiefly, that this property was given to me; it was for those who lived upon it. Therefore I laid out what money I could, not only in getting all the land clearly in its right relation to its owner, but in doing the best I could for those attached to it who could not help themselves. And when I hint to my reader that I had some conscience in paying my curate, though, as they had no children, they did not require so much as I should otherwise have felt compelled to give them, he will easily see that as my family grew up I could not have so much to give away of my own as I should have liked. Therefore this trust of the good Mr Boulderstone was the more acceptable to me.

One word more ere I finish this chapter.—I should not like my friends to think that I had got tired of our Christmas gatherings, because I have made no mention of one this year. It had been pretermitted for the first time, because of my daughter's illness. It was much easier to give them now than when I lived at the vicarage, for there was plenty of room in the old hall. But my curate, Mr Weir, still held a similar gathering there every Easter.

Another one word more about him. Some may wonder

why I have not mentioned him or my sister, especially in connexion with Connie's accident. The fact was, that he had taken, or rather I had given him, a long holiday. Martha had had several disappointing illnesses, and her general health had suffered so much in consequence that there was even some fear of her lungs, and a winter in the south of France had been strongly recommended. Upon this I came in with more than a recommendation, and insisted that they should go. They had started in the beginning of October, and had not returned up to the time of which I am now about to write—somewhere in the beginning of the month of April. But my sister was now almost quite well, and I was not sorry to think that I should soon have a little more leisure for such small literary pursuits as I delighted in—to my own enrichment, and consequently to the good of my parishioners and friends.

CHAPTER X.

AN IMPORTANT LETTER.

T was, then, in the beginning of April that I received one morning an epistle from an old college friend of mine, with whom I had renewed my acquaintance of late, through the pleasure which he was kind enough to say he had derived from reading a little book of mine upon the relation of the mind of St Paul to the gospel story. His name was Shepherd—a good name for a clergyman. In his case both Christian name and patronymic might remind him well of his duty. David Shepherd ought to be a good clergyman.

As soon as I had read the letter, I went with it open in my hand to find my wife.

"Here is Shepherd," I said, "with a clerical sore-throat, and forced to give up his duty for a whole summer. He writes to ask me whether, as he understands I have a curate as good as myself—that is what the old fellow says

—it might not suit me to take my family to his place for the summer. He assures me I should like it, and that it would do us all good. His house, he says, is large enough to hold us, and he knows I should not like to be without duty wherever I was. And so on. Read the letter for yourself, and turn it over in your mind, Weir will come back so fresh and active that it will be no oppression to him to take the whole of the duty here. I will run and ask Turner whether it would be safe to move Connie, and whether the sea-air would be good for her."

"One would think you were only twenty, husband—you make up your mind so quickly, and are in such a hurry."

The fact was, a vision of the sea had rushed in upon me. It was many years since I had seen the sea, and the thought of looking on it once more, in its most glorious show, the Atlantic itself, with nothing between us and America but the round of the ridgy water, had excited me so that my wife's reproof, if reproof it was, was quite necessary to bring me to my usually quiet and sober senses. I laughed, begged old grannie's pardon, and set off to see Turner notwithstanding, leaving her to read and ponder Shepherd's letter.

"What do you think, Turner?" I said, and told him the case.

He looked rather grave.

"When would you think of going?" he asked.

"About the beginning of June."

"Nearly two months," he said, thoughtfully. "And

Miss Connie was not the worse for getting on the sofa yesterday?"

"The better, I do think."

"Has she had any increase of pain since?"

"None, I quite believe; for I questioned her as to that."

He thought again. He was a careful man, although young.

"It is a long journey."

"She could make it by easy stages."

"It would certainly do her good to breathe the sea-air and have such a thorough change in every way—if only it could be managed without fatigue and suffering. I think, if you can get her up every day between this and that, we shall be justified in trying it at least. The sooner you get her out of doors the better too; but the weather is scarcely fit for that yet."

"A good deal will depend on how she is inclined, I suppose."

"Yes. But in her case you must not mind that too much. An invalid's instincts as to eating and drinking are more to be depended upon than those of a healthy person; but it is not so, I think, with regard to anything involving effort. That she must sometimes be urged to. She must not judge that by inclination. I have had, in my short practice, two patients who considered themselves *bedlars*, as you will find the common people in the part you are going to, call them—bedridden, that is. One of them I persuaded to make the attempt to rise, and although her sense of inability was anything but feigned, and she will be a sufferer to the end of her days, yet she goes about the house without much inconvenience, and I suspect is not only physically but morally the better for it. The other would not consent to try, and I believe lies there still."

"The will has more to with most things than people generally suppose," I said. "Could you manage, now, do you think, supposing we resolve to make the experiment, to accompany us the first stage or two?"

"It is very likely I could. Only you must not depend upon me. I cannot tell beforehand. You yourself would teach me that I must not be a respecter of persons, you know."

I returned to my wife. She was in Connie's room.

"Well, my dear," I said, "what do you think of it?"

"Of what?" she asked.

"Why, of Shepherd's letter, of course," I answered.

"I've been ordering the dinner since, Harry."

"The dinner!" I returned, with some show of contempt, for I knew my wife was only teasing me. "What's the dinner to the Atlantic?"

"What do you mean by the Atlantic, papa?" said Connie, from whose roguish eyes I could see that her mother had told her all about it, and that *she* was not disinclined to get up, if only she could.

"The Atlantic, my dear, is the name given to that portion of the waters of the globe which divides Europe from America. I will fetch you the Universal Gazetteer, if you would like to consult it on the subject."

"Oh, papa!" laughed Connie; "you know what I mean."

"Yes; and you know what I mean too, you squirrel!"

"But do you really mean, papa," she said, "that you will take me to the Atlantic?"

"If you will only oblige me by getting well enough to go as soon as possible."

The poor child half rose on her elbow, but sank back again with a moan, which I took for a cry of pain. I was beside her in a moment.

"My darling! You have hurt yourself!"

"Oh no, papa. I felt for the moment as if I could get up if I liked. But I soon found that I hadn't any back or legs. Oh! what a plague I am to you!"

"On the contrary, you are the nicest plaything in the world, Connie. One always knows where to find you."

She half-laughed and half-cried, and the two halves made a very bewitching whole.

"But," I went on, "I mean to try whether my dolly won't bear moving. One thing is clear, I can't go without it. Do you think you could be got on the sofa to-day without hurting you?"

"I am sure I could, papa. I feel better to-day than I have felt yet. Mamma, do send for Susan, and get me up before dinner."

When I went in after a couple of hours or so, I found her lying on the couch, propped up with pillows. She lay looking out of the window on the lawn at the back of the house. A smile hovered about her bloodless lips, and the blue of her eyes, though very gray, looked sunny. Her white face showed the whiter because her dark brown hair was all about it. We had had to cut her hair, but it had grown to her neck again.

"I have been trying to count the daisies on the lawn," she said.

"What a sharp sight you must have, child!"

"I see them all as clear as if they were enamelled on that table before me."

I was not so anxious to get rid of the daisies as some people are. Neither did I keep the grass quite so close shaved.

"But," she went on, "I could not count them, for it gave me the fidgets in my feet."

"You don't say so!" I exclaimed.

She looked at me with some surprise, but concluding that I was only making a little of my mild fun at her expense, she laughed.

"Yes. Isn't it a wonderful fact?" she said.

"It is a fact, my dear, that I feel ready to go on my knees and thank God for. I may be wrong, but I take it as a sign that you are beginning to recover a little. But we mustn't make too much of it, lest I should be mistaken," I added, checking myself, for I feared exciting her too much.

But she lay very still; only the tears rose slowly and lay shimmering in her eyes. After about five minutes, during which we were both silent,—

"Oh, papa!" she said, "to think of ever walking out with you again, and feeling the wind on my face! I can hardly believe it possible."

"It is so mild, I think you might have half that pleasure at once," I answered.

And I opened the window, let the spring air gently move her hair for one moment, and then shut it again. Connie breathed deep, and said after a little pause,—

"I had no idea how delightful it was. To think that I have been in the way of breathing that every moment for so many years, and never thought about it!"

"It is not always just like that in this climate. But I ought not to have made that remark when I wanted to make this other: that I suspect we shall find some day that the loss of the human paradise consists chiefly in the closing of the human eyes; that at least far more of it than people think remains about us still, only we are so filled with foolish desires and evil cares, that we cannot see or hear, cannot even smell or taste the pleasant things round about us. We have need to pray in regard to the right receiving of the things of the senses even, 'Lord, open thou our hearts to understand thy word;' for each of these things is as certainly a word of God as Jesus is The Word of God. He has made nothing in vain. All is for our teaching. Shall I tell you what such a breath of fresh air makes me think of?"

"It comes to me," said Connie, "like forgiveness when I was a little girl and was naughty. I used to feel just like that.

"It is the same kind of thing I feel," I said—"as if life from the Spirit of God were coming into my soul: I think of the wind that bloweth where it listeth. Wind and spirit are the same word in the Greek; and the Latin word *spirit* comes even nearer to what we are saying, for it is the wind as *breathed*. And now, Connie, I will tell you—and you will see how I am growing able to talk to you like quite an old friend—what put me in such a delight with Mr Shepherd's letter, and so exposed me to be teased by mamma and you. As I read it, there rose up before me a vision of one sight of the sea which I had when I was a young man, long before I saw your mamma. I had gone out for a walk along some high downs. But I ought to tell you that I had been working rather hard at Cambridge, and the life seemed to be all gone out of me. Though my holidays had come, they did not feel quite like holidays—not as holidays used to feel when I was a boy. Even when walking along those downs, with the scents of sixteen grasses or so in my brain, like a melody with the odour of the earth for the accompaniment upon which it floated, and with just enough of wind to stir them up and set them in motion, I could not feel at all. I remembered something of what I had used to feel in such places, but instead of believing in that, I doubted now whether it had not been all a trick that I played myself—a fancied pleasure only. I was walking along, then, with the sea behind me. It was a warm, cloudy day—I had had no sunshine since I came out. All at once I turned—I don't know why. There lay the gray sea, but not as I had seen it last, not all gray. It was dotted, spotted, and splashed all over with drops, pools, and lakes of light, of all shades of depth, from a light shimmer of tremulous gray, through a half-light that turned the prevailing lead colour into translucent green that seemed to grow out of its depths—through this, I say, to brilliant light, deepening and deepening till my very soul was stung by the triumph of the intensity of its molten silver. There was no sun upon me. But there were breaks in the clouds over the sea, through which, the air being filled with vapour, I could see the long lines of the sun-rays descending on the waters like rain—so like a rain of light that the water seemed to plash up in light under their fall. I questioned the past no more; the present seized upon me, and I knew that the past was true, and that nature was more lovely, more awful in her loveliness than I could grasp. It was a lonely place! I fell on my knees, and worshipped the God that made the glory and my soul."

While I spoke Connie's tears had been flowing quietly.

"And mamma and I were making fun while you were seeing such things as those!" she said, pitifully.

"You didn't hurt them one bit, my darling—neither mamma nor you. If I had been the least cross about it, as I should have been when I was as young as at the time of which I was thinking, that would have ruined the vision entirely. But your merriment only made me enjoy it more. And, my Connie, I hope you will see the Atlantic before long; and if one vision should come as brilliant as that, we shall be fortunate indeed—if we went all the way to the west to see that only."

"O papa! I dare hardly think of it—it is too delightful. But do you think we shall really go?"

"I do. Here comes your mamma.—I am going to

say to Shepherd, my dear, that I will take his parish in hand, and if I cannot, after all, go myself, will find some one, so that he need be in no anxiety from the uncertainty which must hang over our movements even till the experiment itself is made."

"Very well, husband. I am quite satisfied."

And as I watched Connie, I saw that hope and expectation did much to prepare her.

CHAPTER XI.

CONNIE'S DREAM.

R TURNER, being a good mechanic as well as surgeon, proceeded to invent, and with his own hands in a great measure construct, a kind of litter, which, with a water-bed laid upon it, could be placed in our own carriage for Connie to lie upon, and from that lifted, without disturbing her, and placed in a similar manner in the railway carriage. He had laid Connie repeatedly upon it before he was satisfied that the arrangement of the springs, &c., was successful. But at length she declared that it was perfect, and that she would not mind being carried across the Arabian desert on a camel's back with that under her.

As the season advanced she continued to improve. I shall never forget the first time she was carried out upon the lawn. If you can imagine an infant coming into the world capable of the observation and delight of a child of eight or ten, you will have some idea of how Connie received the new impressions of everything around her. They were almost too much for her at first, however. She who had been used to scamper about like a wild thing on her pony, found the delight of a breath of wind almost more than she could bear. After she was laid down she closed her eyes, and the smile that flickered about her mouth was of a sort that harmonized entirely with the two great tears that crept softly out from under her eyelids, and sank, rather than ran, down her cheeks. She lay so that she faced a rich tract of gently-receding upland, plentifully wooded to the horizon's edge, and through the wood peeped the white and red houses of a little hamlet, with the square tower of its church just rising above the trees. A kind of frame was made to the whole picture by the nearer trees of our own woods, through an opening in which, evidently made or left for its sake, the distant prospect was visible. It was a morning in early summer, when the leaves were not quite full-grown, but almost, and their green was shining and pure as the blue of the sky, when the air had no touch of bitterness or of lassitude, but was thoroughly warm, and yet filled the lungs with the reviving as of a draught of cold water. We had fastened the carriage umbrella to the sofa, so that it should shade her perfectly without obscuring her prospect; and behind this we all crept, leaving her to come to herself without being looked at, for emotion is a shy and sacred thing, and should be tenderly hidden by those who are near. The bees kept very *beesy* all about us.

To see one huge fellow, as big as three ordinary ones, with pieces of red and yellow about him, as if he were the beadle of all bee-dom, and overgrown in consequence —to see him, I say, down in a little tuft of white clover, rolling about in it, hardly able to move for fatness, yet bumming away as if his business was to express the delight of the whole creation—was a sight! Then there were the butterflies, so light that they seemed to tumble up into the air, and get down again with difficulty! They bewildered me with their inscrutable variations of purpose. "If I could but see once, for an hour, into the mind of a butterfly," I thought, "it would be to me worth all the natural history I ever read. If I could but see why he changes his mind so often and so suddenly—what he saw about that flower to make him seek it—then why, on a nearer approach, he should decline further acquaintance with it, and go rocking away through the air, to do the same fifty times over again—it would give me an insight into all animal and vegetable life that ages of study could not bring me up to." I was thinking all this behind my daughter's umbrella, while a lark, whose body had melted quite away in the heavenly spaces, was scattering bright beads of ringing melody straight down upon our heads; while a cock was crowing like a clarion from the home-farm, as if in defiance of the golden glitter of his silent brother on the roof of the stable; while a little stream that scampered down the same slope as the lawn lay upon, from a well in the stable-yard, mingled its sweet undertone of contentment with the jubilation of the lark and the business-like hum of the bees; and while white

Page 123.

clouds floated in the majesty of silence across the blue deeps of the heavens. The air was so full of life and reviving, that it seemed like the crude substance that God might take to make babies' souls of—only the very simile smells of materialism, and therefore I do not like it.

"Papa," said Connie at length, and I was beside her in a moment. Her face looked almost glorified with delight: there was a hush of that awe upon it which is perhaps one of the deepest kinds of delight. She put out her thin white hand, took hold of a button of my coat, drew me down towards her, and said in a whisper:

"Don't you think God is here, papa?"

"Yes, I do, my darling," I answered.

"Doesn't *he* enjoy this?"

"Yes, my dear. He wouldn't make us enjoy it if he did not enjoy it. It would be to deceive us to make us glad and blessed, while our Father did not care about it, or how it came to us. At least it would amount to making us no longer his children."

"I am so glad you think so. I do. And I shall enjoy it so much more now."

She could hardly finish her sentence, but burst out sobbing so that I was afraid she would hurt herself. I saw, however, that it was best to leave her to quiet herself, and motioned to the rest to keep back and let her recover as she could. The emotion passed off in a summer shower, and when I went round once more, her face was shining just like a wet landscape after the sun has come out and Nature has begun to make gentle game of her own past sorrows. In a little while, she was merry—merrier, notwithstanding her weakness, than I think I had ever seen her before.

"Look at that comical sparrow," she said. "Look how he cocks his head first on one side and then on the other. Does he want us to see him? Is he bumptious, or what?"

"I hardly know, my dear. I think sparrows are very like schoolboys; and I suspect that if we understood the one class thoroughly, we should understand the other. But I confess I do not yet understand either."

"Perhaps you will when Charlie and Harry are old enough to go to school," said Connie.

"It is my only chance of making any true acquaintance with the sparrows," I answered. "Look at them now," I exclaimed, as a little crowd of them suddenly appeared where only one had stood a moment before, and exploded in objurgation and general unintelligible excitement. After some obscure fluttering of wings and pecking, they all vanished except two, which walked about in a dignified manner, trying apparently to seem quite unconscious each of the other's presence.

"I think it was a political meeting of some sort," said Connie, laughing merrily.

"Well, they have this advantage over us," I answered, "that they get through their business, whatever it may be, with considerably greater expedition than we get through ours."

A short silence followed, during which Connie lay contemplating everything.

"What do you think we girls are like, then, papa?" she asked at length. "Don't say you don't know, now."

"I ought to know something more about you than I do about schoolboys. And I think I do know a little about girls—not much, though. They puzzle me a good deal sometimes. I know what a great-hearted woman is, Connie."

"You can't help doing that, papa," interrupted Connie, adding with her old roguishness, "You must'nt pass yourself off for very knowing for that. By the time Wynnie is quite grown up, your skill will be tried."

"I hope I shall understand her then, and you too, Connie."

A shadow, just like the shadow of one of those white clouds above us, passed over her face, and she said, trying to smile:

"I shall never grow up, papa. If I live, I shall only be a girl at best—a creature you can't understand."

"On the contrary, Connie, I think I understand you almost as well as mamma. But there isn't so much to understand yet, you know, as there will be."

Her merriment returned.

"Tell me what girls are like, then, or I shall sulk all day because you say there isn't so much in me as in mamma."

"Well, I think, if the boys are like sparrows, the girls are like swallows. Did you ever watch them before rain, Connie, skimming about over the lawn as if it were water, low towards its surface, but never alighting? You never see them grubbing after worms. Nothing less than things with wings like themselves will satisfy them. They will be obliged to the earth only for a little mud to build themselves nests with. For the rest, they live in the air, and on the creatures of the air. And then, when they fancy the air begins to be uncivil, sending little shoots of cold through their warm feathers, they vanish. They won't stand it. They're off to a warmer climate, and you never know till you find they're not there any more. There, Connie!"

"I don't know, papa, whether you are making game of us or not. If you are not, then I wish all you say were quite true of us. If you are, then I think it is not quite like you to be satirical."

"I am no believer in satire, Connie. And I didn't mean any. The swallows are lovely creatures, and there would be no harm if the girls were a little steadier than the swallows. Further satire than that I am innocent of."

"I don't mind that much, papa. Only *I*'m steady enough—and no thanks to me for it," she added with a sigh.

"Connie," I said, "it's all for the sake of your wings that you're kept in your nest."

She did not stay out long this first day, for the life the air gave her soon tired her weak body. But the next morning she was brighter and better, and longing to get up and go out again. When she was once more laid on her couch on the lawn, in the midst of the world of light and busy-ness, in which the light was the busiest of all, she said to me:

"Papa, I had such a strange dream last night: shall I tell it you?"

"If you please, my dear. I am very fond of dreams that have any sense in them—or even of any that have good nonsense in them. I woke this morning, saying to myself, 'Dante, the poet, must have been a respectable man, for he was permitted by the council of Florence to carry the Nicene Creed and the Multiplication Table in his coat of arms.' Now tell me your dream."

Connie laughed. All the household tried to make Connie laugh, and generally succeeded. It was quite a triumph to Charley or Harry, and was sure to be recounted with glee at the next meal, when he succeeded in making Connie laugh.

"Mine wasn't a dream to make me laugh. It was too dreadful at first, and too delightful afterwards. I suppose it was getting out for the first time yesterday that made me dream it. I thought I was lying quite still, without breathing even, with my hands straight down by my sides and my eyes closed. I did not choose to open them, for I knew that if I did I should see nothing but the inside of the lid of my coffin. I did not mind it much at first, for I was very quiet, and not uncomfortable. Everything was as silent as it should be, for I was ten feet and a half under the surface of the earth in the churchyard. Old Rogers was not far from me on one side, and that was a comfort; only there was a thick wall of earth between. But as the time went on, I began to get uncomfortable. I could not help thinking how long I should have to wait for the resurrection. Somehow I had forgotten all that you teach us about that. Perhaps it was a punishment—the dream—for forgetting it."

"Silly child! Your dream is far better than your reflections."

"Well, I'll go on with my dream. I lay a long time till I got very tired, and wanted to get up, oh, so much! But still I lay, and although I tried, I could not move hand or foot. At last I burst out crying. I was ashamed of crying in my coffin, but I couldn't bear it any longer. I thought I was quite disgraced, for everybody was expected to be perfectly quiet and patient down there. But the moment I began to cry, I heard a sound. And when I listened it was the sound of spades and pickaxes. It went on and on, and came nearer and nearer. And then—it was so strange—I was dreadfully frightened at the idea of the light and the wind, and of the people seeing me in my coffin and my night-dress, and tried to persuade myself that it was somebody else they were digging for, or that they were only going to lay another coffin over mine. And I thought that if it was you, papa, I shouldn't mind how long I lay there, for I shouldn't feel a bit lonely, even though we could not speak a word to each other all the time. But the sounds came on, nearer and nearer, and at last a pickaxe struck, with a blow that jarred me all through, upon the lid of the coffin, right over my head.

"'Here she is, poor thing!' I heard a sweet voice say.

"'I'm so glad we've found her,' said another voice.

"'She couldn't bear it any longer,' said a third more pitiful voice than either of the others. 'I heard her first,' it went on. 'I was away up in Orion, when I thought I heard a woman crying that oughtn't to be crying. And I stopped and listened. And I heard her again. Then I knew that it was one of the buried ones, and that she had been buried long enough, and was ready for the resurrection. So as any business can wait except that, I flew here and there till I fell in with the rest of you.'

"I think, papa, that this must have been because of what you were saying the other evening about the mysticism of St Paul; that while he defended with all his might the actual resurrection of Christ and the resurrection of those he came to save, he used it as meaning something more yet, as a symbol for our coming out of the death of sin into the life of truth. Isn't that right, papa?"

"Yes, my dear; I believe so. But I want to hear your dream first, and then your way of accounting for it."

"There isn't much more of it now."

"There must be the best of it."

"Yes. I allow that. Well, while they spoke—it was a wonderfully clear and connected dream: I never had one like it for that, or for anything else—they were clearing away the earth and stones from the top of my coffin. And I lay trembling and expecting to be looked at, like a thing in a box as I was, every moment. But they lifted me, coffin and all, out of the grave, for I felt the motion of it up. Then they set it down, and I heard them taking the lid off. But after the lid was off, it did not seem to make much difference to me. I could not open my eyes. I saw no light, and felt no wind blowing upon me. But I heard whispering about me. Then I felt warm, soft hands washing my face, and then I felt wafts of wind coming on my face, and thought they came from the waving of wings. And when they had washed my eyes, the air came upon them, so sweet and cool! and I opened them, I thought, and here I was lying on this couch, with butterflies and bees flitting and buzzing about me, the brook singing somewhere near me, and a lark up in the sky. But there were no angels—only plenty of light and wind and living creatures. And I don't think I ever knew before what happiness meant. Wasn't it a resurrection, papa, to come out of the grave into such a world as this?"

"Indeed it was, my darling—and a very beautiful and true dream. There is no need for me to moralize it to you, for you have done so for yourself already. But not only do I think that the coming out of sin into goodness, out of unbelief into faith in God, is like your dream; but I do expect that no dream of such delight can come up to the sense of fresh life and being that we shall have, when we get on the higher body after this one won't serve our purpose any longer, and is worn out and cast aside. The very ability of the mind, whether of itself or by some inspiration of the Almighty, to dream such things, is a proof of our capacity for such things, a proof, I think, that for such things we were made. Here comes in the chance for faith in God—the confidence in his being and perfection, that he would not have made us capable without meaning to fill that capacity. If he is able to make us capable, that is the harder half done already. The other he can easily do. And if he is love he will do it. You should thank God for that dream, Connie."

"I was afraid to do that, papa."

"That is as much as to fear that there is one place to which David might have fled, where God would not find him—the most terrible of all thoughts."

"Where do you mean, papa?"

"Dreamland, my dear. If it is right to thank God for a beautiful thought—I mean a thought of strength and grace giving you fresh life and hope—why should you be less bold to thank him when such thoughts arise in plainer shape—take such vivid forms to your mind that they seem to come through the doors of the eyes into the vestibule of the brain, and thence into the inner chambers of the soul?"

CHAPTER XII.

THE JOURNEY.

OR more than two months Charlie and Harry had been preparing for the journey. The moment they heard of the prospect of it, they began to prepare, accumulate, and pack stores both for the transit and the sojourn. First of all there was an extensive preparation of ginger-beer, consisting, as I was informed in confidence, of brown sugar, ground ginger, and cold water. This store was however, as near as I can judge, exhausted and renewed about twelve times before the day of departure arrived, and when at last the auspicious morning dawned, they remembered with dismay that they had drunk the last drop two days before, and there was none in stock. Then there was a wonderful and more successful hoarding of marbles, of a variety so great that my memory refuses to bear the names of the different kinds, which, I think, must have greatly increased since the time when I too was a boy, when some marbles—one of real white marble with red veins especially—produced in my mind something of the delight that a work of art produces now. These were carefully deposited in one of the many divisions of a huge old hair-trunk, which they had got their uncle Weir, who could use his father's tools with pleasure if not to profit, to fit up for them with a multiplicity of boxes, and cupboards, and drawers, and trays, and slides, that was quite bewildering. In this same box was stowed also a quantity of hair, the gleanings of all the horse-tails upon the premises. This was for making fishing-tackle, with a vague notion on the part of Harry that it was to be employed in catching whales and crocodiles. Then all their favourite books were stowed away in the same chest; in especial a packet of a dozen penny books, of which I think I could give a complete list now. For, one afternoon as I searched about in the lumber-room after a set of old library steps, which I wanted to get repaired, I came upon the chest, and opening it, discovered my boys' hoard, and in it this packet of books: I sat down on the top of the chest and read them all through, from Jack the Giant-killer down tc Hop o' my Thumb, without rising, and this in the broad daylight, with the yellow sunshine nestling beside me on the rose-coloured silken seat, richly worked, of a large stately-looking chair with three golden legs. Yes I could tell you all those stories, not to say the names of them, over yet. Only I knew every one of them before; finding now that they had fared like good vintages, for if they had lost something in potency, they had gained much in flavour. Harry could not read these, and Charlie not very well, but they put confidence in them notwithstanding, in virtue of the red, blue, and yellow prints. Then there was a box of sawdust, the design of which I have not yet discovered; a huge ball of string; a rabbit's skin; a Noah's ark; an American clock, that refused to go for all the variety of treatment they gave it; a box of lead soldiers, and twenty other things, amongst which was a huge gilt ball having an eagle of brass with outspread wings on the top of it.

Great was their consternation and dismay when they found that this magazine could not be taken in the post-chaise in which they were to follow us to the station. A good part of our luggage had been sent on before us, but the boys had intended the precious box to go with themselves. Knowing well, however, how little they would miss it, and with what shouts of south-sea discovery they would greet the forgotten treasure when they returned, I insisted on the lumbering article being left in peace. So that, as man goeth treasureless to his grave, whatever he may have accumulated before the fatal moment, they had to set off for the far country without chest or ginger-beer—not therefore altogether so desolate and unprovided for as they imagined. The abandoned treasure was forgotten the moment the few tears it had occasioned were wiped away.

It was the loveliest of mornings when we started upon our journey. The sun shone, the wind was quiet, and everything was glad. The swallows were twittering from the corbels they had added to the adornment of the dear old house.

"I'm sorry to leave the swallows behind," said Wynnie, as she stepped into the carriage after her mother. Connie, of course, was already there, eager and strong-hearted for the journey.

We set off. Connie was in delight with everything, especially with all forms of animal life and enjoyment that we saw on the road. She seemed to enter into the spirit of the cows feeding on the rich green grass of the meadows, of the donkeys eating by the roadside, of the horses we met, bravely diligent at their day's work, as they trudged along the road with waggon or cart behind them. I sat by the coachman, but so that I could see her face by the slightest turning of my head. I knew by its expression that she gave a silent blessing to the little troop of a brown-faced gipsy family, which came out of a dingy tent to look at the passing carriage. A fleet of ducklings in a pool, paddling along under the convoy of the parent duck, next attracted her.

"Look; look. Isn't that delicious?" she cried.

"I don't think I should like it though," said Wynnie.

"What shouldn't you like, Wynnie?" asked her mother.

"To be in the water and not feel it wet. Those feathers!"

"They feel it with their legs and their webby toes,' said Connie.

"Yes, that is some consolation," answered Wynnie.

"And if you were a duck, you would feel the good of

your feathers in winter, when you got into your cold bath of a morning."

I give all this chat for the sake of showing how Connie's illness had not in the least withdrawn her from nature and her sympathies—had rather, as it were, made all the fibres of her being more delicate and sympathetic, so that the things around her could enter her soul even more easily than before, and what had seemed to shut her out had in reality brought her into closer contact with the movements of all vitality.

We had to pass through the village to reach the railway station. Everybody almost was out to bid us good-bye. I did not want, for Connie's sake chiefly, to have any scene, but recalling something I had forgotten to say to one of my people, I stopped the carriage to speak to him. The same instant there was a crowd of women about us. But Connie was the centre of all their regards. They hardly looked at her mother or sister. Had she been a martyr who had stood the test and received her aureole, she could hardly have been more regarded. The common use of the word martyr is a curious instance of how words get degraded. The sufferings involved in martyrdom, and not the pure will giving occasion to that suffering, is fixed upon by the common mind as the martyrdom. The witness-bearing is lost sight of, except we can suppose that "a martyr to the toothache" means a witness of the fact of the toothache and its tortures. But while *martyrdom* really means a bearing for the sake of the truth, yet there is a way in which any suffering, even that we have brought upon ourselves, may become martyrdom. When it is so borne that the sufferer therein bears witness to the presence and fatherhood of God, in quiet hopeful submission to his will, in gentle endurance, and that effort after cheerfulness which is not seldom to be seen where the effort is hardest to make; more than all, perhaps, and rarest of all, when it is accepted as the just and merciful consequence of wrong-doing, and is endured humbly, and with righteous shame, as the cleansing of the Father's hand, indicating that repentance unto life which lifts the sinner out of his sins, and makes him such that the holiest men of old would talk to him with gladness and respect, then indeed it may be called a martyrdom. This latter could not be Connie's case, but the former was hers, and so far she might be called a martyr, even as the old women of the village designated her.

After we had again started, our ears were invaded with shouts from the post-chaise behind us, in which Charlie and Harry, their grief at the abandoned chest forgotten as if it had never been, were yelling in the exuberance of their gladness. Dora, more staid as became her years, was trying to act the matron with them in vain, and old nursey had enough to do with Miss Connie's baby to heed what the young gentlemen were about so long as explosions of noise was all the mischief. Walter, the man-servant, who had been with us ten years, and was the main prop of the establishment, looking after everything, and putting his hand to everything, with an indefinite charge ranging from the nursery to the wine-cellar, and from the corn-bin to the pig-trough, and who, as we could not possibly get on without him, sat on the box of the post-chaise beside the driver from the Griffin, rather connived, I fear, than otherwise at the noise of the youngsters.

"Good-bye, Marshmallows," they were shouting at the top of their voices, as if they had just been released from a prison, where they had spent a wretched childhood; and as it could hardly offend anybody's ears on the open country road, I allowed them to shout till they were tired, which condition fortunately arrived before we reached the station, so that there was no occasion for me to interfere. I always sought to give them as much liberty as could be afforded them.

At the station we found Weir waiting to see us off, with my sister, now in wonderful health. Turner was likewise there, and ready to accompany us a good part of the way. But beyond the valuable assistance he lent us in moving her, no occasion arose for the exercise of his professional skill. She bore the journey wonderfully, slept not unfrequently, and only at the end showed herself at length wearied. We stopped three times on the way; first at Salisbury, where the streams running through the streets delighted her. There we remained one whole day, but sent the children and servants, all but my wife's maid, on before us, under the charge of Walter. This left us more at our ease. At Exeter, we stopped only the night, for Connie found herself quite able to go on the next morning. Here Turner left us, and we missed him very much. Connie looked a little out of spirits after his departure, but soon recovered herself. The next night we spent at a small town on the borders of Devonshire, which was the limit of our railway travelling. Here we remained for another whole day, for the remnant of the journey across part of Devonshire and Cornwall to the shore, must be posted, and was a good five hours' work. We started about eleven o'clock, full of spirits at the thought that we had all but accomplished the only part of the undertaking about which we had had any uneasiness. Connie was quite merry. The air was thoroughly warm. We had an open carriage with a hood. Wynnie sat opposite her mother, Dora and Eliza the maid in the rumble, and I by the coachman. The road being very hilly, we had four horses; and with four horses, sunshine, a gentle wind, hope, and thankfulness, who would not be happy?

There is a strange delight in motion, which I am not sure that I altogether understand. The hope of the end as bringing fresh enjoyment has something to do with it, no doubt; the accompaniments of the motion, the change of scene, the mystery that lies beyond the next hill or the next turn in the road, the breath of the summer wind, the scent of the pine-trees especially, and of all the earth, the tinkling jangle of the harness as you pass the trees on the roadside, the life of the horses, the glitter and the shadow, the cottages and the roses and the rosy faces, the scent of burning wood or peat from the chimneys,—these and a thousand other things combine to make such a journey delightful. But I believe it needs something more than this—something even closer to the human life—to account for the pleasure that motion gives us. I suspect it is its living symbolism; the hidden relations which it bears to the eternal soul in its aspirations and longings—ever following after, ever attaining, never satisfied. Do not misunderstand me, my reader. A man, you will allow, perhaps, may be content although he is not and cannot be happy: I feel inclined to turn all this the other way, saying that a man ought always to be happy, never to be content. You will see I do not say *contented;* I say *content.* Here comes in his faith: his life is hid with Christ in God, measureless, unbounded. All things are his, to become his by blessed, lovely gradations of gift, as his being enlarges to receive; and if ever the shadow of his own necessary incompleteness falls upon the man, he has only to remember that in God's idea he is complete, only his life is hid from himself with Christ in God the Infinite. If any one accuses me here of mysticism, I plead guilty with gladness: I only hope it may be of that true mysticism which, inasmuch as he makes constant use of it, St Paul would understand at once. I leave it, however.

I think I must have been the very happiest of the party myself. No doubt I was younger much than I am now, but then I was quite middle-aged, with full confession thereof, in gray hairs and wrinkles. Why should not a man be happy when he is growing old, so long as his faith strengthens the feeble knees which chiefly suffer in the process of going down the hill? True, the fever heat is over, and the oil burns more slowly in the lamp of life; but if there is less fervour, there is more pervading warmth; if less of fire, more of sunshine;

there is less smoke and more light. Verily, youth is good, but old age is better—to the man who forsakes not his youth when his youth forsakes him. The sweet visitings of nature do not depend upon youth or romance, but upon that quiet spirit whose meekness inherits the earth. The smell of that field of beans gives me more delight now than ever it could have given me when I was a youth. And if I ask myself why, I find it is simply because I have more faith now than I had then. It came to me then as an accident of nature—a passing pleasure flung to me only as the dogs' share of the crumbs. Now, I believe that God *means* that odour of the bean-field; that when Jesus smelled such a scent about Jerusalem or in Galilee, he thought of his Father. And if God means it, it is mine, even if I should never smell it again. The music of the spheres is mine if old age should make me deaf as the adder. Am I mystical again, reader? Then I hope you are too, or will be before you have done with this same beautiful mystical life of ours. More and more nature becomes to me one of God's books of poetry—not his grandest—that is history—but his loveliest, perhaps.

And ought I not to have been happy when all who were with me were happy? I will not run the risk of wearying even my contemplative reader by describing to him the various reflexes of happiness that shone from the countenances behind me in the carriage, but I will try to hit each off in a word or a single simile. My Ethelwyn's face was bright with the brightness of a pale silvery moon that has done her harvest work, and, a little weary, lifts herself again into the deeper heavens from stooping towards the earth. Wynnie's face was bright with the brightness of the morning star, ever growing pale and faint over the amber ocean that brightens at the sun's approach; for life looked to Wynnie severe in its light, and somewhat sad because severe. Connie's face was bright with the brightness of a lake in the rosy evening, the sound of the river flowing in and the sound of the river flowing forth just audible, but itself still, and content to be still and mirror the sunset. Dora's was bright with the brightness of a marigoid that follows the sun without knowing it; and Eliza's was bright with the brightness of a half-blown cabbage rose, radiating good-humour. This last is not a good simile, but I cannot find a better. I confess failure, and go on.

After stopping once to bait, during which operation Connie begged to be carried into the parlour of the little inn, that she might see the china figures that were certain to be on the chimney-piece, as indeed they were, where she drank a whole tumbler of new milk before we lifted her to carry her back, we came upon a wide high moorland country, the roads through which were lined with gorse in full golden bloom, while patches of heather all about were showing their bells, though not yet in their autumnal outburst of purple fire. Here I began to be reminded of Scotland, in which I had travelled a good deal between the ages of twenty and five-and-twenty. The further I went the stronger I felt the resemblance. The look of the fields, the stone fences that divided them, the shape and colour and materials of the houses, the aspect of the people, the feeling of the air, and of the earth and sky generally, made me imagine myself in a milder and more favoured Scotland. The west wind was fresh, but had none of that sharp edge which one can so often detect in otherwise warm winds blowing under a hot sun. Though she had already travelled so many miles, Connie brightened up within a few minutes after we got on this moor; and we had not gone much farther before a shout from the rumble informed us that keen-eyed little Dora had discovered the Atlantic: a dip in the high coast revealed it blue and bright. We soon lost sight of it again, but in Connie's eyes it seemed to linger still. As often as I looked round, the blue of them seemed the reflection of the sea in their little convex mirrors. Ethelwyn's eyes, too, were full of it, and a flush on her generally pale cheek showed that she too expected the ocean. After a few miles along this breezy expanse, we began to descend towards the sea-level. Down the winding of a gradual slope interrupted by steep descents, we approached this new chapter in our history. We came again upon a few trees here and there, all with their tops cut off in a plane inclined upwards away from the sea. For the sea-winds, like a sweeping scythe, bend the trees all away towards the land, and keep their tops mown with their sharp rushing, keen with salt spray off the crests of the broken waves. Then we passed through some ancient villages, with streets narrow and steep and sharp-angled, that needed careful driving and the frequent pressure of the brake upon the wheel. And now the sea shone upon us with nearer greeting, and we began to fancy we could hear its talk with the shore. At length we descended a sharp hill, reached the last level, drove over a bridge and down the line of the stream, saw the land vanish in the sea—a wide bay; then drove over another wooden drawbridge, and along the side of a canal, in which lay half-a-dozen sloops and schooners. Then came a row of pretty cottages; then a gate, and an ascent; and ere we reached the rectory, we were aware of its proximity by loud shouts, and the sight of Charlie and Harry scampering along the top of a stone wall to meet us. This made their mother nervous, but she kept quiet, knowing that unrestrained anxiety is always in danger of bringing about the evil it fears. A moment after, we drew up at a long porch, leading through the segment of a circle to the door of the house. The journey was over. We got down in the little village of Kilkhaven, in the county of Cornwall.

CHAPTER XIII.

WHAT WE DID WHEN WE ARRIVED.

WE carried Connie in first of all, of course, and into the room which nurse had fixed upon for her—the best in the house, of course, again. She did seem tired now, and no wonder She had a cup of tea at once, and in half-an-hour dinner was ready, of which we were all very glad. After dinner, I went up to Connie's room. There I found her fast asleep on the sofa, and Wynnie as fast asleep on the floor beside her. The drive and the sea air had had the same effect on both of them. But pleased as I was to see Connie sleeping so sweetly, I was even more pleased to see Wynnie asleep on the floor. What a wonderful satisfaction it may give to a father and mother to see this or that child asleep! It is when her kittens are asleep that the cat creeps away to look after her own comforts. Our cat chose to have her kittens in my study once, and as I would not have her further disturbed than to give them another cushion to lie on in place of that which belonged to my sofa, I had many opportunities of watching them as I wrote, or prepared my sermons. But I must not talk about the cat and her kittens now. When parents see their children asleep, especially if they have been suffering in any way, they breathe more freely; a load is lifted off their minds; their responsibility seems over; the children have gone back to their Father, and he alone is looking after them for a while. Now, I had not been comfortable about Wynnie for some time, and especially during our journey, and still more especially during the last part of our journey. There was something amiss with her. She seemed constantly more or less dejected, as if she had something to think about that was too much for her, although, to tell the truth, I really believe now that she had not quite enough to think about. Some people can thrive tolerably without much thought: at least, they both live comfortably without it, and do not seem to be capable of effecting it if it were required of them; while for others a large amount of mental and spiritual operation is necessary for the health of both body and mind, and when the matter or occasion for so much is not afforded them, the consequence is analogous to what follows when a healthy physical system is not supplied with sufficient food: the oxygen, the source of life, begins to consume the life itself; it tears up the timbers of the house to burn against the cold. Or, to use a different simile, when the Moses-rod of circumstance does not strike the rock and make the waters flow, such a mind—one that must think to live—will go digging into itself, and is in danger of injuring the very fountain of thought, by drawing away its living water into ditches and stagnant pools. This was, I say, the case in part with my Wynnie, although I did not understand it at that moment. She did not look quite happy, did not always meet a smile with a smile, looked almost reprovingly upon the frolics of the little brother-imps, and though kindness itself when any real hurt or grief befell them, had reverted to her old, somewhat dictatorial manner, of which I have already spoken as interrupted by Connie's accident. To her mother and me she was service itself, only service without the smile which is as the flame of the sacrifice and makes it holy. So we were both a little uneasy about her, for we did not understand her. On the journey she had seemed almost annoyed at Connie's ecstasies, and said to Dora many times—"Do be quiet, Dora;" although there was not a single creature but ourselves within hearing, and poor Connie seemed only delighted with the child's explosions. So I was—but although I say *so*, I hardly know why I was pleased to see her thus, except it was from a vague belief in the anodyne of slumber. But this pleasure did not last long; for as I stood regarding my two treasures, even as if my eyes had made her uncomfortable, she suddenly opened hers, and started to her feet, with the words, "I beg your pardon, papa," looking almost guiltily round her, and putting up her hair hurriedly, as if she had committed an impropriety in being caught untidy. This was fresh sign of a condition of mind that was not healthy.

"My dear," I said, "what do you beg my pardon for? I was so pleased to see you asleep! and you look as if you thought I were going to scold you."

"O papa," she said, laying her head on my shoulder, "I am afraid I must be very naughty. I so often feel now as if I were doing something wrong, or rather as if you would think I was doing something wrong. I am sure there must be something wicked in me somewhere, though I do not clearly know what it is. When I woke up now, I felt as if I had neglected something, and yon had come to find fault with me. *Is* there anything papa?"

"Nothing whatever, my child. But you cannot be well when you feel like that."

"I am perfectly well, so far as I know. I was so cross to Dora to-day! Why shouldn't I feel happy when everybody else is? I must be wicked, papa."

Here Connie woke up.

"There now! I 've waked Connie," Wynnie resumed. "I 'm always doing something I ought not to do. Please go to sleep again, Connie, and take that sin off my poor conscience."

"What nonsense is Wynnie talking about being wicked?" asked Connie.

"It isn 't nonsense, Connie. You know I am."

"I know nothing of the sort, Wynnie. If it were me now! And yet I don't *feel* wicked."

"My dear children," I said, "we must all pray to God

for his Spirit, and then we shall feel just as we ought to feel. It is not for any one to say to himself how he ought to feel at any given moment; still less for one man to say to another how he ought to feel; that is in the former case to do as St Paul says he had learned to give up doing—to judge our own selves, which ought to be left to God; in the latter case it is to do what our Lord has told us expressly we are not to do—to judge other people. You get your bonnet, Wynnie, and come out with me. I am going to explore a little of this desert island upon which we have been cast away. And you, Connie, just to please Wynnie, must try and go to sleep again."

Wynnie ran for her bonnet, a little afraid perhaps that I was going to talk seriously to her, but showing no reluctance anyhow to accompany me.

Now I wonder whether it will be better to tell what we saw, or only what we talked about, and give what we saw in the shape in which we reported it to Connie, when we came back into her room, bearing, like the spies who went to search the land, our bunch of grapes, that is, of sweet news of nature, to her who could not go to gather them for herself. I think it will be the best plan to take part of both plans.

When we left the door of the house, we went up the few steps of a stair leading on to the downs, against and amidst, and indeed *in*, the rocks buttressing the sea-edge of which our new abode was built. A life for a big-winged angel seemed waiting us upon those downs. The wind still blew from the west, both warm and strong—I mean strength-giving—and the wind was the first thing we were aware of. The ground underfoot was green and soft and springy, and sprinkled all over with the bright flowers, chiefly yellow, that live amidst the short grasses of the downs, the shadows of whose unequal surface were now beginning to be thrown east, for the sun was going seawards. I stood up, stretched out my arms, threw back my shoulders and my head, and filled my chest with a draught of the delicious wind, feeling thereafter like a giant refreshed with wine. Wynnie stood apparently unmoved amidst the life-nectar, thoughtful, and turning her eyes hither and thither.

"That makes me feel young again," I said.

"I wish it would make me feel old then," said Wynnie.

"What do you mean, my child?"

"Because then I should have a chance of knowing what it is like to feel young," she answered rather enigmatically. I did not reply. We were walking up the brow which hid the sea from us. The smell of the down-turf was indescribable in its homely delicacy; and by the time we had reached the top, almost every sense was filled with its own delight. The top of the hill was the edge of the great shore-cliff; and the sun was hanging on the face of the mightier sky-cliff opposite, and the sea stretched for visible miles and miles along the shore on either hand, its wide blue mantle fringed with lovely white wherever it met the land, and scalloped into all fantastic curves, according to the whim of the nether fires which had formed its bed; and the rush of the waves, as they bore the rising tide up on the shore, was the one music fit for the whole. Ear and eye, touch and smell, were alike invaded with blessedness. I ought to have kept this to give my reader in Connie's room; but he shall share with her presently. The sense of space—of mighty room for life and growth filled my soul, and I thanked God in my heart. The wind seemed to bear that growth into my soul, even as the wind of God first breathed into man's nostrils the breath of life, and the sun was the pledge of the fulfilment of every aspiration. I turned and looked at Wynnie. She stood pleased but listless amidst that which lifted me into the heaven of the Presence.

"Don't you enjoy all this grandeur, Wynnie?"

"I told you I was very wicked, papa."

"And I told you not to say so, Wynnie."

"You see I cannot enjoy it, papa. I wonder why it is."

"I suspect it is because you haven't room, Wynnie."

"I know you mean something more than I know, papa."

"I mean, my dear, that it is not because you are wicked, but because you do not know God well enough, and therefore your being, which can only live in him, is 'cabined, cribbed, confined, bound in.' It is only in him that the soul has room. In knowing him, is life and its gladness. The secret of your own heart you can never know; but you can know Him who knows its secret. Look up, my darling; see the heavens and the earth. You do not feel them, and I do not call upon you to feel them. It would be both useless and absurd to do so. But just let them look at you for a moment, and then tell me whether it must not be a blessed life that creates such a glory as this All."

She stood silent for a moment, looked up at the sky, looked round on the earth, looked far across the sea to the setting sun, and then turned her eyes upon me. They were filled with tears, but whether from feeling or sorrow that she could not feel, I would not inquire. I made haste to speak again.

"As this world of delight surrounds and enters your bodily frame, so does God surround your soul and live in it. To be at home with the awful source of your being, through the child-like faith which he not only permits, but requires, and is ever teaching you, or rather seeking to rouse up in you, is the only cure for such feelings as those that trouble you. Do not say it is too high for you. God made you in his own image, therefore capable of understanding him. For this final end he sent his Son, that the Father might with him come into you, and dwell with you. Till he does so, the temple of your soul is vacant; there is no light behind the veil, no cloudy pillar over it; and the priests, your thoughts, feelings, loves, and desires, moan and are troubled—for where is the work of the priest when the god is not there? When He comes to you, no mystery, no unknown feeling will any longer distress you. You will say, 'He knows, though I do not.' And you will be at the secret of the things he has made. You will feel what they are, and that which his will created in gladness you will receive in joy. One glimmer of the present God in this glory would send you home singing. But do not think I blame you, Wynnie, for feeling sad. I take it rather as the sign of a large life in you, that will not be satisfied with little things. I do not know when or how it may please God to give you the quiet of mind that you need; but I tell you that I believe it is to be had; and, in the meantime, you must go on doing your work, trusting in God even for this. Tell him to look at your sorrow, ask him to come and set it right, making the joy go up in your heart by his presence. I do not know when this may be, I say, but you must have patience, and till he lays his hand on your head, you must be content to wash his feet with your tears. Only he will be better pleased if your faith keep you from weeping and from going about your duties mournful. Try to be brave and cheerful for the sake of Christ, and for the sake of your confidence in the beautiful teaching of God, whose course and scope you cannot yet understand. Trust, my daughter, and let that give you courage and strength."

Now the sky and the sea and the earth must have made me able to say these things to her; but I knew that, whatever the immediate occasion of her sadness, such was its only real cure. Other things might, in virtue of the will of God that was in them, give her occupation and interest enough for a time, but nothing would do finally, but God himself. Here I was sure I was safe; here I knew lay the hunger of humanity. Humanity may, like other vital forms, diseased systems, fix on this or that as the object not merely of its desire but of its need: it can never be stilled by less than the bread of life—the very presence in the innermost nature of the Father and the Son.

We walked on together. Wynnie made me no reply, but, weeping silently, clung to my arm. We walked a long way by the edge of the cliffs, beheld the sun go down, and then turned and went home. When we reached the house, Wynnie left me, saying only, "Thank you, papa. I think it is all true. I will try to be a better girl."

I went straight to Connie's room: she was lying as I saw her last, looking out of her window.

"Connie," I said, "Wynnie and I have had such a treat—such a sunset!"

"I've seen a little of the light of it on the waves in the bay there, but the high ground kept me from seeing the sunset itself. Did it set in the sea?"

"You do want the General Gazetteer, after all, Connie. Is that water the Atlantic, or is it not? And if it be, where on earth could the sun set but in it?"

"Of course, papa. What a goose I am! But don't make game of me—*please.* I am too deliciously happy to be made game of to-night."

"I won't make game of you, my darling. I will tell you about the sunset—the colours of it, at least. This must be one of the best places in the whole world to see sunsets."

"But you have had no tea, papa. I thought you would come and have your tea with me. But you were so long that mamma would not let me wait any longer."

"Oh, never mind the tea, my dear. But Wynnie has had none. You 've got a tea-caddy of your own, haven't you?"

"Yes, and a teapot; and there 's the kettle on the hob—for I can't do without a little fire in the evenings."

"Then I 'll make some tea for Wynnie and myself, and tell you at the same time about the sunset. I never saw such colours. I cannot tell you what it was like while the sun was yet going down, for the glory of it has burned the memory of it out of me. But after the sun was down, the sky remained thinking about him; and the thought of the sky was in delicate translucent green on the horizon, just the colour of the earth etherealised and glorified—a broad band; then came another broad band of pale rose-colour; and above that came the sky's own eternal blue, pale likewise, but so sure and changeless. I never saw the green and the blue divided and harmonised by the rose-colour before. It was a wonderful sight. If it is warm enough to-morrow, we will carry you out on the height, that you may see what the evening will bring."

"There is one thing about sunsets," returned Connie—"two things, that make me rather sad—about themselves, not about anything else. Shall I tell you them?"

"Do, my love. There are few things more precious to learn than the effects of Nature upon individual minds. And there is not a feeling of yours, my child, that is not of value to me."

"You are so kind, papa! I am so glad of my accident! I think I should never have known how good you are but for that. But my thoughts seem so little worth after you say so much about them."

"Let me be judge of that, my dear."

"Well, one thing is, that we shall never, never, never see the same sunset again."

"That is true. But why should we? God does not care to do the same thing over again. When it is once done, it is done, and he goes on doing something new. For, to all eternity, he never will have done showing himself by new, fresh things. It would be a loss to do the same thing again."

"But that just brings me to my second trouble. The thing is lost. I forget it. Do what I can, I cannot remember sunsets. I try to fix them fast in my memory, that I may recall them when I want them; but just as they fade out of the sky, all into blue or gray, so they fade out of my mind, and leave it as if they had never been there—except perhaps two or three. Now, though I did not see this one, yet, after you have talked about it, I shall never forget *it*."

"It is not, and never will be, as if they had never been. They have their influence, and leave that far deeper than your memory—in your very being, Connie. But I have more to say about it, although it is only an idea, hardly an assurance. Our brain is necessarily an imperfect instrument. For its right work, perhaps it is needful that it should forget in part. But there are grounds for believing that nothing is ever really forgotten. I think that, when we have a higher existence than we have now, when we are clothed with that spiritual body of which St Paul speaks, you will be able to recall any sunset you have ever seen, with an intensity proportioned to the degree of regard and attention you gave it when it was present to you. But here comes Wynnie to see how you are. I 've been making some tea for you, Wynnie, my love."

"Oh, thank you, papa—I shall be so glad of some tea!" said Wynnie, the paleness of whose face showed the red rims of her eyes the more plainly. She had had what girls call a good cry, and was clearly the better for it.

The same moment my wife came in.

"Why didn't you send for me, Harry, to get your tea?" she said.

"I did not deserve any, seeing I had disregarded proper times and seasons. But I knew you must be busy."

"I have been superintending the arrangement of bed-rooms, and the unpacking, and twenty different things," said Ethelwyn. "We shall be so comfortable! It is such a curious house! Have you had a nice walk?"

"Mamma, I never had such a walk in my life," returned Wynnie. "You would think the shore had been built for the sake of the show—just for a platform to see sunsets from. And the sea! Only the cliffs will be rather dangerous for the children."

"I have just been telling Connie about the sunset. She could see something of the co ours on the water, but not much more."

"Oh, Connie, it will be so delightful to get you out here! Everything is so big! There is such room everywhere! But it must be awfully windy in winter," said Wynnie, whose nature was always a little prospective, if nor apprehensive.

But I must not keep my reader longer upon mere family chat.

CHAPTER XIV.

MORE ABOUT KILKHAVEN.

UR dining-room was one story below the level at which we had entered the parsonage; for, as I have said, the house was built into the face of the cliff, just where it sunk nearly to the level of the shores of the bay. While at dinner, on the evening of our arrival, I kept looking from the window, of course, and saw before me, first a little bit of garden, mostly in turf, then a low stone wall; beyond, over the top of the wall, the blue water of the bay; then beyond the water, all alive with light and motion, the rocks and sand-hills of the opposite side of the little bay, not a quarter of a mile across. I could likewise see where the shore went sweeping out and away to the north, with rock after rock standing far into the water, as if gazing over the awful wild, where there was nothing to break the deathly waste between Cornwall and Newfoundland. But for the moment I did not

regard the huge power lying outside so much as the merry blue bay between me and those rocks and sand-hills. If I moved my head a little to the right, I saw, over the top of the low wall already mentioned, and apparently quite close to it, the slender yellow masts of a schooner, her mainsail hanging loose from the gaff, whose peak was lowered. We must, I thought, be on the very harbour-quay. When I went out for my walk with Wynnie, I had turned from the bay, and gone to the brow of the cliffs overhanging the open sea on our side of it.

When I came down to breakfast in the same room next morning, I stared. The blue had changed to yellow. The life of the water was gone. Nothing met my eyes but a wide expanse of dead sand. You could walk straight across the bay to the hills opposite From the look of the rocks, from the perpendicular cliffs on the coast, I had almost, without thinking, concluded that we were on the shore of a deep-water bay. It was high-water, or nearly so, then; and now, when I looked westward, it was over a long reach of sands, on the far border of which the white fringe of the waves was visible, as if there was their *hitherto*, and further towards us they could not come. Beyond the fringe lay the low hill of the Atlantic. To add to my confusion, when I looked to the right, that is, up the bay towards the land, there was no schooner there. I went out at the window, which opened from the room upon the little lawn, to look, and then saw in a moment how it was.

"Do you know, my dear," I said to my wife, "we

are just at the mouth of that canal we saw as we came along? There are gates and a lock just outside there. The schooner that was under this window last night must have gone in with the tide. She is lying in the basin above now."

"Oh, yes, papa," Charlie and Harry broke in together. "We saw it go up this morning. We 've been out ever so long. It was so funny," Charlie went on—everything was *funny* with Charlie—"to see it rise up like a Jack-in-the-box, and then slip into the quiet water through the other gates!"

And when I thought about the waves tumbling and breaking away out there, and the wide yellow sands between, it was wonderful—which was what Charlie meant by funny—to see the little vessel lying so many feet above it all, in a still plenty of repose, gathering strength, one might fancy, to rush out again, when its time was come, into the turmoil beyond, and dash its way through the breasts of the billows.

After breakfast we had prayers, as usual, and after a visit to Connie, whom I found tired, but wonderfully well, I went out for a walk by myself, to explore the neighbourhood, find the church, and, in a word, do something to shake myself into my new garments. The day was glorious. I wandered along a green path, in the opposite direction from our walk the evening before, with a fir-wood on my right hand, and a belt of feathery tamarisks on my left, behind which lay gardens sloping steeply to a lower road, where stood a few pretty cottages. Turning a corner, I came suddenly in sight of the church, on the green down above me—a sheltered yet commanding situation; for, while the hill rose above it, protecting it from the east, it looked down the bay, and the Atlantic lay open before it. All the earth seemed to lie behind it, and all its gaze to be fixed on the symbol of the infinite. It stood as the church ought to stand, leading men up the mount of vision, to the verge of the eternal, to send them back with their hearts full of the strength that springs from hope, by which alone the true work of the world can be done. And when I saw it, I rejoiced to think that once more I was favoured with a church that had a history. Of course it is a happy thing to see new churches built wherever there is need of such; but to the full idea of the building it is necessary that it should be one in which the hopes and fears, the cares and consolations, the loves and desires of our forefathers should have been roofed; where the hearts of those through whom our country has become that which it is—from whom not merely the life-blood of our bodies, but the life-blood of our spirits, has come down to us, whose existence and whose efforts have made it possible for us to be that which we are—have before us worshipped that Spirit from whose fountain the whole torrent of being flows, who ever pours fresh streams into the wearying waters of humanity, so ready to settle down into a stagnant repose. Therefore, I would far rather, when I may, worship in an old church, whose very stones are a history of how men strove to realize the infinite, compelling even the powers of nature into the task as I soon found on the very doorway of this church, where the ripples of the outspread ocean, and grotesque imaginations of the monsters of its deeps, fixed, as it might seem, for ever in stone, gave a distorted reflex, from the little mirror of the artist's mind, of that mighty water, so awful, so significant to the human eye, which yet lies in the hollow of the Father's palm, like the handful that the weary traveller lifts from the brook by the way. It is in virtue of the truth that went forth in such and such like attempts that we are able to hold our portion of the infinite reality which God only knows. They have founded our Church for us, and such a church as this will stand for the symbol of it; for here we too can worship the God of Abraham, of Isaac, and of Jacob—the God of Sidney, of Hooker, of Herbert. This church of Kilkhaven, old and worn, rose before me a history in stone—so beaten and swept about by the "wild west wind,"

> "For whose path the Atlantic's level powers
> Cleave themselves into chasms,"

and so streamed upon, and washed, and dissolved, by the waters lifted from the sea and borne against it on the upper tide of the wind, that you could almost fancy it one of those churches that have been buried for ages beneath the encroaching waters, lifted again, by some mighty revulsion of nature's heart, into the air of the sweet heavens, there to stand marked for ever with the tide-flows of the nether world—scooped, and hollowed, and worn like æonian rocks that have slowly but for ever responded to the swirl and eddy of the wearing waters. So, from the most troublous of times will the

Church of our land arise, in virtue of what truth she holds, and in spite, if she rises at all, of the worldliness of those who, instead of seeking her service, have sought and gained the dignities which, if it be good that she have it in her power to bestow them, need the corrective of a sharply wholesome persecution, which of late times she has not known. But God knows, and the fire will come in its course—first in the form of just indignation, it may be, against her professed servants, and then in the form of the furnace seven times heated, in which the true builders shall yet walk unhurt save as to their mortal part.

I looked about for some cottage where the sexton might be supposed to live, and spied a slated roof, nearly on a level with the road, at a little distance in front of me. I could at least inquire there. Before I reached it, however, an elderly woman came out and approached me. She was dressed in a white cap and a dark-coloured gown. On her face lay a certain repose which attracted me. She looked as if she had suffered, but had consented to it, and therefore could smile. Her smile lay near the surface. A kind word was enough to draw it up from the well where it lay shimmering: you could always see the smile there, whether it was born or not. But even when she smiled, in the very glimmering of that moonbeam, you could see the deep, still, perhaps dark, waters under. Oh! if one could but understand what goes on in the souls that have no words, perhaps no inclination to set it forth! What had she endured? How had she learned to have that smile always near? What had consoled her, and yet left her her grief—turned it, perhaps, into hope? Should I ever know?

She drew near me, as if she would have passed me, as she would have done, had I not spoken. I think she came towards me to give me the opportunity of speaking if I wished, but she would not address me.

"Good morning," I said. "Can you tell me where to find the sexton?"

"Well, sir," she answered, with a gleam of the smile brightening underneath her old skin, as it were, "I be all the sexton you be likely to find this mornin', sir. My husband, he be gone out to see one o' Squire Tregarva's hounds as was took ill last night. So if you want to see the old church, sir, you'll have to be content with an old woman to show you, sir."

"I shall be quite content, I assure you," I answered "Will you go and get the key?"

"I have the key in my pocket, sir; for I thought that would be what you'd be after, sir. And by the time you come to my age, sir, you'll learn to think of your old bones, sir. I beg your pardon for making so free. For mayhap, says I to myself, he be the gentleman as be come to take Mr Shepherd's duty for him. Be ye now, sir?"

All this was said in a slow sweet subdued tone, nearly of one pitch. You would have felt that she claimed the privilege of age with a kind of mournful gaiety, but was careful, and anxious even, not to presume upon it, and therefore gentle as a young girl.

"Yes," I answered. "My name is Walton. I have come to take the place of my friend Mr Shepherd; and, of course, I want to see the church."

"Well, she be a bee-utiful old church. Some things, I think, sir, grows more beautiful the older they grows. But it ain't us, sir."

"I'm not so sure of that," I said. "What do you mean?"

'Well, sir, there's my little grandson in the cottage there: he'll never be so beautiful again. Them children du be the loves. But we all grows uglier as we grows older. Churches don't seem to, sir."

'm not so sure about all that," I said again.

"They did say, sir, that I was a pretty girl once. I'm not much to look at now."

And she smiled with such a gracious amusement, that I felt at once that if there was any vanity left in this memory of her past loveliness, it was as sweet as the memory of their old fragrance left in the withered leaves of the roses.

"But it du not matter, du it, sir? Beauty is only skin-deep."

"I don't believe that," I answered. "Beauty is as deep as the heart at least."

"Well, to be sure, my old husband du say I be as handsome in his eyes as ever I be. But I beg your pardon, sir, for talkin' about myself. I believe it was the old church—she set us on to it."

"The old church didn't lead you into any harm then," I answered. "The beauty that is in the heart will shine out of the face again some day—be sure of that. And after all, there is just the same kind of beauty in a good old face that there is in an old church. You can't say the church is so trim and neat as it was the day that the first blast of the organ filled it as with a living soul. The carving is not quite so sharp, the timbers are not quite so clean. There is a good deal of mould and worm-eating and cobwebs about the old place. Yet both you and I think it more beautiful now than it was then. Well, I believe it is, as nearly as possible, the same with an old face. It has got stained, and weather-beaten, and worn; but if the organ of truth has been playing on inside the temple of the Lord, which St Paul says our bodies are, there is in the old face, though both form and complexion are gone, just the beauty of the music inside. The wrinkles and the brownness can't spoil it. A light shines through it all—that of the indwelling spirit. I wish we all grew old like the old churches."

She did not reply, but I thought I saw in her face that she understood my mysticism. We had been walking very slowly, had passed through the quaint lych-gate, and now the old woman had got the key in the lock of the door, whose archway was figured and fashioned as I have described above, with a dozen mouldings or more, most of them "carved so curiously."

CHAPTER XV.

THE OLD CHURCH.

HE awe that dwells in churches fell upon me as I crossed the threshold—an awe I never fail to feel—heightened, in many cases, no doubt, by the sense of antiquity and of art, but an awe which I have felt all the same in crossing the threshold of an old Puritan conventicle, as the place where men worship and have worshipped the God of their fathers, although for art there was only the science of common bricklaying, and for beauty staring ugliness. To the involuntary fancy, the air of petition and of holy need seems to linger in the place, and the uncovered head acknowledges the sacred symbols of human aspiration and divine revealing. But this was no ordinary church into which I followed the gentlewoman who was my guide. As entering I turned my eyes eastward, a flush of subdued glory invaded them from the chancel, all the windows of which were of richly-stained glass, and the roof of carved oak lavishly gilded. I had my thoughts about this chancel, and thence about chancels generally, which may appear in another part of my story. Now I have to do only with the church, not with the cogitations to which it gave rise. But I will not trouble my reader with even what I could tell him of the blending and contradicting of styles and modes of architectural thought in the edifice. Age is to the work of contesting human hands a wonderful harmonizer of differences. As nature brings into harmony all fractures of her frame, and even positive intrusions upon her realm, clothes and discolours them, in the old sense of the word, so that at length there is no immediate shock at sight of that which in itself was crude, and is yet coarse, so the various architecture of this building had been gone over after the builders by the musical hand of Eld, with wonder of delicate transition and change of key, that one could almost fancy the music of its exquisite organ had been at work *informing* the building, half-melting the sutures, wearing the sharpness, and blending the angles, until in some parts there was but the gentle flickering of the original conception left, all its self-assertion vanished under the file of the air and the gnawing of the worm. True, the hand of the restorer had been busy, but it had wrought lovingly and gently, and wherein it had erred, the same influences of nature, though as yet their effects were invisible, were already at work—of the many making one. I will not trouble my reader, I say, with any architectural description, which, possibly even more than a detailed description of natural beauty dissociated from human feeling, would only weary him, even if it were not unintelligible. When we are reading a poem, we do not first of all examine the construction and dwell on the rhymes and rhythms; all that comes after, if we find that the poem itself is so good that its parts are therefor worth examining, as being probably good in themselves, and elucidatory of the main work. There were carvings on the ends of the benches all along the aisle on both sides well worth examination, and some of them even of description; but I shall not linger on these. A word only about the columns: they supported arches of different fashion on the opposite sides, but they were themselves similar in matter and construction, both remarkable. They were of coarse granite of the country, chiselled, but very far from smooth, not to say polished. Each pillar was a single stone, with chamfered sides.

Walking softly through the ancient house, forgetting in the many thoughts that arose within me that I had a companion, I came at length into the tower, the basement of which was open, forming part of the body of the church. There hung many ropes through holes in a ceiling above, for bell-ringing was encouraged and indeed practised by my friend Shepherd. And as I regarded them, I thought within myself how delightful it would be if in these days, as in those of Samuel, the word of God was precious; so that when it came to the minister of his people—a fresh vision of his glory, a discovery of his meaning—he might make haste to the church and into the tower, lay hold of the rope that hung from the deepest-toned bell of all, and constrain it by the force of strong arms to utter its voice of call, "Come hither, come hear, my people, for God hath spoken;" and from the streets or the lanes would troop the eager folk; the plough be left in the furrow, the cream in the churn; and the crowding people bring faces into the church, all with one question upon them —"What hath the Lord spoken?" But now it would be answer sufficient to such a call to say, "But what will become of the butter?" or, "An hour's ploughing will be lost." And the clergy—how would they bring about such a time? They do not even believe that God has a word to his people through them. They think that his word is petrified for use in the Bible and Prayer-book; that the wise men of old heard so much of the word of God, and have so set it down, that there is no need for any more words of the Lord coming to the prophets of a land; therefore they look down upon the prophesying—that is, the preaching of the word—make light of it, the best of them, say these prayers are everything, or all but everything: *their* hearts are not set upon hearing what God the Lord will speak, that they may speak it abroad to his people again. Therefore it is no wonder if the church bells are obedient only to the clock, are no longer subject to the spirit of the minister, and have nothing to do in telegraphing between heaven and earth. They make little of this part of their duty; and no wonder, if what is to be spoken must remain such as they speak. They put the Church for God, and the prayers, which are the word of man to God, for the word of God to man. But when the prophets see no vision, how should they have any word to speak?

These thoughts were passing through my mind when my eye fell upon my guide. She was seated against the south wall of the tower, on a stool, I thought, or small table. While I was wandering about the church she had taken her stocking and wires out of her pocket, and was now knitting busily. How her needles did go! Her eyes never regarded them, however, but, fixed on the slabs that paved the tower at a yard or two from her feet, seemed to be gazing far out to sea, for they had an infinite objectless outlook. To try her, I took for the moment the position of an accuser.

"So you don't mind working in church?" I said.

When I spoke she instantly rose, her eyes turned as from the far sea-waves to my face, and light came out of them. With a smile she answered—

"The church knows me, sir."

"But what has that to do with it?"

"I don't think she minds it. We are told to be diligent in business, you know, sir."

"Yes, but it does not say in church and out of church. You could be diligent somewhere else, couldn't you?"

As soon as I said this, I began to fear she would think I meant it. But she only smiled and said, "It won't hurt she, sir; and my good man, who does all he can to keep her tidy, is out at toes and heels, and if I don't keep he warm he'll be laid up, and then the church won't be kep' nice, sir, till he's up again."

I was tempted to go on.

"But you could have sat down outside—there are some nice gravestones near—and waited till I came out."

"But what's the church for, sir? The sun's werry hot to-day, sir; and Mr Shepherd, he say, sir, that the church is like the shadow of a great rock in a weary land. So, you see, if I was to sit out in the sun, instead of comin' in here to the cool o' the shadow, I wouldn't be takin' the church at her word. It does my heart good to sit in the old church, sir. There's a something do seem to come out o' the old walls and settle down like the cool o' the day upon my old heart that's nearly tired o' crying, and would fain keep its eyes dry for the rest o' the journey. My old man's stockin' won't hurt the church, sir; and, bein' a good deed, as I suppose it is, it's none the worse for the place. I think, if He was to come by wi' the whip o' small cords, I wouldn't be afeard of his layin' it upo' my old back. Do you think he would, sir?"

Thus driven to speak as I thought, I made haste to reply, more delighted with the result of my experiment than I cared to let her know.

"Indeed I do not. I was only talking. It is but selfish, cheating, or ill-done work that the church's Master drives away. All our work ought to be done in the shadow of the church."

"I thought you be only having a talk about it, sir," she said, smiling her sweet old smile. "Nobody knows what this old church is to me."

Now the old woman had a good husband, apparently:

the sorrows which had left their mark even upon her smile, must have come from her family, I thought.

"You have had a family?" I said, interrogatively.

"I've had thirteen," she answered. "Six bys and seven maidens."

"Why, you are rich!" I returned. "And where are they all?"

"Four maidens be lying in the churchyard, sir; two be married, and one be down in the mill, there."

"And your boys?"

"One of them be lyin' beside his sisters—drownded afore my eyes, sir. Three o' them be at sea, and two o' them in it, sir."

At sea! I thought. What a wide *where!* As vague to the imagination, almost, as *in the other world*. How a mother's thoughts must go roaming about the waste, like birds that have lost their nest, to find them!

As this thought kept me silent for a few moments, she resumed.

"It be no wonder, be it, sir, that I like to creep into the church with my knitting? Many's the stormy night, when my husband couldn't keep still, but would be out on the cliffs or on the breakwater, for no good in life, but just to hear the roar of the waves that he could only see by the white of them, with the balls o' foam flying in his face in the dark—many's the such a night that I have left the house after he was gone, with this blessed key in my hand, and crept into the old church here, and sat down where I'm sittin' now—leastways where I was sittin' when your reverence spoke to me—and hearkened to the wind howling about the place. The church windows never rattle, sir—like the cottage windows, as I suppose you know, sir. Somehow, I feel safe in the church."

"But if you had sons at sea," said I, again wishing to draw her out, "it would not be of much good to you to feel safe yourself, so long as they were in danger."

"Oh! yes, it be, sir. What's the good of feeling safe yourself but it let you know other people be safe too? It's when you don't feel safe yourself that you feel other people ben't safe."

"But," I said—and such confidence I had from what she had already uttered, that I was sure the experiment was not a cruel one—"some of your sons *were* drowned for all that you say about their safety."

"Well, sir," she answered, with a sigh, "I trust they're none the less safe for that. It would be a strange thing for an old woman like me, well-nigh threescore and ten, to suppose that safety lay not in being drownded. Why, they might ha' been cast on a desert island, and wasted to skin and bone, and got home again wi' the loss of half the wits they set out with. Wouldn't that ha' been worse than being drownded right off? And that wouldn't ha' been the worst, either. The church she seem to tell me all the time, that for all the roaring outside, there be really no danger after all. What matter if they go to the bottom? What is the bottom of the sea, sir? You bein' a clergyman can tell that, sir. I shouldn't ha' known it if I hadn't had bys o' my own at sea, sir. But you can tell, sir, though you 'ain't got none there."

And though she was putting her parson to his catechism, the smile that returned on her face was as modest as if she had only been listening to his instruction. I had not long to look for my answer.

"The hollow of his hand," I said, and said no more.

"I thought you would know it, sir," she returned, with a little glow of triumph in her tone. "Well, then, that 's just what the church tells me, when I come in here in the stormy nights. I bring my knitting then too, sir, for I can knit in the dark as well as in the light almost; and when they come home, if they do come home, they 're none the worse that I went to the old church to pray for them. There it goes roaring about them, poor dears, all out there; and their old mother sitting still as a stone almost in the quiet old church, a caring for them. And then it do come across me, sir, that God be a-sitting in his own house at home, hearing all the noise and all the roaring in which his children are tossed about in the world, watching it all, letting it drown some o' them and take them back to him, and keeping it from going too far with others of them that are not quite ready for that same. I have my thoughts, you see, sir, though I be an old woman, and not nice to look at."

I had come upon a genius. How nature laughs at our schools sometimes! Education, so-called, is a fine thing, and might be a better thing; but there is an education, that of life, which when seconded by a pure will to learn, leaves the schools behind, even as the horse of the desert would leave behind the slow pomposity of the common-fed goose. For life is God's school, and they that will listen to the Master there will learn at God's speed. For one moment, I am ashamed to say, I was envious of Shepherd, and repined that, now old Rogers was gone, I had no such glorious old stained-glass-window in my church to let in the eternal upon my light-thirsty soul. I must say for myself that the feeling lasted but for a moment, and that no sooner had the shadow of it passed, and the true light shined after it, than I was heartily ashamed of it. Why should not Shepherd have the old woman as well as I? True, Shepherd was more of what would now be called a ritualist than I; true, I thought my doctrine simpler and therefore better than his; but was this any reason why I should have all the grand people to minister to in my parish! Recovering myself, I found her last words still in my ears.

"You are very nice to look at," I said. "You must not find fault with the work of God, because you would like better to be young and pretty than to be as you now are. Time and time's rents and furrows are all his making and his doing. God makes nothing ugly."

"Are you quite sure of that, sir?"

I paused. Such a question from such a woman "must give us pause." And, as I paused, the thought of certain animals flashed into my mind, and I could not insist that God had never made anything ugly.

"No; I am not sure of it," I answered. For of all things my soul recoiled from, any professional pretence of knowing more than I did know seemed to me the most repugnant to the spirit and mind of the Master, whose servants we are, or but the servants of mere priestly delusion and self-seeking. "But if he does," I went on to say, "it must be that we may see what it is like, and therefore not like it."

Then, unwilling all at once to plunge with her into such an abyss as the question opened, I turned the conversation to an object on which my eyes had been for some time resting half-unconsciously. It was the sort of stool or bench on which my guide had been sitting. I now thought it was some kind of box or chest. It was curiously carved in old oak, very much like the ends of the benches and book-boards.

"What is that you are sitting on?" I asked. "A chest or what?"

"It be there when we come to this place, and that be nigh fifty years agone, sir. But what it be, you'll be better able to tell than I be, sir."

"Perhaps a chest for holding the communion-plate in old time," I said. "But how should it then come to be banished to the tower?"

"No, sir; it can't be that. It be some sort of ancient musical piano, I be thinking."

I stooped and saw that its lid was shaped like the cover of an organ. With some difficulty I opened it; and there, to be sure, was a row of huge keys, fit for the fingers of a Cyclops. I pressed upon them, one after another, but no sound followed. They were stiff to the touch; and once down, so they mostly remained until lifted again. I looked if there was any sign of a bellows, thinking it must have been some primitive kind of reed-instrument, like what we call a seraphine or harmonium now-a-days. But there was no hole through which there could have been any communication with or from a bellows, although there might have been a small one inside. There were, however, a dozen little round holes in the fixed part of the top, which might afford some clue to the mystery of its former life. I could not find any way of reaching the inside of it, so strongly was it put together; therefore I was left, I thought, to the efforts of my imagination alone for any hope of discovery with regard to the instrument, seeing further observation was impossible. But here I found that I was mistaken in two important conclusions, the latter of which depended on the former. The first of these was that it was an instrument: it was only one end of an instrument; therefore, secondly, there might be room for observation still. But I found this out by accident, which has had a share in most discoveries, and which, meaning a something that falls into our hands unlooked for, is so far an unobjectionable word even to the man who does not believe in chance. I had for the time given up the question as insoluble, and was gazing about the place, when, glancing up at the holes in the ceiling through which the bell-ropes went, I spied two or three thick wires hanging through the same ceiling close to the wall, and right over the box with the keys. The vague suspicion of a discovery dawned upon me.

"Have you got the key of the tower?" I asked.

"No, sir. But I'll run home for it at once," she answered. And rising, she went out in haste.

"Run!" thought I, looking after her. "It is a word of the will and the feeling, not of the body." But I was mistaken. The dear old creature had no sooner got outside of the churchyard, within which, I presume, she felt that she must be decorous, than she did run, and ran well too. I was on the point of starting after her at full speed, to prevent her from hurting herself, but reflecting that her own judgment ought to be as good as mine in such a case, I returned, and sitting down on her seat, awaited her reappearance, gazing at the ceiling. There I either saw, or imagined I saw, signs of openings corresponding in number and position with those in the lid under me. In about three minutes the old woman returned, panting but not distressed, with a great crooked old key in her hand. Why are all the keys of a church so crooked? I did not ask her that question, though. What I said to her was—

"You shouldn't run like that. I am in no hurry."

"Be you not, sir? I thought, by the way you spoke, you be taken with a longing to get a-top o' the tower, and see all about you like. For you see, sir, fond as I be of the old church, I du feel sometimes as if she'd smother me; and then nothing will do, but I must get at the top of the old tower. And then, what with the sun, if there be any sun, and what with the fresh air which there al-ways be up there, sir—it du always be fresh up there, sir," she repeated, "I come back down again blessing the old church for its tower."

As she spoke she was toiling up the winding staircase

after me, where there was just room enough for my shoulders to get through by turning themselves a little across the lie of the steps. They were very high, but she kept up with me bravely, bearing out her statement that she was no stranger to them. As I ascended, however I was not thinking of her, but of what she had said. Strange to tell, the significance of the towers or spires of our churches had never been clear to me before. True, I was quite awake to their significance, at least to that of the spires, as fingers pointing ever upwards to

> "regions mild of calm and serene air,
> Above the smoke and stir of this dim spot,
> Which men call Earth;"

but I had not thought of their symbolism as lifting one up above the church itself into a region where no church is wanted, because the Lord God almighty and the Lamb are the temple of it. Happy church, indeed, if it destroys the need of itself by lifting men up into the eternal kingdom! Would that I and all her servants lived pervaded with the sense of this her high end, her one high calling! We need the church towers to remind us that the mephitic airs in the church below are from the churchyard at its feet, which so many take for the church, worshipping over the graves and believing in death—or at least in the material substance over which alone death has power. Thus the church, even in her corruption, lifts us out of her corruption, sending us up her towers and her spires to admonish us that she too lives in the air of truth; that her form too must pass away, while the truth that is embodied in her lives beyond forms and customs and prejudices, shining as the stars for ever and ever. He whom the church does not lift up above the church is not worthy to be a doorkeeper therein.

Such thoughts passed through me, satisfied me, and left me peaceful, so that before I had reached the top, I was thanking the Lord—not for his church-tower, but for his sexton's wife. The old woman was a jewel. If her husband was like her, which was too much to expect—if he believed in her, it would be enough, quite—then indeed the little child, who answered on being questioned thereanent, as the Scotch would say, that the three orders of ministers in the church were the parson, clerk, and sexton, might not be so far wrong in respect of this individual case. So in the ascent, and the thinking associated therewith, I forgot all about the special object for which I had requested the key of the tower, and led the way myself up to the summit, where stepping out of a little door, which being turned only heavenwards had no pretence for, or claim upon a curiously crooked key, but opened to the hand laid upon the latch, I thought of the words of the judicious Hooker, that "the assembling of the church to learn" was "the receiving of angels descended from above;" and in such a whimsical turn as our thoughts will often take when we are not heeding them, I wondered for a moment whether that was why the upper door was left on the latch, forgetting that that could not be of much use, if the door in the basement was kept locked with the crooked key. But the whole suggested something true about my own heart and that of my fellows, if not about the church. Revelation is not enough, the open top-door is not enough, if the door of the heart is not open likewise.

As soon, however, as I stepped out upon the roof of the tower, I forgot again all that had thus passed through my mind, swift as a dream. For, filling the west, lay the ocean beneath, with a dark curtain of storm hanging in perpendicular lines over part of its horizon, and on the other side was the peaceful solid land, with its numberless shades of green, its heights and hollows, its farms and wooded vales—there was not much wood—its scattered villages and country dwellings, lighted and shadowed by the sun and the clouds. Beyond lay the blue heights of Dartmoor. And over all, bathing us as it passed, moved the wind, the life-bearing spirit of the whole, the servant of the sun. The old woman stood beside me, silently enjoying my enjoyment, with a still smile that seemed to say, in kindly triumph, "Was I not right about the tower and the wind that dwells among its pinnacles?" I drank deep of the universal flood, the outspread peace, the glory of the sun, and the haunting shadow of the sea that lay beyond like the visual image of the eternal silence—as it looks to us—that rounds our little earthly life.

There were a good many trees in the churchyard, and as I looked down, the tops of them in their richest foliage hid all the graves directly below me, except a single flat stone looking up through an opening in the leaves, which seemed to have been just made for it to let it see the top of the tower. Upon the stone a child was seated playing with a few flowers she had gathered, not once looking up to the gilded vanes that rose from the four pinnacles at the corners of the tower. I turned to the eastern side, and looked over upon the church roof. It lay far below—looking very narrow and small, but long, with the four ridges of four steep roofs stretching away to the eastern end. It was in excellent repair, for the parish was almost all in one lord's possession, and he was proud of his church: between them he and Mr Shepherd had made it beautiful to behold, and strong to endure.

When I turned to look again, the little child was gone. Some butterfly fancy had seized her, and she was away. A little lamb was in her place, nibbling at the grass that grew on the side of the next mound. And when I looked seaward there was a sloop, like a white-winged sea-bird, rounding the end of a high projecting rock from the south, to bear up the little channel that led to the gates of the harbour canal. Out of the circling waters it had flown home, not from a long voyage, but hardly the less welcome therefore to those that waited and looked for her signal from the barrier rock.

Re-entering by the angels' door to descend the narrow cork-screw stair, so dark and cool, I caught a glimpse, one turn down, by the feeble light that came through its chinks after it was shut behind us, of a tiny maiden-hair fern growing out of the wall. I stopped and said to the old woman—

"I have a sick daughter at home, or I wouldn't rob your tower of this lovely little thing."

"Well, sir, what eyes you have! I never saw the thing before. Do take it home to miss. It'll do her good to see it. I be main sorry to hear you've got a sick maiden. She ben't a bedlar, be she, sir?"

I was busy with my knife getting out all the roots I could without hurting them, and before I had succeeded I had remembered Turner's using the word.

"Not quite that," I answered, "but she can't even sit up, and must be carried everywhere."

"Poor dear! Every one has their troubles, sir. The sea's been mine."

She continued talking and asking kind questions about Connie as we went down the stair. Not till she opened a little door I had passed without observing it as we came up, was I reminded of my first object in ascending the tower. For this door revealed a number of bells hanging in silent power in the brown twilight of the place. I entered carefully, for there were only some planks laid upon the joists to keep one's feet from going through the ceiling. In a few moments I had satisfied myself that my conjecture about the keys below was correct. The small iron rods I had seen from beneath hung down from this place. There were more of them hanging shorter above, and there was yet enough of a further mechanism remaining to prove that those keys, by means of the looped and cranked rods, had been in connexion with hammers, one of them indeed remaining also, which struck the bells, so that a tune could be played upon them as upon any other keyed instrument. This was the first contrivance of the kind I had ever seen, though I have heard of it in other churches since.

"If I could find a clever blacksmith in the neighbourhood, now," I said to myself, "I would get this all repaired, so that it should not interfere with the bell-ringing when the ringers were to be had, and yet Shepherd could play a psalm tune to his parish at large when he pleased." For Shepherd was a very fair musician, and gave a good deal of time to the organ. "It's a grand notion, to think of him sitting here in the gloom, with that great musical instrument towering above him, whence he sends forth the voice of gladness, almost of song to his people, while they are mowing the grass, binding the sheaves, or gazing abroad over the stormy ocean in doubt, anxiety, and fear. 'There's the parson at his bells,' they would say, and stop and listen; and some phrase might sink into their hearts, waking some memory, or giving birth to some hope or faint aspiration. I will see what can be done." Having come to this conclusion, I left the abode of the bells, descended to the church, bade my conductress good morning, saying I would visit her soon in her own house, and bore home to my chiid the spoil which, without kirk-rapine, I had torn from the wall of the sanctuary. By this time the stormy veil had lifted from the horizon, and the sun was shining in full power without one darkening cloud.

Ere I left the churchyard I would have a glance at the stone which ever seemed to lie gazing up at the tower. I soon found it, because it was the only one in that quarter from which I could see the top of the tower. It recorded the life and death of an aged pair who had been married fifty years, concluding with the couplet—

"A long time this may seem to be,
But it did not seem long to we."

The whole story of a human life lay in that last verse. True, it was not good grammar; but they had got through fifty years of wedded life probably without any knowledge of grammar to harmonize or to shorten them, and I daresay, had they been acquainted with the lesson he had put into their dumb mouths, they would have been aware of no ground of quarrel with the poetic stone-cutter, who most likely had thrown the verses in when he made his claim for the stone and the cutting. Having learned this one by heart, I went about looking for anything more in the shape of sepulchral flora that might interest or amuse my crippled darling; nor had I searched long before I found one, the sole but triumphant recommendation of which was the thorough "puzzle-headedness" of its construction. I quite reckoned on seeing Connie trying to make it out looking as bewildered over its excellent grammar as the poet of the other ought to have looked over his rhymes, ere he gave in to the use of the nominative after a preposition.

"If you could view the heavenly shore,
Where heart's content you hope to find,
You would not murmur were you gone before,
But grieve that you are left behind."

CHAPTER XVI.

CONNIE'S WATCH-TOWER.

S I walked home, the rush of the rising tide was in my ears. To my fancy, the ocean awaking from a swoon in which its life had ebbed to its heart, was sending that life abroad to its extremities, and waves breaking in white were the beats of its reviving pulse, the flashes of returning light. But so gentle was its motion, and so lovely its hue, that I could not help contrasting it with its reflex in the mind of her who took refuge from the tumult of its noises in the hollow of the old church. To her, let it look as blue as the sky, as peaceful and as moveless, it was a wild, reckless, false, devouring creature, a prey to its own moods, and to that of the blind winds which, careless of consequences, urged it to raving fury. Only, while the sea took this form to her imagination, she believed in that which held the sea, and knew that, when it pleased God to part his confining fingers, there would be no more sea.

When I reached home, I went straight to Connie's room. Now, the house was one of a class to every individual of which, whatever be its style or shape, I instantly become attached almost as if it possessed a measure of the life which it has sheltered. This class of human dwellings consists of the houses that have *grown*. They have not been built after a straight-up-and-down model of uninteresting convenience or money-loving pinchedness. They must have had some plan, good, bad, or indifferent, as the case may be, at first, I suppose; but that plan they have left far behind, having grown with the necessities or ambitions of succeeding possessors, until the fact that they have a history is as plainly written on their aspect as on that of any son or daughter of Adam. These are the houses which the fairies used to haunt, and if there is any truth in ghost-stories, the houses which ghosts will yet haunt; and hence perhaps the sense of soothing comfort which pervades us when we cross their thresholds. You do not know, the moment you have cast a glance about the hall, where the dining-room, drawing-room, and best bedroom are. You have got it all to find out, just as the character of a man; and thus had I to find out this house of my friend Shepherd. It had formerly been a kind of manor-house, though altogether unlike any other manor-house I ever saw; for after exercising all my constructive ingenuity reversed in pulling it to pieces in my mind, I came to the conclusion that the germ-cell of it was a cottage of the simplest sort, which had grown by the addition of other cells, till it had reached the development in which we found it.

I have said that the dining-room was almost on the level of the shore. Certainly some of the flat stones that coped the low wall in front of it were thrown into the garden before the next winter by the waves. But Connie's room looked out on a little flower garden almost on the downs, only sheltered a little by the rise of a short grassy slope above it. This, however, left the prospect from her window down the bay and out to sea, almost open. To reach this room I had now to go up but one simple cottage stair; for the door of the house entered on the first floor—that is, as regards the building, midway between heaven and earth. It had a large bay window; and in this window Connie was lying on her couch, with the lower sash wide open, through which the breeze entered, smelling of sea-weed tempered with sweet grasses and the wall-flowers and stocks that were in the little plot under it. I thought I could see an improvement in her already. Certainly she looked very happy.

"Oh, papa!" she said, "isn't it delightful?"

"What is, my dear?"

"Oh, everything. The wind, and the sky, and the sea, and the smell of the flowers. Do look at that sea-bird. His wings are like the barb of a terrible arrow. How he goes undulating, neck and body, up and down as he flies. I never felt before that a bird moves his wings. It always looked as if the wings flew with the bird. But I see the effort in him."

"An easy effort, though, I should certainly think."

"No doubt. But I see that he chooses and means to fly, and so does it. It makes one almost reconciled to the idea of wings. Do angels really have wings, papa?"

"It is generally so represented, I think, in the Bible. But whether it is meant as a natural fact about them, is more than I take upon me to decide. For one thing, I should have to examine whether in simple narrative they are ever represented with them, as, I think, in records of visions they are never represented without them. But wings are very beautiful things, and I do not exactly see why you should need reconciling to them."

Connie gave a little shrug of her shoulders.

"I don't like the notion of them growing out at my shoulder-blades. And how ever would you get on your clothes? If you put them over your wings, they would be of no use, and would, besides, make you hump-backed; and if you did not, everything would have to be buttoned round the roots of them. You could not do it yourself, and even on Wynnie I don't think I could bear to touch the things—I don't mean the feathers, but the skinny, folding-up bits of them."

I laughed at her fastidious fancy.

"You want to fly, I suppose?" I said.

"Oh, yes; I should like that."

"And you don't want to have wings?"

"Well, I shouldn't mind the wings exactly; but how ever would one be able to keep them nice?"

"There you go; starting from one thing to another, like a real bird already. When you can't answer one thing, off to another, and, from your new perch on the hawthorn, talk as if you were still on the topmost branch of the lilac!"

"Oh yes, papa! That's what I've heard you say to mamma twenty times."

"And did I ever say to your mamma anything but the truth? or to you either, you puss?"

I had not yet discovered that when I used this epithet to my Connie, she always thought she had gone too far. She looked troubled. I hastened to relieve her.

"When women have wings," I said, "their logic will be good."

"How do you make that out, papa?" she asked, a little re-assured.

"Because then every shadow of feeling that turns your speech aside from the straight course will be recognized in that speech; the whole utterance will be instinct not only with the meaning of what you are thinking, but with the reflex of the forces in you that make the utterance take this or that shape; just as to a perfect palate, the source and course of a stream would be revealed in every draught of its water."

"I have just a glimmering of your meaning, papa. Would you like to have wings?"

"I should like to fly like a bird, to swim like a fish, to gallop like a horse, to creep like a serpent; but I suspect the good of all these is to be got without doing any of them."

"I know what you mean now but I can't put it in words."

"I mean by a perfect sympathy with the creatures that do these things: what it may please God to give to ourselves, we can quite comfortably leave to him. A higher stratum of the same kind is the need we feel of knowing our fellow-creatures through and through, of walking into and out of their worlds as if we were, because we are, perfectly at home in them. But I am talking what the people who do not understand such things lump all together as mysticism, which is their name for a kind of spiritual ashpit, whither they consign dust and stones, never asking whether they may not be gold-dust and rubies, all in a heap. You had better begin to think about getting out, Connie."

"Think about it, papa! I have been thinking about it ever since daylight."

"I will go and see what your mother is doing then, and if she is ready to go out with us."

In a few moments all was arranged. Without killing more than a snail or two, which we could not take time to beware of, Walter and I—finding that the window did not open down to the ground in French fashion, for which there were two good reasons, one the fierceness of the winds in winter, the other, the fact that the means of egress were elsewise provided—lifted the sofa, Connie and all, out over the window-sill, and then there was only a little door in the garden-wall to get her through before we found ourselves upon the down. I think the ascent of this hill was the first experience I had—a little to my humiliation, nothing to my sorrow—that I was descending another hill. I had to set down the precious burden rather oftener before we reached the brow of the cliffs than would have been necessary ten years before. But this was all right, and the newly-discovered weakness then was strength to the power which carries me about on my two legs now. It is all right still. I shall be stronger by and by.

We carried her high enough for her to see the brilliant waters lying many feet below her, with the sea-birds of which we had talked winging their undulating way between heaven and ocean. It is when first you have a chance of looking a bird in the face on the wing that you know what the marvel of flight is. There it hangs or rests, which you please, borne up, as far as eye or any of the senses can witness, by its own will alone. This Connie, quicker than I in her observation of nature, had already observed. Seated on the warm grass by her side, while neither talked, but both regarded the blue spaces, I saw one of those barb-winged birds rest over my head, regarding me from above, as if doubtful whether I did not afford some claim to his theory of treasure-trove. I knew at once that what Connie had been saying to me just before was true.

She lay silent a long time. I too was silent. At length I spoke.

"Are you longing to be running about amongst the rocks, my Connie?"

"No, papa; not a bit. I don't know how it is, but I don't think I ever wished much for anything I knew I could not have. I am enjoying everything more than I can tell you. I wish Wynnie were as happy as I am."

"Why? Do you think she 's not happy, my dear?"

"That doesn't want any thinking, papa. You can see that."

"I am afraid you 're right, Connie. What do you think is the cause of it?"

"I think it is because she can't wait. She 's always going out to meet things; and then when they 're not there waiting for her, she thinks they 're nowhere. But I always think her way is finer than mine. If everybody were like me, there wouldn't be much done in the world, would there, papa?"

"At all events, my dear, your way is wise for you, and I am glad you do not judge your sister."

"Judge Wynnie, papa! That would be cool impudence. She 's worth ten of me. Don't you think, papa," she added, after a pause, "that if Mary had said the smallest word against Martha, as Martha did against Mary, Jesus would have had a word to say on Martha's side next?"

"Indeed I do, my dear. And I think that Mary did not sit very long without asking Jesus if she mightn't go and help her sister. There is but one thing needful—that is, the will of God; and when people love that above everything, they soon come to see that to everything else there are two sides, and that only the will of God gives fair play, as we call it, to both of them."

Another silence followed. Then Connie spoke.

"Is it not strange, papa, that the only thing here that makes me want to get up to look, is nothing of all the grand things round about me? I am just lying like the convex mirror in the school-room at home, letting them all paint themselves in me."

"What is it then that makes you wish to get up and go and see?" I asked with real curiosity.

"Do you see down there—away across the bay—amongst the rocks at the other side, a man sitting sketching?"

I looked for sometime before I could discover him.

"Your sight is good, Connie: I see the man, but I could not tell what he was doing."

"Don't you see him lifting his head every now and then for a moment, and then keeping it down for a longer while?"

"I cannot distinguish that. But then I am short-sighted rather, you know."

"I wonder how you see so many little things that nobody else seems to notice, then, papa."

"That is because I have trained myself to observe. The degree of power in the sight is of less consequence than the habit of seeing. But you have not yet told me what it is that makes you desirous of getting up."

"I want to look over his shoulder, and see what he is doing. Is it not strange that in the midst of all this plenty of beautifulness, I should want to rise to look at a few lines and scratches, or smears of colour, upon a bit of paper?"

"No, my dear; I don't think it is strange. There a new element of interest is introduced—the human. No doubt there is deep humanity in all this around us. No doubt all the world, in all its moods, is human, as those for whose abode and instruction it was made. No doubt, it would be void of both beauty and significance to our eyes, were it not that it is one crowd of pictures of the human mind, blended in one living fluctuating whole. But these meanings are there in solution as it were. The individual is a centre of crystallization to this solution. Around him meanings gather, are separated from other meanings; and if he be an artist, by which I mean true painter, true poet, or true musician, as the case may be, he so isolates and re-presents them, that we see them—not what nature shows to us, but what nature has shown to him, determined by his nature and choice. With it is mingled therefore so much of his own individuality, manifested both in this choice and certain modifications determined by his way of working, that you have not only a representation of an aspect of nature, as far as that may be with limited powers and materials, but a revelation of the man's own mind and nature. Consequently there is a human interest in every true attempt to reproduce nature, an interest of individuality which does not belong to nature herself, who is for all and every man. You have just been saying that you were lying there like a convex mirror reflecting all nature around you. Every man is such a convex mirror; and his drawing, if he can make one, is an attempt to show what is in this little mirror of his, kindled there by the grand world outside. And the human mirrors being all differently formed, vary infinitely in what they would thus represent of the same scene. I have been greatly interested in looking alternately over the shoulders of two artists, both sketching in colour the same, absolutely the same scene, both trying to represent it with all the truth in their power. How different, notwithstanding, the two representations came out!"

"I think I understand you, papa. But look a little farther off. Don't you see over the top of another rock a lady's bonnet? I do believe that's Wynnie. I know she took her box of water-colours out with her this morning, just before you came home. Dora went with her."

"Can't you tell by her ribbons, Connie? You seem sharp-sighted enough to see her face if she would show it. I don't even see the bonnet. If I were like some people I know, I should feel justified in denying its presence, attributing the whole to your fancy, and refusing anything to superiority of vision."

"That wouldn't be like you, papa."

"I hope not; for I have no fancy for being shut up in my own blindness, when other people offer me their eyes to eke out the defects of my own with. But here comes mamma at last."

Connie's face brightened as if she had not seen her mother for a fortnight. My Ethelwyn always brought the home-gladness that her name signified with her. She was a centre of radiating peace.

"Mamma, don't you think that's Wynnie's bonnet over that black rock there, just beyond where you see that man drawing?"

"You absurd child! How should I know Wynnie's bonnet at this distance?"

"Can't you see the little white feather you gave her out of your wardrobe just before we left? She put it in this morning before she went out."

"I think I do see something white. But I want you to look out there, towards what they call the Chapel Rock, at the other end of that long mound they call the breakwater. You will soon see a boat appear full of the coastguard. I saw them going on board just as I left the house to come up to you. Their officer came down with his sword, and each of the men had a cutlas. I wonder what it can mean."

We looked. But before the boat made its appearance, Connie cried out—

"Look there! What a big boat that is rowing for the land, away northwards there!"

I turned my eyes in the direction she indicated, and saw a long boat with some half-dozen oars, full of men, rowing hard, apparently for some spot on the shore at a considerable distance to the north of our bay.

"Ah!" I said, "that boat has something to do with the coastguard and their cutlases. You'll see that, as soon as they get out of the bay, they will row in the same direction."

So it was. Our boat appeared presently from under the concealment of the heights on which we were, and made at full speed after the other boat.

"Surely they can't be smugglers," I said. "I thought all that was over and done with."

In the course of another twenty minutes, during which we watched their progress, both boats had disappeared behind the headland to the northward. Then, thinking Connie had had nearly enough of the sea air for her first experience of its influences, I went and fetched Walter, and we carried her back as we had brought her. She had not been in the shadow of her own room for five minutes before she was fast asleep.

It was now nearly time for our early dinner. We always dined early when we could, that we might eat along with our children. We were both convinced that the only way to make them behave like ladies and gentlemen was to have them always with us at meals. We had seen very unpleasant results in the children of those who allowed them to dine with no other supervision than the nursery afforded: they were a constant anxiety and occasional horror to those whom they visited—snatching like monkeys and devouring like jackals, as selfishly as if they were mere animals.

"Oh! we've seen such a nice gentleman!" said Dora, becoming lively under the influence of her soup.

"Have you, Dora? Where?"

"Sitting on the rocks, taking a portrait of the sea."

"What makes you say he was a nice gentleman?"

"He had such beautiful boots!" answered Dora, at which there was a great laugh about the table.

"Oh! we must run and tell Connie that," said Harry. "It will make her laugh."

"What will you tell Connie, then, Harry?"

"Oh, what was it, Charlie? I've forgotten."

Another laugh followed at Harry's expense now, and

we were all very merry, when Dora, who sat opposite to the window, called out clapping her hands—

"There's Niceboots again! There's Niceboots again!"

The same moment the head of a young man appeared over the wall that separated the garden from the little beach that lay by the entrance of the canal. I saw at once that he must be more than ordinarily tall to show his face, for he was not close to the wall. It was a dark countenance, with a long beard, which few at that time wore, though now it is getting not uncommon, even in my own profession—a noble, handsome face, a little sad, with downbent eyes, which, released from their more immediate duty towards nature, had now bent themselves upon the earth.

"Counting the aewy pebbles, fixed in thought."

"I suppose he's contemplating his boots," said Wynnie, with apparent maliciousness.

"That's too bad of you, Wynnie," I said, and the child blushed.

"I didn't mean anything, papa. It was only following up Dora's wise discrimination," said Wynnie.

"He is a fine-looking fellow," said I, "and ought, with that face and head, to be able to paint good pictures."

"I should like to see what he has done," said Wynnie; "for, by the way we were sitting, I should think we were attempting the same thing."

"And what was that then, Wynnie?" I asked.

"A rock," she answered, "that you could not see from

where you were sitting. I saw you on the top of the cliff."

"Connie said it was you, by your bonnet. She, too, was wishing she could look over the shoulder of the artist at work beside you."

"Not beside me. There were yards and yards of solid rock between us."

"Space, you see, in removing things from the beholder, seems always to bring them nearer to each other, and the most differing things are classed under one name by the man who knows nothing about them. But what sort of a rock was it you were trying to draw?"

"A strange-looking, conical rock, that stands alone in front of one of the ridges that project from the shore into the water. Three sea-birds, with long white wings, were flying about it, and the little waves of the rising tide were beating themselves against it and breaking in white plashes. So the rock stood between the blue and white below and the blue and white above; for, though there were no clouds, the birds gave the touches of white to the upper sea."

"Now, Dora," I said, "I don't know if you are old enough to understand me; but sometimes little people are long in understanding just because the older people think they can't, and don't try them. Do you see, Dora, why I want you to learn to draw? Look how Wynnie sees things. That is, in a great measure, because she draws things, and has, by that, learned to watch in order to find out. It is a great thing to have your eyes open."

Dora's eyes were large, and she opened them to their full width, as if she would take in the universe at their little doors. Whether that indicated that she did not in the least understand what I had been saying, or that she was in sympathy with it, I cannot tell.

"Now let us go up to Connie, and tell her about the rock and everything else you have seen since you went out. We are all her messengers, sent out to discover things, and bring back news of them."

After a little talk with Connie, I retired to the study, which was on the same floor as her room, completing, indeed, the whole of that part of the house, which, seen from without, looked like a separate building; for it had a roof of its own, and stood higher up the rock than the rest of the dwelling. Here I began to glance over his books. To have the run of another man's library, especially if it has all been gathered by himself, is like having a pass-key into the chambers of his thought. Only, one must be wary, when he opens them, what marks on the books he takes for those of the present owner. A mistake here would breed considerable confusion and falsehood in any judgment formed from the library. I found, however, one thing plain enough, that Shepherd had kept up that love for an older English literature which had been one of the cords to draw us towards each other when we were students together. There had been one point on which we especially agreed—that a true knowledge of the present, in literature, as in everything else, could only be founded upon a knowledge of what had gone before; therefore, that any judgment, in regard to the literature of the present day, was of no value, which was not guided and influenced by a real acquaintance with the best of what had gone before, being liable to be dazzled and misled by novelty of form and other qualities which, whatever might be the real worth of the substance, were, in themselves, purely ephemeral. I had taken down a last century edition of the poems of the brothers Fletcher, and, having begun to read a lovely passage in "Christ's Victory and Triumph," had gone into what I can only call an intellectual rage at the impudence of the editor, who had altered innumerable words and phrases to suit the degenerate taste of his own time,—when a knock came to the door, and Charlie entered, breathless with eagerness.

"There 's the boat with the men with the swords in it, and another boat behind them, twice as big."

I hurried out upon the road, and there, close under our windows, were the two boats we had seen in the morning, landing their crews on the little beach. The second boat was full of weather-beaten men, in all kinds of attire, some in blue jerseys, some in red shirts, some in ragged coats. One man, who looked their superior, was dressed in blue from head to foot.

"What 's the matter?" I asked the officer of the coast-guard, a sedate, thoughtful-looking man.

"Vessel foundered, sir," he answered. "Sprung a leak on Sunday morning. She was laden with iron, and in a heavy ground swell it shifted and knocked a hole in her. The poor fellows are worn out with the pump and rowing, upon little or nothing to eat."

They were trooping past us by this time, looking rather dismal, though not by any means abject.

"What are you going to do with them now?"

"They'll be taken in by the people. We'll get up a little subscription for them, but they all belong to the society the sailors have for sending the shipwrecked to their homes, or where they want to go."

"Well, here's something to help," I said.

"Thank you, sir. They'll be very glad of it."

"And if there's anything wanted that I can do for them, you must let me know."

"I will, sir. But I don't think there will be any occasion to trouble you. You are our new clergyman, I believe."

"Not exactly that. Only for a little while, till my friend Mr Shepherd is able to come back to you."

"We don't want to lose Mr Shepherd, sir. He's what they call high in these parts, but he's a great favourite with all the poor people, because you see he understands them as if he was of the same flesh and blood with themselves—as, for that matter, I suppose we all are."

"If we weren't there would be nothing to say at all. Will any of these men be at church to-morrow, do you suppose? I am afraid sailors are not much in the way of going to church?"

"I am afraid not. You see they are all anxious to get home. Most likely they'll be all travelling to-morrow. It's a pity. It would be a good chance for saying something to them that they might think of again. But

I often think that, perhaps—it's only my own fancy, and I don't set it up for anything—that sailors won't be judged exactly like other people. They're so knocked about, you see, sir."

"Of course not. Nobody will be judged like any other body. To his own Master, who knows all about him, every man stands or falls. Depend upon it, God likes fair-play, to use a homely phrase, far better than any sailor of them all. But that's not exactly the question. It seems to me the question is this: shall we, who know what a blessed thing life is because we know what God is like, who can trust in him with all our hearts because he is the Father of our Lord Jesus Christ, the friend of sinners, shall we not try all we can to let them, too, know the blessedness of trusting in their Father in heaven? If we could only get them to say the Lord's prayer, *meaning* it, think what that would be! Look here! This can't be called bribery, for they are in want of it, and it will show them I am friendly. Here's another sovereign. Give them my compliments, and say that if any of them happen to be in Kilkhaven to morrow, I shall be quite pleased to welcome them to church. Tell them I will give them of my best there if they will come. Make the invitation merrily, you know. No long faces and solemn speech. I will give them the solemn speech when they come to church. But even there I hope God will keep the long face far from me. That is fittest for fear and suffering. And the house of God is the casket that holds the antidote against all fear and most suffering. But I am preaching my sermon on Saturday instead of Sunday, and keeping you from your ministration to the poor fellows. Good-bye."

"I will give them your message as near as I can," he said, and we shook hands and parted.

This was the first experience we had of the might and battle of the ocean. To our eyes it lay quiet as a baby asleep. On that Sunday morning there had been no commotion here. Yet now at last, on the Saturday morning, home come the conquered and spoiled of the sea. As if with a mock she takes all they have, and flings them on shore again, with her weeds, and her shells, and her sand. Before the winter was over we had learned—how much more of that awful power that surrounds the habitable earth! By slow degrees the sense of its might grew upon us, first by the vision of its many aspects and moods, and then by the more awful things that followed; for there are few coasts upon which the sea rages so wildly as upon this, the whole force of the Atlantic breaking upon it. Even when there is no storm within perhaps hundreds of miles, when all is still as a church on land, the storm which raves somewhere out upon the vast waste, will drive the waves in upon the shore with such fury that not even a lifeboat could make its way through the yawning hollows, and their fierce, shattered, and tumbling crests.

CHAPTER XVII.

MY FIRST SERMON IN THE SEABOARD PARISH.

N the hope that some of the shipwrecked mariners might be present in the church the next day, I proceeded to consider my morning's sermon for the occasion. There was no difficulty in taking care at the same time that it should be suitable to the congregation, whether those sailors were there or not. I turned over in my mind several subjects. I thought, for instance of showing them how this ocean that lay watchful and ready all about our island, all about the earth, was but a visible type or symbol of two other oceans, one very still, the other very awful and fierce; in fact, that three oceans surrounded us: one of the known world, one of the unseen world, that is, of death; one of the spirit—the devouring ocean of evil—and might I not have added yet another, encompassing and silencing all the rest—that of *truth!* The visible ocean seemed to make war upon the land,

and the dwellers thereon. Restrained by the will of God, and by him made subject more and more to the advancing knowledge of those who were created to rule over it, it was yet like a half-tamed beast, ever ready to break loose and devour its masters. Of course this would have been but one aspect or appearance of it—for it was in truth all service; but this was the aspect I knew it must bear to those, seafaring themselves or not, to whom I had to speak. Then I thought I might show, that its power, like that of all things that man is ready to fear, had one barrier over which no commotion, no might of driving wind, could carry it, beyond which its loudest waves were dumb—the barrier of death. Hitherto and no further could its power reach. It could kill the body. It could dash in pieces the last little cock-boat to which the man clung, but thus it swept the man beyond its own region into the second sea of stillness, which we call death, out upon which the thoughts of those that are left behind can follow him only in great longings, vague conjectures, and mighty faith. Then I thought I could show them how, raving in fear, or lying still in calm deceit, there lay about the life of a man a far more fearful ocean than that which threatened his body; for this would cast, could it but get hold of him, both body and soul into hell—the sea of evil, of vice, of sin, of wrong-doing—they might call it by what name they pleased. This made war against the very essence of life, against God who is the truth, against love, against fairness, against fatherhood, motherhood, sisterhood, brotherhood, manhood, womanhood, against tenderness and grace and beauty, gathering into one pulp of festering death all that is noble, lovely, worshipful in the human nature made so divine that the one fearless man, the Lord Jesus Christ, shared it with us. This, I thought I might make them understand, was the only terrible sea, the only hopeless ocean from whose awful shore we must shrink and flee, the end of every voyage upon whose bosom was the bottom of its filthy waters, beyond the reach of all that is thought or spoken in the light, beyond life itself, but for the hand that reaches down from the upper ocean of truth, the hand of the Redeemer of men. I thought, I say, for a while, that I could make this, not definite, but very real to them. But I did not feel quite confident about it. Might they not in the symbolism forget the thing symbolized? And would not the symbol itself be ready to fade quite from their memory, or to return only in the vaguest shadow? And with the thought I perceived a far more excellent way. For the power of the truth lies of course in its revelation to the mind, and while for this there are a thousand means, none are so mighty as its embodiment in human beings and human life. There it is itself alive and active. And amongst these, what embodiment comes near to that in him who was perfect man in virtue of being at the root of the secret of humanity, in virtue of being the eternal Son of God? We are his sons in time: he is his Son in eternity, of whose sea time is but the broken sparkle. Therefore, I would talk to them about—but I will treat my reader now as if he were not my reader, but one of my congregation on that bright Sunday, my first in the

Seaboard Parish, with the sea outside the church, flashing in the sunlight.

While I stood at the lectern, which was in front of the altar-screen, I could see little of my congregation, partly from my being on a level with them, partly from the necessity for keeping my eyes and thoughts upon that which I read. When, however, I rose from prayer in the pulpit, then I felt, as usual with me, that I was personally present for personal influence with my people, and then I saw, to my great pleasure, that one long bench nearly in the middle of the church was full of such sunburnt men as could not be mistaken for any but mariners, even if their torn and worn garments had not revealed that they must be the very men about whom we had been so much interested. Not only were they behaving with perfect decorum, but their rough faces wore an aspect of solemnity which I do not suppose was by any means their usual aspect.

I gave them no text. I had one myself, which was the necessary thing. They should have it by-and-bye.

"Once upon a time," I said, "a man went up a mountain, and stayed there till it was dark, and stayed on. Now, a man who finds himself on a mountain as the sun is going down, especially if he is alone, makes haste to get down before it is dark. But this man went up when the sun was going down, and, as I say, continued there for a good long while after it was dark. You will want to know why. I will tell you. He wished to be alone. He hadn't a house of his own. He never had all the time he lived. He hadn't even a room of his own into which he could go, and bolt the door of it. True, he had kind friends, who gave him a bed: but they were all poor people, and their houses were small, and very likely they had large families, and he could not always find a quiet place to go into. And I daresay, if he had had a room, he would have been a little troubled with the children constantly coming to find him; for however much he loved them—and no man was ever so fond of children as he was—he needed to be left quiet sometimes. So, upon this occasion, he went up the mountain just to be quiet. He had been all day with a crowd of people, and he felt that it was time to be alone. For he had been talking with men all day, which tires and sometimes confuses a man's thoughts, and now he wanted to talk with God—for that makes a man strong, and puts all the confusion in order again, and lets a man know what he is about. So he went to the top of the hill. That was his secret chamber. It had no door; but that did not matter—no one could see him but God. There he stayed for hours—sometimes, I suppose, kneeling in his prayer to God; sometimes sitting, tired with his own thinking, on a stone; sometimes walking about, looking forward to what would come next—not anxious about it, but contemplating it. For just before he came up here, some of the people who had been with him wanted to make him a king; and this would not do—this was not what God wanted of him, and therefore he got rid of them, and came up here to talk to God. It was so quiet up here! The earth had almost vanished. He could see just the bare hill-top beneath him, a glimmer below, and the sky and the stars over his head. The people had all gone away to their own homes, and perhaps next day would hardly think about him at all, busy catching fish, or digging their gardens, or making things for their houses. But he knew that God would not forget him the next day any more than this day, and that God had sent him not to be the king that these people wanted him to be, but their servant. So, to make his heart strong, I say, he went up into the mountain alone to have a talk with his Father. How quiet it all was up here, I say, and how noisy it had been down there a little while ago! But God had been in the noise then as much as he was in the quiet now—the only difference being that he could not then be alone with him. I need not tell you who this man was—it was the king of men, the servant of men, the Lord Jesus Christ, the everlasting Son of our Father in heaven.

"Now this mountain on which he was praying had a small lake at the foot of it—that is, about thirteen miles long, and five miles broad. Not wanting even his usual companions to be with him this evening—partly, I presume, because they were of the same mind as those who desired to take him by force and make him a king—he had sent them away in their boat, to go across this water to the other side, where were their homes and their families. Now, it was not pitch dark either on the mountain-top or on the water down below; yet I doubt if any other man than he would have been keen-eyed enough to discover that little boat down in the middle of the lake, much distressed by the west wind that blew right in their teeth. But he loved every man in it so much, that I think even as he was talking to his Father, his eyes would now and then go looking for and finding it—watching it on its way across to the other side. You must remember that it was a little boat; and there are often tremendous storms upon these small lakes with great mountains about them. For the wind will come all at once, rushing down through the clefts in as sudden a squall as ever overtook a sailor at sea. And then, you know, there is no sea-room. If the wind get the better of them, they are on the shore in a few minutes, whichever way the wind may blow. He saw them worn out at the oar, toiling in rowing, for the wind was contrary unto them. So the time for loneliness and prayer was over, and the time to go down out of his secret chamber and help his brethren was come. He did not need to turn and say good-bye to his Father, as if he dwelt on that mountain-top alone: his Father was down there on the lake as well. He went straight down. Could not his Father, if he too was down on the lake, help them without him? Yes. But he wanted him to do it, that they might see that he did it. Otherwise they could only have thought that the wind fell and the waves lay down, without supposing for a moment that their Master or his Father had had anything to do with it. They would have done just as people do now-a-days: they think that the help comes of itself, instead of by the will of him who determined from the first that men should be helped. So the Master went down the hill. When he reached the border of the lake, the wind being from the other side, he must have found the waves breaking furiously upon the rocks. But that made no difference to him. He looked out as he stood alone on the edge amidst the rushing wind and the noise of the water, out over the waves under the clear starry sky, saw where the tiny boat was tossed about like a nutshell, and set out."

The mariners had been staring at me up to this point, leaning forward on their benches, for sailors are nearly as fond of a good yarn as they are of tobacco; and I heard afterwards that they had voted parson's yarn a good one. Now, however, I saw one of them, probably more ignorant than the others, cast a questioning glance at his neighbour. It was not returned, and he fell again into a listening attitude. He had no idea of what was coming. He probably thought parson had forgotten to say how Jesus had come by a boat.

"The companions of our Lord had not been willing to go away and leave him behind. Now, I dare say, they wished more than ever that he had been with them—not that they thought he could do anything with a storm, only that somehow they would have been less afraid with his face to look at. They had seen him cure men of dreadful diseases; they had seen him turn water into wine—some of them; they had seen him feed five thousand people the day before with five loaves and two small fishes; but had one of their number suggested that if he had been with them, they would have been safe from the storm, they would not have talked any nonsense about the laws of nature, not having learned that kind of nonsense, but they would have said that was quite a different thing—altogether too much to expect or believe: *nobody* could make the wind mind what it was about, or keep the water from drowning you if you fell into it and couldn't swim; or such like.

"At length, when they were nearly worn out, taking feebler and feebler strokes, sometimes missing the water altogether, at other times burying their oars in it up to the handles—as they rose on the crest of a huge wave, one of them gave a cry, and they all stopped rowing and stared, leaning forward to peer through the darkness. And through the spray which the wind tore from the tops of the waves and scattered before it like dust, they saw, perhaps a hundred yards or so from the boat, something standing up from the surface of the water. It seemed to move towards them. It was a shape like a man. They all cried out with fear, as was natural, for they thought it must be a ghost."

How the faces of the sailors strained towards me at this part of the story! I was afraid one of them especially was on the point of getting up to speak, as we have heard of sailors doing in church. I went on.

"But then, over the noise of the wind and the waters came the voice they knew so well. It said, 'Be of good cheer; it is I. Be not afraid.' I should think, between wonder and gladness, they hardly knew for some moments where they were or what they were about. Peter was the first to recover himself apparently. In the first flush of his delight he felt strong and full of courage. 'Lord, if it be thou,' he said, 'bid me come unto thee on the water.' Jesus just said, 'Come;' and Peter unshipped his oar, and scrambled over the gunwale on to the sea. But when he let go his hold of the boat, and began to look about him, and saw how the wind was tearing the water, and how it tossed and raved between him and Jesus, he began to be afraid. And as soon as he began to be afraid he began to sink; but he had, notwithstanding his fear, just sense enough to do the one sensible thing: he cried out, 'Lord, save me.' And Jesus put out his hand, and took hold of him, and lifted him out of the water, and said to him, 'O thou of little faith, wherefore didst thou doubt?' And then they got into the boat, and the wind fell all at once and altogether.

"Now, you will not think that Peter was a coward, will you? It wasn't that he hadn't courage, but that he hadn't enough of it. And why was it that he hadn't enough of it? Because he hadn't faith enough. Peter was always very easily impressed with the look of things. It wasn't at all likely that a man should be able to walk on the water; and yet Peter found himself standing on the water: you would have thought that when once he found himself standing on the water, he need not be afraid of the wind and the waves that lay between him and Jesus. But they looked so ugly that the fearfulness of them took hold of his heart, and his courage went. You would have thought that the greatest trial of his courage was over when he got out of the boat, and that there was comparatively little more ahead of him. Yet the sight of the waves and the blast of the boisterous wind were too much for him. I will tell you how I fancy it was; and I think there are several instances of the same kind of thing in Peter's life. When he got out of the boat, and found himself standing on the water, he began to think much of himself for being able to do so, and fancy himself better and greater than his companions, and an especial favourite of God above them. Now, there is nothing that kills faith sooner than pride. The two are directly against each other. The moment that Peter grew proud, and began to think about himself instead of about his Master, he began to lose his faith, and then he grew afraid, and then he began to sink—and that brought him to his senses. Then he forgot himself and remembered his Master, and then the hand of the Lord caught him, and the voice of the Lord gently rebuked him for the smallness of his faith, asking, 'Wherefore didst thou doubt?' I wonder if Peter was able to read his own heart sufficiently well to answer that *wherefore.* I do not think it likely at this period of his history. But God has immeasurable patience, and before he had done teaching Peter, even in this life, he had made him know quite well that pride and conceit were at the root of all his failures. Jesus did not point it out to him now. Faith was the only thing that would reveal that to him, as well as cure him of it; and was, therefore, the only thing he required of him in his rebuke. I suspect Peter was helped back into the boat by the eager hands of his companions, already in a humbler state of mind than when he left it; but before his pride would be quite overcome, it would need that same voice of loving-kindness to call him Satan, and the voice of the cock to bring to his mind his loud boast, and his sneaking denial; nay, even the voice of one who had never seen the Lord till after his death, but was yet a readier disciple than he—the voice of St Paul, to rebuke him because he dissembled, and was not downright honest. But at the last even he gained the crown of martyrdom, enduring all extremes, nailed to the cross like his Master, rather than deny his name. This should teach us to distrust ourselves, and yet have great hope for ourselves, and endless patience with other people. But to return to the story, and what the story itself teaches us.

"If the disciples had known that Jesus saw them from the top of the mountain, and was watching them all the time, would they have been frightened at the storm, as I have little doubt they were, for they were only fresh-water fishermen, you know? Well, to answer my own question"—I went on in haste, for I saw one or two of the sailors with an audible answer hovering on their lips—"I don't know that, as they then were, it would have made so much difference to them; for none of them had risen much above the look of the things nearest them yet. But supposing you, who know something about him, were alone on the sea, and expecting your boat to be swamped every moment—if you found out all at once, that he was looking down at you from some lofty hill-top, and seeing all round about you in time and space too, would you be afraid? He might mean you to go to the bottom, you know. Would you mind going to the bottom with him looking at you? I do not think I should mind it myself. But I must take care lest I be boastful like Peter.

"Why should we be afraid of anything with him looking at us who is the Saviour of men? But we are afraid of him instead, because we do not believe that he is what he says he is—the Saviour of men. We do not believe what he offers us is salvation. We think it is slavery, and therefore continue slaves. Friends, I will speak to you who think you do believe in him. I am not going to say that you do not believe in him; but I hope I am going to make you say to yourselves that you too deserve to have those words of the Saviour spoken to you that were spoken to Peter, 'O ye of little faith!' Floating on the sea of your troubles, all kinds of fears and anxieties assailing you, is he not on the mountain-top? Sees he not the little boat of your fortunes tossed with the waves and the contrary wind? Assuredly he will come to you walking on the waters. It may not be in the way you wish, but if not, you will say at last, 'This is better.' It may be he will come in a form that will make you cry out for fear in the weakness of your faith, as the disciples cried out—not believing any more than they did that it can be he. But will not each of you arouse his courage, that to you also he may say, as to the woman with the sick daughter whose confidence he so sorely tried, 'Great is thy faith'? Will you not rouse yourself, I say, that you may do him justice, and cast off the slavery of your own dread? O ye of little faith, wherefore will ye doubt? Do not think that the Lord sees and will not come. Down the mountain assuredly he will come, and you are now as safe in your troubles as the disciples were in theirs with Jesus looking on. They did not know it, but it was so: the Lord was watching them. And when you look back upon your past lives, cannot you see some instances of the same kind—when you felt and acted as if the Lord had forgotten you, and found afterwards that he had been watching you all the time?

"But the reason why you do not trust him more is that you obey him so little. If you would only ask what God would have you to do, you would soon find your confidence growing. It is because you are proud, and envious, and greedy after gain, that you do not trust him more. Ah! trust him if it were only to get rid of these evil things, and be clean and beautiful in heart.

"O sailors with me on the ocean of life, will you, knowing that he is watching you from his mountain-top, do and say the things that hurt, and wrong, and disappoint him? Sailors on the waters that surround this globe, though there be no great mountain that overlooks the little lake on which you float, not the less does he behold you, and care for you, and watch over you. Will you do that which is unpleasing, distressful to him? Will you be irreverent, cruel, coarse? Will you say evil things, lie, and delight in vile stories and reports, with his eye on you, watching your ship on its watery ways, ever ready to come over the waves to help you? It is a fine thing, sailors, to fear nothing; but it would be far finer to fear nothing *because* he is above all, and over all, and in you all. For his sake and for his love, give up everything bad, and take him for your captain. He will be both captain and pilot to you, and steer you safe into the port of glory. Now to God the Father," &c.

This is very nearly the sermon I preached that first Sunday morning. I followed it up with a short enforcement in the afternoon.

CHAPTER XVIII.

ANOTHER SUNDAY EVENING.

IN the evening we met in Connie's room, as usual, to have our talk. And this is what came out of it.

The window was open. The sun was in the west. We sat a little aside out of the course of his radiance, and let him look full into the room. Only Wynnie sat back in a dark corner, as if she would get out of his way. Below him the sea lay bluer than you could believe even when you saw it—blue with a delicate yet deep silky blue, the exquisiteness of which was thrown up by the brilliant white lines of its lapping on the high coast, to the northward. We had just sat down, when Dora broke out with—

"I saw Niceboots at church. He did stare at you, papa, as if he had never heard a sermon before."

"I dare say he never heard such a sermon before!" said Connie, with the perfect confidence of inexperience and partiality—not to say ignorance, seeing she had not heard the sermon herself.

Here Wynnie spoke from her dark corner, apparently forcing herself to speak, and thereby giving what seemed an unpleasant tone to what she said.

"Well, papa, I don't know what to think. You are always telling us to trust in Him—but how can we, if we are not good?"

"The first good thing you can do, is to look up to him. That is the beginning of trust in him, and the most sensible thing that it is possible for us to do. That is faith."

"But it's no use sometimes."

"How do you know that?"

"Because you—I mean I—can't feel good, or care about it at all."

"But is that any ground for saying that it is no use—that he does not heed you? that he disregards the look cast up to him? that till the heart goes with the will, he who made himself strong to be the helper of the weak, who pities most those who are most destitute—and who so destitute as those who do not love what they want to love—except, indeed, those who don't want to love?—that till you are well on towards all right by earnestly seeking it, he won't help you? You are to judge him from yourself, are you?—forgetting that all the misery in you is just because you have not got his grand presence with you?"

I spoke so earnestly as to be somewhat incoherent in words. But my reader will understand. Wynnie was silent. Connie, as if partly to help her sister, followed on the same side.

"I don't know exactly how to say what I mean, papa, but I wish I could get this lovely afternoon, all full of sunshine and blue, into unity with all that you teach us about Jesus Christ. I wish this beautiful day came in with my thought of him, like the frame—gold, and red, and blue—that you have to that picture of him at home. Why doesn't it?"

"Just because you have not enough of faith in him, my dear. You do not know him well enough yet. You do not yet believe that he means you all gladness, heartily, honestly, thoroughly."

"And no suffering, papa?"

"I did not say that, my dear. There you are on your couch and can't move. But he does mean you such gladness, such a full sunny air and blue sea of blessedness that this suffering shall count for little in it; nay, more, shall be taken in for part, and, like the rocks that interfere with the roll of the sea, flash out the white that glorifies and intensifies the whole—to pass away by and by, I trust, none the less. What a chance you have, my Connie, of believing in him, of offering upon his altar!"

"But," said my wife, "are not these feelings in a great measure dependent upon the state of one's health? I find it so different when the sunshine is inside me as well as outside me."

"Not a doubt of it, my dear. But that is only the more reason for rising above all that. From the way some people speak of physical difficulties—I don't mean you, wife—you would think that they were not merely the inevitable which they are, but the insurmountable which they are not. That they are physical and not spiritual, is not only a great consolation, but a strong argument for overcoming them. For all that is physical is put or is in the process of being put under the feet of the spiritual. Do not mistake me. I do not say you can make yourself merry or happy, when you are in a physical condition which is contrary to such mental condition. But you can withdraw from it—not all at once; but by practice and effort, you can learn to withdraw from it, refusing to allow your judgments and actions to be ruled by it. You can climb up out of the fogs, and sit quiet in the sunlight on the hill-side of faith. You cannot be merry down below in the fog, for there is the fog; but you can every now and then fly with the dove-wings of the soul up into the clear, to remind yourself that all this passes away, is but an accident, and that the sun shines always, although it may not at any given moment be shining on you. 'What does that matter?' you will learn to say. 'It is enough for me to know that the sun does shine, and that this is only a weary fog that is round about me for the moment. I shall come out into the light beyond presently.' This is faith—faith in God, who is the light, and is all in all. I believe that the most glorious instances of calmness in suffering are thus achieved; that the sufferers really do not suffer what one of us would if thrown into their physical condition without the refuge of their spiritual condition as well; for they have taken refuge in the inner chamber. Out of the spring of their life a power goes forth that quenches the flames of the furnace of their suffering, so far at least that it does not touch the deep life, cannot make them miserable, does not drive them from the possession of their soul in patience, which is the divine citadel of the suffering. Do you understand me, Connie?"

"I do, papa. I think, perfectly."

"Still less, then, is the fact that the difficulty is physical to be used as an excuse for giving way to ill-temper, and, in fact, leaving ourselves to be tossed and shaken by every tremble of our nerves. That is as if a man should give himself into the hands and will and caprice of an organ-grinder, to work upon him, not with the music of the spheres, but with the wretched growling of the streets."

"But," said Wynnie, "I have heard you yourself, papa, make excuse for people's ill-temper on this very ground, that they were out of health. Indeed," she went on, half-crying, "I have heard you do so for myself when you did not know that I was within hearing."

"Yes, my dear, most assuredly. It is no fiction, but a real difference that lies between excusing ourselves and excusing other people. No doubt the same excuse is just for ourselves that is just for other people. But we can do something to put ourselves right upon a higher principle, and therefore we should not waste our time in excusing, or even in condemning ourselves, but make haste up the hill. Where we cannot work—that is, in the life of another—we have time to make all the excuse we can. Nay, more; it is only justice there. We are not bound to insist on our own rights, even of excuse; the wisest thing often is to forego them. But we are bound by heaven, earth, and hell, to give them to other people. And, besides, what a comfort to ourselves to be able to say, 'It is true So-and-so was cross to-day. But it wasn't in the least that he wasn't friendly, or didn't like me; it was only that he had eaten something that hadn't agreed with him. I could see it in his eye. He had one of his headaches.' Thus, you see, justice to our neighbour, and comfort to ourselves, is one and the same thing. But it would be a sad thing to have to think that when we found ourselves in the same ungracious condition, from whatever cause, we had only to submit to it saying, 'It is a law of nature,' as even those who talk most about laws will not do, when those laws come between them and their own comfort. They are ready enough then to call in the aid of higher laws, which, so far from being contradictory, overrule the lower to get things into something like habitable, endurable condition. It may be a law of nature, but what has the Law of the Spirit of Life to *propound anent* it? as the Scotch lawyers would say."

A little pause followed, during which I hope some of us were thinking. That Wynnie, at least, was, her next question made evident.

"What you say about a law of nature and a law of the Spirit, makes me think again how that walking on the water has always been a puzzle to me."

"It could hardly be other, seeing that we cannot possibly understand it," I answered.

"But I find it so hard to believe. Can't you say something, papa, to help me to believe it?"

"I think if you admit what goes before, you will find there is nothing against reason in the story."

"Tell me, please, what you mean."

"If all things were made by Jesus, the Word of God, would it be reasonable that the water that he had created should be able to drown him?"

"It might drown his body."

"It would if he had not the power over it still, to prevent it from laying hold of him. But just think for a moment. God is a spirit. Spirit is greater than matter. Spirit makes matter. Think what it was for a human body to have such a divine creative power dwelling in it as that which dwelt in the human form of Jesus! What power, and influence, and utter rule that spirit must have over the body in which it dwells! We cannot imagine how much; but if we have so much power over our bodies, how much more must the pure, divine Jesus have had over his! I suspect this miracle was wrought, not through anything done to the water, but through the power of the spirit over the body of Jesus, which was all obedient thereto. I am not explaining the miracle, for that I cannot do. One day I think it will be plain common sense to us. But now I am only showing you what seems to me to bring us a step nearer to the essential region of the miracle, and so far make it easier to believe. If we look at the history of our Lord, we shall find that, true real human body as his was, it was yet used by his spirit after a fashion in which we cannot yet use our bodies. And this is only reasonable. Let me give you an instance. You remember how, on the Mount of Transfiguration, that body shone so that the light of it illuminated all his garments. You do not surely suppose that this shine was external—physical light, as we say, *merely?* No doubt it was physical light, for how else would their eyes have seen it? But where did it come from? What was its source? I think it was a natural outburst of glory from the mind of Jesus, filled with the perfect life of communion with his Father—the light of his divine blessedness taking form in physical radiance that permeated and glorified all that surrounded him. As the body is the expression of the soul, as the face of Jesus himself was the expression of the being, the thought, the love of Jesus, in like manner this radiance was the natural expression of his gladness, even in the face of that of which they had been talking—Moses, Elias, and he—namely, the decease that he should accomplish at Jerusalem. Again, after his resurrection, he convinced the hands, as well as the eyes, of doubting Thomas, that he was indeed there in the body; and yet that body could appear and disappear as the Lord willed. All this is full of marvel, I grant you; but probably far more intelligible to us in a further state of existence than some of the most simple facts with regard to our own bodies are to us now, only that we are so used to them that we never think how unintelligible they really are."

"But then about Peter, papa? What you have been saying will not apply to Peter's body, you know."

"I confess there is more difficulty there. But if you can suppose that such power were indwelling in Jesus, you cannot limit the sphere of its action. As he is the head of the body, his church, in all spiritual things, so I firmly believe, however little we can understand about it, is he in all natural things as well. Peter's faith in him brought even Peter's body within the sphere of the outgoing power of the Master. Do you suppose that because Peter ceased to be brave and trusting, therefore Jesus withdrew from him some sustaining power, and allowed him to sink? I do not believe it. I believe Peter's sinking followed naturally upon his loss of confidence. Thus he fell away from the life of the Master; was no longer, in that way I mean, connected with the Head, was instantly under the dominion of the natural law of gravitation, as we call it, and began to sink. Therefore the Lord must take other means to save him. He must draw nigh to him in a bodily manner. The pride of Peter had withdrawn him from the immediate spiritual influence of Christ, conquering his matter; and therefore the Lord must come over the stormy space between, come nearer to him in the body, and from his own height of safety above the sphere of the natural law, stretch out to him the arm of physical aid, lift him up, lead him to the boat. The whole salvation of the human race is figured in this story. It is all Christ, my love. Does this help you to believe at all?"

"I think it does, papa. But it wants thinking over

a good deal. I always find as I think, that lighter bits shine out here and there in a thing I have no hope of understanding altogether. That always helps me to believe that the rest might be understood too, if I were only clever enough."

"Simple enough, not clever enough, my dear."

"But there's one thing," said my wife, "that is more interesting to me than what you have been talking about. It is the other instances in the life of St Peter in which you said he failed in a similar manner from pride or self-satisfaction."

"One, at least, seems to me very clear. You have often remarked to me, Ethel, how little praise servants can stand; how almost invariably after you have commended the diligence or skill of any of your household, as you felt bound to do, one of the first visible results was either a falling away in the performance by which she had gained the praise, or a more or less violent access, according to the nature of the individual, of self-conceit, soon breaking out in bad temper or impertinence. Now you will see precisely the same kind of thing in Peter."

Here I opened my New Testament, and read fragmentarily,—"'But whom say ye that I am? . . . Thou art the Christ, the Son of the living God. . . . Blessed art thou, Simon. . . . My Father hath revealed that unto thee. I will give unto thee the keys of the kingdom of heaven. . . . I must suffer many things, and be killed, and be raised again the third day. . . . Be it far from thee, Lord. This shall not be unto thee. . . . Get thee behind me, Satan. Thou art an offence unto me. Just contemplate the change here in the words of our Lord. 'Blessed art thou.' 'Thou art an offence unto me.' Think what change has passed on Peter's mood before the second of these words could be addressed to him to whom the first had just been spoken. The Lord had praised him. Peter grew self-sufficient, even to the rebuking of him whose praise had so uplifted him. But it is ever so. A man will gain a great moral victory: glad first, then uplifted, he will fall before a paltry temptation. I have sometimes wondered, too, whether his denial of our Lord had anything to do with his satisfaction with himself for making that onslaught upon the high priest's servant. It was a brave thing and a faithful to draw a single sword against a multitude. In his fiery eagerness and inexperience, the blow, well meant to cleave Malchus's head, missed, and only cut off his ear; but Peter had herein justified his confident saying that he would not deny him. He was not one to deny his Lord who had been the first to confess him! Yet ere the cock had crowed, ere the morning had dawned, the vulgar grandeur of the palace of the high priest, (for let it be art itself, it was vulgar grandeur beside that grandeur which it caused Peter to deny,) and the accusing tone of a maid-servant, were enough to make him quail whom the crowd with lanterns, and torches, and weapons, had only roused to fight. True, he was excited then, and now he was cold in the middle of the night, with Jesus gone from his sight a prisoner, and for the faces of friends that had there surrounded him and strengthened him with their sympathy, now only the faces of those who were, or whom at least Peter thought to be on the other side, looking at him curiously, as a strange intruder into their domains. Alas, that the courage which led him to follow the Lord should have thus led him, not to deny him, but into the denial of him! Yet why should I say *alas?* If the denial of our Lord lay in his heart a possible thing, only prevented by his being kept in favourable circumstances for confessing him, it was a thousand times better that he should deny him, and thus know what a poor weak thing that heart of his was, trust it no more, and give it up to the Master to make it strong, and pure, and grand. For such an end the Lord was willing to bear all the pain of Peter's denial. Oh, the love of that Son of Man, who in the midst of all the wretched weaknesses of those who surrounded him, loved the best in them, and looked forward to his own victory for them that thev might become all that they were meant to be—like him; that the lovely glimmerings of truth and love that were in them now—the breakings forth of the light that lighteneth every man—might grow into the perfect human day; loving them even the more that they were so helpless, so oppressed, so far from that ideal which was their life, and which all their dim desires were reaching after!"

Here I ceased, and a little overcome with the great picture in my soul to which I had been able only to give the poorest expression, rose, and retired to my own room. There I could only fall on my knees and pray that the Lord Christ, who had died for me, might have his own way with me—that it might be worth his while to have done what he did and what he was doing now for me. To my Elder Brother, my Lord, and my God, I gave myself yet again, confidently, because he cared to have me, and my very breath was his. I *would* be what he wanted, who knew all about it, and had done everything that I might be a son of God—a living glory of gladness.

CHAPTER XIX.

NICEBOOTS.

HE next morning the captain of the lost vessel called upon me early to thank me for himself and his men. He was a fine, honest-looking, burly fellow, dressed in blue from head to heel. He might have sat for a portrait of Chaucer's shipman as far as his hue and the first look of him went. It was clear that "in many a tempest had his beard be shake," and certainly "the hote somer had made his hew all broun;" but farther the likeness would hardly go, for the "good fellow" which Chaucer applies with such irony to the shipman of his time, who would filch wine, and drown all the captives he made in a sea-fight, was clearly applicable in good earnest to this shipman. Still I thought I had something to bring against him, and therefore before we parted I said to him—

"They tell me captain, that your vessel was not

seaworthy, and that you could not but have known that."

"She was my own craft, sir, and I judged her fit for several voyages more. If she had been A 1 she couldn't have been mine; and a man must do what he can for his family.

"But you were risking your life, you know."

"A few chances more or less don't much signify to a sailor, sir. There ain't nothing to be done without risk. You 'll find an old tub go voyage after voyage, and she beyond bail, and a clipper fresh off the stocks go down in the harbour. It 's all in the luck, sir, I assure you."

"Well, if it were your own life I should have nothing to say, seeing you have a family to look after; but what about the poor fellows who made the voyage with you? Did they know what kind of a vessel they were embarking in?"

"Wherever the captain's ready to go he 'll always find men ready to follow him. Bless you, sir, they never ask no questions. If a sailor was always to be thinking of the chances, he 'd never set his foot off shore."

"Still I don't think it 's right they shouldn't know."

"I daresay they knowed all about the old brig as well as I did myself. You gets to know all about a craft just as you do about her captain. She 's got a character of her own, and she can't hide it long, any more than you can hide yours, sir, begging your pardon."

"I dare say that 's all correct, but still I shouldn't like any one to say to me, 'You ought to have told me, captain.' Therefore, you see, I 'm telling you, captain, and now I'm clear.—Have a glass of wine before you go?" I concluded, ringing the bell.

"Thank you, sir. I'll turn over what you've been saying, and anyhow I take it kind of you."

So we parted. I have never seen him since, and shall not most likely in this world. But he looked like a man that could understand why and wherefore I spoke as I did. And I had the advantage of having had a chance of doing something for him first of all. Let no man who wants to do anything for the soul of a man lose a chance of doing something for his body. He ought to be willing, and ready, which is more than willing, to do that whether or not; but there are those who need this reminder. Of many a soul Jesus laid hold by healing the suffering the body brought upon it. No one but himself can tell how much the nucleus of the church was composed of and by those who had received health from his hands, loving-kindness from the word of his mouth. My own opinion is, that herein lay the very germ of the kernel of what is now the ancient, was then the infant church; that from them, next to the disciples themselves, went forth the chief power of life in love, for they too had seen the Lord, and in their own humble way could preach and teach concerning him. What memories of him theirs must have been!

Things went on very quietly, that is, as I mean now, from the view-point of a historian, without much to record bearing notably upon after events, for the greater part of the next week. I wandered about my parish, making acquaintance with different people in an outside sort of way, only now and then finding an opportunity of seeing into their souls except by conclusion. But I enjoyed endlessly the aspects of the country. It was not picturesque except in parts. There was little wood and there were no hills, only undulations, though many of them were steep enough even from a pedestrian's point of view. Neither, however, were there any plains except high moorland tracts. But the impression of the whole country was large, airy, sunshiny, and it was clasped in the arms of the infinite, awful, yet how bountiful sea—if one will look at the ocean in its world-wide, not to say its eternal aspects, and not out of the fears of a hide-bound love of life! The sea and the sky, I must confess, dwarfed the earth, made it of small account beside them; but who could complain of such an influence? At least, not I.

My children bathed in this sea every day, and gathered strength and knowledge from it. It was, as I have indicated, a dangerous coast to bathe upon. The sweep of the tides varied with the varying sands that were cast up. There was now in one place, now in another, a strong *undertow*, as they called it—a reflux, that is, of the inflowing waters, which was quite sufficient to carry those who could not swim out into the great deep, and rendered much exertion necessary, even in those who could, to regain the shore. But there was a fine, strong Cornish woman to take charge of the ladies and the little boys, and she, watching the ways of the wild monster, knew the when and the where, and all about it.

Connie got out upon the downs every day. She improved in health certainly, and we thought a little even in her powers of motion. The weather continued superb. What rain there was fell at night, just enough for Nature to wash her face with, and so look quite fresh in the morning. We contrived a dinner on the sands on the other side of the bay, for the Friday of this same week.

The morning rose gloriously. Harry and Charlie were turning the house upside down, to judge by their noise, long before I was in the humour to get up, for I had been reading late the night before. I never made much objection to mere noise, knowing that I could stop it the moment I pleased, and knowing, which was of more consequence, that so far from there being anything wrong in making a noise, the sea would make noise enough in our ears before we left Kilkhaven. The moment, however, that I heard a thread of whining or a burst of anger in the noise, I would interfere at once—treating these just as things that must be dismissed at once. Harry and Charlie were, I say, to use their own form of speech, making such a row that morning, however, that I was afraid of some injury to the house or furniture, which were not our own. So I opened my door, and called out—

"Harry! Charlie! What on earth are you about?"

"Nothing, papa,' answered Charlie. "Only it's so jolly!"

"What is jolly, my boy?" I asked.

"Oh, I don't know, papa! It's *so* jolly!"

"Is it the sunshine?" thought I; "and the wind!

God's world all over? The God of gladness in the hearts of the lads? Is it that? No wonder, then, that they cannot tell what it is!"

I withdrew into my room; and so far from seeking to put an end to the noise—I knew Connie did not mind it—listened to it with a kind of reverence, as the outcome of a gladness which the God of joy had kindled in their hearts. Soon after, however, I heard certain dim growls of expostulation from Harry, and having, from experience, ground for believing that the elder was tyrannising over the younger, I stopped that and the noise together, sending Charlie to find out where the tide would be between one and two o'clock, and Harry to run to the top of the hill, and find out the direction of the wind. Before I was dressed, Charlie was knocking at my door with the news that it would be half-tide about one; and Harry speedily followed with the discovery that the wind was north-east by south-west, which of course determined that the sun would shine all day.

As the dinner-hour drew near, the servants went over, with Walter at their head, to choose a rock convenient for a table, under the shelter of the rocks on the sands across the bay. Thither, when Walter returned, we bore our Connie, carrying her litter close by the edge of the retreating tide, which sometimes broke in a ripple of music under her, wetting our feet with innocuous rush. The child's delight was extreme, as she thus skimmed the edge of the ocean, with the little ones gamboling about her, and her mamma and Wynnie walking quietly on the landward side, for she wished to have no one between her and the sea.

After scrambling with difficulty over some rocky ledges, and stopping, at Connie's request, to let her look into a deep pool in the sand, which somehow or other retained the water after the rest had retreated, we set her down near the mouth of a cave, in the shadow of a rock. And there was our dinner nicely laid for us on a flat rock in front of the cave. The cliffs rose behind us, with curiously-curved and variously-angled strata. The sun in his full splendour threw dark shadows on the brilliant yellow sand, more and more of which appeared as the bright blue water withdrew itself, now rippling over it as if it meant to hide it all up again, now uncovering more as it withdrew for another rush. Before we had finished our dinner, the foremost wavelets appeared so far away over the plain of the sand, that it seemed a long walk to the edge that had been almost at our feet a little while ago. Between us and it lay a lovely desert of glittering sand.

When even Charley and Harry had arrived at the conclusion that it was time to stop eating, we left the shadow and went out into the sun, carrying Connie and laying her down in the midst of "the ribbed sea-sand," which was very ribby to-day. On a shawl a little way off from her lay her baby, crowing and kicking with the same jollity that had possessed the boys ever since the morning. I wandered about with Wynnie on the sands, picking up, amongst other things, strange creatures in thin shells ending in vegetable-like tufts, if I remember rightly. My wife sat on the end of Connie's litter, and Dora and the boys, a little way off, were trying how far the full force of three wooden spades could, in digging a hole, keep ahead of the water which was ever tumbling in the sand from the sides of the same. Behind, the servants were busy washing the plates in a pool, and burying the fragments of the feast; for I made it a rule wherever we went that the fair face of nature was not to be defiled. I have always taken the part of excursionists in these latter days of running to and fro, against those who complain that the loveliest places are being destroyed by their inroads. But there is one most offensive, even disgusting habit amongst them—that of leaving bones, fragments of meat pies, and worse than all, pieces of greasy paper about the place, which I cannot excuse, or at least defend. Even the surface of Cumberland and Westmoreland lakes will be defiled with these floating abominations—not abominations at all if they are decently burned or buried when done with, but certainly abominations when left to be cast hither and thither in the wind, over the grass, or on the eddy and ripple of the pure water, for days after those who have thus left their shame behind them have returned to their shops or factories. I forgive them for trampling down the grass and the ferns. That cannot be helped, and in comparison of the good they get, is not to be considered at all. But why should they leave such a savage trail behind them as this, forgetting too, that though they have done with the spot, there are others coming after them to whom these remnants must be an offence.

At length in our roaming, Wynnie and I approached a long low ridge of rock, rising towards the sea into which it ran. Crossing this, we came suddenly upon the painter whom Dora had called Niceboots, sitting with a small easel before him. We were right above him ere we knew. He had his back towards us, so that we saw at once what he was painting.

"Oh, papa!" cried Wynnie involuntarily, and the painter looked round.

"I beg your pardon," I said. "We came over from the other side, and did not see you before. I hope we have not disturbed you much."

"Not in the least," he answered courteously, and rose as he spoke.

I saw that the subject on his easel suggested that of which Wynnie had been making a sketch at the same time, on the day when Connie first lay on the top of the opposite cliff. But he was not even looking in the same direction now.

"Do you mind having your work seen before it is finished?"

"Not in the least, if the spectators will do me the favour to remember that most processes have to go through a seemingly chaotic stage," answered he.

I was struck with the mode and tone of the remark.

"Here is no common man," I said to myself, and responded to him in something of a similar style.

"I wish we could always keep that in mind with regard to human beings themselves, as well as their works," I said aloud.

The painter looked at me, and I looked at him.

"We speak each from the experience of his own profession, I presume," he said.

"But," I returned, glancing at the little picture in oils upon his easel, "your work here, though my knowledge of painting is next to nothing—perhaps I ought to say nothing at all—this picture must have long ago passed the chaotic stage."

"It is nearly as much finished as I care to make it," he returned. "I hardly count this work at all. I am chiefly amusing, or rather pleasing, my own fancy at present."

"Apparently," I remarked, "you had the conical rock outside the bay for your model, and now you are finishing it with your back turned towards it. How is that?"

"I will soon explain," he answered. "The moment I saw this rock it reminded me of Dante's Purgatory."

"Ah, you are a reader of Dante?" I said. "In the original, I hope."

"Yes. A friend of mine, a brother painter, an Italian, set me going with that, and once going with Dante, nobody could well stop. I never knew what intensity *per se* was till I began to read Dante."

"That is quite my own feeling. Now, to return to your picture."

"Without departing at all from natural forms, I thought to make it suggest the Purgatorio to any one who remembered the description given of the place *ab extra* by Ulysses, in the end of the twenty-sixth canto of the

Inferno. Of course, that thing there is a mere rock, yet it has certain mountain forms about it. I have put it at a much greater distance, you see, and have sought to make it look a solitary mountain in the midst of a great water. You will discover even now that the circles of the Purgatory are suggested without any approach, I think, to artificial structure; and there are occasional hints at figures, which you cannot definitely detach from the rocks—which, by the way, you must remember, were in one part full of sculptures. I have kept the mountain near enough, however, to indicate the great expanse of wild flowers on the top, which Matilda was so busy gathering. I want to indicate too the wind up there in the terrestrial paradise, ever and always blowing one way. You remember, Mr Walton?"—for the young man, getting animated, began to talk as if we had known each other for some time—and here he repeated the purport of Dante's words in English:—

> "An air of sweetness, changeless in its flow,
> With no more strength than in a soft wind lies,
> Smote peacefully against me on the brow.
> By which the leaves all trembling, level-wise,
> Did every one bend thitherward to where
> The high mount throws its shadow at sunrise."

"I thought you said you did not use translations?"

"I thought it possible that—Miss Walton (?)" interrogatively this—"might not follow the Italian so easily, and I feared to seem pedantic."

"She won't lag far behind, I flatter myself," I returned. "Whose translation do you quote?"

He hesitated a moment; then said carelessly:

"I have cobbled a few passages after that fashion myself."

"It has the merit of being near the original at least," I returned; "and that seems to me one of the chief merits a translation can possess."

"Then," the painter resumed, rather hastily, as if to avoid any further remark upon his verses, "you see those white things in the air above?" Here he turned to Wynnie. "Miss Walton will remember—I think she was making a drawing of the rock at the same time I was—how the sea-gulls, or some such birds—only two or three of them—kept flitting about the top of it?"

"I remember quite well," answered Wynnie, with a look of appeal to me.

"Yes," I interposed; "my daughter in describing what she had been attempting to draw, spoke especially of the birds over the rock. For she said the white lapping of the waves looked like spirits trying to get loose, and the white birds like foam that had broken its chains, and risen in triumph into the air."

Here Mr Niceboots, for as yet I did not know what else to call him, looked at Wynnie almost with a start.

"How wonderfully that falls in with my fancy about the rock!" he said. "Purgatory indeed! with imprisoned souls lapping at its foot, and the free souls winging their way aloft in ether. Well, this world is a kind of purgatory anyhow—is it not, Mr Walton?"

"Certainly it is. We are here tried as by fire, to see

what our work is—whether wood, hay, and stubble, or gold and silver and precious stones."

"You see," resumed the painter, "if anybody only glanced at my little picture, he would take those for sea-birds; but if he looked into it, and began to suspect me, he would find out that they were Dante and Beatrice on their way to the sphere of the moon."

"In one respect at least, then, your picture has the merit of corresponding to fact; for what thing is there in the world, or what group of things, in which the natural man will not see merely the things of nature, but the spiritual man the things of the spirit?"

"I am no theologian," said the painter, turning away; I thought somewhat coldly.

But I could see that Wynnie was greatly interested in him. Perhaps she thought that here was some enlightenment of the riddle of the world for her, if she could but get at what he was thinking. She was used to my way of it: here might be something new.

"If I can be of any service to Miss Walton with her drawing, I shall be happy," he said, turning again towards me.

But his last gesture had made me a little distrustful of him, and I received his advances on this point with a coldness which I did not wish to make more marked than his own towards my last observation.

"You are very kind," I said; "but Miss Walton does not presume to be an artist."

I saw a slight shade pass over Wynnie's countenance. When I turned to Mr Niceboots, a shade of a different sort was on his. Surely I had said something wrong to cast a gloom on two young faces. I made haste to make amends.

"We are just going to have some coffee," I said, "for my servants, I see, have managed to kindle a fire. Will you come and allow me to introduce you to Mrs Walton?"

"With much pleasure," he answered, rising from the rock whereon, as he spoke about his picture, he had again seated himself. He was a fine-built, black-bearded, sunburnt fellow, with clear grey eyes notwithstanding, a rather Roman nose, and good features generally. But there was an air of suppression, if not of sadness, about him, which, however, did not in the least interfere with the manliness of his countenance, or of its expression.

"But," I said, "how am I to effect an introduction, seeing I do not yet know your name?"

I had had to keep a sharp look-out on myself lest I should call him Mr Niceboots. He smiled very graciously, and replied—

"My name is Percivale—Charles Percivale."

"A descendant of Sir Percivale of King Arthur's Round Table?"

"I cannot count quite so far back," he answered, "as that—not quite to the Conquest," he added, with a slight deepening of his sunburnt hue. "I do come of a fighting race, but I cannot claim Sir Percivale."

We were now walking along the edge of the still retreating waves towards the group upon the sands, Mr Percivale and I foremost, and Wynnie lingering behind.

"Oh, do look here, papa!" she cried, from some little distance.

We turned, and saw her gazing at something on the sand at her feet. Hastening back, we found it to be a little narrow line of foam-bubbles, which the water had left behind it on the sand, slowly breaking and passing out of sight. Why there should be foam-bubbles there then, and not always, I do not know. But there they were—and such colours! deep rose and grassy green and ultramarine blue; and above all, one dark, yet brilliant and intensely-burnished, metallic gold. All of them were of a solid-looking burnished colour, like opaque body-colour laid on behind translucent crystal. Those little ocean bubbles were well worth turning to see; and so I said to Wynnie. But, as we gazed, they went on vanishing, one by one. Every moment a heavenly glory of hue burst, and was nowhere.

We walked away again towards the rest of our party.

"Don't you think those bubbles more beautiful than any precious stones you ever saw, papa?"

"Yes, my love, I think they are, except it be the opal. In the opal, God seems to have fixed the evanescent and made the vanishing eternal."

"And flowers are more beautiful things than jewels?" she said, interrogatively.

"Many—perhaps most flowers are," I granted.

"And did you ever see such curves and delicate textures anywhere else as in the clouds, papa?"

"I think not—in the cirrhous clouds at least—the

frozen ones. But what are you putting me to my catechism for in this way, my child?"

"Oh, papa, I could go on a long time with that catechism; but I will end with one question more, which you will perhaps find a little harder to answer. Only, I daresay you have had an answer ready for years lest one of us should ask you some day."

"No, my love. I never got an answer ready for anything lest one of my children should ask me. But it is not surprising either that children should be puzzled about the things that have puzzled their father, or that by the time they are able to put the questions, he should have found out some sort of an answer to most of them. Go on with your catechism, Wynnie. Now for your puzzle!"

"It's not a funny question, papa; it's a very serious one. I can't think why the unchanging God should have made all the most beautiful things wither and grow ugly, or burst and vanish, or die somehow and be no more. Mamma is not so beautiful as she once was, is she?"

"In one way no, but in another and better way much more so. But we will not talk about her kind of beauty just now: we will keep to the more material loveliness of which you have been speaking—though, in truth, no loveliness can be only material.—Well, then, for my answer: it is, I think, because God loves the beauty so much that he makes all beautiful things vanish quickly."

"I do not understand you, papa."

"I daresay not, my dear. But I will explain to you a little, if Mr Percivale will excuse me."

"On the contrary, I am greatly interested, both in the question and the answer."

"Well, then, Wynnie: everything has a soul and a body, or something like them. By the body we know the soul. But we are always ready to love the body instead of the soul. Therefore, God makes the body die continually, that we may learn to love the soul indeed. The world is full of beautiful things, but God has saved many men from loving the mere bodies of them, by making them poor; and more still by reminding them that if they be as rich as Crœsus all their lives, they will be as poor as Diogenes—poorer, without even a tub—when this world with all its pictures, scenery, books, and—alas for some Christians!—bibles even, shall have vanished away."

"Why do you say *alas*, papa—if they are Christians especially?"

"I say *alas* only from their point of view, not from mine. I mean such as are always talking and arguing from the Bible, and never giving themselves any trouble to do what it tells them. They insist on the anise and cummin, and forget the judgment, mercy, and faith. These worship the body of the truth and forget the soul of it. If the flowers were not perishable, we should cease to contemplate their beauty, either blinded by the passion for hoarding the bodies of them, or dulled by the hebetude of commonplaceness that the constant presence of them would occasion. To compare great things with small, the flowers wither, the bubbles break, the clouds and sunsets pass, for the very same holy reason, in the degree of its application to them, for which the Lord withdrew from his disciples and ascended again to his Father—that the Comforter, the Spirit of Truth, the Soul of things, might come to them and abide with them, and so, the Son return, and the Father be revealed. The flower is not its loveliness, and its loveliness we must love, else we shall only treat them as flower-greedy children, who gather and gather, and fill hands and baskets from a mere desire of acquisition, excusable enough in them, but the same in kind, however harmless in mode, and degree, and object, as the avarice of the miser. Therefore God, that we may always have them, and ever learn to love their beauty, and yet more their truth, sends the beneficent winter that we may think about what we have lost, and welcome them when they come again with greater tenderness and love, with clearer eyes to see, and purer hearts to understand, the spirit that dwells in them. We cannot do without the 'winter of our discontent.' Shakespeare surely saw that when he makes Titania say in 'A Midsummer Night's Dream,'—

'The human mortals want their winter here'—

namely, to set things right; and none of those editors who would alter the line seem to have been capable of understanding its import."

"I think I understand you a little," answered Wynnie. Then, changing her tone—"I told you, papa, you would have an answer ready: didn't I?"

"Yes, my child—but with this difference: I found the answer to meet my own necessities, not yours."

"And so you had it ready for me when I wanted it."

"Just so. That is the only certainty you have in regard to what you give away. No one who has not tasted it and found it good has a right to offer any spiritual dish to his neighbour."

Mr Percivale took no part in our conversation. The moment I had presented him to Mrs Walton and Connie, and he had paid his respects by a somewhat stately old-world obeisance, he merged the salutation into a farewell, and, either forgetting my offer of coffee, or having changed his mind, withdrew, a little to my disappointment, for, notwithstanding his lack of response where some things he said would have led me to expect it, I had begun to feel much interested in him.

He was scarcely beyond hearing when Dora came up to me from her digging with an eager look on her sunny face.

"Hasn't he got nice boots, papa?"

"Indeed, my dear, I am unable to support you in that assertion, for I never saw his boots."

"I did then," returned the child; "and I never saw such nice boots."

"I accept the statement willingly," I replied, and we heard no more of the boots, for his name was now substituted for his nickname. Nor did I see himself again for some days—not in fact till next Sunday—though why he should come to church at all was something of a puzzle to me, especially when I knew him better.

CHAPTER XX.

THE BLACKSMITH.

HE next day I set out after breakfast to inquire about a blacksmith. It was not every or any blacksmith that would do. I must not fix on the first to do my work because he was the first. There was one in the village, I soon learned; but I found him an ordinary man, who, I have no doubt, could shoe a horse and avoid the quick, but from whom any greater delicacy of touch was not to be expected. Inquiring further, I heard of a young smith who had lately settled in a hamlet a couple of miles distant, but still within the parish. In the afternoon I set out to find him. To my surprise, he was a pale-faced, thoughtful-looking man, with a huge frame, which appeared worn rather than naturally thin, and large eyes that looked at the anvil as if it was the horizon of the world. He had got a horse-shoe in his tongs when I entered. Nothwithstanding the fire that glowed on the hearth, and the sparks that flew like a nimbus in eruption from about his person, the place looked very dark to me entering from the glorious blaze of the almost noontide sun, and felt cool after the deep lane through which I had come, and which had seemed a very reservoir of sunbeams. I could see the smith by the glow of his horse-shoe; but all between me and the shoe was dark.

"Good morning," I said. "It is a good thing to find a man by his work. I heard you half-a-mile off or so, and now I see you, but only by the glow of your work. It is a grand thing to work in fire."

He lifted his hammered hand to his forehead courteously, and as lightly as if the hammer had been the butt-end o a whip.

"I don't know if you would say the same i. you had to work at it in weather like this," he answered.

"If I did not," I returned, "that would be the fault of my weakness, and would not affect the assertion I have just made, that it is a fine thing to work in fire."

"Well, you may be right," he rejoined with a sigh, as, throwing the horse-shoe he had been fashioning from the tongs on the ground, he next let the hammer drop beside the anvil, and leaning against it, held his head for a moment between his hands, and regarded the floor. "It does not much matter to me," he went on, "if I only get through my work and have done with it. No man shall say I shirked what I'd got to do. And then when it's over there won't be a word to say agen me, or"——

He did not finish the sentence. And now I could see

the sunlight lying in a somewhat dreary patch, if the word *dreary* can be truly used with respect to any mani festation of sunlight, on the dark clay floor.

"I hope you are not ill," I said.

He made no answer, but taking up his tongs caught with it from a beam one of a number of roughly finished horse-shoes which hung there, and put it on the fire to be fashioned to a certain fit. While he turned it in the fire, and blew the bellows, I stood regarding him. "This man will do for my work," I said to myself; "though I should not wonder from the look of him if it was the last piece of work he ever did under the New Jerusalem." The smith's words broke in on my meditations.

"When I was a little boy," he said, "I once wanted to stay at home from school. I had, I believe, a little headache, but nothing worth minding. I told my mother that I had a headache, and she kept me, and I helped her at her spinning, which was what I liked best of anything. But in the afternoon the Methodist preacher came in to see my mother, and he asked me what was the matter with me, and my mother answered for me that I had a bad head, and he looked at me; and as my head was quite well by this time, I could not help feeling guilty. And he saw my look, I suppose, sir, for I can't account for what he said any other way, and he turned to me, and he said to me, solemn-like, 'Is your head bad enough to send you to the Lord Jesus to make you whole?' I could not speak a word, partly from bashfulness, I suppose, for I was but ten years old. So he followed it up, as they say: 'Then you ought to be at school,' says he. I said nothing, because I couldn't. But never since then have I given in as long as I could stand. And I can stand now, and lift my hammer too," he said, as he took the horse-shoe from the forge, laid it on the anvil, and again made a nimbus of coruscating iron.

"You are just the man I want," I said. "I've got a job for you, down to Kilkhaven, as you say in these parts."

"What is it, sir? Something about the church? I should ha' thought the church was all spick and span by this time."

"I see you know who I am," I said.

"Of course I do," he answered. "I don't go to church myself, being brought up a Methodist; but anything that happens in the parish is known the next day all over it."

"You won't mind doing my job though you are a Methodist, will you?" I asked.

"Not I, sir. If I've read right, it's the fault of the Church that we don't pull all alongside. You turned us out, sir; we didn't go out of ourselves. At least, if all they say is true, which I can't be sure of you know, in this world."

"You are quite right there though," I answered. "And in doing so, the Church had the worst of it—as all that judge and punish their neighbours have. But you have been the worse for it, too: all of which is to be laid to the charge of the Church. For there is not one clergyman I know—mind, I say, that I know—who would have made such a cruel speech to a boy as that the Methodist parson made to you."

"But it did me good, sir."

"Are you sure of that? I am not. Are you sure, first of all, it did not make you proud? Are you sure it has not made you work beyond your strength—I don't mean your strength of arm, for clearly that is all that could be wished, but of your chest, your lungs? Is there not some danger of your leaving some one who is dependent on you too soon unprovided for? Is there not some danger of your having worked as if God were a hard master?—of your having worked fiercely, indignantly, as if he wronged you by not caring for you, not understanding you?"

He returned me no answer, but hammered momently on his anvil. Whether he felt what I meant, or was offended at my remark, I could not then tell. I thought it best to conclude the interview with business.

"I have a delicate little job that wants nice handling, and I fancy you are just the man to do it to my mind," I said.

"What is it, sir?" he asked, in a friendly manner enough.

"If you will excuse me, I would rather show it to you than talk about it," I returned.

"As you please, sir. When do you want me?"

"The first hour you can come."

"To-morrow morning?"

"If you feel inclined."

"For that matter, I 'd rather go to bed."

"Come to me instead: it's light work."

"I will, sir—at ten o'clock."

"If you please."

And so it was arranged.

CHAPTER XXI.

THE LIFE-BOAT.

HE next day rose glorious. Indeed, early as the sun rose, I saw him rise—saw him, from the down above the house, over the land to the east and north, ascend triumphant into his own light, which had prepared the way for him; while the clouds that hung over the sea glowed out with a faint flush, as anticipating the hour when the west should clasp the declining glory in a richer though less dazzling splendour, and shine out the bride of the bridegroom east, which behold each other from afar across the intervening world, and never mingle but in the sight of the eyes. The clear pure light of the morning made me long for the truth in my heart, which alone could make me pure and clear as the morning, tune me up to the concert-pitch of the nature around me. And the wind that blew from the sunrise made me hope in the God who had first breathed into my nostrils the breath of life,

that he would at length so fill me with his breath, his wind, his spirit, that I should think only his thoughts and live his life, finding therein my own life, only glorified infinitely.

After breakfast and prayers, I would go to the church to await the arrival of my new acquaintance the smith. In order to obtain entrance, I had, however, to go to the cottage of the sexton. This was not my first visit there, so that I may now venture to take my reader with me. To reach the door, I had to cross a hollow by a bridge, built, for the sake of the road, over what had once been the course of a rivulet from the heights above. Now it was a kind of little glen, or what would in Scotland be called a den, I think, grown with grass and wild flowers and ferns, some of them rare and fine. The roof of the cottage came down to the road, and, until you came quite near, you could not but wonder where the body that supported this head could be. But you soon saw that the ground fell suddenly away, leaving a bank against which the cottage was built. Crossing a garden of the smallest, the principal flowers of which were the stonecrop on its walls, by a flag-paved path, you entered the building, and, to your surprise, found yourself, not in a little cottage kitchen, as you expected, but in a waste-looking space, that seemed to have forgotten the use for which it had been built. There was a sort of loft along one side of it, and it was heaped with indescribable lumber-looking stuff, with here and there a hint at possible machinery. The place had been a mill for grinding corn, and its wheel had been driven by the stream which had run for ages in the hollow of which I have already spoken. But when the canal came to be constructed, the stream had to be turned aside from its former course, and indeed was now employed upon occasion to feed the canal; so that the mill of necessity had fallen into disuse and decay. Crossing this floor, you entered another door, and turning sharp to the left, went down a few steps of a ladder sort of stair, and after knocking your hat against a beam, emerged in the comfortable quaint little cottage kitchen you had expected earlier. A cheerful though small fire burns in the grate —for even here the hearth-fire has vanished from the records of cottage-life—and is pleasant here even in the height of summer, though it is counted needful only for cooking purposes. The ceiling, which consists only of the joists and the boards that floor the bedroom above, is so low, that necessity, if not politeness, would compel you to take off your already-bruised hat. Some of these joists, you will find, are made further useful by supporting each a shelf, before which hangs a little curtain of printed cotton, concealing the few stores and postponed eatables of the house—forming, in fact, both store-room and larder of the family. On the walls hang several coloured prints, and within a deep glazed frame the figure of a ship in full dress, carved in rather high relief in sycamore.

As I now entered, Mrs Coombes rose from a high-backed settle near the fire, and bade me good morning with a courtesy.

"What a lovely day it is, Mrs Coombes! It is so

bright over the sea," I said, going to the one little window which looked out on the great Atlantic, "that one almost expects a great merchant navy to come sailing into Kilkhaven— sunk to the water's edge with silks, and ivory, and spices, and apes, and peacocks, like the ships of Solomon that we read about—just as the sun gets up the noonstead."

Before I record her answer, I turn to my reader, who in the spirit accompanies me, and have a little talk with him. I always make it a rule to speak freely with the less as with the more educated of my friends. I never *talk down* to them, except I be expressly explaining something to them. The law of the world is as the law of the family. Those children grow much the faster who hear all that is going on in the house. Reaching ever above themselves, they arrive at an understanding at fifteen which, in the usual way of things, they would not reach before five-and-twenty or thirty; and this in a natural way, and without any necessary priggishness, except such as may belong to their parents. Therefore I always spoke to the poor and uneducated, as to my own people, freely, not much caring whether I should be quite understood or not; for I believed in influences not to be measured by the measure of the understanding.

But what was the old woman's answer? It was this:—

"I know, sir. And when I was as young as you"—I was not so very young, my reader may well think—"I thought like that about the sea myself. Everything come from the sea. For my boy Willie he du bring me home the beautifullest parrot and the talkingest you ever see, and the red shawl all worked over with flowers: I'll show it to you some day, sir, when you have time. He made that ship you see in the frame there, sir, all with his own knife, out on a bit o' wood that he got at the Marishes, as they calls it, sir—a bit of an island somewheres in the great sea. But the parrot's gone dead like the rest of them, sir.—Where am I? and what am I talking about?" she added, looking down at her knitting as if she had dropped a stitch, or rather as if she had forgotten what she was making, and therefore what was to come next.

"You were telling me how you used to think of the sea"——

"When I was as young as you. I remember, sir. Well, that lasted a long time—lasted till my third boy fell asleep in the wide water; for it du call it falling asleep, don't it, sir?"

"The Bible certainly does," I answered.

"It's the Bible I be meaning, of course," she returned. "Well, after that, but I don't know what began it, only I did begin to think about the sea as something that took away things and didn't bring them no more. And somehow or other she never look so blue after that, and she give me the shivers. But now, sir, she always looks to me like one o' the shining ones that come to fetch the pilgrims. You've heard tell of the 'Pilgrim's Progress,' I daresay, sir, among the poor people; for they du say it was written by a tinker, though there be a power o' good things in it that I think the gentle folk would like if they knowed it."

"I do know the book—nearly as well as I know the Bible," I answered; "and the shining ones are very beautiful in it. I am glad you can think of the sea that way."

"It's looking in at the window all day as I go about the house," she answered, "and all night too when I'm asleep; and if I hadn't learned to think of it that way, it would have driven me mad, I du believe. I was forced to think that way about it, or not think at all. And that wouldn't be easy, with the sound of it in your ears the last thing at night and the first thing in the morning."

"The truth of things is indeed the only refuge from the look of things," I replied. "But now I want the key of the church, if you will trust me with it, for I have something to do there this morning; and the key of the tower as well, if you please."

With her old smile, ripened only by age, she reached the ponderous keys from the nail where they hung, and gave them into my hand. I left her in the shadow of her dwelling, and stepped forth into the sunlight. The first thing I observed was the blacksmith waiting for me at the church door.

Now that I saw him in the full light of day, and now that he wore his morning face upon which the blackness of labour had not yet gathered, I could see more plainly how far he was from well. There was a flush on his thin cheek by which the less used exercise of walking revealed his inward weakness, and the light in his eyes had something of the far-country in them—"the light that never was on sea or shore." But his speech was cheerful, for he had been walking in the light of this world, and that had done something to make the light within him shine a little more freely.

"How do you find yourself to-day?" I asked.

"Quite well, sir, I thank you," he answered. "A day like this does a man good. But," he added, and his countenance fell, "the heart knoweth its own bitterness."

"It may know it too much," I returned, "just because it refuses to let a stranger intermeddle therewith."

He made no reply. I turned the key in the great lock, and the iron-studded oak opened and let us into the solemn gloom.

It did not require many minutes to make the man understand what I wanted of him.

"We must begin at the bells and work down," he said.

So we went up into the tower, where, with the help of a candle I fetched for him from the cottage, he made a good many minute measurements; found that carpenter's work was necessary for the adjustment of the hammers and cranks and the leading of the rods, undertook the management of the whole, and in the course of an hour and a half went home to do what had to be done before any fixing could be commenced, assuring me that he had no doubt of bringing the job to a satisfactory conclusion, although the force of the blow on the bell would doubtless have to be regulated afterwards by repeated trials.

"In a fortnight, I hope you will be able to play a tune to the parish, sir," he added as he took his leave.

I resolved, if possible, to know more of the man, and

find out his trouble, if haply I might be able to give him any comfort, for I was all but certain that there was a deeper cause for his gloom than the state of his health.

When he was gone I stood with the key of the church in my hand, and looked about me. Nature at least was in glorious health—sunshine in her eyes, light fantastic cloud-images passing through her brain, her breath coming and going in soft breezes perfumed with the scents of meadows and wild flowers, and her green robe shining in the motions of her gladness. I turned to lock the church door, though in my heart I greatly disapproved of locking the doors of churches, and only did so now because it was not my church, and I had no business to force my opinions upon other customs. But when I turned I received a kind of questioning shock. There was the fallen world, as men call it, shining in glory and gladness, because God was there: here was the way into the lost Paradise, yea, the door into an infinitely higher Eden than that ever had or ever could have been, iron-clamped and riveted, gloomy and low-browed like the entrance to a sepulchre, and surrounded with the grim heads of grotesque monsters of the deep. What did it mean? Here was contrast enough to require harmonizing, or if that might not be, then accounting for. Perhaps it was enough to say that although God made both the kingdom of nature and the kingdom of grace, yet the symbol of the latter was the work of man, and might not altogether correspond to God's idea of the matter. I turned away thoughtful, and went through the churchyard with my eye on the graves.

Page 269.

As I left the churchyard, still looking to the earth, the sound of voices reached my ear. I looked up. There, down below me, at the foot of the high bank on which I stood, lay a gorgeous shining thing upon the bosom of the canal, full of men, and surrounded by men, women, and children, delighting in its beauty. I had never seen such a thing before, but I knew at once, as if by instinct, which of course it could not have been, that it was the life-boat. But in its gorgeous colours, red and white and green, it looked more like the galley that bore Cleopatra to Actium. Nor, floating so light on the top of the water, and broad in the beam withal, curved upward and ornamented at stern and stem, did it look at all like a creature formed to battle with the fierce elements. A pleasure boat for floating between river banks it seemed, drawn by swans mayhap, and regarded in its course by fair eyes from green terrace-walks, or oriel windows of ancient houses on verdant lawns. Ten men sat on the thwarts, and one in the stern by the yet useless rudder, while men and boys drew the showy thing by a rope downward to the lock-gates. The men in the boat wore blue jerseys, but you could see little of the colour for strange unshapely things that they wore above them, like an armour cut out of a row of organ pipes. They were their cork-jackets. For every man had to be made into a life-boat himself. I descended the bank, and stood on the edge of the canal as it drew near. Then I saw that every oar was loosely but firmly fastened to the rowlock, so that it could be dropped and caught again in a moment; and that the gay sides of the unwieldly looking creature were festooned with ropes from the gunwale, for the men to lay hold of when she capsized, for the earlier custom of fastening the men to their seats had been quite given up, because their weight under the water might prevent the boat from righting itself again, and the men could not come to the surface. Now they had a better chance in their freedom, though why they should not be loosely attached to the boat, I do not quite see.

They towed the shining thing through the upper gate of the lock, and slowly she sank from my sight, and for some moments was no more to be seen, for I had remained standing where first she passed me. All at once there she was beyond the covert of the lock-head, abroad and free, fleeting from the strokes of ten swift oars over the still waters of the bay towards the waves that roared further out where the ground-swell was broken by the rise of the sandy coast. There was no vessel in danger now, as the talk of the spectators informed me; it was only for exercise and show that they went out. It seemed all child's play for a time; but when they got among the broken waves, then it looked quite another thing. The motion of the waters laid hold upon her, and soon tossed her fearfully, now revealing the whole of her capacity on the near side of one of their slopes, now hiding her whole bulk in one of their hollows beyond. She, careless as a child in the troubles of the world, floated about amongst them with what appeared too much buoyancy for the promise of a safe return. Again and again she was driven from her course towards the low rocks on the other side of the bay; and again and again returned to disport herself, like a sea-animal, as it seemed, upon the backs of the wild, rolling and bursting billows.

"Can she go no further!" I asked of the captain of the coastguard, whom I found standing by my side.

"Not without some danger," he answered.

"What, then, must it be in a storm!" I remarked.

"Then of course," he returned, "they must take their chance. But there is no good in running risks for nothing. That swell is quite enough for exercise."

"But is it enough to accustom them to face the danger that will come?" I asked.

"With danger comes courage," said the old sailor.

"Were you ever afraid?"

"No, sir. I don't think I ever was afraid. Yes, I believe I was once for one moment, no more, when I fell from the maintop-gallant yard, and felt myself falling. But it was soon over, for I only fell into the maintop. I was expecting the smash on deck when I was brought up there. But," he resumed, "I don't care much about the life-boat. My rockets are worth a good deal more, as you may see, sir, before the winter is over; for seldom does a winter pass without at least two or three wrecks close by here on this coast. The full force of the Atlantic breaks here, sir. I *have* seen a life-boat—not that one—*she's* done nothing yet—pitched stern over stem; not capsized, you know, sir, in the ordinary way, but struck by a wave behind while she was just hanging in the balance on the knife-edge of a wave, and flung a somerset, as I say, stern over stem, and four of her men lost."

While we spoke I saw on the pier-head the tall figure of the painter looking earnestly at the boat. I thought he was regarding it chiefly from an artistic point of view, but I became aware before long that that would not have been consistent with the character of Charles Percivale. He had been, I learned afterwards, a crack oarsman at Oxford, and had belonged to the University boat, so that he had some almost class-sympathy with the doings of the crew.

In a little while the boat sped swiftly back, entered the lock, was lifted above the level of the storm-heaved ocean, and floated up the smooth canal calmly as if she had never known what trouble was. Away up to the pretty little Tudor-fashioned house in which she lay—one could almost fancy dreaming of storms to come—she went, as softly as if moved only by her "own sweet will," in the calm consolation for her imprisonment of having tried her strength, and found therein good hope of success for the time when she should rush to the rescue of men from that to which, as a monster that begets monsters, she a watching Perseis, lay ready to offer battle. The poor little boat lying in her little house watching the ocean, was something significant in my eyes, and not less so after what came in the course of changing seasons and gathered storms.

All this time I had the keys in my hand, and now went back to the cottage to restore them to their place upon the wall. When I entered, there was a young woman of a sweet interesting countenance talking to Mrs Coombes. Now as it happened, I had never yet seen the daughter who lived with her, and thought this was she.

"I've found your daughter at last then?" I said approaching them.

"Not yet, sir. She goes out to work, and her hands be pretty full at present. But this be almost my daughter, sir," she added. "This is my next daughter, Mary Trehern, from the south. She's got a place near by, to be near her mother that is to be, that's me."

Mary was hanging her head and blushing, as the old woman spoke.

"I understand," I said. "And when are you going to get your new mother, Mary? Soon, I hope."

But she gave me no reply—only hung her head lower and blushed deeper.

Mrs Coombes spoke for her.

"She's shy, you see, sir. But if she was to speak her mind, she would ask you whether you wouldn't marry her and Willie when he comes home from his next voyage."

Mary's hands were trembling now, and she turned half away.

"With all my heart," I said.

The girl tried to turn towards me, but could not. I looked at her face a little more closely. Through all its tremor, there was a look of constancy that greatly pleased me. I tried to make her speak.

"When do you expect Willie home?" I said.

She made a little gasp and murmur, but no articulate words came.

"Don't be frightened, Mary," said her mother, as I found she always called her. "The gentleman won't be sharp with you."

She lifted a pair of soft brown eyes with one glance and a smile, and then sank them again.

"He 'll be home in about a month, we think," answered the mother. "She 's a good ship he 's aboard of, and makes good voyages."

"It is time to think about the banns, then," I said.

"If you please, sir," said the mother.

"Just come to me about it, and I will attend to it—when you think proper."

I thought I could hear a murmured "Thank you, sir," from the girl, but I could not be certain that she spoke. I shook hands with them, and went for a stroll on the other side of the bay.

CHAPTER XXII.

MR PERCIVALE.

WHEN I reached home I found that Connie was already on her watch-tower. For while I was away, they had carried her out that she might see the life-boat. I followed her, and found the whole family about her couch, and with them Mr Percivale, who was showing her some sketches that he had made in the neighbourhood. Connie knew nothing of drawing; but she seemed to me always to catch the feeling of a thing. Her remarks therefore were generally worth listening to, and Mr Percivale was evidently interested in them. Wynnie stood behind Connie, looking over her shoulder at the drawing in her hand.

"How do you get that shade of green?" I heard her ask as I came up.

And then Mr Percivale proceeded to tell her; from

which beginning they went on to other things, till Mr Percivale said—

"But it is hardly fair, Miss Walton, to criticize my work while you keep your own under cover."

"I wasn't criticizing, Mr Percivale: was I, Connie?"

"I didn't hear her make a single remark, Mr Percivale," said Connie, taking her sister's side.

To my surprise they were talking away with the young man as if they had known him for years, and my wife was seated at the foot of the couch, apparently taking no exception to the suddenness of the intimacy. I am afraid, when I think of it, that a good many springs would be missing from the world's history if they might not flow till the papas gave their wise consideration to everything about the course they were to take.

"I think, though," added Connie, "it is only fair that Mr Percivale *should* see your work, Wynnie."

"Then I will fetch my portfolio, if Mr Percivale will promise to remember that I have no opinion of it. At the same time, if I could do what I wanted to do, I think I should not be ashamed of showing my drawings even to him."

And now I was surprised to find how like grown women my daughters could talk. To me they always spoke like the children they were; but when I heard them now, it seemed as if they had started all at once into ladies experienced in the ways of society. There they were chatting lightly, airily, and yet decidedly, a slight tone of badinage interwoven, with a young man of grace and dignity, whom they had only seen once before, and who had advanced no farther, with Connie at least, than a stately bow. They had, however, been a whole hour together before I arrived, and their mother had been with them all the while, which gives great courage to good girls, while, I am told, it shuts the mouths of those who are sly. But then it must be remembered that there are as great differences in mothers as in girls. And besides, I believe wise girls have an instinct about men that all the experience of other men cannot overtake. But yet again, there are many girls foolish enough to mistake a mere impulse for instinct, and vanity for insight.

As Wynnie spoke, she turned and went back to the house to fetch some of her work. Now, had she been going a message for me, she would have gone like the wind; but on this occasion she stepped along in a stately manner, far from devoid of grace, but equally free from frolic or eagerness. And I could not help noting as well that Mr Percivale's eyes followed her. What I felt or fancied is of no consequence to anybody. I do not think, even if I were writing an autobiography, I should be forced to tell *all* about myself. But an autobiography is further from my fancy, however much I may have trenched upon its limits, than any other form of literature with which I am acquainted.

She was not long in returning, however, though she came back with the same dignified motion.

"There is nothing really worth either showing or concealing," she said to Mr Percivale, as she handed him the portfolio, to help himself, as it were. She then turned away, as if a little feeling of shyness had come over her, and began to look for something to do about Connie. I could see that, although she had hitherto been almost indifferent about the merit of her drawings, she had a new-born wish that they might not appear altogether contemptible in the eyes of Mr Percivale. And I saw, too, that Connie's wide eyes were taking in everything. It was wonderful how Connie's deprivations had made her keen in observing. Now she hastened to her sister's rescue even from such a slight inconvenience as the shadow of embarrassment in which she found herself—perhaps from having seen some unusual expression in my face, of which I was unconscious, though conscious enough of what might have occasioned such.

"Give me you hand, Wynnie," said Connie, "and help me to move one inch further on my side. I may move just that much on my side, mayn't I, papa?"

"I think you had better not, my dear, if you can do without it," I answered; for the doctor's injunctions had been strong.

"Very well, papa; but I feel as if it would do me good."

"Mr Turner will be here next week, you know; and you must try to stick to his rules till he comes to see you. Perhaps he will let you relax a little."

Connie smiled very sweetly and lay still, while Wynnie stood holding her hand.

Meantime Mr Percivale, having received the drawings, had walked away with them towards what they called the storm tower—a little building standing square to the points of the compass, from little windows in which the coastguard could see with their telescopes along the coast on both sides and far out to sea. This tower stood on the very edge of the cliff, but behind it there was a steep descent, to reach which apparently he went round the tower and disappeared. He evidently wanted to make a leisurely examination of the drawings—somewhat formidable for Wynnie, I thought. At the same time, it impressed me favourably with regard to the young man that he was not inclined to pay a set of stupid and untrue compliments the instant the portfolio was opened, but, on the contrary, in order to speak what was real about them, would take the trouble to make himself in some adequate measure acquainted with them. I therefore, to Wynnie's relief, I fear, strolled after him, seeing no harm in taking a peep at his person while he was taking a peep at my daughter's mind. I went round the tower to the other side, and there saw him at a little distance below me, but further out on a great rock that overhung the sea, connected with the cliff by a long narrow isthmus, a few yards lower than the cliff itself, only just broad enough to admit of a footpath along its top, and on one side going sheer down with a smooth hard rock-face to the sands below. The other side was less steep, and had some grass upon it. But the path was too narrow, and the precipice too steep, for me to trust my head with the business of guiding my feet along it. So I stood and saw him from the mainland—saw his head at least bent over the drawings; saw how slowly he turned from one to the other; saw how, after having gone over them once, he turned to the beginning and went over them again, even more slowly than before; saw how he turned the third time to the first. Then, getting tired, I went back to the group on the down; caught sight of Charlie and Harry turning heels over head down the slope toward the house; found that my wife had gone home—in fact, that only Connie and Wynnie were left. The sun had disappeared under a cloud, and the sea had turned a little slaty; the yellow flowers in the short down-grass no longer caught the eye with their gold, and the wind that bent their tops had just the suspicion of an edge in it. And Wynnie's face looked a little cloudy too, I thought, and I feared that it was my fault. I fancied there was just a tinge of beseeching in Connie's eye as I looked at her, thinking there might be danger for her in the sunlessness of the wind. But I do not know that all this, even the clouding of the sun, may not have come out of my own mind, the result of my not being quite satisfied with myself because of the mood I had been in. My feeling had altered considerably in the meantime.

"Run, Wynnie, and ask Mr Percivale, with my compliments, to come and lunch with us," I said—more to let her see I was not displeased, however I might have looked, than for any other reason. She went—sedately as before.

Almost as soon as she was gone, I saw that I had put her in a difficulty. For I had discovered, very soon after coming into these parts, that her head was no more steady than my own upon high places, for she had never been used to such in our own level country, except, indeed, on the stair that led down to the old quarry and the well, where, I can remember now, she always laid her hand on the balustrade with some degree of tremor, although she had been in the way of going up and down from childhood. But if she could not cross that narrow and really dangerous isthmus, still less could she call to a man she had never seen but once, across the intervening chasm. I therefore set off after her, leaving Connie lying there in loneliness, between the sea and the sky. But when I got to the other side of the little tower, instead of finding her standing hesitating on the brink of action, there she was on the rock beyond. Mr Percivale had risen, and was evidently giving an answer to my invitation; at least, the next moment she turned to come back, and he followed. I stood trembling almost to see her cross the knife-back of that ledge. If I had not been almost fascinated, I should have turned and left them to come together, lest the evil fancy should cross her mind that I was watching them, for it was one thing to watch him with her drawings, and quite another to watch him with herself. But I stood and stared as she crossed. In the middle of the path, however—up to which point she had been walking with perfect steadiness and composure—she lifted her eyes—by what influence I cannot tell—saw me, looked as if she saw a ghost, half-lifted her arms, swayed as if she would fall, and, indeed, was falling over the precipice, when Percivale, who was close behind her, caught her in his arms, almost too late for both of them. So nearly down was she already, that her weight bent him over the rocky side till it seemed as if he must yield, or his body snap. For he bent from the waist, and looked as if his feet only kept a hold on the ground. It was all over in a moment, but in that moment it made a sun-picture on my brain, which returns ever and again, with such vivid agony that I cannot hope to get rid of it till I get rid of the brain itself in which lies the impress. In another moment they were at my side—she with a wan, terrified smile, he in a ruddy alarm. I was unable to speak, and could only, with trembling steps, lead the way from the dreadful spot. I reproached myself afterwards for my want of faith in God; but I had not had time to correct myself yet. Without a word on their side either, they followed me. Before we reached Connie, I recovered myself sufficiently to say, "Not a word to Connie," and they understood me. I told Wynnie to run to the house, and send Walter to help me to carry Connie home. She went, and, until Walter came, I talked to Mr Percivale as if nothing had happened. And what made me feel yet more friendly towards him was, that he did not do as some young men wishing to ingratiate themselves would have done: he did not offer to help me to carry Connie home, I saw that the offer rose in his mind, and that he repressed it. He understood that I must consider such a permission as a privilege not to be accorded to the acquaintance of a day; that I must know him better before I could allow the weight of my child to rest on his strength. I was even grateful to him for this knowledge of human nature. But he responded cordially to my invitation to lunch with us, and walked by my side as Walter and I bore the precious burden home

During our meal, he made himself quite agreeable; talked well on the topics of the day, not altogether as a man who had made up his mind, but not the less, rather the more, as a man who had thought about them, and one who did not find it so easy to come to a conclusion as most people do—or possibly as not feeling the necessity of coming to a conclusion, and therefore preferring to allow the conclusion to grow instead of constructing one for immediate use. This I rather liked than otherwise. His behaviour, I need hardly say, after what I have told of him already, was entirely that of a gentleman; and his education was good. But what I did not like was, that as often as the conversation made a bend in the direction of religious matters, he was sure to bend it away in some other direction as soon as ever he laid his next hold upon it. This, however, might have various reasons to account for it, and I would wait.

After lunch, as we rose from the table, he took Wynnie's portfolio from the side-table where he had laid it, and with no more than a bow and thanks returned it to her. She, I thought, looked a little disappointed, though she said as lightly as she could—

"I am afraid you have not found anything worthy of criticism in my poor attempts, Mr Percivale?"

"On the contrary, I shall be most happy to tell you what I think of them if you would like to hear the impression they have made upon me." he replied, holding out his hand to take the portfolio again.

"I shall be greatly obliged to you," she said, returning it, "for I have had no one to help me since I left school, except a book called 'Modern Painters,' which I think has the most beautiful things in it I ever read, but which I lay down every now and then with a kind of despair, as if I never could do anything worth doing. How long the next volume is in coming! Do you know the author, Mr Percivale?"

"I wish I did. He has given me much help. I do not say I can agree with everything he writes; but when I do not, I have such a respect for him that I always feel as if he must be right whether he seems to me to be right or not. And if he is severe, it is with the severity of love that will speak only the truth."

This last speech fell on my ear like the tone of a church bell. "That will do, my friend," thought I. But I said nothing to interrupt.

By this time he had laid the portfolio open on the side-table, and placed a chair in front of it for my daughter. Then seating himself by her side, but without the least approach to familiarity, he began to talk to her about her drawings, praising, in general, the feeling, but finding fault with the want of nicety in the execution—at least so it appeared to me from what I could understand of the conversation.

"But," said my daughter, "it seems to me that if you get the feeling right, that is the main thing."

"No doubt," returned Mr Percivale; "so much the main thing that any imperfection or coarseness or untruth which interferes with it becomes of the greatest consequence."

"But can it really interfere with the feeling?"

"Perhaps not with most people, simply because most people observe so badly that their recollections of nature are all blurred and blotted and indistinct, and therefore the imperfections we are speaking of do not affect them. But with the more cultivated it is otherwise. It is for them you ought to work, for you do not thereby lose the others. Besides, the feeling is always intensified by the finish, for that belongs to the feeling too, and must, I should think, have some influence even where it is not noted."

"But is it not a hopeless thing to attempt the finish of nature?"

"Not at all; to the degree, that is, in which you can represent anything else of nature. But in this drawing now you have no representative of, nothing to hint at or recall the feeling of the exquisiteness of nature's finish. Why should you not at least have drawn a true horizon-line there? Has the absolute truth of the meeting of sea and sky nothing to do with the feeling which such a landscape produces? I should have thought you would have learned that, if anything, from Mr Ruskin."

Mr Percivale spoke earnestly. Wynnie, either from disappointment or despair, probably from a mixture of both, apparently fancied that, or rather felt as if, he was scolding her, and got cross. This was anything but dignified, especially with a stranger, and one who was doing his best to help her. And yet somehow, I must with shame confess, I was not altogether sorry to see it. In fact, my reader, I must just uncover my sin, and say that I felt a little jealous of Mr Percivale. The negative reason was that I had not yet learned to love him. The only cure for jealousy is love. But I was ashamed too of Wynnie's behaving so childishly. Her face flushed, the tears came in her eyes, and she rose, saying with a little choke in her voice—

"I see it's no use trying. I won't intrude any more into things I am incapable of. I am much obliged to you, Mr Percivale, for showing me how presumptuous I have been."

The painter rose as she rose, looking greatly concerned. But he did not attempt to answer her. Indeed she gave him no time. He could only spring after her to open the door for her. A more than respectful bow as she left the room was his only adieu. But when he turned his face again towards me, it expressed even a degree of consternation.

"I fear," he said, approaching me with an almost military step, much at variance with the shadow upon his countenance, "I fear I have been rude to Miss Walton, but nothing was farther"——

"You mistake entirely, Mr Percivale. I heard all you were saying, and you were not in the least rude. On the contrary, I consider you were very kind to take the trouble with her you did. Allow me to make the apology for my daughter which I am sure she will wish made when she recovers from the disappointment of finding more obstacles in the way of her favourite pursuit than she had previously supposed. She is only too ready to lose heart, and she paid too little attention to your approbation and too much, in proportion, I mean, to your —criticism. She felt discouraged and lost her temper, but more with herself and her poor attempts, I venture to assure you, than with your remarks upon them. She is too much given to despising her own efforts."

"But I must have been to blame if I caused any such feeling with regard to those drawings, for I assure you they contain great promise."

"I am glad you think so. That I should myself be of the same opinion can be of no consequence."

"Miss Walton at least sees what ought to be represented. All she needs is greater severity in the quality of representation. And that would have grown without any remark from onlookers. Only a friendly criticism is sometimes a great help. It opens the eyes a little sooner than they would have opened of themselves. And time," he added, with a half-sigh and with an appeal in his tone, as if he would justify himself to my conscience, "is half the battle in this world. It is over so soon."

"No sooner than it ought to be," I rejoined.

"So it may appear to you," he returned; "for you, I presume to conjecture, have worked hard and done much. I may or may not have worked hard—sometimes I think I have, sometimes I think I have not—but I certainly have done little. Here I am nearly thirty, and have made no mark on the world yet."

"I don't know that that is of so much consequence,"

I said. "I have never hoped for more than to rub out a few of the marks already made."

"Perhaps you are right," he returned. "Every man has something he can do, and more, I suppose, that he can't do. But I have no right to turn a visit into a visitation. Will you please tell Miss Walton that I am very sorry I presumed on the privileges of a drawing-master, and gave her pain. It was so far from my intention that it will be a lesson to me for the future."

With these words he took his leave, and I could not help being greatly pleased both with them and with his bearing. He was clearly anything but a common man.

CHAPTER XXIII.

THE SHADOW OF DEATH.

WHEN Wynnie appeared at dinner she looked ashamed of herself, and her face betrayed that she had been crying. But I said nothing, for I had confidence that all she needed was time to come to herself, that the voice that speaks louder than any thunder might make its stillness heard. And when I came home from my walk the next morning I found Mr Percivale once more in the group about Connie, and evidently on the best possible terms with all. The same afternoon Wynnie went out sketching with Dora. I had no doubt that she had made some sort of apology to Mr Percivale; but I did not make the slightest attempt to discover what had passed between them, for though it is of all things desirable that children should be quite open with their parents, I was most anxious to lay upon them no burden of obligation.

For such burden lies against the door of utterance, and makes it the more difficult to open. It paralyses the speech of the soul. What I desired was, that they should trust me so that faith should overcome all difficulty that might lie in the way of their being open with me. That end is not to be gained by any urging of admonition. Against such, growing years at least, if nothing else, will bring a strong reaction. Nor even, if so gained, would the gain be at all of the right sort. The openness would not be faith. Besides, a parent must respect the spiritual person of his child, and approach it with reverence, for that too looks the Father in the face, and has an audience with him into which no earthly parent can enter even if he dared to desire it. Therefore I trusted my child. And when I saw that she looked at me a little shyly when we next met, I only sought to show her the more tenderness and confidence, telling her all about my plans with the bells, and my talks with the smith and Mrs Coombes. She listened with just such interest as I had always been accustomed to see in her, asking such questions, and making such remarks as I might have expected, but I still felt that there was the thread of a little uneasiness through the web of our intercourse,—such a thread of a false colour as one may sometimes find wandering through the labour of the loom, and seek with pains to draw from the woven stuff. But it was for Wynnie to take it out, not for me. And she did not leave it long. For as she bade me good night in my study, she said suddenly, yet with hesitating openness,

"Papa, I told Mr Percivale that I was sorry I had behaved so badly about the drawings."

"You did right, my child," I replied. At the same moment a pang of anxiety passed through me lest under the influence of her repentance she should have said anything more than becoming. But I banished the doubt instantly as faithlessness in the womanly instincts of my child. For we men are always so ready and anxious to keep women right, like the wretched creature, Laertes, in *Hamlet*, who reads his sister such a lesson on her maidenly duties, but declines almost with contempt to listen to a word from her as to any co-relative obligation on his side!

And here I may remark in regard to one of the vexed questions of the day—the rights of women—that what women demand it is not for men to withhold. It is not their business to lay down the law for women. That women must lay down for themselves. I confess that, although I must herein seem to many of my readers old-fashioned and conservative, I should not like to see any woman I cared much for either in parliament or in an anatomical class-room; but on the other hand I feel that women must be left free to settle that matter. If it is not good, good women will find it out and recoil from it. If it is good, then God give them good speed. One thing they *have* a right to—a far wider and more valuable education than they have been in the way of receiving. When the mothers are well taught the generations will grow in knowledge at a fourfold rate. But still the teaching of life is better than all the schools, and common-sense than all learning. This common-sense is a rare gift, scantier in none than in those who lay claim to it on the ground of following commonplace, worldly, and prudential maxims. But I must return to my Wynnie.

"And what did Mr Percivale say?" I resumed, for she was silent.

"He took the blame all on himself, papa."

"Like a gentleman," I said.

"But I could not leave it so, you know, papa, because that was not the truth."

"Well?"

"I told him that I had lost my temper from disappointment; that I had thought I did not care for my drawings because I was so far from satisfied with them, but when he made me feel that they were worth nothing, then I found from the vexation I felt that I had cared for them. But I do think, papa, I was more ashamed of having shown them, and vexed with myself, than cross with him. But I was very silly."

"Well, and what did he say?"

"He began to praise them then. But you know I could not take much of that, for what could he do?"

"You might give him credit for a little honesty, at least."

"Yes; but things may be true in a way, you know, and not mean much."

"He seems to have succeeded in reconciling you to the prosecution of your efforts, however; for I saw you go out with your sketching apparatus this afternoon."

"Yes," she answered, shyly. "He was so kind, that somehow I got heart to try again. He 's very nice, isn't he?"

My answer was not quite ready.

"Don't you like him, papa?"

"Well—I like him—yes. But we must not be in haste with our judgments, you know. I have had very little opportunity of seeing into him. There is much in him that I like, but"——

"But what, please, papa?"

"To tell the truth then, Wynnie, for I can speak my mind to you, my child, there is a certain shyness of approaching the subject of religion; so that I have my fears lest he should belong to any of these new schools of a fragmentary philosophy which acknowledge no source of truth but the testimony of the senses and the deductions made therefrom by the intellect."

"But is not that a hasty conclusion, papa?"

"That is a hasty question, my dear. I have come to no conclusion. I was only speaking confidentially about my fears."

"Perhaps, papa, it 's only that he 's not sure enough, and is afraid of appearing to profess more than he believes. I 'm sure, if that 's it, I have the greatest sympathy with him."

I looked at her, and saw the tears gathering fast in her eyes.

"Pray to God on the chance of his hearing you, my darling, and go to sleep," I said. "I will not think hardly of you because you cannot be so sure as I am. How could you be? You have not had my experience. Perhaps you are right about Mr Percivale too. But it would be an awkward thing to get intimate with him, you know, and then find out that we did not like him after all. You couldn't like a man much, could you, who did not believe in anything greater than himself, anything marvellous, grand, beyond our understanding—who thought that he had come out of the dirt and was going back to the dirt?"

"I could, papa, if he tried to do his duty notwithstanding—for I am sure I couldn't. I should cry myself to death."

"You are right, my child. I should honour him too. But I should be very sorry for him. For he would be so disappointed in himself."

I do not know whether this was the best answer to make, but I had little time to think.

"But you don't know that he 's like that."

"I do not, my dear. And more, I will not associate the idea with him till I know for certain. We will leave it to ignorant old ladies who lay claim to an instinct for theology to jump at conclusions, and reserve ours—as even such a man as we have been supposing might well teach us—till we have sufficient facts from which to draw them. Now go to bed, my child.

"Good-night then, dear papa," she said, and left me with a kiss.

I was not altogether comfortable after this conversation. I had tried to be fair to the young man both in word and thought, but I could not relish the idea of my daughter falling in love with him, which looked likely enough, before I knew more about him, and found that *more* good and hope-giving. There was but one rational thing left to do, and that was to cast my care on him that careth for us—on the Father who loved my child more than even I could love her—and loved the young man too, and regarded my anxiety, and would take its cause upon himself. After I had lifted up my heart to him I was at ease, read a canto of Dante's Paradise, and then went to bed. The prematurity of a conversation with my wife, in which I found that she was very favourably impressed with Mr Percivale, must be pardoned to the forecasting hearts of fathers and mothers.

As I went out for my walk the next morning, I caught sight of the sexton, with whom as yet I had had but little communication, busily trimming some of the newer graves in the churchyard. I turned in through the nearer gate, which was fashioned like a lychgate, with seats on the sides and a stone table in the centre, but had no roof. The one on the other side of the church was roofed, but probably they had found that here no roof could resist the sea-blasts in winter. The top of the wall where the roof should have rested, was simply covered with flat slates to protect it from the rain.

"Good morning, Coombes," I said.

He turned up a wizened, humorous, old face, the very type of a gravedigger's, and with one hand leaning on the edge of the green mound, upon which he had been cropping with a pair of shears the too long and too thin grass, touched his cap with the other, and bade me a cheerful good morning in return.

"You 're making things tidy," I said.

"It take time to make them all comfortable, you see, sir," he returned, taking up his shears again, and clipping away at the top and sides of the mound.

"You mean the dead, Coombes?"

"Yes, sir; to be sure, sir."

"You don't think it makes much difference to their comfort, do you, whether the grass is one length or another upon their graves?"

"Well no, sir. I don't suppose it makes *much* difference to them. But it look more comfortable, you know. And I like things to look comfortable. Don't you, sir?"

"To be sure I do, Coombes. And you are quite right. The resting-place of the body, although the person it belonged to be far away, should be respected."

"That 's what I think, though I don't get no credit for it. I du believe the people hereabouts thinks me only a single hair better than a Jack Ketch. But I 'm sure I do my best to make the poor things comfortable."

He seemed unable to rid his mind of the idea that the comfort of the departed was dependent upon his ministrations.

"The trouble I have with them sometimes! There 's now this same one as lies here, old Jonathan Giles. He have the gout so bad! and just as I come within a couple o' inches o' the right depth, out come the edge of a great stone in the near corner at the foot of the bed. Thinks

I, he 'll never lie comfortable with that same under his gouty toe. But the trouble I had to get out that stone! I du assure you, sir, it took me nigh half the day.—But this be one of the nicest places to lie in all up and down the coast—a nice gravelly soil, you see, sir; dry, and warm, and comfortable. Them poor things as comes out of the sea must quite enjoy the change, sir."

There was something grotesque in the man's persistence in regarding the objects of his interest from this point of view. It was a curious way for the humanity that was in him to find expression; but I did not like to let him go on thus. It was so much opposed to all that I believed and felt about the change from this world to the next!

"But, Coombes," I said, "why will you go on talking as if it made an atom of difference to the dead bodies where they were buried? They care no more about it than your old coat would care where it was thrown after you had done with it."

He turned and regarded his coat where it hung beside him on the headstone of the same grave at which he was working, shook his head with a smile that seemed to hint a doubt whether the said old coat would be altogether so indifferent to its treatment when it was past use as I had implied. Then he turned again to his work, and after a moment's silence began to approach me from another side. I confess he had the better of me before I was aware of what he was about.

"The church of Boscastle stands high on the cliff. You've been to Boscastle, sir?"

I told him I had not yet, but hoped to go before the summer was over.

"Ah, you should see Boscastle, sir. It's a wonderful place. That's where I was born, sir. When I was a by that church was haunted, sir. It's a damp place, and the wind in it awful. I du believe it stand higher than any church in the country, and have got more wind in it of a stormy night than any church whatsomever. Well they said it was haunted; and sure enough every now and then there was a knocking heard down below. And this always took place of a stormy night, as if there was some poor thing down in the low wouts, (*vaults*,) and he wasn't comfortable and wanted to get out. Well, one night it was so plain and so fearful it was that the sexton he went and took the blacksmith and a ship's carpenter down to the harbour, and they go up together and they hearken all over the floor, and they open one of the old family wouts that belongs to the Penhaligans, and they go down with a light. Now the wind it was a-blowing all as usual, only worse than common. And there to be sure what do they see but the wout half full of sea-water, and nows and thens a great spout coming in through a hole in the rock, for it was high water and a wind off the sea, as I tell you. And there was a coffin afloat on the water, and every time the spout come through, it set it knocking agen the side o' the wout, and that was the ghost."

"What a horrible idea!" I said, with a half-shudder at the unrest of the dead.

The old man uttered a queer long-drawn sound, neither

a chuckle, a crow, nor a laugh, but a mixture of all three, and turned himself yet again to the work which, as he approached the end of his narration, he had suspended, that he might make his story *tell*, I suppose, by looking me in the face. And as he turned he said, "I thought you would like to be comfortable then as well as other people, sir."

I could not help laughing to see how the cunning old fellow had caught me. I have not yet been able to find out how much of truth there was in his story. From the twinkle of his eye I cannot help suspecting that if he did not invent the tale, he embellished it at least, in order to produce the effect which he certainly did produce. Humour was clearly his predominant disposition, the reflex of which was to be seen, after a mild lunar fashion, on the countenance of his wife. Neither could I help thinking with pleasure, as I turned away, how the merry little old man would enjoy telling his companions how he had posed the new parson. Very welcome was he to his laugh for my part. Yet I gladly left the churchyard, with its sunshine above and its darkness below. Indeed I had to look up to the glittering vanes on the four pinnacles of the church tower, dwelling aloft in the clean sunny air, to get the feeling of the dark vault, and the floating coffin, and the knocking heard in the windy church, out of my brain. But the thing that did free me was the reflection with what supreme disregard the disincarcerated spirit would look upon any possible vicissitudes of its abandoned vault. For in proportion as the body of man's revelation ceases to be in harmony with the spirit that dwells therein, it becomes a vault, a prison, from which it must be freedom to escape at length. The house we like best would be a prison of awful sort if doors and windows were built up. Man's abode, as age begins to draw nigh, fares thus. Age is in fact the mason that builds up the doors and the windows, and death is the angel that breaks the prison-house, and lets the captives free. Thus I got something out of the sexton's horrible story.

But before the week was over, death came near indeed—in far other fashion than any funereal tale could have brought it.

One day, after lunch, I had retired to my study, and was dozing in my chair, for the day was hot, when I was waked by Charlie rushing into the room with the cry, "Papa, papa, there 's a man drowning!"

I started up, and hurried down to the drawing-room which looked out over the bay. I could see nothing but people running about on the edge of the quiet waves. No sign of human being was on the water. But the one boat belonging to the pilot was coming out from the shelter of the lock of the canal where it usually lay, and my friend of the coastguard was running down from the tower on the cliff with ropes in his hand. He would not stop the boat even for the moment it would need to take him on board, but threw them in and urged to haste. I stood at the window and watched. Every now and then I fancied I saw something white heaved up on the swell of a wave, and as often was satisfied that I had but fancied it. The boat seemed to be floating about lazily, if not idly. The eagerness to help made it appear as if nothing was going on. Could it, after all, have been a false alarm? Was there, after all, no insensible form swinging about in the sweep of those waves, with life gradually oozing away? Long, long, as it seemed to me, I watched, and still the boat kept moving from place to place, so far out that I could see nothing distinctly of the motions of its crew. At length I saw something. Yes; a long white thing rose from the water slowly, and was drawn into the boat. It rowed swiftly to the shore. There was but one place fit to land upon, a little patch of sand, nearly covered at high water, but now lying yellow in the sun, under the window at which I stood, and immediately under our garden-wall. Thither the boat shot along; and there my friend of the coastguard, earnest and sad, was waiting to use, though without hope, every appliance so well known to him from the frequent occurrence of such necessity in the course of his watchful duties along miles and miles of stormy coast.

I will not linger over the sad details of vain endeavour. The honoured head of a family, he had departed, and left a good name behind him. But even in the midst of my poor attentions to the quiet, speechless, pale-faced wife, who sat at the head of the corpse, I could not help feeling anxious about the effect on my Connie. It was impossible to keep the matter concealed from her. The undoubted concern on the faces of the two boys was enough to reveal that something serious and painful had occurred; while my wife and Wynnie, and indeed the whole household, were busy in attending to every remotest suggestion of aid that reached them from the little crowd gathered about the body. At length it was concluded, on the verdict of the medical man who had been sent for, that all further effort was useless. The body was borne away, and I led the poor lady to her lodging, and remained there with her till I found that, as she lay on the sofa, the sleep that so often dogs the steps of sorrow had at length thrown its veil over her consciousness, and put her for the time to rest. There is a gentle consolation in the firmness of the grasp of the inevitable, known but to those who are led through the valley of the shadow. I left her with her son and daughter, and returned to my own family. They too were of course in the skirts of the cloud. Had they only heard of the occurrence, it would have had little effect; but death had appeared to them. Every one but Connie had seen the dead lying there; and before the day was over, I wished that she too had seen the dead. For I found from what she said at intervals, and from the shudder that now and then passed through her, that her imagination was at work, showing but the horrors that belong to death; for the enfolding peace that accompanies it can be known but by sight of the dead. When I spoke to her, she seemed, and I suppose for the time felt tolerably quiet and comfortable; but I could see that the words she had heard fall in the going and coming, and the communications of Charlie and Harry to each other, had made as it were an excoriation on her fancy, to which her consciousness was ever returning. And now I became more grateful than I had yet been for the gift of that gipsy-child. For I felt no anxiety about Connie so long as she was with her. The presence even of her mother could not relieve her, for she and Wynnie were both clouded with the same awe, and its reflex in Connie was distorted by her fancy. But the sweet ignorance of the baby, which, rightly considered, is more than a type or symbol of faith, operated most healingly; for she appeared in her sweet merry ways—no baby was ever more filled with the mere gladness of life than Connie's baby—to the mood in which they all were, like a little sunny window in a cathedral crypt, telling of a whole universe of sunshine and motion beyond those oppressed pillars and low-groined arches. And why should not the baby know best? I believe the babies do know best. I therefore favoured her having the child more than I might otherwise have thought good for her, being anxious to get the dreary, unhealthy impression healed as soon as possible, lest it should, in the delicate physical condition in which she was, turn to a sore.

But my wife suffered for a time nearly as much as Connie. As long as she was going about the house or attending to the wants of her family, she was free; but no sooner did she lay her head on the pillow than in rushed the cry of the sea, fierce, unkind, craving like a wild beast. Again and again she spoke of it to me, for it came to her mingled with the voice of the tempter, saying, "*Cruel chance*," over and over again. For although the two words contradict each other when put together thus, each in its turn would assert itself.

A great part of the doubt in the world comes from the fact that there are in it so many more of the impressible as compared with the originating minds. Where the openness to impression is balanced by the power of production, the painful questions of the world are speedily met by their answers; where such is not the case, there are often long periods of suffering till the child-answer of truth is brought to the birth. Hence the need for every impressible mind to be, by reading or speech, held in living association with an original mind able to combat those suggestions of doubt and even unbelief, which the look of things must often occasion—a look which comes from our inability to gain other than fragmentary visions of the work that the Father worketh hitherto. When the kingdom of heaven is at hand, one sign thereof will be that all clergymen will be more or less of the latter sort, and mere receptive goodness, no more than education and moral character, will be considered sufficient reason for a man's occupying the high position of an instructor of his fellows. But even now this possession of original power is not by any means to be limited to those who make public show of the same. In many a humble parish priest it shows itself at the bedside of the suffering, or in the admonition of the closet, although as yet there are many of the clergy who, so far from being able to console wisely, are incapable of understanding the condition of those that need consolation.

"It is all a fancy, my dear," I said to her. "There is nothing more terrible in this than in any other death

On the contrary, I can hardly imagine a less fearful one. A big wave falls on the man's head and stuns him, and without further suffering he floats gently out on the sea of the unknown."

"But it is so terrible for those left behind!"

"Had you seen the face of his widow, so gentle, so loving, so resigned in its pallor, you would not have thought it so *terrible*."

But though she always seemed satisfied, and no doubt felt nearly so, after any conversation of the sort, yet every night she would call out once and again, "Oh, that sea, out there!" I was very glad indeed when Mr Turner, who had arranged to spend a short holiday with us, arrived.

He was concerned at the news I gave him of the shock both Connie and her mother had received, and counselled an immediate change, that time might, in the absence of surrounding associations, obliterate something of the impression that had been made. The consequence was, that we resolved to remove our household, for a short time, to some place not too far off to permit of my attending to my duties at Kilkhaven, but out of the sight and sound of the sea. It was Thursday when Mr Turner arrived, and he spent the next two days in inquiring and looking about for a suitable spot to which we might repair as early in the week as possible.

On the Saturday, the blacksmith was busy in the church tower, and I went in to see how he was getting on.

"You had a sad business here the last week, sir," he said, after we had done talking about the repairs.

"A very sad business, indeed," I answered.

"It was a warning to us all," he said.

"We may well take it so," I returned. "But it seems to me that we are too ready to think of such remarkable things only by themselves, instead of being roused by them to regard everything, common and uncommon, as ordered by the same care and wisdom."

"One of our local preachers made a grand use of it."

I made no reply. He resumed.

"They tell me you took no notice of it last Sunday, sir."

"I made no immediate allusion to it certainly. But I preached under the influence of it. And I thought it better that those who could reflect on the matter should be thus led to think for themselves than that they should be subjected to the reception of my thoughts and feelings about it; for in the main it is life and not death that we have to preach."

"I don't quite understand you, sir. But then you don't care much for preaching in your church."

"I confess," I answered, "that there has been much indifference on that point. I could, however, mention to you many and grand exceptions. Still there is, even in some of the best in the church, a great amount of disbelief in the efficacy of preaching. And I allow that a great deal of what is called preaching partakes of its nature only in the remotest degree. But, while I hold a strong opinion of its value—that is where it is genuine—I venture just to suggest that the nature of the preaching to which the body you belong to has resorted, has had something to do, by way of a reaction, in driving the church to the other extreme."

"How do you mean that, sir?"

"You try to work upon people's feelings without reference to their judgment. Any one who can preach what you call rousing sermons, is considered a grand preacher amongst you, and there is a great danger of his being led thereby to talk more nonsense than sense. And then when the excitement goes off, there is no seed left in the soil to grow in peace, and they are always craving after more excitement."

"Well, there is the preacher to rouse them up again."

"And the consequence is, that they continue like children—the good ones, I mean—and have hardly a chance of making a calm, deliberate choice of that which is good; while those who have been only excited and nothing more, are hardened and seared by the recurrence of such feeling as is neither aroused by truth nor followed by action."

"You daren't talk like that if you knew the kind of people in this country that the Methodists, as you call them, have got a hold of. They tell me it was like hell itself down in those mines before Wesley come among them."

"I should be a fool or a bigot to doubt that the Wesleyans have done incalculable good in the country. And that not alone to the people who never went to church. The whole Church of England is under obligations to Methodism such as no words can overstate."

"I wonder you can say such things against them then."

"Now there you show the evil of thinking too much about the party you belong to. It makes a man touchy; and then he fancies, when another is merely, it may be, analysing a difference, or insisting strongly on some great truth, that he is talking against his party."

"But you said, sir, that our clergy don't care about moving our judgments, only our feelings. Now I know preachers amongst us of whom that would be anything but true."

"Of course there must be. But there is what I say: your party-feeling makes you touchy. A man can't always be saying in the press of utterance—'*Of course there are exceptions.*' That is understood. I confess I do not know much about your clergy, for I have not had the opportunity. But I do know this, that some of the best and most liberal people I have ever known have belonged to your community."

"They do gather a deal of money for good purposes."

"Yes. But that was not what I meant by *liberal.* It is far easier to give money than to be generous in judgment. I meant by *liberal,* able to see the good and true in people that differ from you—glad to be roused to the reception of truth in God's name from whatever quarter it may come, and not readily finding offence where a remark may have chanced to be too sweeping or unguarded. But I see that I ought to be more careful, for I have made you, who certainly are not one of the quarrelsome people I have been speaking of, misunderstand me."

"I beg your pardon, sir. I was hasty. But I do think I am more ready to lose my temper since"——

Here he stopped. A fit of coughing came on, and, to my concern, was followed by what I saw plainly could be the result only of a rupture in the lungs. I insisted on his dropping his work and coming home with me, where I made him rest the remainder of the day and all Sunday, sending word to his mother that I could not let him go home. When we left on the Monday morning, we took him with us in the carriage hired for the journey, and set him down at his mother's, apparently no worse than usual.

CHAPTER XXIV.

AT THE FARM.

EAVING the younger members of the family at home with the servants, we set out for a farm-house, some twenty miles off, which Turner had discovered for us. Connie had stood the journey down so well, and was now so much stronger, that we had no anxiety about her so far as regarded the travelling. Through deep lanes with many cottages and here and there a very ugly little chapel, over steep hills, up which Turner and Wynnie and I walked, and along sterile moors we drove, stopping at roadside inns, and often besides to raise Connie and let her look about upon the extended prospect, so that it was drawing towards evening before we arrived at our destination. On the way Turner had warned us that we were not to expect a beautiful country, although the place was within reach of much that was remarkable. Therefore we were not surprised when we drew up at the door of a

bare-looking, shelterless house, with scarcely a tree in sight, and a stretch of undulating fields on every side.

"A dreary place in winter, Turner," I said, after we had seen Connie comfortably deposited in the nice white-curtained parlour, smelling of dried roses even in the height of the fresh ones, and had strolled out while our tea-dinner was being got ready for us.

"Not a doubt of it; but just the place I wanted for Miss Connie," he replied. "We are high above the sea, and the air is very bracing, and not, at this season, too cold. A month later I should not on any account have brought her here."

"I think even now there is a certain freshness in the wind that calls up a kind of will in the nerves to meet it."

"That is precisely what I wanted for you all. You observe there is no rasp in its touch, however. There are regions in this island of ours where even in the hottest day in summer you would frequently discover a certain unfriendly edge in the air, that would set you wondering whether the seasons had not changed since you were a boy, and used to lie on the grass half the idle day."

"I often do wonder whether it may not be so. But I always come to the conclusion that even this is but an example of the involuntary tendency of the mind of man towards the ideal. He forgets all that comes between and divides the hints of perfection scattered here and there along the scope of his experience. I especially remember one summer day in my childhood, which has coloured all my ideas of summer and bliss and fulfilment of content. It is made up of only mossy grass, and the scent of the earth and wild flowers, and hot sun, and perfect sky—deep and blue, and traversed by blinding white clouds. I could not have been more than five or six, I think, from the kind of dress I wore, the very pearl buttons of which, encircled on their face with a ring of half-spherical hollows, have their undeniable relation in my memory to the heavens and the earth, to the march of the glorious clouds, and the tender scent of the rooted flowers; and, indeed, when I think of it, must, by the delight they gave me, have opened my mind the more to the enjoyment of the eternal paradise around me. What a thing it is to please a child!"

"I know what you mean perfectly," answered Turner. "It is as I get older that I understand what Wordsworth says about childhood. It is indeed a mercy that we were not born grown men, with what we consider our wits about us. They are blinding things those wits we gather. I fancy that the single thread by which God sometimes keeps hold of a man is such an impression of his childhood as that of which you have been speaking."

"I do not doubt it. For conscience is so near in all those memories to which you refer! The whole surrounding of them is so at variance with sin! A sense of purity, not in himself, for the child is not feeling that he is pure, is all about him; and when afterwards the condition returns upon him, returns when he is conscious of so much that is evil and so much that is unsatisfied in him, it brings with it a longing after the high clear air of moral well-being."

"Do you think, then, that it is only by association that nature thus impresses us? that she has no power of meaning these things?"

"Not at all. No doubt there is something in the recollection of the associations of childhood to strengthen the power of nature upon us, but the power is in nature herself, else it would be but a poor weak thing to what it is. There *is* purity and state in that sky. There *is* a peace now in this wide still earth—not so very beautiful, you own—and in that overhanging blue, which my heart cries out that it needs and cannot be well till it gains—gains in the truth, gains in God, who is the power of truth, the living and causing truth. There is indeed a rest that remaineth, a rest pictured out even here this night, to rouse my dull heart to desire it and follow after it, a rest that consists in thinking the thoughts of Him who is the Peace because the Unity, in being filled with that spirit which now pictures itself forth in this repose of the heavens and the earth."

"True," said Turner, after a pause. "I must think more about such things. The science the present day is going wild about will not give us that rest."

"No; but that rest will do much to give you that science. A man with this repose in his heart will do more by far, other capabilities being equal, to find out the laws that govern things. For all law is living rest."

"What you have been saying," resumed Turner, after

another pause, "reminds me much of one of Words-worth's poems. I do not mean the famous ode."

"You mean the Ninth Evening Voluntary, I know—one of his finest and truest and deepest poems. It begins, *Had this effulgence disappeared.*"

"Yes, that is the one I mean. I shall read it again when I go home. But you don't agree with Wordsworth, do you, about our having had an existence previous to this?"

He gave a little laugh as he asked the question.

"Not in the least. But an opinion held by such men as Plato, Origen, and Wordsworth, is not to be laughed at, Mr Turner. It cannot be in its nature absurd. I might have mentioned Shelley as holding it, too, had his opinion been worth anything."

"Then you don't think much of Shelley?"

"I think his *feeling* most valuable; his *opinion* nearly worthless."

"Well, perhaps I had no business to laugh at it; but"——

"Do not suppose for a moment that I even lean to it. I dislike it. It would make me unhappy to think there was the least of sound argument for it. But I respect the men who have held it, and know there must be *something* good in it, else they could not have held it."

"Are you able then to sympathize with that ode of Wordsworth's? Does it not depend for all its worth on the admission of this theory?"

"Not in the least. Is it necessary to admit that we

must have had a conscious life before this life to find meaning in the words,—

> 'But trailing clouds of glory do we come
> From God who is our home?'

Is not all the good in us his image? Imperfect and sinful as we are, is not all the foundation of our being his image? Is not the sin all ours, and the life in us all God's? We cannot be the creatures of God without partaking of his nature. Every motion of our conscience, every admiration of what is pure and noble, is a sign and a result of this. Is not every self-accusation a proof of the presence of his spirit? That comes not of ourselves —that is not without him. These are the clouds of glory we come trailing from him. All feelings of beauty and peace and loveliness and right and goodness, we trail with us from our home. God is the only home of the human soul. To interpret in this manner what Wordsworth says, will enable us to enter into perfect sympathy with all that grandest of his poems. I do not say this is what he meant; but I think it includes what he meant by being greater and wider than what he meant. Nor am I guilty of presumption in saying so, for surely the idea that we are born of God is a greater idea than that we have lived with him a life before this life. But Wordsworth is not the first among our religious poets to give us at least what is valuable in the notion. I came upon a volume amongst my friend Shepherd's books, with which I had made no acquaintance before—Henry Vaughan's poems. I brought it with me, for it has finer lines, I almost think, than any in George Herbert, though not so fine poems by any means as his best. When we go into the house, I will read one of them to you."

"Thank you," said Turner. "I wish I could have such talk once a week. The shades of the prison house, you know, Mr Walton, are always trying to close about us, and shut out the vision of the glories we have come from, as Wordsworth says."

"A man," I answered, "who ministers to the miserable necessities of his fellows has even more need than another to believe in the light and the gladness—else a poor Job's comforter will he be. *I* don't want to be treated like a musical snuff-box."

The doctor laughed.

"No man can *prove*," he said, "that there is not a being inside the snuff-box, existing in virtue of the harmony of its parts, comfortable when they go well, sick when they go badly, and dying when it is dismembered, or even when it stops."

"No," I answered. "No man can prove it. But no man can convince a human being of it. And just as little can any one convince me that my conscience, making me do sometimes what I *don't* like, comes from a harmonious action of the particles of my brain. But it is time we went in, for by the law of things in general, I being ready for my dinner, my dinner ought to be ready for me."

"A law with more exceptions than instances, I fear," said Turner.

"I doubt that," I answered. "The readiness is everything, and that we constantly blunder in. But we had better see whether we are really ready for it by trying whether it is ready for us."

Connie went to bed early, as indeed we all did, and she was rather better than worse the next morning. My wife, for the first time for many nights, said nothing about the crying of the sea. The following day Turner and I set out to explore the neighbourhood. The rest remained quietly at home.

It was, as I have said, a high bare country. The fields lay side by side, parted from each other chiefly, as so often in Scotland, by stone walls; and these stones being of a laminated nature, the walls were not unfrequently built by laying thin plates on their edges, which gave a neatness to them not found in other parts of the country as far as I am aware. In the middle of the fields came here and there patches of yet unreclaimed moorland.

Now in a region like this, beauty must be looked for below the surface. There is a probability of finding hollows of repose, sunken spots of loveliness, hidden away altogether from the general aspect of sternness, or perhaps sterility, that meets the eye in glancing over the outspread landscape; just as in the natures of stern men you may expect to find, if opportunity should be afforded you, sunny spots of tender verdure, kept ever green by that very sternness which is turned towards the common gaze—thus existent because they are below the surface, and not laid bare to the sweep of the cold winds that roam the world. How often have not men started with amaze at the discovery of some feminine sweetness, some grace of protection in the man whom they had judged cold and hard and rugged, inaccessible to the more genial influences of humanity! It may be that such men are only fighting against the wind, and keep their hearts open to the sun.

I knew this; and when Turner and I set out that morning to explore, I expected to light upon some instance of it—some mine or other in which nature had hidden away rare jewels; but I was not prepared to find such as I did find. With our hearts full of a glad secret we returned home, but we said nothing about it, in order that Ethelwyn and Wynnie might enjoy the discovery even as we had enjoyed it.

There was another grand fact with regard to the neighbourhood about which we judged it better to be silent for a few days, that the inland influences might be free to work. We were considerably nearer the ocean than my wife and daughters supposed, for we had made a great round in order to arrive from the land-side. We were, however, out of the sound of its waves, which broke along the shore, in this part, at the foot of tremendous cliffs. What cliffs they were we shall soon find.

CHAPTER XXV.

THE KEEVE.

"OW, my dear! now, Wynnie!" I said, after prayers the next morning, "you must come out for a walk as soon as ever you can get your bonnets on."

"But we can't leave Connie, papa," objected Wynnie.

"Oh, yes, you can, quite well. There's nursie to look after her. What do you say, Connie?"

For, for some time now, Connie had been able to get up so early, that it was no unusual thing to have prayers in her room.

"I am entirely independent of help from my family," returned Connie, grandiloquently. "I am a woman of independent means," she added. "If you say another word, I will rise and leave the room."

And she made a movement as if she would actually do as she had said. Seized with an involuntary terror, I rushed towards her, and the impertinent girl burst out laughing in my face—threw herself back on her pillows, and laughed delightedly.

"Take care, papa," she said. "I carry a terrible club for rebellious people." Then, her mood changing, she added, as if to suppress the tears gathering in her eyes, "I am the queen—of luxury and self-will—and I won't have anybody come near me till dinner-time. I mean to enjoy myself."

So the matter was settled, and we went out for our walk. Ethelwyn was not such a good walker as she had been; but even if she had retained the strength of her youth, we should not have got on much the better for it—so often did she and Wynnie stop to grub ferns out of the chinks and roots of the stone walls. Now, I admire ferns as much as anybody—that is, not, I fear, so much as my wife and daughter, but quite enough notwithstanding—but I do not quite enjoy being pulled up like a fern at every turn.

"Now, my dear, what is the use of stopping to torture that harmless vegetable?' I say, but say in vain. "It is much more beautiful where it is than it will be anywhere where you can put it. Besides, you know they never come to anything with you. They *always* die."

Thereupon my wife reminds me of this fern and that fern, gathered in such and such places, and now in such and such corners of the garden or the greenhouse, or under glass-shades in this or that room, of the very existence of which I am ignorant, whether from original inattention, or merely from forgetfulness, I do not know.

Certainly, out of their own place I do not care much for them.

At length, partly by the inducement I held out to them of a much greater variety of ferns where we were bound, I succeeded in getting them over the two miles in little more than two hours. After passing from the lanes into the fields, our way led downwards till we reached a very steep large slope, with a delightful southern exposure, and covered with the sweetest down-grasses. It was just the place to lie in, as on the edge of the earth, and look abroad upon the universe of air and floating worlds.

"Let us have a rest here, Ethel," I said. "I am sure this is much more delightful than uprooting ferns. What an awful thing to think that here we are on this great round tumbling ball of a world, held by the feet, and lifting up the head into infinite space—without choice or wish of our own—compelled to think and to be, whether we will or not! Just God must know it to be very good, or he would not have taken it in his hands to make individual lives without a possible will of theirs. He must be our Father, or we are wretched creatures—the slaves of a fatal necessity! Did it ever strike you, Turner, that each one of us stands on the apex of the world? With a sphere, you know, it must be so. And thus is typified, as it seems to me, that each one of us must look up for himself to find God, and then look abroad to find his fellows."

"I think I know what you mean," was all Turner's reply.

"No doubt," I resumed, "the apprehension of this truth has, in otherwise ill-ordered minds, given rise to all sorts of fierce and grotesque fanaticism. But the minds which have thus conceived the truth, would have been immeasurably worse without it; nay, this truth affords at last the only possible door out of the miseries of their own chaos, whether inherited or the result of their own misconduct."

"What's that in the grass?" cried Wynnie, in a tone of alarm.

I looked where she indicated, and saw a slow-worm, or blind-worm, lying basking in the sun. I rose and went towards it.

"Here's your stick," said Turner.

"What for?" I asked. "Why should I kill it? It is perfectly harmless, and, to my mind, beautiful."

I took it in my hands, and brought it to my wife. She gave an involuntary shudder as it came near her.

"I assure you it is harmless," I said, "though it has a forked tongue." And I opened its mouth as I spoke. "I do not think the serpent form is essentially ugly."

"It makes me feel ugly," said Wynnie.

"I allow I do not quite understand the mystery of it," I said. "But you never saw lovelier ornamentation than these silvery scales, with all the neatness of what you ladies call a set pattern, and none of the stiffness, for there are not two of them the same in form. And you never saw lovelier curves than this little patient creature, which does not even try to get away from me, makes with the queer long thin body of him."

"I wonder how it can look after its tail, it is so far off," said Wynnie.

"It does though—better than you ladies look after your long dresses. I wonder whether it is descended from creatures that once had feet, and did not make a good use of them. Perhaps they had wings even, and would not use them at all, and so lost them. Its ancestors may have had poison-fangs: it is innocent enough. But it is a terrible thing to be all feet, is it not? There is an awful significance in the condemnation of the serpent—'On thy belly shalt thou go, and eat dust.'—But it is better to talk of beautiful things. *My* soul at least has dropped from its world apex. Let us go on. Come, wife. Come, Turner."

They did not seem willing to rise. But the glen drew me. I rose, and my wife followed my example with the help of my hand. She returned to the subject, however, as we descended the slope.

"Is it possible that in the course of ever so many ages wings and feet should be both lost?" she said.

"The most presumptuous thing in the world is to pronounce on the possible and the impossible. I do not know what is possible and what is impossible. I can only tell a little of what is true and what is untrue. But I do say this, that between the condition of many decent members of society and that for the sake of which God made them, there is a gulf quite as vast as that between a serpent and a bird. I get peeps now and then into the condition of my own heart, which, for the moment, make it seem impossible that I should ever rise into a true state of nature—that is, into the simplicity of God's will concerning me. The only hope for ourselves and for others lies in him—in the power the creating spirit has over the spirits he has made."

By this time the descent on the grass was getting too steep and slippery to admit of our continuing to advance in that direction. We turned, therefore, down the valley in the direction of the sea. It was but a narrow cleft, and narrowed much towards a deeper cleft, in which we now saw the tops of trees, and from which we heard the rush of water. Nor had we gone far in this direction before we came upon a gate in a stone wall, which led into what seemed a neglected garden. We entered, and found a path turning and winding, among small trees, and luxuriant ferns, and great stones, and fragments of ruins down towards the bottom of the chasm. The noise of falling water increased as we went on, and at length, after some scrambling and several sharp turns, we found ourselves with a nearly precipitous wall on each side, clothed with shrubs and ivy, and creeping things of the vegetable world. Up this cleft there was no advance. The head of it was a precipice down which shot the stream from the vale above, pouring out of a deep slit it had itself cut in the rock as with a knife. Half-way down, it tumbled into a great basin of hollowed stone, and flowing from a chasm in its side, which left part of the lip of the basin standing like the arch of a vanished bridge, it fell into a black pool below, whence it crept as if half-stunned or weary down the gentle decline of the ravine. It was a perfect little picture. I, for my part, had never seen such a picturesque fall. It was a little gem of nature, complete in effect. The ladies were full of pleasure. Wynnie, forgetting her usual reserve, broke out in frantic exclamations of delight.

We stood for a while regarding the ceaseless pour of the water down the precipice, here shot slanting in a little trough of the rock, full of force and purpose, here falling in great curls of green and gray, with an expression of absolute helplessness and conscious perdition, as if sheer to the centre, but rejoicing the next moment to find itself brought up boiling and bubbling in the basin, to issue in the gathered hope of experience. Then we turned down the stream a little way, crossed it by a plank, and stood again to regard it from the opposite side. Small as the whole affair was—not more than about a hundred and fifty feet in height—it was so full of variety that I saw it was all my memory could do, if it carried away anything like a correct picture or its aspect. I was contemplating it fixedly, when a little stifled cry from Wynnie made me start and look round. Her face was flushed, yet she was trying to look unconcerned.

"I thought we were quite alone, papa," she said; "but I see a gentleman sketching."

I looked whither she indicated. A little way down, the bed of the ravine widened considerably, and was no doubt filled with water in rainy weather. Now it was swampy—full of reeds and willow bushes. But on the opposite side of the stream, with a little canal from it going all around it, lay a great flat rectangular stone, not more than a foot above the level of the water, and upon a camp-stool in the centre of this stone sat a gentleman sketching. I had no doubt that Wynnie had recognized him at once. And I was annoyed, and indeed, angry, to think that Mr Percivale had followed us here. But while I regarded him, he looked up, rose very quietly, and, with his pencil in his hand, came towards us. With no nearer approach to familiarity than a bow, and no expression of either much pleasure or any surprise, he said—

"I have seen your party for some time, Mr Walton—since you crossed the stream; but I would not break in upon your enjoyment with the surprise which my presence here must cause you."

I suppose I answered with a bow of some sort; for I could not say with truth that I was glad to see him. He resumed, doubtless penetrating my suspicion—

"I have been here almost a week. I certainly had no expectation of the pleasure of seeing you."

This he said lightly, though no doubt with the object of clearing himself. And I was, if not reassured, yet disarmed, by his statement; for I could not believe, from what I knew of him, that he would be guilty of such a white lie as many a gentleman would have thought justifiable on the occasion. Still, I suppose he found me a little stiff, for presently he said—

"If you will excuse me, I will return to my work."

Then I felt as if I must say something, for I had shown him no courtesy during the interview.

"It must be a great pleasure to carry away such talismans with you—capable of bringing the place back to your mental vision at any moment."

"To tell the truth," he answered, "I am a little ashamed of being found sketching here. Such bits of scenery are not of my favourite studies. But it is a change."

"It is very beautiful here," I said, in a tone of contravention.

"It is very pretty," he answered—"very lovely, if you will—not very *beautiful*, I think. I would keep that word for things of larger regard. Beauty requires width, and here is none. I had almost said this place was fanciful—the work of imagination in her play-hours, not in her large serious moods. It affects me like the face of a woman only pretty, about which boys and guardsmen will rave—to me not very interesting, save for its single lines."

"Why, then, do you sketch the place?"

"A very fair question," he returned, with a smile. "Just because it is soothing from the very absence of beauty. I would far rather, however, if I were only following my taste, take the barest bit of the moor above, with a streak of the cold sky over it. That gives room."

"You would like to put a skylark in it, wouldn't you?"

"That I would if I knew how. I see you know what I mean. But the mere romantic I never had much taste for; though if you saw the kind of pictures I try to paint, you would not wonder that I take sketches of places like this, while in my heart of hearts I do not care much for them. They are so different, and just *therefore* they are good for me. I am not working now. I am only playing."

"With a view to working better afterwards, I have no doubt," I answered.

"You are right there, I hope," was his quiet reply, as he turned and walked back to the island.

He had not made a step towards joining us. He had only taken his hat off to the ladies. He was gaining ground upon me rapidly.

"Have you quarrelled with our new friend, Harry?" said my wife, as I came up to her.

She was sitting on a stone. Turner and Wynnie were farther off towards the foot of the fall.

"Not in the least," I answered, slightly outraged—I did not at first know why—by the question. "He is only gone to his work, which is a duty belonging both to the first and second tables of the law."

"I hope you have asked him to come home to our early dinner, then," she rejoined.

"I have not. That remains for you to do. Come, I will take you to him."

Ethelwyn rose at once, put her hand in mine, and with a little help, soon reached the table-rock. When Percivale saw that she was really on a visit to him on his island-perch, he rose, and when she came near enough, held out his hand. It was but a step, and she was beside him in a moment. After the usual greetings, which on her part, although very quiet, like every motion and word of hers, were yet indubitably cordial and kind, she said—

"When you get back to London, Mr Percivale, might I ask you to allow some friends of mine to call at your studio, and see your paintings?"

"With all my heart," answered Percivale. "I must warn you, however, that I have not much they will care to see. They will perhaps go away less happy than they entered. Not many people care to see my pictures twice."

"I would not send you any one I thought unworthy of the honour," answered my wife.

Percivale bowed—one of his stately, old-world bows, which I greatly liked.

"Any friend of yours—that is guarantee sufficient," he answered.

There was this peculiarity about any compliment that Percivale paid, that you had not a doubt of its being genuine.

"Will you come and take an early dinner with us?" said my wife. "My invalid daughter will be very pleased to see you."

"I will with pleasure," he answered, but in a tone of some hesitation, as he glanced from Ethelwyn to me.

"My wife speaks for us all," I said. "It will give us all pleasure."

"I am only afraid it will break in upon your morning's work," remarked Ethelwyn.

"Oh! that is not of the least consequence," he rejoined. "In fact, as I have just been saying to Mr

Walton, I am not working at all at present. This is pure recreation."

As he spoke, he turned towards his easel, and began hastily to bundle up his things.

"We 're not quite ready to go yet," said my wife, loath to leave the lovely spot. "What a curious flat stone this is!" she added.

"It is," said Percivale. "The man to whom the place belongs, a worthy yeoman of the old school, says that this wider part of the channel must have been the fish-pond, and that the portly monks stood on this stone and fished in the pond."

"Then was there a monastery here?" I asked.

"Certainly. The ruins of the chapel, one of the smallest, are on the top, just above the fall—rather a fearful place to look down from. I wonder you did not observe them as you came. They say it had a silver bell in the days of its glory, which now lies in a deep hole under the basin, half-way between the top and bottom of the fall. But the old man says that nothing will make him look, or let any one else lift the huge stone; for he is much better pleased to believe that it may be there, than he would be to know it was not there; for certainly, if it were found, it would not be left there long."

As he spoke Percivale had continued packing his gear. He now led our party up to the chapel, and thence down a few yards to the edge of the chasm, where the water fell headlong. I turned away with that fear of high places which is one of my many weaknesses, and when I turned again towards the spot, there was Wynnie on the very edge, looking over into the flash and tumult of the water below, but with a nervous grasp of the hand of Percivale, who stood a little further back.

In going home, the painter led us by an easier way out of the valley, left his little easel and other things at a cottage, and then walked on in front between my wife and daughter, while Turner and I followed. He seemed quite at his ease with them, and plenty of talk and laughter rose on the way. I, however, was chiefly occupied with finding out Turner's impression of Connie's condition.

"She is certainly better," he said. "I wonder you do not see it as plainly as I do. The pain is nearly gone from her spine, and she can move herself a good deal more, I am certain, than she could when she left. She asked me yesterday if she might not turn upon one side. 'Do you think you could?' I asked.—'I think so,' she answered. 'At any rate, I have often a great inclination to try; only papa said I had better wait till you came.' I do think she might be allowed a little more change of posture now."

"Then you have really some hope of her final recovery?"

"I have *hope* most certainly. But what is hope in me, you must not allow to become certainty in you. I am nearly sure, though, that she can never be other than an invalid; that is, if I am to judge by what I know of such cases."

"I am thankful for the hope," I answered. "You need

not be afraid of my turning upon you, should the hope never pass into sight. I should do so only if I found that you had been treating me irrationally—inspiring me with hope which you knew to be false. The element of uncertainty is essential to hope, and for all true hope, even as hope, man has to be unspeakably thankful."

CHAPTER XXVI.

THE WALK TO CHURCH.

WAS glad to be able to arrange with a young clergyman who was on a visit to Kilkhaven, that he should take my duty for me the next Sunday, for that was the only one Turner could spend with us. He and I and Wynnie walked together two miles to church. It was a lovely morning, with just a tint of autumn in the air. But even that tint, though all else was of the summer, brought a shadow, I could see, on Wynnie's face.

"You said you would show me a poem of—Vaughan, I think you said, was the name of the writer. I am too ignorant of our older literature," said Turner.

"I have only just made acquaintance with him," I answered. "But I think I can repeat the poem. You shall judge whether it is not like Wordsworth's ode.

> 'Happy those early days, when I
> Shined in my angel infancy;

Before I understood the place
Appointed for my second race,
Or taught my soul to fancy ought
But a white, celestial thought;
When yet I had not walked above
A mile or two from my first love,
And looking back, at that short space,
Could see a glimpse of his bright face;
When on some gilded cloud or flower
My gazing soul would dwell an hour,
And in those weaker glories spy
Some shadows of eternity;
Before I taught my tongue to wound
My conscience with a sinful sound,
But felt through all this fleshly dress
Bright shoots of everlastingness.
O how I long to travel back' "——

But here I broke down, for I could not remember the rest with even approximate accuracy.

"When did this Vaughan live?" asked Turner.

"He was born, I find, in 1621—five years, that is, after Shakspeare's death, and when Milton was about thirteen years old. He lived to the age of seventy-three, but seems to have been little known. In politics he was on the Cavalier side. By the way, he was a medical man, like you, Turner—an M.D. We 'll have a glance at the little book when we go back. Don't let me forget to show it you. A good many of your profession have distinguished themselves in literature, and as profound believers, too."

"I should have thought the profession had been chiefly remarkable for such as believe only in the evidence of the senses."

"As if having searched into the innermost recesses of the body, and not having found a soul, they considered themselves justified in declaring there was none."

"Just so."

"Well, that is true of the commonplace amongst them, I do believe. You will find the exceptions have been men of fine minds and characters—not such as he of whom Chaucer says,—

> His study was but little on the Bible;

for if you look at the rest of the description of the man, you will find that he was in alliance with his apothecary for their mutual advantage, that he was a money-loving man, and that some of Chaucer's keenest irony is spent on him in an off-hand, quiet manner. Compare the tone in which he writes of the doctor of physic, with the profound reverence wherewith he bows himself before the poor country parson."

Here Wynnie spoke, though with some tremor in her voice.

"I never know, papa, what people mean by talking about childhood in that way. I never seem to have been a bit younger and more innocent than I am."

"Don't you remember a time, Wynnie, when the things about you—the sky and the earth, say—seemed to you much grander than they seem now? You are old enough to have lost something."

She thought for a little while before she answered.

"My dreams were, I know. I cannot say so of anything else."

I in my turn had to be silent, for I did not see the true answer, though I was sure there was one somewhere, if I could only find it. All I could reply, however, even after I had meditated a good while, was—and perhaps, after all, it was the best thing I could have said—

"Then you must make a good use of your dreams, my child."

'Why, papa?"

"Because they are the only memorials of childhood you have left."

"How am I to make a good use of them? I don't know what to do with my silly old dreams."

But she gave a sigh as she spoke that testified her silly old dreams had a charm for her still.

"If your dreams, my child, have ever testified to you of a condition of things beyond that which you see around you; if they have been to you the hints of a wonder and glory beyond what visits you now, you must not call them silly, for they are just what the scents of Paradise borne on the air were to Adam and Eve as they delved and spun, reminding them that they must aspire yet again through labour into that childhood of obedience which is the only paradise of humanity—into that oneness with the will of the Father, which our race our individual selves, need just as much as if we had personally fallen with Adam, and from which we fall every time we are disobedient to the voice of the Father within our souls—to the conscience which is his making and his witness. If you have had no childhood, my Wynnie, yet permit your old father to say that everything I see in you indicates more strongly in you than in most people that it is this childhood after which you are blindly longing, without which you find that life is hardly to be endured. Thank God for your dreams, my child. In him you will find that the essence of those dreams is fulfilled. We are saved by hope, Turner. Never man hoped too much, or repented that he had hoped. The plague is that we don't hope in God half enough. The very fact that hope is strength, and strength the outcome, the body of life, shows that hope is at one with life, with the very essence of what says 'I am'—yea, of what doubts and says 'Am I? and therefore is reasonable to creatures who cannot even doubt save in that they live."

By this time, for I have of course, only given the outlines, or rather salient points, of our conversation, we had reached the church, where, if I found the sermon neither healing nor inspiring, I found the prayers full of hope and consolation. They at least are safe beyond human caprice, conceit, or incapacity. Upon them, too, the man who is distressed at the thought of how little of the needful food he had been able to provide for his people, may fall back for comfort, in the thought that there at least was what ought to have done them good, what it was well worth their while to go to church for. But I did think they were too long for any individual Christian soul to sympathise with from beginning to end, that is, to respond to, like organ-tube to the fingered key, in every touch of the utterance of the general

Christian soul. For my reader must remember that it is one thing to read prayers and another to respond; and that I had had very few opportunities of being in the position of the latter duty. I had had suspicions before, and now they were confirmed—that the present crowding of services was most inexpedient. And as I pondered on the matter, instead of trying to go on praying after I had already uttered my soul, which is but a heathenish attempt after much speaking, I thought how our Lord had given us such a short prayer to pray, and I began to wonder when or how the services came to be so heaped the one on the back of the other as they now were. No doubt many people defended them; no doubt many people could sit them out; but how many people could pray from beginning to end of them? On this point we had some talk as we went home. Wynnie was opposed to any change of the present use on the ground that we should only have the longer sermons.

"Still," I said, "I do not think even that so great an evil. A sensitive conscience will not reproach itself so much for not listening to the whole of a sermon, as for kneeling in prayer and not praying. I think myself, however, that after the prayers are over, every one should be at liberty to go out and leave the sermon unheard, if he pleases. I think the result would be in the end a good one both for parson and people. It would break through the deadness of this custom, this use and wont. Many a young mind is turned for life against the influences of church-going—one of the most sacred influences when *pure*, that is, unmingled with non-essentials—just by the feeling that he *must* do so and so, that he must go through a certain round of duty. It is a willing service that the lord wants; no forced devotions are either acceptable to him, or other than injurious to the worshipper, if such he can be called."

After an early dinner, I said to Turner,—

"Come out with me, and we will read that poem of Vaughan's in which I broke down to-day."

"Oh, papa!" said Connie, in a tone of injury from the sofa.

"What is it, my dear?" I asked.

"Wouldn't it be as good for us as for Mr Turner?"

"Quite, my dear. Well, I will keep it for the evening, and meantime Mr Turner and I will go and see if we can find out anything about the change in the church-service."

For I had thrown into my bag as I left the rectory a copy of "The Clergyman's Vade Mecum"—a treatise occupied with the externals of the churchman's relations—in which I soon came upon the following passage:—

"So then it appears that the common practice of reading all three together, is an innovation, and if an ancient or infirm clergyman do read them at two or three several times, he is more strictly conformable: however, this is much better than to omit any part of the liturgy, or to read all three offices into one, as is now commonly done, without any pause or distinction."

"On the part of the clergyman, you see, Turner," I said, when I had finished reading the whole passage to him. "There is no care taken of the delicate women of the congregation, but only of the ancient or infirm clergyman. And the logic, to say the least, is rather queer: is it only in virtue of his antiquity and infirmity that he is to be upheld in being more strictly conformable? The writer's honesty has its heels trodden upon by the fear of giving offence. Nevertheless there should perhaps be a certain slowness to admit change, even back to a more ancient form."

"I don't know that I can quite agree with you there," said Turner. "If the form is better, no one should hesitate to advocate the change. If it is worse, then slowness is not sufficient: utter obstinacy is the right condition."

"You are right, Turner. For the right must be the rule, and where *the right* is beyond our understanding or our reach, then *the better*, as indeed not only right compared with the other, but the sole ascent towards the right."

In the evening I took Henry Vaughan's poems into the common sitting-room, and to Connie's great delight read the whole of the lovely, though unequal little poem, called "The Retreat," in recalling which I had failed in the morning. She was especially delighted with the "white celestial thought," and the "bright shoots of everlastingness." Then I gave a few lines from another yet more unequal poem, worthy in themselves of the best of the other. I quote the first strophe entire.

CHILDHOOD.

"I cannot reach it; and my striving eye
Dazzles at it, as at eternity.

Were now that chronicle alive,
Those white designs which children drive,
And the thoughts of each harmless hour,
With their content too in my power,
Quickly would I make my path even,
And by mere playing go to heaven.

. . . . . .

And yet the practice worldlings call
Business and weighty action all,
Checking the poor child for his play,
But gravely cast themselves away.

. . . . .

An age of mysteries! which he
Must live twice that would God's face see,
Which angels guard, and with it play,
Angels! which foul men drive away.
How do I study now, and scan
Thee more than ere I studied man,
And only see through a long night
Thy edges and thy bordering light!
O for thy centre and midday!
For sure that is the *narrow way!*"

"For of such is the kingdom of heaven," said my wife softly, as I closed the book.

"May I have the book, papa?" said Connie, holding out her thin white cloud of a hand to take it.

"Certainly, my child. And if Wynnie would read it with you, she will feel more of the truth of what Mr Percivale was saying to her about finish. Here are the finest, grandest thoughts, set forth sometimes with such carelessness, at least such lack of neatness, that, instead of their falling on the mind with all their power of loveliness, they are like a beautiful face disfigured with patches, and, what is worse, they put the mind out of the right, quiet, unquestioning, open mood, which is the only fit one for the reception of such true things as are embodied in the poems. But they are too beautiful after all to be more than a little spoiled by such a lack of the finish with which Art ends off all her labours. A gentleman, however, thinks it of no little importance to have his nails nice as well as his face and his shirt."

CHAPTER XXVII.

THE OLD CASTLE.

HE place Turner had chosen suited us all so well, that after attending to my duties on the two following Sundays at Kilkhaven, I returned on the Monday or Tuesday to the farmhouse. But Turner left us in the middle of the second week, for he could not be longer absent from his charge at home, and we missed him much. It was some days before Connie was quite as cheerful again as usual. I do not mean that she was in the least gloomy—that she never was; she was only a little less merry. But whether it was that Turner had opened our eyes, or that she had visibly improved since he allowed her to make a little change in her posture—certainly she appeared to us to have made considerable progress, and every now and then we were discovering some little proof of the fact. One evening, while we were still at the farm, she startled us by calling out suddenly,—

"Papa, papa! I moved my big toe! I did indeed."

We were all about her in a moment. But I saw that she was excited, and fearing a reaction I sought to calm her.

"But, my dear," I said, as quietly as I could, "you are probably still aware that you are possessed of two big toes: which of them are we to congratulate on this first stride in the march of improvement?"

She broke out in the merriest laugh. A pause followed in which her face wore a puzzled expression. Then she said all at once, "Papa, it is very odd, but I can't tell which of them," and burst into tears. I was afraid that I had done more harm than good.

"It is not of the slightest consequence, my child," I said. "You have had so little communication with the twins of late, that it is no wonder you should not be able to tell the one from the other."

She smiled again through her sobs, but was silent, with shining face, for the rest of the evening. Our hopes took a fresh start, but we heard no more from her of her power over her big toe. As often as I inquired she said she was afraid she had made a mistake, for she had not had another hint of its existence. Still I thought it could not have been a fancy, and I would cleave to my belief in the good sign.

Percivale called to see us several times, but always appeared anxious not to intrude more of his society upon us than might be agreeable. He grew in my regard, however; and at length I asked him if he would assist me in another surprise which I meditated for my companions, and this time for Connie as well, and which I hoped would prevent the painful influences of the sight of the sea from returning upon them when they went back to Kilkhaven: they must see the sea from a quite different shore first. In a word I would take them to Tintagel, of the near position of which they were not aware, although in some of our walks we had seen the ocean in the distance. An early day was fixed for carrying out our project, and I proceeded to get everything ready. The only difficulty was to find a carriage in the neighbourhood suitable for receiving Connie's litter. In this, however, I at length succeeded, and on the morning of a glorious day of blue and gold, we set out for the little village of Trevenna, now far better known than at the time of which I write. Connie had been out every day since she came, now in one part of the fields, now in another, enjoying the expanse of earth and sky, but she had had no drive, and consequently had seen no variety of scenery. Therefore, believing she was now thoroughly able to bear it, I quite reckoned of the good she would get from the inevitable excitement. We resolved, however, after finding how much she enjoyed the few miles' drive, that we would not demand more of her strength that day, and therefore put up at the little inn, where, after ordering dinner, Percivale and I left the ladies, and sallied forth to reconnoitre.

We walked through the village and down the valley beyond, sloping steeply between hills towards the sea, the opening closed at the end by the blue of the ocean below, and the more ethereal blue of the sky above. But when we reached the mouth of the valley we found that we were not yet on the shore, for a precipice lay between us and the little beach below. On the left a great peninsula of rock stood out into the sea, upon which rose the ruins of the keep of Tintagel, while behind on the mainland stood the ruins of the castle itself, connected with the other only by a narrow isthmus. We had read that this peninsula had once been an island, and that the two parts of the castle were formerly connected by a drawbridge. Looking up at the great gap which now divided the two portions, it seemed at first impossible to believe that they had ever been thus united; but a little reflection cleared up the mystery. The fact was, that the isthmus, of half the height of the two parts connected by it, had been formed entirely by the fall of portions of the rock and soil on each side into the narrow dividing space, through which the waters of the Atlantic had been wont to sweep. And now the fragments of walls stood on the very verge of the precipice, and showed that large portions of the castle itself had fallen into the gulf between. We turned to the left along the edge of the rock, and so by a narrow path reached and crossed to the other side of the isthmus. We then found that the path led to the foot of the rock, formerly island, of the keep, and thence in a zigzag up the face of it to the top. We followed it, and after a great climb reached a door in a modern battlement. Entering, we found ourselves amidst grass, and ruins haggard with age. We turned and surveyed the path by which we had come. It was steep and somewhat difficult. But the outlook was glorious. It was indeed one of God's mounts of vision upon which we stood. The thought, "Oh that Connie could see this!" was swelling in my heart, when Percivale broke the silence—not with any remark on the glory around us, but with the commonplace question—

"You haven't got your man with you, I think, Mr Walton?"

"No," I answered; "we thought it better to leave him to look after the boys."

He was silent for a few minutes, while I gazed in delight.

"Don't you think," he said, "it would be possible to bring Miss Constance up here?"

I almost started at the idea, and had not replied before he resumed:

"It would be something for her to recur to with delight all the rest of her life."

"It would, indeed. But it is impossible."

"I do not think so—if you would allow me the honour to assist you. I think we could do it perfectly between us."

I was again silent for a while. Looking down on the way we had come, it seemed an almost dreadful undertaking. Percivale spoke again.

"As we shall come here to-morrow, we need not explore the place now. Shall we go down at once and observe the whole path, with a view to the practicability of carrying her up?"

"There can be no objection to that," I answered, as a little hope, and courage with it, began to dawn in my heart. "But you must allow it does not look very practicable."

"Perhaps it would seem more so to you, if you had come up with the idea in your head all the way, as I did. Any path seems more difficult in looking back than at the time when the difficulties themselves have to be met and overcome."

"Yes, but then you must remember that we have to take the way back whether we will or no, if we once take the way forward."

"True; and now I will go down with the descent in my head as well as under my feet."

"Well, there can be no harm in reconnoitring it at least. Let us go."

"You know we can rest almost as often as we please," said Percivale, and turned to lead the way.

It certainly was steep, and required care even in our own descent; but for a man who had climbed mountains, as I had done in my youth, it could hardly be called difficult even in middle age. By the time we had got again into the valley road I was all but convinced of the practicability of the proposal. I was a little vexed, however, I must confess, that a stranger should have thought of giving such a pleasure to Connie, when the bare wish that she might have enjoyed it had alone arisen in my mind. I comforted myself with the reflection that this was one of the ways in which we were to be weaned from the world and knit the faster to our fellows. For even the middle-aged, in the decay of their daring, must look for the fresh thought and the fresh impulse to the youth which follows at their heels in the march of life. Their part is to *will* the relation and the obligation, and so, by love to and faith in the young, keep themselves in the line along which the electric current flows, till at length they too shall once more be young and daring in the strength of the Lord. A man must always seek to rise above his moods and feelings, to let them move within him, but not allow them to storm or gloom around him. By the time we reached home we had agreed to make the attempt, and to judge by the path to the foot of the rock, which was difficult in parts, whether we should be likely to succeed, without danger, in attempting the rest of the way and the following descent. As soon as we had arrived at this conclusion, I felt so happy in the prospect that I grew quite merry, especially after we had further agreed that, both for the sake of her nerves and for the sake of the lordly surprise, we should bind Connie's eyes so that she should see nothing till we had placed her in a certain position, concerning the preferableness of which we were not of two minds.

"What mischief have you two been about?" said my wife, as we entered our room in the inn, where the cloth was already laid for dinner. "You look just like two school-boys that have been laying some plot, and can hardly hold their tongues about it."

"We have been enjoying our little walk amazingly," I answered. "So much so, that we mean to set out for another the moment dinner is over."

"I hope you will take Wynnie with you then."

"Or you, my love," I returned.

"No; I will stay with Connie."

"Very well. You, and Connie too, shall go out to morrow, for we have found a place we want to take you to. And, indeed, I believe it was our anticipation of the pleasure you and she would have in the view that made us so merry when you accused us of plotting mischief."

My wife replied only with a loving look, and dinner appearing at this moment, we sat down a happy party.

When that was over—and a very good dinner it was, just what I like, homely in material but admirable in cooking—Wynnie and Percivale and I set out again. For as Percivale and I came back in the morning we had seen the church standing far aloft and aloof on the other side of the little valley, and we wanted to go to it. It was rather a steep climb, and Wynnie accepted Percivale's offered arm. I led the way, therefore, and left them to follow—not so far in the rear, however, but that I could take a share in the conversation. It was some little time before any arose, and it was Wynnie who led the way into it.

"What kind of things do you like best to paint, Mr Percivale?" she asked.

He hesitated for several seconds, which between a question and an answer look so long, that most people would call them minutes.

"I would rather you should see some of my pictures —I should prefer that to answering your question," he said, at length.

"But I have seen some of your pictures," she returned.

"Pardon me. Indeed you have not, Miss Walton."

'At least I have seen some of your sketches and studies."

"Some of my sketches—none of my studies."

"But you make use of your sketches for your pictures, do you not?"

"Never of such as you have seen. They are only a slight antidote to my pictures."

"I cannot understand you."

I do not wonder at that. But I would rather, I repeat, say nothing about my pictures till you see some of them."

"But how am I to have that pleasure, then?"

"You go to London, sometimes, do you not?"

"Very rarely. More rarely still when the Royal Academy is open."

"That does not matter much. My pictures are seldom to be found there."

"Do you not care to send them there?"

"I send one at least every year. But they are rarely accepted."

"Why?"

This was a very improper question, I thought; but if Wynnie had thought so she would not have put it. He hesitated a little before he replied.

"It is hardly for me to say why," he answered; 'but I cannot wonder much at it, considering the subjects I choose.—But I daresay," he added, in a lighter tone, "after all, that has little to do with it, and there is something about the things themselves that precludes a favourable judgment. I avoid thinking about it. A man ought to try to look at his own work as if it were none of his, but not as with the eyes of other people. That is an impossibility, and the attempt a bewilderment. It is with his own eyes he must look, with his own judgment he must judge. The only effort is to get it set far away enough from him to be able to use his own eyes and his own judgment upon it."

"I think I see what you mean. A man has but his own eyes and his own judgment. To look with those of other people is but a fancy."

"Quite so. You understand me quite."

He said no more in explanation of his rejection by the Academy. Till we reached the church, nothing more of significance passed between them.

What a waste, bare churchyard that was! It had two or three lych-gates, but they had no roofs. They were just small enclosures, with the low stone tables to rest the living from the weight of the dead, while the clergyman, as the keeper of heaven's wardrobe, came forth to receive the garment they restored—to be laid aside as having ended its work, as having been worn done in the winds, and rains, and labours of the world. Not a tree stood in that churchyard. Rank grass was the sole covering of the soil heaved up with the dead beneath. What blasts from the awful space of the sea must rush athwart the undefended garden! The ancient church stood in the midst, with its low, strong, square tower, and its long, narrow nave, the ridge bowed with age, like the back of a horse worn out in the service of man, and its little homely chancel, like a small cottage that had leaned up against its end for shelter from the western blasts. It was locked, and we could not enter. But of all world-worn, sad-looking churches, that one—sad, even in the sunset—was the dreariest I had ever beheld. Surely, it needed the gospel of the resurrection fervently preached therein, to keep it from sinking to the dust with dismay and weariness. Such a soul alone could keep it from vanishing utterly of dismal old age. Near it was one huge mound of grass-grown rubbish, looking like the grave where some former church of the dead had been buried, when it could stand erect no longer before the onsets of Atlantic winds. I walked round and round it, gathering its architecture, and peeping in at every window I could reach. Suddenly I was aware that I was alone. Returning to the other side, I found that Percivale was seated on the churchyard wall, next the sea—it would have been less dismal had it stood immediately on the cliffs, but they were at some little distance beyond bare downs and rough stone walls: he was sketching the place, and Wynnie stood beside him, looking over his shoulder. I did not interrupt him, but walked among the graves, reading the poor memorials of the dead, and wondering how many of the words of laudation that were inscribed on their tombs were spoken of them while they were yet alive. Yet surely, in the lives of those to whom they applied the least, there had been moments when the true nature, the nature God had given them, broke forth in faith and tenderness, and would have justified the words inscribed on their gravestones! I was yet wandering and reading, and stumbling over the mounds, when my companions joined me, and, without a word, we walked out of the churchyard. We were nearly home before one of us spoke.

"That church is oppressive," said Percivale. "It looks like a great sepulchre, a place built only for the dead—the church of the dead."

"It is only that it partakes with the living," I returned; "suffers with them the buffetings of life, outlasts them, but shows, like the shield of the Red-Cross Knight, the 'old dints of deep wounds.'"

"Still, is it not a dreary place to choose for a church to stand in?"

"The church must stand everywhere. There is no region into which it must not, ought not to enter. If it refuses any earthly spot, it is shrinking from its calling. Here this one stands for the sea as for the land, high-uplifted, looking out over the waters as a sign of the haven from all storms, the rest in God. And down beneath in its storehouse lie the bodies of men—you saw the grave of some of them on the other side—flung ashore from the gulfing sea. It may be a weakness, but one would rather have the bones of his friend laid in the still Sabbath of the churchyard earth, than sweeping and swaying about as Milton imagines the bones of his friend Edward King, in that wonderful 'Lycidas.'" Then I told them the conversation I had had with the sexton at

Kilkhaven. "But," I went on, "these fancies are only the ghostly mists that hang about the eastern hills before the sun rises. We shall look down on all that with a smile by and by; for the Lord tells us that if we believe in him we shall never die."

By this time we were back once more at the inn. We gave Connie a description of what we had seen.

"What a brave old church!" said Connie.

The next day I awoke very early, full of the anticipated attempt. I got up at once, found the weather most promising, and proceeded first of all to have a look at Connie's litter, and see that it was quite sound. Satisfied of this, I rejoiced in the contemplation of its lightness and strength.

After breakfast I went to Connie's room, and told her that Mr Percivale and I had devised a treat for her. Her face shone at once.

"But we want to do it our own way."

"Of course, papa," she answered.

"Will you let us tie your eyes up?"

"Yes; and my ears and my hands too. It would be no good tying my feet, when I don't know one big toe from the other."

And she laughed merrily.

"We'll try to keep up the talk all the way, so that you shan't weary of the journey.

"You're going to carry me somewhere with my eyes tied up. Oh! how jolly! And then I shall see something all at once! Jolly! jolly!—Getting tired!" she repeated. "Even the wind on my face would be pleasure enough for half a day. I shan't get tired so soon as you will—you dear, kind papa! I am afraid I shall be dreadfully heavy. But I shan't jerk your arms much. I will lie so still!"

"And you won't mind letting Mr Percivale help me to carry you?"

"No. Why should I, if he doesn't mind it? He looks strong enough; and I am sure he is nice, and won't think me heavier than I am."

"Very well, then. I will send mamma and Wynnie to dress you at once; and we shall set out as soon as you are ready."

She clapped her hands with delight, then caught me round the neck and gave me one of my own kisses as she called the best she had, and began to call as loud as she could on her mamma and Wynnie to come and dress her.

It was indeed a glorious morning. The wind came in little wafts, like veins of cool, white silver amid the great warm, yellow gold of the sunshine. The sea lay before us, a mound of blue closing up the end of the valley, as if overpowered into quietness by the lordliness of the sun overhead; and the hills between which we went lay like great sheep, with green wool, basking in the blissful heat. The gleam from the waters came up the pass; the grand castle crowned the left-hand steep, seeming to warm its old bones, like the ruins of some awful megatherium in the lighted air; one white sail sped like a glad thought across the spandrel of the sea; the shadows of the rocks lay over our path, like transient, cool, benignant deaths, through which we had to pass again and again to yet higher glory beyond; and one lark was somewhere in whose little breast the whole world was reflected as in the convex mirror of a dewdrop, where it swelled so that he could not hold it, but let it out again through his throat, metamorphosed into music, which he poured forth over all as the libation on the outspread altar of worship.

And of all this we talked to Connie as we went; and every now and then she would clap her hands gently in the fulness of her delight, although she beheld the splendour only as with her ears, or from the kisses of the wind on her cheeks. But she seemed, since her accident, to have approached that condition which Milton represents Samson as longing for in his blindness, wherein the sight should be

> "through all parts diffused,
> That she might look at will through every pore."

I had, however, arranged with the rest of the company that the moment we reached the cliff over the shore, and turned to the left to cross the isthmus, the conversation should no longer be about the things around us: and especially I warned my wife and Wynnie that no exclamation of surprise or delight should break from them before Connie's eyes were uncovered. I had said nothing to either of them about the difficulties of the way, that, seeing us take them as ordinary things, they might take them so too, and not be uneasy.

We never stopped till we reached the foot of the peninsula, *née* island, upon which the keep of Tintagel stands.

There we set Connie down, to take breath and ease our arms before we began the arduous way.

"Now, now!" said Connie, eagerly, lifting her hands in the belief that we were on the point of undoing the bandage from her eyes.

"No, no, my love, not yet," I said, and she lay still again, only she looked more eager than before.

"I am afraid I have tired out you and Mr Percivale, papa," she said.

Percivale laughed so amusedly, that she rejoined roguishly—

"Oh yes! I know every gentleman is a Hercules—at least, he chooses to be considered one! But, notwithstanding my firm faith in the fact, I have a little womanly conscience left that is hard to hoodwink."

There was a speech for my wee Connie to make! The best answer and the best revenge was to lift her and go on. This we did, trying as well as we might to prevent the difference of level between us from tilting the litter too much for her comfort.

"Where *are* you going, papa?" she said once, but without a sign of fear in her voice, as a little slip I made lowered my end of the litter suddenly. "You must be going up a steep place. Don't hurt yourself, dear papa."

We had changed our positions, and were now carrying her, head foremost, up the hill Percivale led, and I followed. Now I could see every change on her lovely face, and it made me strong to endure; for I did find it hard work, I confess, to get to the top. It lay like a little sunny pool on which all the cloudy thoughts that moved in some unseen heaven cast exquisitely delicate changes of light and shade as they floated over it. Percivale strode on as if he bore a feather behind him. I did wish we were at the top, for my arms began to feel like iron-cables, stiff and stark—only I was afraid of my fingers giving way. My heart was beating uncomfortably too. But Percivale, I felt almost inclined to quarrel with him before it was over, he strode on so unconcernedly, turning every corner of the zigzag where I expected him to propose a halt, and striding on again, as if there could be no pretence for any change of procedure. But I held out, strengthened by the play on my daughter's face, delicate as the play on an opal—one that inclines more to the milk than the fire.

When at length we turned in through the gothic door in the battlemented wall, and set our lovely burden down upon the grass—

"Percivale," I said, forgetting the proprieties in the affected humour of being angry with him, so glad was I that we had her at length on the mount of glory, "why did you go on walking like a castle, and pay no heed to me?"

"You didn't speak, did you Mr Walton?" he returned, with just a shadow of solicitude in the question.

"No. Of course not," I rejoined.

"Oh, then," he returned, in a tone of relief, "how could I? You were my captain: how could I give in so long as you were holding on?"

I am afraid the *Percivale*, without the *Mister*, came

again and again after this, though I pulled myself up for it as often as I caught myself.

"Now, papa!" said Connie from the grass.

"Not yet, my dear. Wait till your mamma and Wynnie come. Let us go and meet them, Mr Percivale."

"Oh yes, do, papa. Leave me alone here without knowing where I am or what kind of a place I am in. I should like to know how it feels. I have never been alone in all my life."

"Very well, my dear," I said; and Percivale and I left her alone in the ruins.

We found Ethelwyn toiling up with Wynnie helping her all she could.

"Dear Harry," she said, "how could you think of bringing Connie up such an awful place? I wonder you dared to do it."

"It's done, you see, wife," I answered, "thanks to Mr Percivale, who has nearly torn the breath out of me. But now we must get you up, and you will say that to see Connie's delight, not to mention your own, is quite wages for the labour."

"Isn't she afraid to find herself so high up?"

"She knows nothing about it yet."

"You do not mean you have left the child there with her eyes tied up."

"To be sure. We could not uncover them before you came. It would spoil half the pleasure."

"Do let us make haste then. It is surely dangerous to leave her so."

Page 361.

"Not in the least; but she must be getting tired of the darkness. Take my arm now."

"Don't you think Mrs. Walton had better take my arm?" said Percivale, "and then you can put your hand on her back, and help her a little that way."

We tried the plan, found it a good one, and soon reached the top. The moment our eyes fell upon Connie, we could see that she had found the place neither fearful nor lonely. The sweetest ghost of a smile hovered on her pale face, which shone in the shadow of the old gateway of the keep, with light from within her own sunny soul. She lay in such still expectation, that you would have thought she had just fallen asleep after receiving an answer to a prayer, reminding me of a little-known sonnet of Wordsworth's, in which he describes as the type of Death—

the face of one
Sleeping alone within a mossy cave,
With her face up to heaven; that seemed to have
Pleasing remembrance of a thought foregone;
A lovely beauty in a summer grave.*

But she heard our steps, and her face awoke.

"Is mamma come?"

"Yes, my darling. I am here," said her mother. "How do you feel?"

"Perfectly well, mamma, thank you. Now, papa!"

"One moment more, my love. Now, Percivale."

We carried her to the spot we had agreed upon, and

* Miscellaneous Sonnets. Part I. 28.

while we held her a little inclined that she might see the better, her mother undid the bandage from her head.

"Hold your hands over her eyes, a little way from them," I said to her as she untied the handkerchief, "that the light may reach them by degrees, and not blind her."

Ethelwyn did so for a few moments, then removed them. Still for a moment or two more, it was plain from her look of utter bewilderment, that all was a confused mass of light and colour. Then she gave a little cry, and to my astonishment, almost fear, half rose to a sitting posture. One moment more, and she laid herself gently back, and wept and sobbed.

And now I may admit my reader to a share, though at best but a dim reflex in my poor words, of the glory that made her weep.

Through the gothic-arched door in the battlemented wall, which stood on the very edge of the precipitous descent, so that nothing of the descent was seen and the door was as a framework to the picture, Connie saw a great gulf at her feet, full to the brim of a splendour of light and colour. Before her rose the great ruins of rock and castle, the ruin of rock with castle; rough stone below, clear green happy grass above, even to the verge of the abrupt and awful precipice; over it the summer sky so clear that it must have been clarified by sorrow and thought; at the foot of the rocks, hundreds of feet below, the blue waters breaking in white upon the dark gray sands; all full of the gladness of the sun overflowing in speechless delight, and reflected in fresh gladness from stone, and water, and flower, like new springs of light rippling forth from the earth itself to swell the universal tide of glory—all this seen through the narrow gothic archway of a door in a wall—up—down—on either hand. But the main marvel was the look sheer below into the abyss full of light, and air, and colour, its sides lined with rock and grass, and its bottom lined with blue ripples and sand. Was it any wonder that my Connie should cry aloud when the vision dawned upon her, and then weep to ease a heart ready to burst with delight? "O Lord God!" I said, almost involuntarily, "thou art very rich. Thou art the one poet, the one maker. We worship thee. Make but our souls as full of glory in thy sight as this chasm is to our eyes glorious with the forms which thou hast cloven and carved out of nothingness, and we shall be worthy to worship thee, O Lord, our God." For I was carried beyond myself with delight, and with sympathy with Connie's delight and with the calm worship of gladness in my wife's countenance. But when my eye fell on Wynnie, I saw a trouble mingled with her admiration, a self-accusation, I think, that she did not and could not enjoy it more; and when I turned from her, there were the eyes of Percivale fixed on me in wonderment; and for the moment I felt as David must have felt when, in his dance of undignified delight that he had got the ark home again, he saw the contemptuous eyes of Michal fixed on him from the window. But I could not leave it so. I said to him—coldly I daresay,—

"Excuse me, Mr Percivale; I forgot for the moment that I was not amongst my own family."

Percivale took his hat off.

"Forgive my seeming rudeness, Mr Walton. I was half envying and half wondering. You would not be surprised at my unconscious behaviour if you had seen as much of the wrong side of the stuff as I have seen in London."

I had some idea of what he meant; but this was no time to enter upon a discussion. I could only say,—

"My heart was full, Mr Percivale, and I let it overflow."

"Let me at least share in its overflow," he rejoined, and nothing more passed on the subject.

For the next ten minutes we stood in absolute silence. We had set Connie down on the grass again, but propped up so that she could see through the doorway. And she lay in still ecstasy. But there was more to be seen ere we descended. There was the rest of the little islet with its crop of down-grass, on which the horses of all the knights of King Arthur's round table might have fed for a week--yes, for a fortnight, without, by any means, encountering the short commons of war. There were the ruins of the castle so built of plates of the laminated stone of the rocks on which they stood, and so woven in, or more properly incorporated with, the outstanding rocks themselves, that in some parts I found it impossible to tell which was building and which was rock—the walls themselves seeming like a growth out of the island itself, so perfectly were they in harmony with, and in kind the same as, the natural ground upon which and of which they had been constructed. And this would seem to me to be the perfection of architecture. The work of man's hands should be so in harmony with the place where it stands that it must look as if it had grown out of the soil. But the walls were in some parts so thin that one wondered how they could have stood so long. They must have been built before the time of any formidable artillery—enough only for defence from arrows. But then the island was nowhere commanded, and its own steep cliffs would be more easily defended than any erections upon it. Clearly the intention was that no enemy should thereon find rest for the sole of his foot, for if he was able to land, farewell to the notion of any further defence. Then there was outside the walls the little chapel—such a tiny chapel! of which little more than the foundation remained, with the ruins of the altar still standing, and outside the chancel, nestling by its wall, a coffin hollowed in the rock; then the churchyard a little way off full of graves, which, I presume, would have vanished long ago were it not that the very graves were founded on the rock. There still stood old worn-out headstones of thin slate, but no memorials were left. Then there was the fragment of arched passage underground laid open to the air in the centre of the islet; and last, and grandest of all, the awful edges of the rock, broken by time, and carved by the winds and the waters into grotesque shapes and threatening forms. Over all the surface of the islet we carried Connie, and from three sides of this sea-fortress she looked abroad over "the

Atlantic's level powers." It blew a gentle ethereal breeze on the top; but had there been such a wind as I have since stood against on that fearful citadel of nature, I should have been in terror lest we should all be blown into the deep. Over the edge she peeped at the strange fantastic needle-rock, and round the corner she peeped to see Wynnie and her mother seated in what they call Arthur's chair—a canopied hollow wrought in the plated rock by the mightiest of all solvents—air and water; till at length it was time that we should take our leave of the few sheep that fed over the place, and issuing by the gothic door, wind away down the dangerous path to the safe ground below.

"I think we had better tie up your eyes again, Connie?" I said.

"Why?" she asked, in wonderment. "There's nothing higher yet, is there?"

"No, my love. If there were, you would hardly be able for it to-day, I should think. It is only to keep you from being frightened at the precipice as you go down."

"But I shan't be frightened, papa."

"How do you know that?"

"Because you are going to carry me."

"But what if I should slip? I might, you know."

"I don't mind. I shan't mind being tumbled over the precipice, if you do it. I shan't be to blame, and I'm sure you won't, papa." Then she drew my head down and whispered in my ear, "If I get as much more by being killed, as I have got by having my poor back hurt, I'm sure it will be well worth it."

I tried to smile a reply, for I could not speak one. We took her just as she was, and with some tremor on my part, but not a single slip, we bore her down the winding path, her face showing all the time that, instead of being afraid, she was in a state of ecstatic delight. My wife, I could see, was nervous, however; and she breathed a sigh of relief when we were once more at the foot.

"Well, I'm glad that's over," she said.

"So am I," I returned as we set down the litter.

"Poor papa! I've pulled his arms to pieces! and Mr Percivale's too!"

Percivale answered first by taking up a huge piece of stone. Then turning towards her, he said—"Look here, Miss Connie;" and flung it far out from the isthmus on which we were resting. We heard it strike on a rock below, and then fall in a shower of fragments. "My arms are all right, you see," he said.

Meantime, Wynnie had scrambled down to the shore, where we had not yet been. In a few minutes, we still lingering, she came running back to us out of breath with the news—

"Papa! Mr Percivale! there's such a grand cave down there! It goes right through under the island."

Connie looked so eager, that Percivale and I glanced at each other, and without a word, lifted her, and followed Wynnie. It was a little way that we had to carry her down, but it was very broken, and insomuch more difficult than the other. At length we stood in the cavern. What a contrast to the vision overhead!—

nothing to be seen but the cool, dark vault of the cave, long and winding, with the fresh seaweed lying on its pebbly floor, and its walls wet with the last tide, for every tide rolled through in rising and falling—the waters on the opposite sides of the islet greeting through this cave; the blue shimmer of the rising sea, and the forms of huge outlying rocks, looking in at the further end, where the roof rose like a grand cathedral arch; and the green gleam of veins rich with copper, dashing and streaking the darkness in gloomy little chapels, where the floor of heaped-up pebbles rose and rose within till it met the descending roof. It was like a going-down from Paradise into the grave—but a cool, friendly, brown-lighted grave, which even in its darkest recesses bore some witness to the wind of God outside, in the occasional ripple of shadowed light, from the play of the sun on the waves, that, flected and reflected, wandered across its jagged roof. But we dared not keep Connie long in the damp coolness; and I have given my reader quite enough of description for one hour's reading. He can scarcely be equal to more.

My invalids had now beheld the sea in such a different aspect, that I no longer feared to go back to Kilkhaven. Thither we went three days after, and at my invitation, Percivale took Turner's place in the carriage.

CHAPTER XXVIII.

JOE AND HIS TROUBLE.

HOW bright the yellow shores of Kilkhaven looked after the dark sands of Tintagel! But how low and tame its highest cliffs after the mighty rampart of rocks which there face the sea like a cordon of fierce guardians! It was pleasant to settle down again in what had begun to look like home, and was indeed made such by the boisterous welcome of Dora and the boys. Connie's baby crowed aloud, and stretched forth her chubby arms at sight of her. The wind blew gently around us, full both of the freshness of the clean waters and the scents of the down-grasses, to welcome us back. And the dread vision of the shore had now receded so far into the past, that it was no longer able to hurt.

We had called at the blacksmith's house on our way home, and found that he was so far better as to be working at his forge again. His mother said he was used to such attacks, and soon got over them. I, however, feared that they indicated an approaching break-down.

"Indeed, sir," she said, "Joe might be well enough if he liked. It's all his own fault."

"What do you mean?" I asked. "I cannot believe that your son is in any way guilty of his own illness."

"He's a well-behaved lad, my Joe," she answered; "but he hasn't learned what I had to learn long ago."

"What is that?" I asked.

"To make up his mind, and stick to it. To do one thing or the other."

She was a woman with a long upper lip and a judicial face, and as she spoke, her lip grew longer and longer; and when she closed her mouth in mark of her own resolution, that lip seemed to occupy two-thirds of all her face under the nose.

"And what is it he won't do?"

"I don't mind whether he does it or not, if he would only make—up—his—mind—and—stick—to— it."

"What is it you want him to do, then?"

"I don't want him to do it, I'm sure. It's no good to me—and wouldn't be much to him, that I'll be bound. Howsomever, he must please himself."

I thought it not very wonderful that he looked gloomy, if there was no more sunshine for him at home than his mother's face indicated. Few things can make a man so strong and able for his work as a sun indoors, whose rays are smiles, ever ready to shine upon him when he opens the door,—the face of wife or mother or sister. Now his mother's face certainly was not sunny. No doubt it must have shone upon him when he was a baby. God has made that provision for babies, who need sunshine so much that a mother's face cannot help being sunny to them: why should the sunshine depart as the child grows older?

"Well, I suppose I must not ask. But I fear your son is very far from well. Such attacks do not often occur without serious mischief somewhere. And if there is anything troubling him, he is less likely to get over it."

"If he would let somebody make up his mind for him, and then stick to it,"——

"Oh! but that is impossible, you know. A man must must make up his own mind."

"That's just what he won't do."

All the time she looked naughty, only after a self-righteous fashion. It was evident that whatever was the cause of it, she was not in sympathy with her son, and therefore could not help him out of any difficulty he might be in. I made no further attempt to learn from her the cause of her son's discomfort, clearly a deeper cause than his illness. In passing his workshop, we stopped for a moment, and I made an arrangement to meet him at the church the next day.

I was there before him, and found that he had done a good deal since we left. Little remained except to get the keys put to rights, and the rods attached to the cranks in the box. To-day he was to bring a carpenter, a cousin of his own, with him.

They soon arrived, and a small consultation followed.

The cousin was a bright-eyed, cheruby-cheeked little man, with a ready smile and white teeth: I thought he might help me to understand what was amiss in Joseph's affairs. But I would not make the attempt except openly. I therefore said, half in a jocular fashion, as with gloomy, self-withdrawn countenance the smith was fitting one loop into another in two of his iron rods,—

"I wish we could get this cousin of yours to look a little more cheerful. You would think he had quarrelled with the sunshine."

The carpenter showed his white teeth between his rosy lips.

"Well, sir, if you'll excuse me, you see my cousin Joe is not like the rest of us. He's a religious man, is Joe."

"But I don't see how that should make him miserable. It hasn't made me miserable. I hope I'm a religious man myself. It makes me happy every day of my life."

"Ah, well," returned the carpenter, in a thoughtful tone, as he worked away gently to get the inside out of the oak-chest without hurting it, "I don't say it's the religion, for I don't know; but perhaps it's the way he takes it up. He don't look after hisself enough; he's always thinking about other people, you see, sir; and it seems to me, sir, that if you don't look after yourself, why, who is to look after you? That's common sense, *I* think."

It was a curious contrast—the merry friendly face, which shone good-fellowship to all mankind, accusing the sombre, pale, sad, severe, even somewhat bitter countenance beside him, of thinking too much about other people, and too little about himself. Of course it might be correct in a way. There is all the difference between a comfortable, healthy inclination, and a pained conscientious principle. It was a smile very unlike his cousin's with which Joe heard his remarks on himself.

"But," I said, "you will allow, at least, that if everybody would take Joe's way of it, there would then be no occasion for taking care of yourself."

"I don't see why, sir."

"Why, because everybody would take care of everybody else."

"Not so well, I doubt, sir."

"Yes, and a great deal better."

"At any rate, that 's a long way off; and meantime, *who*'s to take care of the odd man like Joe there, that don't look after hisself?"

"Why, God, of course."

"Well, there 's just where I 'm out. I don't know nothing about that branch, sir."

I saw a grateful light mount up in Joe's gloomy eyes, as I spoke thus upon his side of the question. He said nothing, however; and his cousin volunteering no further information, I did not push any advantage I might have gained.

At noon I made them leave their work, and come home with me to have their dinner: they hoped to finish the job before dusk Harry Cobb and I dropped behind, and Joe Harper walked on in front, apparently sunk in meditation.

Scarcely were we out of the churchyard, and on the road leading to the rectory, when I saw the sexton's daughter meeting us. She had almost come up to Joe before he saw her, for his gaze was bent on the ground, and he started. They shook hands in what seemed to me an odd, constrained, yet familiar fashion, and then stood as if they wanted to talk, but without speaking. Harry and I passed, both with a nod of recognition to the young woman, but neither of us had the ill manners to look behind. I glanced at Harry, and he answered me with a queer look. When we reached the turning that would hide them from our view, I looked back almost involuntarily, and there they were still standing. But before we reached the door of the rectory, Joe got up with us.

There was something remarkable in the appearance of Agnes Coombes, the sexton's daughter. She was about six and twenty, I should imagine, the youngest of the family, with a sallow, rather sickly complexion, somewhat sorrowful eyes, a smile rare and sweet, a fine figure, tall and slender, and a graceful gait. I now saw, I thought, a good hair's-breadth further into the smith's affairs. Beyond the hair's-breadth, however, all was dark. But I saw likewise that the well of truth, whence I might draw the whole business, must be the girl's mother.

After the men had had their dinner and rested a while, they went back to the church, and I went to the sexton's cottage. I found the old man seated at the window, with his pot of beer on the sill, and an empty plate beside it.

"Come in, sir," he said, rising, as I put my head in at the door. "The mis'ess ben't in, but she'll be here in a few minutes."

"Oh, it's of no consequence," I said. "Are they all well?"

"All comfortable, sir. It be fine dry weather for them, this, sir. It be in winter it be worst for them."

"But it's a snug enough shelter you've got here. It seems such, anyhow; though, to be sure, it is the blasts of winter that find out the weak places both in house and body."

"It ben't the wind touch *them*," he said; "they be safe enough from the wind. It be the wet, sir. There ben't much snow in these parts; but when it du come, that be very bad for them, poor things!"

Could it be that he was harping on the old theme again?

"But at least this cottage keeps out the wet," I said. "If not, we must have it seen to."

"This cottage du well enough, sir. It'll last my time, anyhow."

"Then why are you pitying your family for having to live in it?"

"Bless your heart, sir! It's not them. They du well enough. It's my people out yonder. You've got the souls to look after, and I've got the bodies. That's what it be, sir. To be sure!"

The last exclamation was uttered in a tone of impatient

surprise at my stupidity in giving all my thoughts and sympathies to the living, and none to the dead. I pursued the subject no further, but as I lay in bed that night, it began to dawn upon me as a lovable kind of hallucination in which the man indulged. He too had an office in the church of God, and he would magnify that office. He could not bear that there should be no further outcome of his labour; that the burying of the dead out of sight should be "the be-all and the end-all." He was God's vicar, the gardener in God's Acre, as the Germans call the churchyard. When all others had forsaken the dead, he remained their friend, caring for what little comfort yet remained possible to them. Hence in all changes of air and sky above, he attributed to them some knowledge of the same, and some share in their consequences even down in the darkness of the tomb. It was his way of keeping up the relation between the living and the dead. Finding I made him no reply, he took up the word again.

"You 've got your part, sir, and I 've got mine. You up into the pulpit, and I down into the grave. But it 'll be all the same by and by."

"I hope it will," I answered. "But when you do go down into your own grave, you 'll know a good deal less about it than you do now. You 'll find you 've got other things to think about. But here comes your wife. She'll talk about the living rather than the dead."

"That 's natural, sir. She brought 'em to life, and I buried 'em—at least the best part of 'em. If only I had the other two safe down with the rest!"

I remembered what the old woman had told me—that she had two boys *in* the sea; and I knew therefore what he meant. He regarded his drowned boys as still tossed about in the weary wet cold ocean, and would have gladly laid them to rest in the warm dry churchyard.

He wiped a tear from the corner of his eye with the back of his hand, and saying, "Well, I must be off to my gardening," left me with his wife. I saw then that, humourist as the old man might be, his humour, like that of all true humourists, lay close about the wells of weeping.

"The old man seems a little out of sorts," I said to his wife.

"Well, sir," she answered, with her usual gentleness, a gentleness which obedient suffering had perfected, "this be the day he buried our Nancy, this day two years; and to-day Agnes be come home from her work poorly; and the two things together they've upset him a bit."

"I met Agnes coming this way. Where is she?"

"I believe she be in the churchyard, sir. I've been to the doctor about her."

"I hope it's nothing serious."

"I hope not, sir; but you see—four on 'em, sir!"

"Well, she's in God's hands, you know."

"That she be, sir."

"I want to ask you about something, Mrs Coombes."

"What be that, sir? If I can tell, I will, you may be sure, sir."

"I want to know what's the matter with Joe Harper, the blacksmith."

"They du say it be a consumption, sir."

"But what has he got on his mind?"

"He's got nothing on his mind, sir. He be as good a by as ever stepped, I assure you, sir."

"But I am sure there is something or other on his mind. He's not so happy as he should be. He's not the man, it seems to me, to be unhappy because he's ill. A man like him would not be miserable because he was going to die. It might make him look sad sometimes, but not gloomy as he looks."

"Well, sir, I believe you be right, and perhaps I know summat. But it's part guessing.—I believe my Agnes and Joe Harper are as fond upon one another as any two in the county."

"Are they not going to be married then?"

"There be the pint, sir. I don't believe Joe ever said a word o' the sort to Aggy. She never could ha' kep it from me, sir."

"Why doesn't he then?"

"That's the pint again, sir. All as knows him says it's because he be in such bad health, and he thinks he oughtn't to go marrying with one foot in the grave. He never said so to me; but I think very likely that be it."

"For that matter, Mrs Coombes, we've all got one foot in the grave, I think."

"That be very true, sir."

"And what does your daughter think?"

"I believe she thinks the same. And so they go on talking to each other, quiet-like, like old married folks, not like lovers at all, sir. But I can't help fancying it have something to do with my Aggy's pale face."

"And something to do with Joe's pale face too, Mrs Coombes," I said. "Thank you. You've told me more than I expected. It explains everything. I must have it out with Joe now."

"Oh deary me! sir, don't go and tell him I said anything, as if I wanted him to marry my daughter."

"Don't you be afraid. I'll take good care of that. And don't fancy I'm fond of meddling with other people's affairs. But this is a case in which I ought to do something. Joe's a fine fellow."

"That he be, sir. I couldn't wish a better for a son-in-law."

I put on my hat.

"You won't get me into no trouble with Joe, will ye sir?"

"Indeed I will not, Mrs Coombes. I should be doing a great deal more harm than good if I said a word to make him doubt you."

I went straight to the church. There were the two men working away in the shadowy tower, and there was Agnes standing beside, knitting like her mother, so quiet, so solemn even, that it did indeed look as if she were a long-married wife, hovering about her husband at his work. Harry was saying something to her as I went in, but when they saw me they were silent, and Agnes gently withdrew.

"Do you think you will get through to-night?" I asked.

"Sure of it, sir," answered Harry.

"You shouldn't be sure of anything, Harry. We are told in the New Testament that we ought to say *If the Lord will*," said Joe.

"Now, Joe, you're too hard upon Harry," I said. "You don't think that the Bible means to pull a man up every step like that, till he's afraid to speak a word? It was about a long journey and a year's residence that the Apostle James was speaking."

"No doubt, sir. But the principle's the same. Harry can no more be sure of finishing his work before it be dark, than those people could be of going their long journey."

"That is perfectly true. But you are taking the letter for the spirit, and that, I suspect, in more ways than one. The religion does not lie in not being sure about anything, but in a loving desire that the will of God in the matter, whatever it be, may be done. And if Harry has not learned yet to care about the will of God, what is the good of coming down upon him that way, as if that would teach him in the least. When he loves God, then, and not till then, will he care about his will. Nor does the religion lie in saying, *if the Lord will*, every time anything is to be done. It is a most dangerous thing to use sacred words often. It makes them so common to our ear that at length, when used most solemnly, they have not half the effect they ought to have, and that is a serious loss. What the Apostle means is, that we should always be in the mood of looking up to God and having regard to his will, not always writing D.V. for instance, as so many do—most irreverently, I think—using a Latin contraction for the beautiful words, just as if they were a charm, or as if God would take offence if they did not make the salvo of acknowledgment. It seems to me quite heathenish. Our hearts ought ever to be in the spirit of those words; our lips ought to utter them rarely. Besides, there are some things a man might be pretty sure the Lord wills."

"It sounds fine, sir; but I'm not sure that I understand what you mean to say. It sounds to me like a darkening of wisdom."

I saw I had irritated him, and so had in some measure lost ground. But Harry struck in—

"How *can* you say that now, Joe? *I* know what the parson means well enough, and everybody knows I 'ain't got half the brains you 've got."

"The reason is, Harry, that he 's got something in his head that stands in the way."

"And there 's nothing in my head *to* stand in the way!" returned Harry, laughing.

This made me laugh too, and even Joe could not help a sympathetic grin. By this time it was getting dark.

"I 'm afraid, Harry, after all, you won't get through to-night."

"I begin to think so too, sir. And there 's Joe saying, 'I told you so,' over and over to himself, though he won't say it out like a man."

Joe answered only with another grin.

"I tell you what it is, Harry," I said—"you must come again on Monday. And on your way home just look in and tell Joe's mother that I have kept him over to-morrow. The change will do him good."

"No, sir, that can't be. I haven't got a clean shirt."

"You can have a shirt of mine," I said. "But I 'm afraid you 'll want your Sunday clothes."

"I 'll bring them for you, Joe—before you 're up," interposed Harry. "And then you can go to church with Aggy Coombes, you know."

Here was just what I wanted.

"Hold your tongue, Harry," said Joe angrily. "You 're talking of what you don't know anything about."

"Well, Joe, I ben't a fool, if I ben't so religious as you be. You ben't a bad fellow, though you be a Methodist, and I ben't a fool, though I be Harry Cobb."

"What do you mean, Harry? Do hold your tongue."

"Well, I 'll tell you what I mean first, and then I 'll hold my tongue. I mean this—that nobody with two eyes, or one eye, for that matter, in his head, could help seeing the eyes you and Aggy make at each other, and why you don't port your helm and board her—I won't say it 's more than I know, but I du say it be more than I think be fair to the young woman."

"Hold your tongue, Harry."

"I said I would when I 'd answered you as to what I

meaned. So no more at present; but I 'll be over with your clothes afore you 're up in the morning."

As Harry spoke he was busy gathering his tools.

"They won't be in the way, will they, sir?" he said, as he heaped them together in the furthest corner of the tower.

"Not in the least," I returned. "If I had my way, all the tools used in building the church should be carved on the posts and pillars of it, to indicate the sacredness of labour, and the worship of God that lies, not in building the church merely, but in every honest trade honestly pursued for the good of mankind and the need of the workman. For a necessity of God is laid upon every workman as well as on St Paul. Only St Paul saw it, and every workman doesn't, Harry."

"Thank you, sir. I like that way of it. I almost think I could be a little bit religious after your way of it, sir."

"Almost, Harry!" growled Joe, not unkindly.

"Now you hold your tongue, Joe," I said. "Leave Harry to me. You may take him, if you like, after I 've done with him."

Laughing merrily, but making no other reply than a hearty good-night, Harry strode away out of the church, and Joe and I went home together.

When he had had his tea, I asked him to go out with me for a walk.

The sun was shining aslant upon the downs from over the sea. We rose out of the shadowy hollow to the sunlit brow. I was a little in advance of Joe. Happening to turn, I saw the light full on his head and face, while the rest of his body had not yet emerged from the shadow.

"Stop, Joe," I said. "I want to see you so for a moment."

He stood—a little surprised.

"You look just like a man rising from the dead, Joe," I said.

"I don't know what you mean, sir," he returned.

"I will describe yourself to you. Your head and face are full of sunlight, the rest of your body is still buried in the shadow. Look; I will stand where you are now; and you come here. You will soon see what I mean."

We changed places. Joe stared for a moment. Then his face brightened.

"I see what you mean, sir," he said. "I fancy you don't mean the resurrection of the body, but the resurrection of righteousness."

"I do, Joe. Did it ever strike you that the whole history of the Christian life is a series of such resurrections? Every time a man bethinks himself that he is not walking in the light, that he has been forgetting himself, and must repent, that he has been asleep and must awake, that he has been letting his garments trail, and must gird up the loins of his mind—every time this takes place, there is a resurrection in the world. Yes, Joe; and every time that a man finds that his heart is troubled, that he is not rejoicing in God, a resurrection must follow—a resurrection out of the night of troubled thoughts into the gladness of the truth. For the truth is, and ever was, and ever must be, gladness, however much the souls on which it shines may be obscured by the clouds of sorrow, troubled by the thunders of fear, or shot through with the lightnings of pain. Now, Joe, will you let me tell you what you are like—I do not know your thoughts; I am only judging from your words and looks?"

"You may if you like, sir," answered Joe, a little sulkily. But I was not to be repelled.

I stood up in the sunlight, so that my eyes caught only about half the sun's disc. Then I bent my face towards the earth.

"What part of me is the light shining on now, Joe?"

"Just the top of your head," answered he.

"There, then," I returned, "that is just what you are like—a man with the light on his head, but not on his face. And why not on your face? Because you hold your head down."

"Isn't it possible, sir, that a man might lose the light on his face, as you put it, by doing his duty?"

"That is a difficult question," I replied. "I must think before I answer it."

"I mean," added Joe—"mightn't his duty be a painful one?"

"Yes. But I think that would rather etherealize than destroy the light. Behind the sorrow would spring a yet greater light from the very duty itself. I have expressed myself badly, but you will see what I mean.—To be frank with you, Joe, I do not see that light in your face. Therefore I think something must be wrong with you. Remember a good man is not necessarily in the right. St Peter was a good man, yet our Lord called him Satan—and meant it of course, for he never said what he did not mean."

"How can I be wrong when all my trouble comes from doing my duty—nothing else, as far as I know?"

"Then," I replied, a sudden light breaking in on my mind, "I doubt whether what you suppose to be your duty can be your duty. If it were, I do not think it would make you so miserable. At least—I may be wrong, but I venture to think so."

"What is a man to go by, then? If he thinks a thing is his duty, is he not to do it?"

"Most assuredly—until he knows better. But it is of the greatest consequence whether the supposed duty be the will of God or the invention of one's own fancy or mistaken judgment. A real duty is always something right in itself. The duty a man makes his for the time, by supposing it to be a duty, may be something quite wrong in itself. The duty of a Hindoo widow is to burn herself on the body of her husband. But that duty lasts no longer than till she sees that, not being the will of God, it is not her duty. A real duty, on the other hand, is a necessity of the human nature, without seeing and doing which a man can never attain to the truth and blessedness of his own being. It was the duty of the early hermits to encourage the growth of vermin upon their bodies, for they supposed that was pleasing to God; but they could not fare so well as if they had seen the truth that the will of God was cleanliness. And there may be far more serious things done by Christian people against the will of God, in the fancy of doing their duty, than such a trifle as swarming with worms. In a word, thinking a thing is your duty makes it your duty only till you know better. And the prime duty of every man is to seek and find, that he may do, the will of God."

"But do you think, sir, that a man is likely to be doing what he ought not, if he is doing what he don't like?"

"Not *so* likely, I allow. But there may be ambition in it. A man must not want to be better than the right. That is the delusion of the anchorite—a delusion in which the man forgets the rights of others for the sake of his own sanctity."

"It might be for the sake of another person, and not for the person's own sake at all."

"It might be; but except it were the will of God for that other person, it would be doing him or her a real injury."

We were coming gradually towards what I wanted to make the point in question. I wished him to tell me all about it himself, however, for I knew that while advice given on request is generally disregarded, to offer advice unasked is worthy only of a fool.

"But how are you to know the will of God in every case?" asked Joe.

"By looking at the general laws of life, and obeying them—except there be anything special in a particular case to bring it under a higher law."

"Ah! but that be just what there is here."

"Well, my dear fellow, that may be; but the special conduct may not be right for the special case for all that. The speciality of the case may not be even sufficient to take it from under the ordinary rule. But it is of no use talking generals. Let us come to particulars. If you can trust me, tell me all about it, and we may be able to let some light in. I am sure there is darkness somewhere."

"I will turn it over in my mind, sir; and if I can bring myself to talk about it, I will. I would rather tell you than any one else."

I said no more. We watched a glorious sunset—there never was a grander place for sunsets—and went home.

CHAPTER XXIX.

A SMALL ADVENTURE.

HE next morning Harry came with the clothes. But Joe did not go to church. Neither did Agnes make her appearance that morning. They were both present at the evening service, however.

When we came out of church, it was cloudy and dark, and the wind was blowing cold from the sea. The sky was covered with one cloud, but the waves tossing themselves against the rocks, flashed whiteness out of the general gloom. As the tide rose the wind increased. It was a night of surly temper—hard and gloomy. Not a star cracked the blue above—there was no blue; and the wind was *gurly:* I once heard that word in Scotland, and never forgot it.

After one of our usual gatherings in Connie's room, which were much shorter here because of the evening service in summer, I withdrew till supper should be ready.

Now I have always had, as I think I have incidentally stated before, a certain peculiar pleasure in the surly aspects of nature. When I was a young man this took form in opposition and defiance; since I had begun to grow old the form had changed into a sense of safety. I welcomed such aspects, partly at least, because they roused my faith to look through and beyond the small region of human conditions in which alone the storm can be and blow, and thus induced a feeling like that of the child who lies in his warm crib and listens to the howling of one of these same storms outside the strong-built house which yet trembles at its fiercer onsets: the house is not in danger; or, if it be, that is his father's business, not his. Hence it came that, after supper, I put on my great-coat and travelling cap, and went out into the ill-tempered night—speaking of it in its human symbolism.

I meant to have a stroll down to the breakwater, of which I have yet said little, but which was a favourite resort both of myself and my children. At the further end of it, always covered at high water, was an outlying cluster of low rocks, in the heart of which the lord of the manor, a noble-hearted Christian gentleman of the old school, had constructed a bath of graduated depth—an open-air swimming pool—the only really safe place for men who were swimmers to bathe in. Thither I was in the habit of taking my two little men every morning, and bathing with them, that I might develop the fish that was in them; for, as George Herbert says—

> Man is everything,
> And more: he is a tree, yet bears no fruit;
> A beast, yet is, or should be, more;"

and he might have gone on to say that he is, or should be, a fish as well.

It will seem strange to any reader who can recall the position of my Connie's room, that the nearest way to the breakwater should be through that room; but so it was. I mention the fact because I want my readers to understand a certain peculiarity of the room. By the side of the window which looked out upon the breakwater was a narrow door, apparently of a closet or cupboard, which communicated, however, with a narrow, curving, wood-built passage, leading into a little wooden hut, the walls of which were by no means impervious to the wind, for they were formed of outside-planks, with the bark still upon them. From this hut one or two little windows looked seaward, and a door led out on the bit of sward in which lay the flower-bed under Connie's window. From this spot again a door in the low wall and thick hedge led out on the downs, where a path wound along the cliffs that formed the side of the bay, till, descending under the storm-tower, it brought you to the root of the breakwater.

This mole stretched its long strong low back to a rock a good way out, breaking the force of the waves, and rendering the channel of a small river, that here flowed into the sea across the sands from the mouth of the canal, a refuge from the Atlantic. But it was a roadway often hard to reach. In fair weather even, the wind falling as the vessel rounded the point of the breakwater into the calm of the projecting headlands, the under-current would sometimes dash her helpless on the rocks. During all this heavenly summer there had been no thought or fear of any such disaster. The present night was a hint of what weather would yet come.

When I went into Connie's room, I found her lying in bed a very picture of peace. But my entrance destroyed the picture.

"Papa," she said, "why have you got your coat on? Surely you are not going out to-night. The wind is blowing dreadfully."

"Not very dreadfully, Connie. It blew much worse the night we found your baby."

"But it is very dark."

"I allow that; but there is a glimmer from the sea. I am only going on the breakwater for a few minutes. You know I like a stormy night quite as much as a fine one."

"I shall be miserable till you come home, papa."

"Nonsense, Connie. You don't think your father hasn't sense to take care of himself! Or rather, Connie, for I grant that is poor ground of comfort, you don't think I can go anywhere without my Father to take care of me?"

"But there is no occasion—is there, papa?"

"Do you think I should be better pleased with my boys if they shrunk from everything involving the least possibility of danger because there was no occasion for it? That is just the way to make cowards. And I am certain God would not like his children to indulge in such moods of self-preservation as that. He might well be ashamed of them. The fearful are far more likely to meet with accidents than the courageous. But really, Connie, I am almost ashamed of talking so. It is all your fault. There is positively no ground for apprehension, and I hope you won't spoil my walk by the thought that my foolish little girl is frightened."

"I will be good—indeed I will, papa," she said, holding up her mouth to kiss me.

I left her room, and went through the wooden passage into the bark hut. The wind roared about it, shook it, and pawed it, and sung and whistled in the chinks of the planks. I went out and shut the door. That moment the wind seized upon me, and I had to fight with it. When I got on the path leading along the edge of the downs, I felt something lighter than any feather fly in my face. When I put up my hand, I found my cheek wet. Again and again I was thus assailed, but when I got to the breakwater, I found what it was. They were flakes of foam, bubbles worked up into little masses of adhering thousands, which the wind blew off the waters and across the downs, carrying some of them miles inland. When I reached the breakwater, and looked along its ridge through the darkness of the night I was bewildered to see a whiteness lying here and there in a great patch upon its top. They were but accumulations of these foam-flakes, like soap-suds, lying so thick that I expected to have to wade through them, only they vanished at the touch of my feet. Till then I had almost believed it was snow I saw. On the edge of the waves, in quieter spots, they lay like yeast, foaming and working. Now and then a little rush of water from a higher wave swept over the top of the broad breakwater, as with head bowed sideways against the wind, I struggled along towards the rock at its end; but I said to myself, "The tide is falling fast, and salt water hurts nobody," and struggled on over the huge rough stones of the mighty heap, outside which the waves were white with wrath, inside which they had fallen asleep, only heaving with the memory of their late unrest. I reached the tall rock at length, climbed the rude stair leading up to the flagstaff, and looked abroad, if looking it could be called, into the thick dark. But the wind blew so strong on the top that I was glad to descend. Between me and the basin where yesterday morning I had bathed in still water and sunshine with my boys, rolled the deathly waves. I wandered on the rough narrow space yet uncovered, stumbling over the stones and the rocky points between which they lay, stood here and there half-meditating, and at length, finding a sheltered nook in a mass of rock, sat with the wind howling and the waves bursting around me. There I fell into a sort of brown study—almost a half-sleep.

But I had not sat long before I came broad awake, for I heard voices, low and earnest. One I recognized as Joe's voice. The other was a woman's. I could not tell what they said for some time, and therefore felt no immediate necessity for disclosing my proximity, but sat debating with myself whether I should speak to them or not. At length, in a lull of the wind, I heard the woman say—I could fancy with a sigh—

"I 'm sure you 'll du what is right, Joe. Don't 'e think o' me, Joe."

"It 's just of you that I do think, Aggy. You know it ben't for my sake. Surely you know that?"

There was no answer for a moment. I was still doubting what I had best do—go away quietly or let them know I was there—when she spoke again. There was a momentary lull now in the noises of both wind and water, and I heard what she said well enough.

"It ben't for me to contradict you, Joe. But I don't think you be going to die. You be no worse than last year. Be you now, Joe?"

It flashed across me how once before, a stormy night and darkness had brought me close to a soul in agony. Then I was in agony myself; now the world was all fair and hopeful around me—the portals of the world beyond ever opening wider as I approached them, and letting out more of their glory to gladden the path to their threshold. But here were two souls straying in a mist which faith might roll away, and leave them walking in the light. The moment was come. I must speak.

"Joe!" I called out.

"Who 's there?" he cried; and I heard him start to his feet.

"Only Mr Walton. Where are you?"

"We can't be very far off," he answered, not in a tone of any pleasure at finding me so nigh.

I rose, and peering about through the darkness, found

that they were a little higher up on the same rock by which I was sheltered.

"You musn't think," I said, "that I have been eaves-dropping. I had no idea any one was near me till I heard your voices, and I did not hear a word till just the last sentence or two."

"I saw some one go up the Castle-rock," said Joe; "but I thought he was gone away again. It will be a lesson to me."

"I 'm no tell-tale, Joe," I returned, as I scrambled up the rock. "You will have no cause to regret that I happened to overhear a little. I am sure, Joe, you will never say anything you need be ashamed of. But what I heard was sufficient to let me into the secret of your trouble. Will you let me talk to Joe, Agnes? I've been young myself, and to tell the truth, I don't think I 'm old yet."

"I am sure, sir," she answered, "you won't be hard on Joe and me. I don't suppose there be anything wrong in liking each other, though we can't be—married."

She spoke in a low tone, and her voice trembled very much; yet there was a certain womanly composure in her utterance. "I 'm sure it 's very bold of me to talk so," she added, "but Joe will tell you all about it."

I was close beside them now, and fancied I saw through the dusk the motion of her hand stealing into his.

"Well, Joe, this is just what I wanted," I said. "A woman can be braver than a big smith sometimes.

Agnes has done her part. Now you do yours, and tell me all about it."

No response followed my adjuration. I must help him.

"I think I know how the matter lies, Joe. You think you are not going to live long, and that therefore you ought not to marry. Am I right?"

"Not far off it, sir," he answered.

"Now, Joe," I said, "can't we talk as friends about this matter? I have no right to intrude into your affairs—none in the least—except what friendship gives me. If you say I am not to talk about it, I shall be silent. To force advice upon you would be as impertinent as useless."

"It 's all the same, I 'm afraid, sir. My mind has been made up for a long time. What right have I to bring other people into trouble? But I take it kind of you, sir, though I mayn't look over-pleased. Agnes wants to hear your way of it. I 'm agreeable."

This was not very encouraging. Still I thought it sufficient ground for proceeding.

"I suppose that you will allow that the root of all Christian behaviour is the will of God?"

"Surely, sir."

"Is it not the will of God, then, that when a man and woman love each other, they should marry?"

"Certainly, sir—where there be no reasons against it."

"Of course. And you judge you see reason for not doing so, else you would?"

"I do see that a man should not bring a woman into trouble for the sake of being comfortable himself for the rest of a few weary days."

Agnes was sobbing gently behind her handkerchief. I knew how gladly she would be Joe's wife, if only to nurse him through his last illness.

"Not except it would make her comfortable too, I grant you, Joe. But listen to me. In the first place, you don't know, and you are not required to know, when you are going to die. In fact, you have nothing to do with it. Many a life has been injured by the constant expectation of death. It is life we have to do with, not death. The best preparation for the night is to work while the day lasts, diligently. The best preparation for death is life. Besides, I have known delicate people who have outlived all their strong relations, and been left alone in the earth—because they had possibly taken too much care of themselves. But marriage is God's will, and death is God's will, and you have no business to set the one over against, as antagonistic to, the other. For anything you know, the gladness and the peace of marriage may be the very means intended for your restoration to health and strength. I suspect your desire to marry, fighting against the idea that you ought not to marry, has a good deal to do with the state of health in which you now find yourself. A man would get over many things if he were happy, that he cannot get over when he is miserable."

"But it's for Aggy. You forget that."

"I do not forget it. What right have you to seek for

her another kind of welfare than you would have yourself? Are you to treat her as if she were worldly when you are not—to provide for her a comfort which yourself you would despise? Why should you not marry because you have to die soon?—if you *are* thus doomed, which to me is by no means clear. Why not have what happiness you may for the rest of your sojourn? If you find at the end of twenty years that here you are after all, you will be rather sorry you did not do as I say."

"And if I find myself dying at the end of six months?"

"You will thank God for those six months. The whole thing, my dear fellow, is a want of faith in God. I do not doubt you think you are doing right, but, I repeat, the whole thing comes from want of faith in God. You will take things into your own hands, and order them after a preventive and self-protective fashion, lest God should have ordained the worst for you, which worst, after all, would be best met by doing his will without inquiry into the future; and which worst is no evil. Death is no more an evil than marriage is."

"But you don't see it as I do," persisted the blacksmith.

"Of course I don't. I think you see it as it is not."

He remained silent for a little. A shower of spray fell upon us. He started.

"What a wave!" he cried. "That spray came over the top of the rock. We shall have to run for it."

I fancied that he only wanted to avoid further conversation.

"There's no hurry," I said. "It was high water an hour and a half ago."

"You don't know this coast, sir," returned he, "or you wouldn't talk like that."

As he spoke he rose, and going from under the shelter of the rock, looked along.

"For God's sake, Aggy!" he cried, in terror, "come at once. Every other wave be rushing across the breakwater as if it was on the level."

So saying, he hurried back, caught her by the hand, and began to draw her along.

"Hadn't we better stay where we are?" I suggested.

"If you can stand the night in the cold. But Aggy here is delicate; and I don't care about being out all night. It's not the tide, sir; it's a ground swell—from a storm somewhere out at sea. That never asks no questions about tide or no tide."

"Come along, then," I said. "But just wait one minute more. It is better to be ready for the worst."

For I remembered that the day before I had seen a crow-bar lying among the stones, and I thought it might be useful. In a moment or two I had found it, and returning, gave it to Joe. Then I took the girl's disengaged hand She thanked me in a voice perfectly calm and firm. Joe took the bar in haste, and drew Agnes towards the breakwater.

Any real thought of danger had not yet crossed my mind. But when I looked along the outstretched back of the mole, and saw a dim sheet of white sweep across it, I felt that there was ground for his anxiety, and prepared myself for a struggle

"Do you know what to do with the crowbar, Joe?" I said, grasping my own stout oak stick more firmly.

"Perfectly," answered Joe. "To stick between the stones and hold on. We must watch our time between the waves."

"You take the command, then, Joe," I returned. "You see better than I do, and you know the ways of that raging wild beast there better than I do. I will obey orders—one of which, no doubt, will be, not for wind or sea to lose hold of Agnes—eh, Joe?"

Joe gave a grim enough laugh in reply, and we started, he carrying his crowbar in his right hand towards the advancing sea, and I my oak stick in my left towards the still water within.

"Quick march!" said Joe, and away we went out on the breakwater.

Now the back of the breakwater was very rugged, for it was formed of huge stones, with wide gaps between, where the waters had washed out the cement, and worn their edges. But what impeded our progress secured our safety.

"Halt!" cried Joe, when we were yet but a few yards beyond the shelter of the rocks. "There's a topper coming."

We halted at the word of command, as a huge wave, with combing crest, rushed against the far outsloping base of the mole, and flung its heavy top right over the middle of the mass, a score or two of yards in front of us.

"Now for it," cried Joe. "Run!"

We did run. In my mind there was just sense enough of danger to add to the pleasure of the excitement. I did not know how much danger there was. Over the rough worn stones we sped, stumbling.

"Halt!" cried the smith once more, and we did halt; but this time, as it turned out, in the middle front of the coming danger.

"God be with us!" I exclaimed, when the huge billow showed itself through the night, rushing towards the mole. The smith stuck his crowbar between two great stones. To this he held on with one hand, and threw the other arm round Agnes's waist. I, too, had got my oak firmly fixed, held on with one hand, and threw the other arm round Agnes. It took but a moment.

"Now then!" cried Joe. "Here she comes! Hold on, sir. Hold on, Aggy!"

But when I saw the height of the water, as it rushed on us up the sloping side of the mound, I cried out, in my turn—

"Down, Joe! Down on your face, and let it over us easy! Down, Agnes!"

They obeyed. We threw ourselves across the break-water, with our heads to the coming foe, and I grasped my stick close to the stones with all the power of a hand that was then strong. Over us burst the mighty wave, floating us up from the stones where we lay. But we held on, the wave passed, and we sprung gasping to our feet.

"Now, now!" cried Joe and I together, and, heavy

as we were, with the water pouring from us, we flew across the remainder of the heap, and arrived, panting and safe, at the other end, ere one wave more had swept the surface. The moment we were in safety we turned and looked back over the danger we had traversed. It was to see a huge billow sweep the breakwater from end to end. We looked at each other for a moment without speaking.

"I believe, sir," said Joe at length, with slow and solemn speech, "if you hadn't taken the command at that moment we should all have been lost."

"It seems likely enough, when I look back on it. For one thing, I was not sure that my stick would stand, so I thought I had better grasp it low down."

"We were awfully near death," said Joe.

"Nearer than you thought, Joe; and yet we escaped it. Things don't go all as we fancy, you see. Faith is as essential to manhood as foresight—believe me, Joe. It is very absurd to trust God for the future, and not trust him for the present. The man who is not anxious is the man most likely to do the right thing. He is cool and collected and ready. Our Lord therefore told his disciples that when they should be brought before kings and rulers, they were to take no thought what answer they should make, for it would be given them when the time came."

We were climbing the steep path up to the downs. Neither of my companions spoke.

"You have escaped one death together," I said, at length: "dare another."

Still neither of them returned an answer. When we came near the parsonage, I said—

"Now, Joe, you must go in and get to bed at once. I will take Agnes home. You can trust me not to say anything against you?"

Joe laughed rather hoarsely, and replied—

"As you please, sir. Good night, Aggy. Mind you get to bed as fast as you can."

When I returned from giving Agnes over to her parents, I made haste to change my clothes, and put on my warm dressing-gown. I may as well mention at once, that not one of us was the worse for our ducking. I then went up to Connie's room.

"Here I am you see, Connie, quite safe."

"I 've been lying listening to every blast of wind since you went out, papa. But all I could do was to trust in God."

"Do you call that *all*, Connie? Believe me, there is more power in that than any human being knows the tenth part of yet. It is indeed *all*."

I said no more then. I told my wife about it that night, but we were well into another month before I told Connie.

When I left her, I went to Joe's room to see how he was, and found him having some gruel. I sat down on the edge of his bed, and said—

"Well, Joe, this is better than under water. I hope you won't be the worse for it."

"I don't much care what comes of me, sir. It will be all over soon."

"But you ought to care what comes of you, Joe. I will tell you why. You are an instrument out of which ought to come praise to God, and, therefore, you ought to care for the instrument."

"That way, yes, sir, I ought."

"And you have no business to be like some children, who say, 'Mamma won't give me so and so,' instead of asking her to give it them."

"I see what you mean, sir. But really you put me out before the young woman. I couldn't say before her what I meant. Suppose, you know, sir, there was to come a family. It might be, you know."

"Of course. What else would you have?"

"But if I was to die, where would she be then?"

"In God's hands; just as she is now."

"But I ought to take care that she is not left with a burden like that to provide for."

"Oh, Joe! how little you know a woman's heart! It would just be the greatest comfort she could have for losing you—that's all. Many a woman has married a man she did not care enough for, just that she might have a child of her own to let out her heart upon. I don't say that is right, you know. Such love cannot be perfect. A woman ought to love her child because it is her husband's more than because it is her own, and because it is God's more than either's. I saw in the papers the other day, that a woman was brought before the Recorder of London for stealing a baby, when the judge himself said that there was no imaginable motive for her action but a motherly passion to possess the child. It is the need of a child that makes so many women take to poor miserable, broken-nosed lap-dogs; for they are self-indulgent, and cannot face the troubles and dangers of adopting a child. They would if they might get one of a good family, or from a respectable home; but they dare not take an orphan out of the dirt, lest it should spoil their silken chairs. But that has nothing to do with our argument. What I mean is this, that if Agnes really loves you, as no one can look in her face and doubt, she will be far happier if you leave her a child—yes, she will be happier if you only leave her your name for hers—than if you died without calling her your wife."

I took Joe's basin from him, and he lay down. He turned his face to the wall. I waited a moment, but finding him silent, bade him good night, and left the room.

A month after, I married them.

CHAPTER XXX.

THE HARVEST.

T was some time before we got the bells to work to our mind, but at last we succeeded. The worst of it was to get the cranks, which at first required strong pressure on the keys, to work easily enough. But neither Joe nor his cousin spared any pains to perfect the attempt, and, as I say, at length we succeeded. I took Wynnie down to the instrument and made her try whether she could not do something, and she succeeded in making the old tower discourse loudly and eloquently.

By this time the thanksgiving for the harvest was at hand: on the morning of that first of all would I summon the folk to their prayers with the sound of the full peal. And I wrote a little hymn of praise to the God of the harvest, modelling it to one of the oldest tunes in that part of the country, and I had it printed on slips of paper and laid plentifully on the benches. What with the calling of the bells, like voices in the highway, and the solemn meditation of the organ within to bear aloft the thoughts of those who heard, and came to the prayer and thanksgiving in common, and the message which God had given me to utter to them, I hoped that we should indeed keep holiday.

Wynnie summoned the parish with the hundredth psalm pealed from aloft, dropping from the airy regions of the tower on village and hamlet and cottage, calling aloud —for who could dissociate the words from the music, though the words are in the Scotch psalms?—written none the less by an Englishman, however English wits may amuse themselves with laughing at their quaintness—calling aloud,—

"All people that on earth do dwell
Sing to the Lord with cheerful voice;
Him serve with mirth, his praise forth tell—
Come ye before him and rejoice."

Then we sang the psalm before the communion service, making bold in the name of the Lord to serve him with *mirth* as in the old version, and not with the *fear* with which some editor, weak in faith, has presumed to alter the line. Then before the sermon we sang the hymn I had prepared—a proceeding justifiable by many an example in the history of the church while she was not only able to number singers amongst her clergy, but those singers were capable of influencing the whole heart and judgment of the nation with their songs. Ethelwyn played the organ.

The song I had prepared was this:—

We praise the Life of All;
From buried seeds so small
Who makes the ordered ranks of autumn stand•
Who stores the corn
In rick and barn
To feed the winter of the land.

We praise the Life of Light!
Who from the brooding night
Draws out the morning holy, calm, and grand;
Veils up the moon,
Sends out the sun,
To glad the face of all the land.

We praise the Life of Work,
Who from sleep's lonely dark
Leads forth his children to arise and stand,
Then go their way,
The live-long day,
To trust and labour in the land.

We praise the Life of Good,
Who breaks sin's lazy mood,
Toilsomely ploughing up the fruitless sand.
The furrowed waste
They leave, and haste
Home, home to till their Father's land.

We praise the Life of Life,
Who in this soil of strife
Casts us at birth, like seed from sower's hand;
To die, and so
Like corn to grow
A golden harvest in his land.

After we had sung this hymn, the meaning of which is far better than the versification, I preached from the words of St Paul, "If by any means I might attain unto the resurrection of the dead. Not as though I had already attained, either were already perfect." And this is something like what I said to them:—

"The world, my friends, is full of resurrections, and it is not always of the same resurrection that St Paul speaks. Every night that folds us up in darkness is a death; and those of you that have been out early and have seen the first of the dawn, will know it—the day rises out of the night like a being that has burst its tomb and escaped into life. That you may feel that the sunrise is a resurrection—the word resurrection just means a rising again—I will read you a little description of it from a sermon by a great writer and great preacher called Jeremy Taylor. Listen. 'But as when the sun approaching towards the gates of the morning, he first opens a little eye of heaven and sends away the spirits of darkness, and gives light to a cock, and calls up the lark to matins, and by and by gilds the fringes of a cloud, and peeps over the eastern hills, thrusting out his golden horns like those which decked the brows of Moses, when he was forced to wear a veil, because himself had seen the face of God; and still, while a man tells the story, the sun gets up higher, till he shows a fair face and a full light, and then he shines one whole day, under a cloud often, and sometimes weeping great and little showers, and sets quickly; so is a man's reason and his life.' Is not this a resurrection of the day out of the night? Or hear how Milton makes his Adam and Eve praise God in the morning,—

'Ye mists and exhalations that now rise
From hill or streaming lake, dusky or gray,

Till the sun paint your fleecy skirts with gold,
In honour to the world's great Author rise,
Whether to deck with clouds the uncoloured sky,
Or wet the thirsty earth with falling showers,
Rising or falling still advance his praise.'

But it is yet more of a resurrection to you. Think of your own condition through the night and in the morning. You die, as it were, every night. The death of darkness comes down over the earth; but a deeper death, the death of sleep, descends on you. A power overshadows you; your eyelids close, you cannot keep them open if you would; your limbs lie moveless; the day is gone; your whole life is gone; you have forgotten everything; an evil man might come and do with your goods as he pleased; you are helpless. But the God of the Resurrection is awake all the time, watching his sleeping men and women, even as a mother who watches her sleeping baby, only with larger eyes and more full of love than hers; and so, you know not how, all at once you know that you are what you are; that there is a world that wants you outside of you, and a God that wants you inside of you; you rise from the death of sleep, not by your own power, for you knew nothing about it; God put his hand over your eyes, and you were dead; he lifted his hand and breathed light on you, and you rose from the dead, thanked the God who raised you up, and went forth to do your work. From darkness to light; from blindness to seeing; from knowing nothing to looking abroad on the mighty world; from helpless submission to willing obedience,—is not this a resurrection indeed? That St Paul saw it to be such may be shown from his using the two things with the same meaning when he says, 'Awake thou that sleepest and arise from the dead, and Christ shall give thee light.' No doubt he meant a great deal more. No man who understands what he is speaking about can well mean only one thing at a time.

"But to return to the resurrections we see around us in nature. Look at the death that falls upon the world in winter. And look how it revives when the sun draws near enough in the spring to wile the life in it once more out of its grave. See how the pale, meek snowdrops come up with their bowed heads, as if full of the memory of the fierce winds they encountered last spring, and yet ready in the strength of their weakness to encounter them again. Up comes the crocus, bringing its gold safe from the dark of its colourless grave into the light of its parent gold. Primroses, and anemones, and blue-bells, and a thousand other children of the spring, hear the resurrection-trumpet of the wind from the west and south, obey, and leave their graves behind to breathe the air of the sweet heavens. Up and up they come till the year is glorious with the rose and the lily, till the trees are not only clothed upon with new garments of loveliest green, but the fruit-tree bringeth forth its fruit, and the little children of men are made glad with apples, and cherries, and hazel-nuts. The earth laughs out in green and gold. The sky shares in the grand resurrection. The garments of its mourning, wherewith it made men sad, its clouds of snow and hail and stormy vapours are swept away, have sunk indeed to the earth, and are now humbly feeding the roots of the flowers whose dead stalks they beat upon all the winter long. Instead, the sky has put on the garments of praise. Her blue, coloured after the sapphire-floor on which stands the throne of him who is the Resurrection and the Life, is dashed and glorified with the pure white of sailing clouds, and at morning and evening prayer, puts on colours in which the human heart drowns itself with delight—green and gold and purple and rose. Even the icebergs floating about in the lonely summer seas of the north are flashing all the glories of the rainbow. But, indeed, is not this whole world itself a monument of the Resurrection? The earth was without form and void. The wind of God moved on the face of the waters, and up arose this fair world. Darkness was on the face of the deep: God said, 'Let there be light,' and there was light.

"In the animal world as well, you behold the goings of the Resurrection. Plainest of all, look at the story of the butterfly—so plain that the pagan Greeks called it and the soul by one name—Psyche. Psyche meant with them a butterfly or the soul, either. Look how the creeping thing, ugly to our eyes, so that we can hardly handle it without a shudder, finding itself growing sick with age, straightway falls a spinning and weaving at its own shroud, coffin, and grave, all in one—to prepare, in fact, for its resurrection; for it is for the sake of the resurrection that death exists. Patiently it spins its strength, but not its life, away, folds itself up decently, that its body may rest in quiet till the new body is formed within it; and at length when the appointed hour has arrived, out of the body of this crawling thing breaks forth the winged splendour of the butterfly—not the same body—a new built out of the ruins of the old—even as St Paul tells us that it is not the same body *we* have in the resurrection, but a nobler body like ourselves, with all the imperfect and evil thing taken away. No more creeping for the butterfly; wings of splendour now. Neither yet has it lost the feet wherewith to alight on all that is lovely and sweet. Think of it—up from the toilsome journey over the low ground, exposed to the foot of every passer-by, destroying the lovely leaves upon which it fed, and the fruit which they should shelter, up to the path at will through the air, and a gathering of food which hurts not the source of it, a food which is but as a tribute from the loveliness of the flowers to the yet higher loveliness of the flower-angel: is not this a resurrection? Its children too shall pass through the same process, to wing the air of a summer noon, and rejoice in the ethereal and the pure.

"To return yet again from the human thoughts suggested by the symbol of the butterfly"—

Here let me pause for a moment—and there was a corresponding pause, though but momentary, in the sermon as I spoke it—to mention a curious, and to me at the moment an interesting fact. At this point of my address, I caught sight of a white butterfly, a belated one, flitting about the church. Absorbed for a moment, my eye wandered after it. It was near the bench where my own people sat, and, for one flash of thought, I longed that the butterfly would alight on my Wynnie, for I was more anxious about her resurrection at the time than about anything else. But the butterfly would not. And then I told myself that God would, and that the butterfly was only the symbol of a grand truth, and of no private interpretation, to make which of it was both selfishness and superstition. But all this passed in a flash, and I resumed my discourse.

—"I come now naturally to speak of what we commonly call the Resurrection. Some say: 'How can the same dust be raised again, when it may be scattered to the winds of heaven?' It is a question I hardly care to answer. The mere difficulty can in reason stand for nothing with God; but the apparent worthlessness of the supposition renders the question uninteresting to me. What is of import is, that I should stand clothed upon, with a body which is *my* body because it serves my ends, justifies my consciousness of identity by being, in all that was good in it, like that which I had before, while now it is tenfold capable of expressing the thoughts and feelings that move within me. How can I care whether the atoms that form a certain inch of bone should be the same as those which formed that bone when I died? All my life-time I never felt or thought of the existence of such a bone! On the other hand, I object to having the same worn muscles, the same shrivelled skin with which I may happen to die. Why give me the same body as that? Why not rather my youthful body, which was strong, and facile, and capable? The matter in the muscle of my arm at death would not serve to make half the muscle I had when young. But I thank God that St Paul says it will *not* be the same body. That body dies—up springs another body. I suspect myself that those are right who say that this body being the seed, the moment it dies in the soil of this world, that moment is the resurrection of the new body. The life in it rises out of it in a new body. This is not after it is put in the mere earth; for it is dead then, and the germ of life gone out of it. If a seed rots, no new body comes of it. The seed dies into a new life, and so does man. Dying and rotting are two very different things.—But I am not sure by any means. As I say, the whole question is rather uninteresting to me. What do I care about my old clothes after I have done with them? What is it to me to know what becomes of an old coat or an old pulpit gown? I have no such clinging to the flesh. It seems to me that people believe their bodies to be themselves, and are therefore very anxious about them—and no wonder then. Enough for me that I shall have eyes to see my friends, a face that they shall know me by, and a mouth to praise God withal. I leave the matter with one remark, that I am well content to rise as Jesus rose, however that was. For me the will of God is so good that I would rather have his will done than my own choice given me.

"But I now come to the last, because infinitely the most important part of my subject—the resurrection for the sake of which all the other resurrections exist—the resurrection unto Life. This is the one of which St Paul speaks in my text. This is the one I am most anxious—indeed, the only one I am anxious to set forth, and impress upon you.

"Think, then, of all the deaths you know; the death of the night, when the sun is gone, when friend says not a word to friend, but both lie drowned and parted in the sea of sleep; the death of the year, when winter lies heavy on the graves of the children of summer, when the leafless trees moan in the blasts from the ocean, when the beasts even look dull and oppressed, when the children go about shivering with cold, when the poor and improvident are miserable with suffering; or think of such a death of disease as befalls us at times, when the man who says, 'Would God it were morning!' changes but his word, and not his tune, when the morning comes, crying, 'Would God it were evening!' when what life is left is known to us only by suffering, and hope is amongst the things which were once and are no more—think of all these, think of them all together, and you will have but the dimmest, faintest picture of the death from which the resurrection of which I have now to speak, is the rising. I shrink from the attempt, knowing how weak words are to set forth *the* death, set forth *the* resurrection. Were I to sit down to yonder organ, and crash out the most horrible dissonances that ever took shape in sound, I should give you but a weak figure of this death; were I capable of drawing from many a row of pipes an exhalation of dulcet symphonies and voices sweet, such as Milton himself could have invaded our ears withal, I could give you but a faint figure of this resurrection. Nevertheless, I must try what I can do in my own way.

"If into the face of the dead body, lying on the bed, waiting for its burial, the soul of the man should begin to dawn again, drawing near from afar to look out once more at those eyes, to smile once again through those lips, the change on that face would be indeed great and wondrous, but nothing for marvel or greatness to that which passes on the countenance, the very outward bodily face of the man who wakes from his sleep, arises from the dead and receives light from Christ. Too often indeed, the reposeful look on the face of the dead body would be troubled, would vanish away at the revisiting of the restless ghost; but when a man's own right true mind, which God made in him, is restored to him again, and he wakes from the death of sin, then comes the repose without the death. It may take long for the new spirit to complete the visible change, but it begins at once, and will be perfected. The bloated look of self-indulgence passes away like the leprosy of Naaman, the cheek grows pure, the lips return to the smile of hope instead of the grin of greed, and the eyes that made innocence shrink and shudder with their yellow leer grow childlike and sweet and faithful. The mammon-eyes, hitherto fixed on the earth, are lifted to meet their kind; the lips that mumbled over figures and sums of gold learn to say words of grace and tenderness. The truculent, repellent, self-satisfied face begins to look thoughtful and doubtful, as if searching for some treasure of whose whereabouts it had no certain sign. The face, anxious, wrinkled, peering, troubled, on whose lines you read the dread of hunger, poverty, and nakedness, thaws into a smile; the eyes reflect in courage the light of the Father's care; the back grows erect under its burden with the assurance that the hairs of its head are all numbered. But the face can with all its changes set but dimly forth the rising from the dead which passes within. The heart, which cared but for itself, becomes aware of surrounding thousands like itself, in the love and care of which it feels a dawning blessedness undreamt of before. From selfishness to love—is not this a rising from the dead? The man whose ambition declares that his way in the world would be to subject everything to his desires, to bring every human care, affection, power, and aspiration to his feet—such a world it would be, and such a king it would have, if individual ambition might work its will! if a man's opinion of himself could be made out in the world, degrading, compelling, oppressing, doing everything for his own glory!—and such a glory!—but a pang of light strikes this man to the heart; an arrow of truth, feathered with suffering and loss and dismay, finds out—the open joint in his armour, I was going to say—no, finds out the joint in the coffin where his heart lies festering in a death so dead that itself calls it life. He trembles, he awakes, he rises from the dead. No more he seeks the slavery of all: where can he find whom to serve? how can he become if but a threshold in the temple of Christ, where all serve all, and no man thinks first of himself? He to whom the mass of his fellows, as he massed them, was common and unclean, bows before every human sign of the presence of the making God. The sun, which was to him but a candle with which to search after his own ends, wealth, power, place, praise—the world, which was but the cavern where he thus searched—are now full of the mystery of loveliness, full of the truth of which sun and wind and land and sea are symbols and signs. From a withered old age of unbelief, the dim eyes of which refuse the glory of things a passage to the heart, he is raised up a child full of admiration, wonder, and gladness. Everything is glorious to him; he can believe, and therefore he sees. It is from the grave into the sunshine, from the night into the morning, from death into life. To come out of the ugly into the beautiful; out of the mean and selfish into the noble and loving; out of the paltry into the great; out of the false into the true; out of the filthy into the clean; out of the commonplace into the glorious; out of the corruption of disease into the fine vigour and gracious movements of health; in a word, out of evil into good—is not this a resurrection indeed—*the* resurrection of all, the resurrection of Life? God grant that with St Paul we may attain to this resurrection of the dead.

"This rising from the dead is often a long and a painful process. Even after he had preached the gospel to the Gentiles, and suffered much for the sake of his Master, Paul sees the resurrection of the dead towering grandly before him, not yet climbed, not yet attained unto—a mountainous splendour and marvel still shining aloft in the air of existence, still, thank God, to be attained, but ever growing in height and beauty as, forgetting those things that are behind, he presses towards the mark, if by any means he may attain to the resurrection of the dead. Every blessed moment in which a man bethinks himself that he has been forgetting his high calling, and sends up to the Father a prayer for aid; every time a man resolves that what he has been doing he will do no more; every time that the love of God, or the feeling of the truth, rouses a man to look first up at the light, then down at the skirts of his own garments—that moment a divine resurrection is wrought in the earth. Yea, every time that a man passes from resentment to forgiveness, from cruelty to compassion, from hardness to tenderness, from indifference to carefulness, from selfishness to honesty, from honesty to generosity, from generosity to love,—a resurrection, the bursting of a fresh bud of life out of the grave of evil gladdens the eye of the Father watching his children. Awake then, thou that sleepest, and arise from the dead, and Christ will give thee light. As the harvest rises from the wintry earth, so rise thou up from the trials of this world a full ear in the harvest of him who sowed thee in the soil that thou mightest rise above it. As the summer rises from the winter, so rise thou from the cares of eating and drinking and clothing into the fearless sunshine of confidence in the Father. As the morning rises out of the night, so rise thou from the darkness of ignorance to do the will of God in the daylight; and as a man feels that he is himself when he wakes from the troubled and grotesque visions of the night into the glory of the sunrise, even so wilt thou feel that then first thou knowest what thy life, the gladness of thy being, is. As from painful tossing in disease, rise into the health of well-being. As from the awful embrace of thy own dead body, burst forth in thy spiritual body. Arise thou, responsive to the indwelling will of the Father, even as thy body will respond to thy indwelling soul.

'White wings are crossing;
Glad waves are tossing;
The earth flames out in crimson and green:
Spring is appearing,
Summer is nearing—
Where hast thou been?

Down in some cavern,
Death's sleepy tavern,
Housing, carousing with spectres of night?
The trumpet is pealing
Sunshine and healing—
Spring to the light.'"

With this quotation from a friend's poem, I closed my sermon, oppressed with a sense of failure; for ever the marvel of simple awaking, the mere type of the resurrection eluded all my efforts to fix it in words. I had to comfort myself with the thought that God is so strong that he can work even with our failures.

CHAPTER XXXI.

A WALK WITH MY WIFE.

THE autumn was creeping up on the earth, with winter holding by its skirts behind; but before I lose my hold of the garments of summer, I must write a chapter about a walk and a talk I had one night with my wife. It had rained a good deal during the day, but as the sun went down the air began to clear, and when the moon shone out, near the full, she walked the heavens, not "like one that hath been led astray," but as "queen and huntress, chaste and fair."

"What a lovely night it is!" said Ethelwyn, who had come into my study—where I always sat with unblinded windows, that the night and her creatures might look in upon me—and had stood gazing out for a moment.

"Shall we go for a little turn?" I said.

"I should like it very much," she answered. "I will go and put on my bonnet at once."

In a minute or two she looked in again, all ready. I rose, laid aside my Plato, and went with her. We turned our steps along the edge of the down, and descended upon the breakwater, where we seated ourselves upon the same spot where, in the darkness, I had heard the voices of Joe and Agnes. What a different night it was from that! The sea lay as quiet as if it could not move for the moonlight that lay upon it. The glory over it was so mighty in its peacefulness, that the wild element beneath was afraid to toss itself even with the motions of its natural unrest. The moon was like the face of a saint before which the stormy people has grown dumb. The rocks stood up solid and dark in the universal æther, and the pulse of the ocean throbbed against them with a lapping gush, soft as the voice of a passionate child soothed into shame of its vanished petulance. But the sky was the glory. Although no breath moved below, there was a gentle wind abroad in the upper regions. The air was full of masses of cloud, the vanishing fragments of the one great vapour which had been pouring down in rain the most of the day. These masses were all setting with one steady motion eastward into the abysses of space; now obscuring the fair moon, now solemnly sweeping away from before her. As they departed, out shone her marvellous radiance, as calm as ever. It was plain that she knew nothing of what we called her covering, her obscuration, the dimming of her glory. She had been busy all the time weaving her lovely opaline damask on the other side of the mass in which we said she was swallowed up.

"Have you ever noticed wifie," I said, "how the eyes of our minds—almost our bodily eyes—are opened sometimes to the cubicalness of nature, as it were?"

"I don't know, Harry, for I don't understand your question," she answered.

"Well, it was a stupid way of expressing what I meant. No human being could have understood it from that. I will make you understand in a moment, though. Sometimes—perhaps, generally—we see the sky as a flat dome, spangled with star-points, and painted blue. *Now* I see it as an awful depth of blue air, depth within depth; and the clouds before me are not passing away to the left, but sinking away from the front of me into the marvellous unknown regions, which, let philosophers say what they will about time and space—and I daresay they are right—are yet very awful to me. Thank God, my dear," I said, catching hold of her arm, as the terror of mere space grew upon me, "for Himself. He is deeper than space, deeper than time; he is the heart of all the cube of history."

"I understand you now, husband," said my wife.

"I knew you would," I answered.

"But," she said again, "is it not something the same with the things inside us? I can't put it in words as you do. Do you understand me now?"

"I am not sure that I do. You must try again."

"You understand me well enough, only you like to make me blunder where you can talk," said my wife, putting her hand in mine. "But I will try. Sometimes, after thinking about something for a long time, you come to a conclusion about it, and you think you have settled it plain and clear to yourself, for ever and a day. You hang it upon your wall, like a picture, and are satisfied for a fortnight. But some day, when you happen to cast a look at it, you find that instead of hanging flat on the wall, your picture has gone through it—opens out into some region you don't know where—shows you far receding distances of air and sea—in short, where you thought one question was settled for ever, a hundred are opened up for the present hour."

"Bravo, wife!" I cried in true delight. "I do indeed understand you now. You have said it better than I could ever have done. That's the plague of you women! You have been taught for centuries and centuries that there is little or nothing to be expected of you, and so you won't try. Therefore we men know no more than you do whether it is in you or not. And when you do try, instead of trying to think, you want to be in Parliament all at once."

"Do you apply that remark to me, sir?" demanded Ethelwyn.

"You must submit to bear the sins of your kind upon occasion," I answered.

"I am content to do that, so long as yours will help mine," she replied.

"Then I may go on?" I said, with interrogation.

"Till sunrise if you like. We were talking of the cubicalness—I believe you called it—of nature."

"And you capped it with the cubicalness of thought.

And quite right too. There are people, as a dear friend of mine used to say, who are so accustomed to regard everything in the *flat*, as dogma cut and—not *always* dried my moral olfactories aver—that if you prove to them the very thing they believe, but after another mode than that they have been accustomed to, they are offended, and count you a heretic. There is no help for it. Even St Paul's chief opposition came from the Judaizing Christians of his time, who did not believe that God *could* love the Gentiles, and therefore regarded him as a teacher of falsehood. We must not be fierce with them. Who knows what wickedness of their ancestors goes to account for their stupidity? For that there are stupid people, and that they are, in very consequence of their stupidity, conceited, who can deny? The worst of it is, that no man who is conceited can be convinced of the fact."

"Don't say that, Harry. That is to deny conversion."

"You are right, Ethelwyn. The moment a man is convinced of his folly, he ceases to be a fool. The moment a man is convinced of his conceit, he ceases to be conceited. But there *must* be a final judgment, and the true man will welcome it, even if he is to appear a convicted fool. A man's business is to see first that he is not acting the part of a fool, and next, to help any honest people who care about the matter to take heed likewise that they be not offering to pull the mote out of their brother's eye. But there are even societies established and supported by good people for the express purpose of pulling out motes.—'The Mote-Pulling Society!'—That ought to take with a certain part of the public."

"Come, come, Harry. You are absurd. Such people don't come near you."

"They can't touch me. No. But they come near good people whom I know, brandishing the long pins with which they pull the motes out, and threatening them with judgment before their time. They are but pins, to be sure—not daggers."

"But you have wandered, Harry, into the narrowest, underground, musty ways, and have forgotten all about 'the cubicalness of nature.'"

"You are right, my love, as you generally are," I answered, laughing. "Look at that great antlered elk, or moose—fit quarry for Diana of the silver bow. Look how it glides solemnly away into the unpastured depths of the aërial deserts. Look again at that reclining giant, half raised upon his arm, with his face turned towards the wilderness. What eyes they must be under those huge brows! On what message to the nations is he borne, as by the slow sweep of ages, on towards his mysterious goal?"

"Stop, stop, Harry," said my wife. "It makes me unhappy to hear grand words clothing only cloudy fancies. Such words ought to be used about the truth, and the truth only."

"If I could carry it no further, my dear, then it would indeed be a degrading of words. But there never was a vagary that uplifted the soul, or made the grand words flow from the gates of speech, that had not its counterpart in truth itself. Man can imagine nothing, even in the clouds of the air, that God has not done, or is not doing. Even as that cloudy giant yields, and is 'shepherded by the slow unwilling wind,' so is each of us borne onward to an unseen destiny—a glorious one if we will but yield to the Spirit of God that bloweth where it listeth—with a grand listing—coming whence we know not, and going whither we know not. The very clouds of the air are hung up as dim pictures of the thoughts and history of man."

"I do not mind how long you talk like that, husband, even if you take the clouds for your text. But it did make me miserable to think that what you were saying had no more basis than the fantastic forms which the clouds assume. I see I was wrong, though."

"The clouds themselves, in such a solemn stately march as this, used to make me sad for the very same reason. I used to think, What is it all for? They are but vapours blown by the wind. They come nowhence, and they go nowhither. But now I see them and all things as ever moving symbols of the motions of man's spirit and destiny."

A pause followed, during which we sat and watched the marvellous depth of the heavens, deep as I do not think I ever saw them before or since, covered with a stately procession of ever-appearing and ever-vanishing forms—great sculpturesque blocks of a shattered storm—the icebergs of the upper sea. These were not far off against a blue background, but floating near us in the heart of a blue-black space, gloriously lighted by a golden rather than silvery moon. At length my wife spoke.

"I hope Mr Percivale is out to-night," she said. "How he must be enjoying it if he is!"

"I wonder the young man is not returning to his professional labours," I said. "Few artists can afford such long holidays as he is taking."

"He is laying in stock, though, I suppose," answered my wife.

"I doubt that, my dear. He said not, on one occasion, you may remember."

"Yes, I remember. But still he must paint better the more familiar he gets with the things God cares to fashion."

"Doubtless. But I am afraid the work of God he is chiefly studying at present is our Wynnie."

"Well, is she not a worthy object of his study?" returned Ethelwyn, looking up in my face with an arch expression.

"Doubtless, again, Ethel; but I hope she is not studying him quite so much in her turn. I have seen her eyes following him about."

My wife made no answer for a moment. Then she said,

"Don't you like him, Harry?"

"Yes. I like him very much."

"Then why should you not like Wynnie to like him?"

"I should like to be surer of his principles, for one thing."

"I should like to be surer of Wynnie's."

I was silent. Ethelwyn resumed.

"Don't you think they might do each other good?"

Still I could not reply.

"They both love the truth, I am sure; only they don't perhaps know what it is yet. I think if they were to fall in love with each other, it would very likely make them both more desirous of finding it still."

"Perhaps," I said at last. "But you are talking about awfully serious things, Ethelwyn."

"Yes, as serious as life," she answered.

"You make me very anxious," I said. "The young man has not, I fear, any means of gaining a livelihood for more than himself."

"Why should he, before he wanted it? I like to see a man who can be content with an art and a living by it."

"I hope I have not been to blame in allowing them to see so much of each other," I said, hardly heeding my wife's words.

"It came about quite naturally," she rejoined. "If you had opposed their meeting, you would have been interfering just as if you had been Providence. And you would have only made them think more about each other."

"He hasn't said anything—has he?" I asked in positive alarm.

"Oh dear no. It may be all my fancy. I am only looking a little ahead. I confess I should like him for a son-in-law. I approve of him," she added, with a sweet laugh.

"Well," I said, "I suppose sons-in-law are possible, however disagreeable, results of having daughters.

I tried to laugh, but hardly succeeded.

"Harry," said my wife, "I don't like you in such a mood. It is not like you at all. It is unworthy of you."

"How can I help being anxious when you speak of such dreadful things as the possibility of having to give away my daughter, my precious wonder that came to me through you, out of the infinite—the tender little darling!"

"'Out of the heart of God,' you used to say, Henry. Yes, and with a destiny he had ordained. It is strange to me how you forget your best and noblest teaching sometimes. You are always telling us to trust in God. Surely it is a poor creed that will only allow us to trust in God for ourselves—a very selfish creed. There must be something wrong there. I should say that the man who can only trust God for himself is not half a Christian. Either he is so selfish that that satisfies him, or he has such a poor notion of God that he cannot trust him with what most concerns him. The former is not your case, Harry: is the latter, then?—You see I must take my turn at the preaching sometimes. Mayn't I, dearest?"

She took my hand in both of hers. The truth arose in my heart. I never loved my wife more than at that moment. And now I could not speak for other reasons. I saw that I had been faithless to my God, and the moment I could command my speech, I hastened to confess it.

"You are right, my dear," I said, "quite right. I have been wicked, for I have been denying my God. I have been putting my providence in the place of his—trying, like an anxious fool, to count the hairs on Wynnie's head, instead of being content that the grand, loving Father should count them. My love, let us pray for Wynnie; for what is prayer but giving her to God and his holy, blessed will?"

We sat hand in hand. Neither spoke aloud for some minutes, but we spoke in our hearts to God, talking to him about Wynnie. Then we rose together, and walked homeward, still in silence. But my heart and hand clung to my wife as to the angel whom God had sent to deliver me out of the prison of my faithlessness. And as we went, lo! the sky was glorious again. It had faded from my sight, had grown flat as a dogma, uninteresting as "a foul and pestilent congregation of vapours;" the moon had been but a round thing with the sun shining upon it, and the stars were only minding their own business. But now the solemn march towards an unseen, unimagined goal had again begun. Wynnie's life was hid with Christ in God. Away strode the cloudy pageant with its banners blowing in the wind, which blew where it grandly listed, marching as to a solemn triumphal music that drew them from afar towards the gates of pearl by which the morning walks out of the New Jerusalem to gladden the nations of the earth. Solitary stars, with all their sparkles drawn in, shone, quiet as human eyes, in the deep solemn clefts of dark blue air. They looked restrained and still, as if they knew all about it —all about the secret of this midnight march. For the moon—she saw the sun, and therefore made the earth glad.

"You have been a moon to me, this night, my wife," I said. "You were looking full at the truth, while I was dark. I saw its light in your face, and believed, and turned my soul to the sun. And now I am both ashamed and glad. God keep me from sinning so again."

"My dear husband, it was only a mood—a passing mood," said Ethelwyn, seeking to comfort me.

"It was a mood, and thank God, it is now past; but it was a wicked one. It was a mood in which the Lord might have called me a devil, as he did St Peter. Such moods have to be grappled with and fought the moment they appear. They must not have their way for a single thought even."

"But we can't help it always, can we, husband?"

"We can't help it out and out, because our wills are not yet free with the freedom God is giving us as fast as we will let him. When we are able to will thoroughly, then we shall do what we will. At least, I think we shall. But there is a mystery in it God only understands. All we know is, that we can struggle and pray. But a mood is an awful oppression sometimes when you least believe in it and most wish to get rid of it. It is like a headache in the soul."

"What do the people do that don't believe in God?" said Ethelwyn.

The same moment Wynnie, who had seen us pass the window, opened the door of the bark-house for us, and we passed into Connie's chamber and found her lying in the moonlight, gazing at the same heavens as her father and mother had been revelling in.

CHAPTER XXXII.

OUR LAST SHORE-DINNER.

THE next day was very lovely. I think it is the last of the kind of which I shall have occasion to write in my narrative of the Seaboard Parish. I wonder if my readers are tired of so much about the common things of Nature. I reason about it something in this way:—We are so easily affected by the smallest things that are of the unpleasant kind, that we ought to train ourselves to the influence of those that are of an opposite nature. The unpleasant ones are like the thorns which make themselves felt as we scramble—for we often do scramble in a very undignified manner—through the thickets of life; and, feeling the thorns, we grumble, and are blind to all but the thorns. The flowers and the lovely leaves and the red berries and the clusters of filberts and the birds'-nests, do not force themselves upon our attention as the thorns do, and the thorns make us forget to look for them. But a scratch would be forgotten—and that in mental hurts is often equivalent to a cure, for a forgotten scratch on the mind or heart will never fester—if we but allowed our being a moment's repose upon any of the quiet, waiting, unobtrusive beauties that lie around the half-trodden way, offering their gentle healing. And when I think how, not unfrequently, otherwise noble characters are anything but admirable when under the influence of trifling irritations, the very paltriness of which seems what the mind, which would at once rouse itself to a noble endurance of any mighty evil, is unable to endure, I would gladly help so with sweet antidotes to defeat the fly in the ointment of the apothecary that the whole pot shall send forth a pure savour. We ought for this to cultivate the friendships of little things. Beauty is one of the surest antidotes to vexation. Often when life looked dreary about me, from some real or fancied injustice or indignity, has a thought of truth been flashed into my mind from a flower, a shape of frost, or even a lingering shadow,—not to mention such glories as angel-winged clouds, rainbows, stars, and sun-rises. Therefore I hope that in my loving delay over such aspects of Nature as impressed themselves upon me in this most memorable part of my history, I shall not prove wearisome to my reader, for therein I should utterly contravene my hope and intent in the recording of them.

This day there was to be an unusually low tide, and we had reckoned of enlarging our acquaintance with the bed of the ocean—of knowing a few yards more of the millions of miles lapt in the mystery of waters. It was to be low water about two o'clock, and we resolved to dine upon the sands. But all the morning the children were out playing on the threshold of old Neptune's palace; for in his quieter mood, he will, like a fierce mastiff, let children do with him what they will. I gave myself a whole holiday—sometimes the most precious part of my life both for myself and those for whom I labour—and wandered about on the shore, now passing the children and assailed with a volley of cries and entreaties to look at this one's castle and that one's ditch, now leaving them behind, with what in its un-graduated flatness might well enough personate an end-less desert of sand between, over the expanse of which I could imagine them disappearing on a far horizon, whence, however, a faint occasional cry of excitement and pleasure would reach my ears. The sea was so calm, and the shore so gently sloping, that you could hardly tell where the sand ceased and the sea began—the water sloped to such a thin pellicle, thinner than any knife edge, upon the shining brown sand, and you saw the sand underneath the water to such a distance out. Yet this depth, which would not drown a red spider, was the ocean. In my mind I followed that bed of shining sand, bared of its hiding waters, out and out, till I was lost in an awful wilderness of chasms, precipices, and mountain peaks, in whose caverns the sea-serpent may dwell, with his breath of pestilence; the kraken, with "his skaly rind," may there be sleeping

"His ancient dreamless, uninvaded sleep,"

while

> "faintest sunlights flee
> About his shadowy sides,"

as he lies

> "Battening upon huge seaworms in his sleep."

There may lie all the horrors that Schiller's diver encountered—the frightful Molch, and that worst of all, to which he gives no name, which came creeping with a hundred knots at once; but here are only the gracious rainbow-woven shells, an evanescent jelly or two, and the queer baby-crabs that crawl out from the holes of the bordering rocks. What awful gradations of gentleness lead from such as these down to those caverns where wallow the inventions of Nature's infancy, when like a child of untutored imagination, she drew on the slate of her fancy creations in which flitting shadows of beauty serve only to heighten the shuddering, gruesome horror? The sweet sun and air, the hand of man, and the growth of the ages, have all but swept such from the upper plains of the earth: what hunter's bow has twanged, what adventurer's rifle has cracked in those leagues of mountain waste, vaster than all the upper world can show, where the beasts of the ocean "graze the sea-weed, their pasture"! Diana of the silver bow herself, when she descends into the interlunar caves of hell, sends no such monsters fleeing from her spells. Yet if such there be, such horrors too must lie in the undiscovered caves of man's nature, of which all this outer world is but a typical analysis. By equally slow gradations may the inner eye descend from the truth of a Cordelia to the falsehood of an Iago. As these golden sands slope from the sun-light into the wallowing abyss of darkness, even so from the love of the child to his holy mother slopes the inclined plane of humanity to the hell of the sensualist. "But with one difference in the moral world," I said aloud, as I paced up and down on the shimmering margin—"that everywhere in the scale the eye of the all-seeing Father can detect the first quiver of the eyelid that would raise itself heavenward, responsive to his waking spirit." I lifted my eyes in the relief of the thought, and saw how the sun of the autumn hung above the waters oppressed with a mist of his own glory; far away to the left a man who had been clambering on a low rock, inaccessible save in such a tide, gathering mussels, threw himself into the sea and swam ashore; above his head the storm-tower stood in the stormless air; the sea glittered and shone, and the long-winged birds knew not which to choose, the balmy air or the cool deep, now flitting like arrow-heads through the one, now alighting eagerly upon the other, to forsake it anew for the thinner element. I thanked God for his glory.

"Oh, papa, it's so jolly! So jolly!" shouted the children as I passed them again.

"What is it that's so jolly, Charlie?" I asked.

"My castle," screeched Harry in reply; "only it's tumbled down. The water *would* keep coming in underneath."

"I tried to stop it with a newspaper," cried Charlie, "but it wouldn't. So we were forced to let it be, and down it went into the ditch."

"We blew it up rather than surrender," said Dora. "We did. Only Harry always forgets, and says it was the water did it."

I drew near the rock that held the bath. I had never approached it from this side before. It was high above my head, and a stream of water was flowing from it. I scrambled up, undressed and plunged into its dark hollow, where I felt like one of the sea-beasts of which I had been dreaming, down in the caves of the unvisited ocean. But the sun was over my head, and the air with an edge of the winter was about me. I dressed quickly, descended on the other side of the rock, and wandered again on the sands to seaward of the breakwater, which lay above looking dry and weary, and worn with years of contest with the waves, which had at length withdrawn defeated to their own country, and left it as if to victory and a useless age of peace. How different was the scene when a raving mountain of water filled all the hollow where I now wandered, and rushed over the top of that mole now so high above me, and I had to cling to its stones to keep me from being carried off like a bit of floating sea-weed! This was the loveliest and strangest part of the shore. Several long low ridges of rock, of whose existence I scarcely knew, worn to a level with the sand, hollowed and channelled with the terrible run of the tide across them, and looking like the old and outworn cheek-teeth of some awful beast of prey, stretched out seawards. Here and there amongst them rose a well-known rock, but now so changed in look by being lifted all the height between the base on the waters, and the second base in the sand, that I wondered at each, walking round and viewing it on all sides. It seemed almost a fresh growth out of the garden of the shore, with uncouth hollows around its fungous root, and a forsaken air about its brows as it stood in the dry sand and looked seaward. But what made the chief delight of the spot, closed in by rocks from the open sands, was the multitude of fairy rivers that flowed across it to the sea. The gladness these streams gave me I cannot communicate. The tide had filled thousands of hollows in the breakwater, hundreds of cracked basins in the rocks, huge sponges of sand; from all of which—from cranny and crack, and oozing sponge—the water flowed in restricted haste back, back to the sea, tumbling in tiny cataracts down the faces of the rocks, bubbling from their roots as from wells, gathering in tanks of sand, and overflowing in broad, shallow streams, curving and sweeping in their sandy channels just like the great rivers of a continent;—here spreading into smooth, silent lakes and reaches, here babbling along in ripples and waves innumerable—flowing, flowing, to lose their small beings in the same ocean that met on the other side the waters of the Mississippi, the Orinoco, the Amazon. All their channels were of golden sand, and the golden sunlight was above and through and in them all: gold and gold met, with the waters between. And what gave an added life to their motion was that all the ripples made shadows on the clear yellow below them. The eye could not see the rippling on the surface; but the sun saw it, and drew it in multitudinous shadowy motion upon the sand, with the play of a thousand fancies of gold burnished and dead, of sunlight and yellow, trembling, melting, curving, blending, vanishing ever, ever renewed. It was as if all the water-marks upon a web of golden silk had been set in wildest yet most graceful curvilinear motion by the breath of a hundred playful zephyrs. My eye could not be filled with seeing. I stood in speechless delight for a while, gazing at the "endless ending" which was "the humour of the game," and thinking how in all God's works the laws of beauty are wrought out in evanishment, in birth and death. There, there is no hoarding, but an ever fresh creating, an eternal flow of life from the heart of the All-beautiful. Hence, even the heart of man cannot hoard. His brain or his hand may gather into its box and hoard; but the moment the thing has passed into the box, the heart has lost it and is hungry again. If man would *have*, it is the giver he must have; the eternal, the original, the ever-outpouring is alone within his reach; the everlasting *creation* is his heritage. Therefore, all that he makes must be free to come and go through the heart of his child; he can enjoy it only as it passes, can enjoy only its life, its soul, its vision, its meaning, not itself. To hoard rubies and sapphires is as useless and hopeless for the heart, as if I were to attempt to hoard this marvel of sand and water and sunlight in the same iron chest with the musty deeds of my wife's inheritance.

"Father," I murmured half aloud, "thou alone art, and I am because thou art. Thy will shall be mine."

I know that I must have spoken aloud, because I remember the start of consciousness and discomposure occasioned by the voice of Percivale greeting me.

"I beg your pardon," he added, "I did not mean to startle you, Mr Walton. I thought you were only looking at Nature's childplay—not thinking."

"I know few things more fit to set one thinking than what you have very well called Nature's childplay," I returned. "Is Nature very heartless now, do you think, to go on with this kind of thing at our feet, when away up yonder lies the awful London with so many sores festering in her heart?"

"You must answer your own question, Mr Walton. You know I cannot. I confess I feel the difficulty deeply. I will go further and confess that the discrepancy makes me doubt many things I would gladly believe. I know *you* are able to distinguish between a glad unbelief and a sorrowful doubt."

"Else were I unworthy of the humblest place in the kingdom—unworthy to be a doorkeeper in the house of my God," I answered, and recoiled from the sound of my own words, for they seemed to imply that I believed myself worthy of the position I occupied. I hastened to correct them. "But do not mistake my thoughts," I said. "I do not dream of worthiness in the way of honour—only of fitness for the work to be done. For that I think God has fitted me in some measure. The doorkeeper's office may be given him not because he has done some great deed worthy of the honour, but because he can sweep the porch and scour the threshold, and will, in the main, try to keep them clean. That is all the worthiness I dare to claim, even to hope that I possess."

"No one who knows you can mistake your words, except wilfully," returned Percivale, courteously.

"Thank you," I said. "Now I will just ask you, in reference to the contrast between human life and nature, how you will go back to your work in London after seeing all this child's and other play of Nature? Suppose you had had nothing here but rain and high winds and sea fogs, would you have been better fitted for doing something to comfort those who know nothing of such influences than you will be now? One of the most important qualifications of a sick nurse is a ready smile. A long-faced nurse in a sick room is a visible embodiment and presence of the disease against which the eager life of the patient is fighting in agony. Such ought to be banished, with their black dresses and their mourning-shop looks, from every sick chamber, and permitted to minister only to the dead, who do not mind looks. With what a power of life and hope does a woman—young or old, I do not care—with a face of the morning, a dress like the spring, a bunch of wild flowers in her hand, with the dew upon them, and perhaps in her eyes too—I don't object to that—that is sympathy, not the worship of darkness,—with what a message from nature and life does she, looking death in the face with a smile, dawn upon the vision of the invalid! She brings a little health, a little strength to fight, a little hope to endure, actually lapt in the folds of her gracious garments. For the soul itself can do more than any medicine, if it be fed with the truth of life."

'But are you not—I beg your pardon for interposing on your eloquence with dull objection," said Percivale—"are you not begging all the question? *Is* life such an affair of sunshine and gladness?"

"If life is not, then I confess all this show of Nature is worse than vanity: it is a vile mockery. Life is gladness: it is the death in it that makes the misery. We call life-in-death life, and hence the mistake. If gladness were not at the root, whence its opposite sorrow against which we arise, from which we recoil, with which we fight? We recognize it as death—the contrary of life. There could be no sorrow but for a recognition of primordial bliss. This in us that fights must be life. It is of the nature of light, not of darkness. Darkness is nothing until the light comes. This very childplay, as you call it, of nature, is her assertion of the secret that life is the deepest—that life shall conquer death: those who believe this must bear the good news to them that sit in darkness and the shadow of death. Our Lord has conquered death—yea, the moral death that he called the world—and now having sown the seed of light, the harvest is springing in human hearts—is springing in this dance of radiance—and will grow and grow until the hearts of the children of the kingdom shall frolic in the sunlight of the Father's presence. Nature has God at her heart. She is but the garment of the Invisible. God wears his singing robes in a day like this, and says to his children, 'Be not afraid: your brothers and sisters up there in

London are in my hands: go and help them. I am with you. Bear to them the message of joy. Tell them to be of good cheer: I have overcome the world. Tell them to endure hunger, and not sin; to endure passion, and not yield; to admire, and not desire. Sorrow and pain are serving my ends; for by them will I slay sin, and save my children.'"

"I wish I could believe as you do, Mr Walton."

"I wish you could. But God will teach you if you are willing to be taught."

"I desire the truth, Mr Walton."

"God bless you. God is blessing you," I said.

"Amen," returned Percivale devoutly, and we strolled away together in silence towards the cliffs.

The recession of the tide allowed us to get far enough away from the face of the rocks to see the general effect. With the lisping of the inch-deep wavelets at our heels we stood and regarded the worn yet defiant, the wasted and jagged yet reposeful face of the guardians of the shore.

"Who could imagine, in weather like this, and with this baby of a tide lying behind us, low at our feet, and shallow as the water a schoolboy pours upon his slate to wash it withal, that those grand cliffs before us bear on their front the scars and dints of centuries, of chiliads of stubborn resistance, of passionate contest with this same creature that is at this moment unable to rock the cradle of an infant? Look behind you, at your feet, Mr Percivale: look before you at the chasms, rents, caves, and hollows, of those rocks."

"I wish you were a painter, Mr Walton," he said.

"I wish I were," I returned. "At least, I know I should rejoice in it, if it had been given me to be one. But why do you say so now?"

"Because you have always some individual predominating idea, which would give interpretation to nature while it gave harmony, reality, and individuality to your representation of her."

"I know what you mean," I answered; "but I have no gift whatever in that direction. I have no idea of drawing, or of producing the effects of light and shade, though I think I have a little notion of colour—perhaps about as much as the little London boy, who stopped a friend of mine once to ask the way to the field where the buttercups grew, had of nature."

"I wish I could ask your opinion of some of my pictures."

"That I should never presume to give. I could only tell you what they made me feel, or perhaps only think. Some day I may have the pleasure of looking at them."

"May I offer you my address?" he said, and took a card from his pocket-book. "It is a poor place, but if you should happen to think of me when you are next in London, I shall be honoured by your paying me a visit."

"I shall be most happy," I returned, taking his card.—"Did it ever occur to you, in reference to the subject we were upon a few minutes ago, how little you can do without shadow in making a picture?"

"Little indeed," answered Percivale. "In fact it would be no picture at all."

"I doubt if the world would fare better without its shadows."

"But it would be a poor satisfaction with regard to the nature of God, to be told that he allowed evil for artistic purposes."

"It would indeed, if you regard the world as a picture. But if you think of his art as expended, not upon the making of a history or a drama, but upon the making of an individual, a being, a character, then I think a great part of the difficulty concerning the existence of evil which oppresses you will vanish. So long as a creature has not sinned, sin is possible to him. Does it seem inconsistent with the character of God that in order that sin should become impossible he should allow sin to come? that, in order that his creatures should choose the good and refuse the evil, in order that they might become such with their whole nature infinitely enlarged, as to turn from sin with a perfect repugnance of the will, he should allow them to fall? that, in order that, from being sweet childish children they should become noble, child-like men and women, he should let them try to walk alone? Why should he not allow the possible in order that it should become impossible? for possible it would ever have been, even in the midst of all the blessedness until it had been, and had been thus destroyed. Thus sin is slain, uprooted. And the war must ever exist it seems to me, where there is creation still going on. How could I be content to guard my children so that they should never have temptation, knowing that in all probability they would fail if at any moment it should cross their path? Would the deepest communion of father and child ever be possible between us? Evil would ever seem to be in the child, so long as it was possible it should be there developed. And if this can be said for the existence of moral evil, the existence of all other evil becomes a comparative trifle; nay, a positive good, for by this the other is combated."

"I think I understand you," returned Percivale. "I will think over what you have said. These are very difficult questions."

"Very. I don't think argument is of much use about them, except as it may help to quiet a man's uneasiness a little, and so give his mind peace to think about duty. For about the doing of duty there can be no question once it is seen. And the doing of duty is the shortest—in very fact, the only way into the light."

As we spoke, we had turned from the cliffs, and wandered back across the salt streams to the sands beyond. From the direction of the house came a little procession of servants, with Walter at their head, bearing the preparations for our dinner—over the gates of the lock, down the sides of the embankment of the canal, and across the sands, in the direction of the children, who were still playing merrily.

"Will you join our early dinner, which is to be out of doors, as you see, somewhere hereabout on the sands?" I said.

"I shall be delighted," he answered, "if you will let

me be of some use first. I presume you mean to bring your invalid out."

"Yes; and you shall help me to carry her, if you will."

"That is what I hoped," said Percivale; and we went together towards the parsonage.

As we approached, I saw Wynnie sitting at the drawing-room window; but when we entered the room, she was gone. My wife was there, however.

"Where is Wynnie?" I asked.

"She saw you coming," she answered, "and went to get Connie ready; for I guessed Mr Percivale had come to help you to carry her out."

But I could not help doubting there might be more than that in Wynnie's disappearance. "What if she should have fallen in love with him," I thought, "and he should never say a word on the subject? That would be dreadful for us all."

They had been repeatedly but not very much together of late, and I was compelled to allow to myself that if they did fall in love with each other it would be very natural on both sides, for there was evidently a great mental resemblance between them, so that they could not help sympathizing with each other's peculiarities. And any one could see what a fine couple they would make.

Wynnie was much taller than Connie—almost the height of her mother. She had a very fair skin, and brown hair, a broad forehead, a wise, thoughtful, often troubled face, a mouth that seldom smiled, but on which a smile seemed always asleep, and round soft cheeks that dimpled like water when she did smile. I have described Percivale before. Why should not two such walk together along the path to the gates of the light? And yet I could not help some anxiety. I did not know anything of his history. I had no testimony concerning him from any one that knew him. His past life was a blank to me; his means of livelihood probably insufficient—certainly, I judged, precarious, and his position in society—but there I checked myself: I had had enough of that kind of thing already. I would not willingly offend in that worldliness again. The God of the whole earth could not choose that I should look at such works of his hands after that fashion. And I was his servant—not Mammon's or Belial's.

All this passed through my mind in about three turns of the winnowing fan of thought. Mr Percivale had begun talking to my wife, who took no pains to conceal that his presence was pleasant to her, and I went up-stairs, almost unconsciously, to Connie's room.

When I opened the door, forgetting to announce my approach as I ought to have done, I saw Wynnie leaning over Connie, and Connie's arm round her waist. Wynnie started back, and Connie gave a little cry, for the jerk thus occasioned had hurt her. Wynnie had turned her head away, but turned it again at Connie's cry, and I saw a tear on her face.

"My darlings, I beg your pardon," I said. "It was very stupid of me not to knock at the door."

Connie looked up at me with large resting eyes, and said—

"It 's nothing, papa. Wynnie is in one of her gloomy moods, and didn't want you to see her crying. She gave me a little pull, that was all. It didn't hurt me much, only I 'm such a goose! I 'm in terror before the pain comes. Look at me," she added, seeing doubtless, some perturbation on my countenance: "I 'm all right now." And she smiled in my face perfectly.

I turned to Wynnie, put my arm about her, kissed her cheek, and left the room. I looked round at the door, and saw that Connie was following me with her eyes, but Wynnie's were hidden in her handkerchief.

I went back to the drawing-room, and in a few minutes Walter came to announce that dinner was about to be served. The same moment Wynnie came to say that Connie was ready. She did not lift her eyes, or approach to give Percivale any greeting, but went again as soon as she had given her message. I saw that he looked first concerned, and then thoughtful.

"Come, Mr Percivale," I said, and he followed me up to Connie's room.

Wynnie was not there, but Connie lay, looking lovely, all ready for going. We lifted her, and carried her by the window out on the down, for the easiest way, though the longest, was by the path to the breakwater, along its broad back, and down from the end of it upon the sands. Before we reached the breakwater, I found that Wynnie was following behind us. We stopped in the middle of it, and set Connie down, as if I wanted to take breath,

But I had thought of something to say to her, which I wanted Wynnie to hear without its being addressed to her.

"Do you see, Connie," I said, "how far off the water is?"

"Yes, papa; it is a long way off. I wish I could get up and run down to it."

"You can hardly believe that all between, all those rocks, and all that sand, will be covered before sunset."

"I know it will be. But it doesn't *look* likely—does it, papa?"

"Not the least likely, my dear. Do you remember that stormy night when I came through your room to go out for a walk in the dark?"

"Remember it, papa? I cannot forget it. Every time I hear the wind blowing when I wake in the night, I fancy you are out in it, and have to wake myself up quite to get rid of the thought."

"Well, Connie, look down into the great hollow there, with rocks and sand at the bottom of it, stretching far away."

"Yes, papa."

"Now, look over the side of your litter. You see those holes all about between the stones."

"Yes, papa."

"Well, one of those little holes saved my life that night, when the great gulf there was full of huge mounds of roaring water, which rushed across this breakwater with force enough to sweep a whole cavalry regiment off its back."

"Papa!" exclaimed Connie, turning pale.

Then first I told her all the story. And Wynnie listened behind.

"Then I *was* right in being frightened, papa!" cried Connie, bursting into tears; for since her accident she could not well command her feelings.

"You were right in trusting in God, Connie."

"But you might have been drowned, papa!" she sobbed.

"Nobody has a right to say that anything might have been other than what has been. Before a thing has happened, we can say might or might not; but that has to do only with our ignorance. Of course I am not speaking of things wherein we ought to exercise will and choice. That is *our* department.—But this does not look like that now, does it? Think what a change,—from the dark night and the roaring water, to this fulness of sunlight and the bare sands, with the water lisping on their edge away there in the distance. Now, I want you to think that in life troubles will come which look as if they would never pass away; the night and the storm look as if they would last for ever, but the calm and the morning cannot be stayed; the storm in its very nature is transient. The effort of Nature, as that of the human heart, ever is to return to its repose, for God is Peace."

"But if you will excuse me, Mr Walton," said Percivale, "you can hardly expect experience to be of use to any but those who have had it. It seems to me that its influences cannot be imparted."

"That depends on the amount of faith in those to

whom its results are offered. Of course, as experience, it can have no weight with another; for it is no longer experience. One remove, and it ceases. But faith in the person who has experienced can draw over or derive —to use an old Italian word—some of its benefits to him who has the faith. Experience may thus, in a sense, be accumulated, and we may go on to fresh experience of our own. At least I can hope that the experience of a father may take the form of hope in the minds of his daughters. Hope never hurt any one—never yet interfered with duty; nay, always strengthens to the performance of duty, gives courage and clears the judgment. St Paul says we are saved by hope. Hope is the most rational thing in the universe. Even the ancient poets, who believed it was delusive, yet regarded it as an antidote given by the mercy of the gods against some at least of the ills of life."

"But they counted it delusive. A wise man cannot consent to be deluded."

"Assuredly not. The sorest truth rather than a false hope! But what is a false hope? Only one that ought not to be fulfilled. The old poets could give themselves little room for hope, and less for its fulfilment; for what were the gods in whom they believed—I cannot say, in whom they trusted? Gods who did the best their own poverty of being was capable of doing for men when they gave them the *illusion* of hope.—But I see they are waiting for us below. One thing I repeat: the waves that foamed across the spot where we now stand are gone away, have sunk and vanished."

"But they will come again, papa," faltered Wynnie.

"And God will come with them, my love," I said, as we lifted the litter.

In a few minutes more we were all seated on the sand around a table-cloth spread upon it. I shall never forget the peace and the light outside and in, as far as I was concerned at least, and I hope the others too, that afternoon. The tide had turned, and the waves were creeping up over the level, soundless almost as thought; but it would be time to go home long before they had reached us. The sun was in the western half of the sky, and now and then a breath of wind came from the sea, with a slight saw-edge in it, but not enough to hurt. Connie could stand much more in that way now. And when I saw how she could move herself on her couch, and thought how much she had improved since first she was laid upon it, hope for her kept fluttering joyously in my heart. I could not help fancying even that I saw her move her legs a little, but I could not be in the least sure; and she, if she did move them, was clearly unconscious of it. Charles and Harry were every now and then starting up from their dinner and running off with a shout, to return with apparently increased appetite for the rest of it: and neither their mother nor I cared to interfere with the indecorum. Dora alone took it upon her to rebuke them. Wynnie was very silent, but looked more cheerful. Connie seemed full of quiet bliss. My wife's face was a picture of heavenly repose. The old nurse was walking about with the baby, occasionally with one hand helping the other servants to wait upon us. They, too, seemed to have a share in the gladness of the hour, and, like Ariel, did their spiriting gently.

"This is the will of God," I said, after the things were removed, and we had sat for a few moments in silence.

"What is the will of God, husband?" asked Ethelwyn.

"Why, this, my love," I answered; "this living air and wind, and sea, and light, and land all about us; thi consenting consorting harmony of Nature, that mirrors a like peace in our souls. The perfection of such visions, the gathering of them all in one was, is, I should say, in the face of Christ Jesus. You will say that face was troubled sometimes. Yes, but with a trouble that broke not the music, but deepened the harmony. When he wept at the grave of Lazarus, you do not think it was for Lazarus himself, or for his own loss of him, that he wept? That could not be, seeing he had the power to call him back when he would. The grief was for the poor troubled hearts left behind, to whom it was so dreadful because they had not faith enough in his Father, the God of life and love, who was looking after it all, full of tenderness and grace, with whom Lazarus was present and blessed. It was the aching, loving heart of humanity for which he wept, that needed God so awfully, and could not yet trust in him. Their brother was only hidden in the skirts of their Father's garment, but they could not believe that: they said he was dead—lost—away—all gone, as the children say. And it was so sad to think of a whole world full of the grief of death, that he could not bear it without the human tears to help his heart, as they help ours. It was for our dark sorrows that he wept. But the peace could be no less plain on the face that saw God. Did you ever think of that wonderful saying: 'Again a little while, and ye shall see me, because I go to the Father?' The heart of man would have joined the 'because I go to the Father' with the former result—the not seeing of him. The heart of man is not able, without more and more light, to understand that all vision is in the light of the Father Because Jesus went to the Father, therefore the disciples saw him tenfold more. His body no longer in their eyes, his very being, his very self was in their hearts—not in their affections only—in their spirits, their heavenly consciousness."

As I said this, a certain hymn, for which I had and have an especial affection, came into my mind, and, without prologue or introduction, I repeated it:—

If I Him but have,
If he be but mine,
If my heart, hence to the grave,
Ne'er forgets his love divine—
Know I nought of sadness,
Feel I nought but worship, love, and gladness.

If I Him but have,
Glad with all I part;
Follow on my pilgrim staff
My Lord only, with true heart;
Leave them, nothing saying,
On broad, bright, and crowded highways straying.

If I Him but have,
Glad I fall asleep;

Aye the flood that his heart gave
Strength within my heart shall keep;
And with soft compelling
Make it tender, through and through it swelling.

If I Him but have,
Mine the world I hail!
Glad as cherub smiling grave,
Holding back the virgin's veil.
Sunk and lost in seeing,
Earthly fears have died from all my being.

Where I have but Him
Is my Fatherland;
And all gifts and graces come
Heritage into my hand:
Brothers long deplored
I in his disciples find restored.

"What a lovely hymn, papa!" exclaimed Connie. She could always speak more easily than either her mother or sister. "Who wrote it?"

"Friedrich von Hardenberg, known, where he is known, as Novalis."

"But he must have written it in German. Did you translate it?"

"Yes. You will find, I think, that I have kept form, thought, and feeling, however I may have failed in making an English poem of it."

"Oh, you dear papa! It is lovely! Is it long since you did it?"

"Years before you were born, Connie."

"To think of you having lived so long, and being one of us!" she returned. "Was he a Roman Catholic, papa?"

"No, he was a Moravian. At least, his parents were. I don't think he belonged to any section of the church in particular."

"But oughtn't he, papa?"

"Certainly not, my dear, except he saw good reason for it. But what is the use of asking such questions, after a hymn like that?"

"Oh, I didn't think anything bad, papa, I assure you. It was only that I wanted to know more about him."

The tears were in her eyes, and I was sorry I had treated as significant what was really not so. But the constant tendency to consider Christianity as associated of necessity with this or that form of it, instead of as obedience to Christ simply, had grown more and more repulsive to me as I had grown myself, for it always seemed like an insult to my brethren in Christ; hence, the least hint of it in my children I was too ready to be down upon like a most unchristian ogre. I took her hand in mine and she was comforted, for she saw in my face that I was sorry, and yet she could see that there was reason at the root of my haste.

"But," said Wynnie, who, I thought afterwards, must have strengthened herself to speak from the instinctive desire to show Percivale how far she was from being out of sympathy with what he might suppose formed a barrier between him and me—"But," she said, "the lovely feeling in that poem seems to me, as in all the rest of such poems, to belong only to the New Testament, and have nothing to do with this world round about us. These things look as if they were only for drawing and painting and being glad in, not as if they had relations with all those awful and solemn things. As soon as I try to get the two together, I lose both of them."

"That is because the human mind must begin with one thing and grow to the rest. At first, Christianity seemed to men to have only to do with their conscience. That was the first relation, of course. But even with art it was regarded as having no relation except for the presentment of its history. Afterwards, men forgot the conscience almost, in trying to make Christianity comprehensible to the understanding. Now, I trust, we are beginning to see that Christianity is everything or nothing. Either the whole is a lovely fable setting forth the loftiest longing of the human soul after the vision of the divine, or it is such a fact as is the heart not only of theology so called, but of history, politics, science, and art: the treasures of the Godhead must be hidden in him, and therefore by him only can be revealed. This will interpret all things, or it has not yet been. Teachers of men have not taught this, because they have not seen it. If we do not find him in Nature, we may conclude either that we do not understand the expression of Nature, or have mistaken ideas or poor feelings about him. It is one great business in our life to find the interpretation which will render this harmony visible. Till we find it, we have not seen him to be all in all. Recognizing a discord when they touched the notes of nature and society, the hermits forsook the instrument altogether, and contented themselves with a partial symphony, lofty, narrow, and weak. Their example, more or less, has been followed by almost all Christians. Exclusion is so much the easier way of getting harmony in the orchestra than study, insight, and interpretation, that most have adopted it. It is for us, and all who have hope in the infinite God, to widen its basis as we may, to search and find the true tone, and right idea, place, and combination of instruments, until to our enraptured ear they all, with one voice of multiform yet harmonious utterance, declare the glory of God and of his Christ."

"A grand idea," said Percivale.

"Therefore likely to be a true one," I returned. "People find it hard to believe grand things; but why? If there be a God, is it not likely everything is grand, save where the reflection of his great thoughts is shaken, broken, distorted by the watery mirrors of our unbelieving and troubled souls? Things ought to be grand, simple, and noble. The ages of eternity will go on showing that such they are and ever have been. God will yet be victorious over our wretched unbeliefs."

I was sitting facing the sea, but with my eyes fixed on the sand, boring holes in it with my stick, for I could talk better when I did not look my familiar faces in the face. I did not feel thus in the pulpit. There I sought the faces of my flock to assist me in speaking to their needs. As I drew to the close of my last monologue, a colder and stronger blast from the sea blew in my face. I lifted my head, and saw that the tide had crept up a long way, and was coming in fast. A luminous fog had sunk down over the western horizon, and almost hidden the sun, had obscured the half of the sea, and destroyed all our hopes of a sunset. A certain veil as of the commonplace, like that which so often settles down over the spirit of man after a season of vision, and glory, and gladness, had dropped over the face of Nature. The wind came in little bitter gusts across the dull waters. It was time to lift Connie and take her home.

This was the last time we ate together on the open shore

CHAPTER XXXIII.

A PASTORAL VISIT.

HE next morning rose neither "cherchef't in a comely cloud," nor "roab'd in flames and amber light," but covered all in a rainy mist, which the wind mingled with salt spray torn from the tops of the waves. Every now and then the wind blew a blastful of larger drops against the window of my study with an angry clatter and clash, as if daring me to go out and meet its ire. The earth was very dreary, for there were no shadows anywhere. The sun was hustled away by the crowding vapours, and earth, sea, and sky were possessed by a gray spirit that threatened wrath. The breakfast bell rang, and I went down, expecting to find my Wynnie, who was always down first to make the tea, standing at the window with a sad face, giving fit response to the aspect of nature without, her soul talking with the gray spirit: I did find her at the window, looking out upon the

restless tossing of the waters, but with no despondent answer to the trouble of nature. On the contrary, her cheek, though neither rosy nor radiant, looked luminous, and her eyes were flashing out upon the ebb-tide which was sinking away into the troubled ocean beyond. Does my girl-reader expect me to tell her next that something had happened? that Percivale had said something to her? or that at least he had just passed the window, and given her a look which she might interpret as she pleased? I must disappoint her. It was nothing of the sort. I knew the heart and feeling of my child. It was only that kind nature was in sympathy with her mood. The girl was always more peaceful in storm than in sunshine. I remembered that now. A movement of life instantly began in her when the obligation of gladness had departed with the light. Her own being arose to provide for its own needs. She could smile now when nature required from her no smile in response to hers. And I could not help saying to myself: "She must marry a poor man some day. She is a creature of the north, and not of the south. The hot sun of prosperity would wither her up. Give her a bleak hill-side, and a glint or two of sunshine between the hail-storms, and she will live and grow. Give her poverty and love, and life will be interesting to her as a romance. Give her money and position, and she will grow dull and haughty; she will believe in nothing that poet can sing or architect build. She will, like Cassius, "scorn her spirit for being moved to smile at anything."

I had stood regarding her for a moment. She turned and saw me, and came forward with her usual morning greeting.

"I beg your pardon, papa: I thought it was Walter."

"I am glad to see a smile on your face, my love."

"Don't think me very disagreeable, papa. I know I am a trouble to you. But I am a trouble to myself first. I fear I have a discontented mind and a complaining temper. But I do try, and I will try hard to overcome it."

"It will not get the better of you, so long as you do the duty of the moment. But I think, as I told you before, that you are not very well, and that your indisposition is going to do you good by making you think about some things you are ready to think about, but which you might have banished if you had been in good health and spirits. You are feeling, as you never felt before, that you need a presence in your soul of which at least you haven't enough yet. But I preached quite enough to you yesterday, and I won't go on the same way to-day again. Only I wanted to comfort you. Come and give me my breakfast."

"You do comfort me, papa," she answered, approaching the table. "I know I don't show what I feel as I ought, but you do comfort me much. Don't you like a day like this, papa?"

"I do, my dear. I always did. And I think you take after me in that, as you do in a good many things besides. That is how I understand you so well."

"Do I really take after you, papa? Are you sure

that you understand me so well?" she asked, brightening up.

"I know I do," I returned, replying to her last question.

"Better than I do myself?" she asked, with an arch smile.

"Considerably, if I mistake not," I answered.

How delightful! To think that I am understood even when I don't understand myself!"

"But even if I am wrong, you are yet understood. The blessedness of life is that we can hide nothing from God. If we could hide anything from God, that hidden thing would by and by turn into a terrible disease. It is the sight of God that keeps and makes things clean. But as we are both, by mutual confession, fond of this kind of weather, what do you say to going out with me? I have to visit a sick woman."

"You don't mean Mrs Coombes, papa?"

'No, my dear. I did not hear she was ill."

"Oh, I daresay it is nothing much. Only old nursey said yesterday she was in bed with a bad cold, or something of that sort."

"We'll call and inquire as we pass,—that is, if you are inclined to go with me."

"How can you put an *if* to that, papa?"

"I have just had a message from that cottage that stands all alone on the corner of Mr Barton's farm —over the cliff, you know—that the woman is ill, and would like to see me. So the sooner we start, the better."

"I shall have done my breakfast in five minutes, papa. Oh! here's mamma. Mamma, I'm going out for a walk in the rain with papa. You won't mind, will you?"

"I don't think it will do you any harm, my dear. That's all I mind, you know. It was only once or twice when you were not well that I objected to it. I quite agree with your papa, that only lazy people are *glad* to stay in-doors when it rains."

"And it does blow so delightfully!" said Wynnie, as she left the room to put on her long cloak and her bonnet.

We called at the sexton's cottage, and found him sitting gloomily by the low window, looking seaward.

"I hope your wife is not *very* poorly, Coombes," I said.

"No, sir. She be very comfortable in bed. Bed's not a bad place to be in in such weather," he answered, turning again a dreary look towards the Atlantic. "Poor things!"

"What a passion for comfort you have, Coombes! How does that come about, do you think?"

"I suppose I was made so, sir."

"To be sure you were. God made you so."

"Surely, sir. Who else?"

"Then I suppose he likes making people comfortable if he makes people like to be comfortable."

"It du look likely enough, sir."

"Then when he takes it out of your hands, you mustn't

think he doesn't look after the people you would make comfortable if you could."

"I must mind my work, you know, sir."

"Yes, surely. And you mustn't want to take his out of his hands, and go grumbling as if you would do it so much better if he would only let you get *your* hand to it."

"I dare say you be right, sir," he said. "I must just go and have a look about though. Here's Agnes. She'll tell you about mother."

He took his spade from the corner, and went out. He often brought his tools into the cottage. He had carved the handle of his spade all over with the names of the people he had buried.

"Tell your mother, Agnes, that I will call in the evening and see her, if she would like to see me. We are going now to see Mrs Stokes. She is very poorly, I hear."

"Let us go through the churchyard, papa," said Wynnie, "and see what the old man is doing."

"Very well, my dear. It is only a few steps round."

"Why do you humour the sexton's foolish fancy so much, papa? It is such nonsense! You taught us it was, surely, in your sermon about the resurrection?"

"Most certainly, my dear. But it would be of no use to try to get it out of his head by any argument. He has a kind of craze in that direction. To get people's hearts right is of much more importance than convincing their judgments. Right judgment will follow. All such fixed ideas should be encountered from the deepest grounds of truth, and not from the outsides of their relations. Coombes has to be taught that God cares for the dead more than he does, and *therefore* it is unreasonable for him to be anxious about them."

When we reached the churchyard, we found the old man kneeling on a grave before its headstone. It was a very old one, with a death's head and cross bones carved upon the top of it in very high relief. With his pocket-knife, he was removing the lumps of green moss out of the hollows of the eyes of the carven skull. We did not interrupt him, but walked past with a nod.

"You saw what he was doing, Wynnie? That reminds me of almost the only thing in Dante's grand poem that troubles me. I cannot think of it without a renewal of my concern, though I have no doubt he is as sorry now as I am that ever he could have written it. When, in the Inferno, he reaches the lowest region of torture, which is a solid lake of ice, he finds the lost plunged in it to various depths, some, if I remember rightly, entirely submerged, and visible only through the ice, transparent as crystal, like the insects found in amber. One man with his head only above the ice, appeals to him as condemned to the same punishment, to take pity on him, and remove the lumps of frozen tears from his eyes, that he may weep a little before they freeze again and stop the relief once more. Dante says to him, 'Tell me who you are, and if I do not assist you, I deserve to lie at the bottom of the ice myself.' The man tells him who he is, and explains to him one awful mystery of these regions. Then he says

'Now stretch forth thy hand, and open my eyes?' 'And,' says Dante, 'I did not open them for him; and rudeness to him was courtesy.'"

"But he promised, you said."

"He did, and yet he did not do it! Pity and truth had abandoned him together. One would think little of it, comparatively, were it not that Dante is so full of tenderness and grand religion. It is very awful, and may teach us many things."

"But what made you think of that now?"

"Merely what Coombes was about. The visual image was all. He was scooping the green moss out of the eyes of the death's head on the gravestone."

By this time we were on the top of the downs, and the wind was buffeting us, and every other minute assailing us with a blast of rain. Wynnie drew her cloak closer about her, bent her head towards the blast, and struggled on bravely by my side. No one who wants to enjoy a walk in the rain must carry an umbrella: it is pure folly. When we came to one of the stone fences, we cowered down by its side for a few moments to recover our breath, and then struggled on again. Anything like conversation was out of the question. At length we dropped into a hollow, which gave us a little repose. Down below, the sea was dashing into the mouth of the glen, or coomb, as they call it there. On the opposite side of the hollow, the little house to which we were going, stood up against the gray sky.

"I begin to doubt whether I ought to have brought you, Wynnie. It was thoughtless of me—I don't mean for your sake, but because your presence may be embarrassing in a small house, for probably the poor woman may prefer seeing me alone."

"I will go back, papa. I shan't mind it a bit."

"No. You had better come on. I shall not be long with her, I daresay. We may find some place that you can wait in. Are you wet?"

"Only my cloak. I am as dry as a tortoise inside."

"Come along then. We shall soon be there."

When we reached the house, I found that Wynnie would not be in the way. I left her seated by the kitchen fire, and was shown into the room where Mrs Stokes lay. I cannot say I perceived, but I guessed somehow, the moment I saw her, that there was something upon her mind. She was a hard-featured woman, with a cold troubled black eye that rolled restlessly about. She lay on her back, moving her head from side to side. When I entered, she only looked at me, and turned her eyes away towards the wall. I approached the bedside, and seated myself by it. I always do so at once; for the patient feels more at rest than if you stand tall up before her. I laid my hand on hers.

"Are you very ill, Mrs Stokes?" I said.

"Yes, very," she answered with a groan. "It be come to the last with me."

"I hope not indeed, Mrs Stokes. It's not come to the last with us, so long as we have a Father in heaven."

"Ah, but it be with me. He can't take any notice of the like of me."

"But indeed he does, whether you think it or not. He takes notice of every thought we think, and every deed we do, and every sin we commit."

I said the last words with emphasis, for I suspected something more than usual upon her conscience. She gave another groan, but made no reply. I therefore went on.

"Our Father in heaven is not like some fathers on earth, who so long as their children don't bother them, let them do anything they like. He will not have them do what is wrong. He loves them too much for that."

"He won't look at me," she said, half murmuring, half sighing it out, so that I could hardly hear what she said.

"It is because he *is* looking at you that you are feeling uncomfortable," I answered. "He wants you to confess your sins. I don't mean to me, but to himself; though if you would like to tell me anything, and I can help you, I shall be *very* glad. You know Jesus Christ came to save us from our sins; and that 's why we call him our Saviour. But he can't save us from our sins if we won't confess that we have any."

"I 'm sure I never said but what I be a great sinner, as well as other people."

'You don't suppose that 's confessing your sins?" I said. "I once knew a woman of very bad character, who allowed to me she was a great sinner; but when I said, 'Yes: you have done so and so,' she would not allow one of those deeds to be worthy of being reckoned amongst her sins. When I asked her what great sins she had been guilty of, then, seeing these counted for nothing, I could get no more out of her than that she was a great sinner, like other people, as you have just been saying."

"I hope you don't be thinking I ha' done anything of that sort!" she said, with wakening energy. "No man or woman dare say I 've done anything to be ashamed of."

"Then you 've committed no sins," I returned. "But why did you send for me? You must have something to say to me."

"I never did send for you. It must ha' been my husband."

"Ah, then, I 'm afraid I 've no business here!" I returned, rising. "I thought you had sent for me."

She returned no answer. I hoped that by retiring I should set her thinking, and make her more willing to listen the next time I came. I think clergymen may do much harm by insisting when people are in a bad mood, as if they had everything to do, and the Spirit of God nothing at all. I bade her good-day, hoped she would be better soon, and returned to Wynnie.

As we walked home together, I said—

"Wynnie, I was right. It would not have done at all to take you into the sick room. Mrs Stokes had not sent for me herself, and rather resented my appearance. But I think she will send for me before many days are over."

CHAPTER XXXIV.

THE ART OF NATURE.

E had a week of hazy weather after this. I spent it chiefly in my study and in Connie's room. A world of mist hung over the sea. It refused to hold any communion with mortals. As if ill-tempered or unhappy, it folded itself in its mantle, and lay still.

What was it thinking about? All Nature is so full of meaning, that we cannot help fancying sometimes that she knows her own meanings. She is busy with every human mood in turn, sometimes with ten of them at once, picturing our own inner world before us, that we may see, understand, develope, reform it.

I was turning over some such thought in my mind one morning, when Dora knocked at the door, saying that Mr Percivale had called, and that mamma was busy, and would I mind if she brought him up to the study.

"Not in the least, my dear," I answered; "I shall be very glad to see him."

"Not much of weather for your sacred craft, Percivale," I said, as he entered. "I suppose if you were asked to make a sketch to-day, it would be much the same as if a stupid woman were to ask you to take her portrait."

Not quite so bad as that," said Percivale.

'Surely the human face is more than nature"

"Nature is never stupid."

'The woman might be pretty."

'Nature is full of beauty in her worst moods; while the prettier such a woman, the more stupid she would look, and the more irksome you would feel the task, for you could not help making claims upon her which you would never think of making upon Nature."

"I daresay you are right. Such stupidity has a good deal to do with moral causes. You do not ever feel that Nature is to blame."

"Nature is never ugly. She may be dull, sorrowful, troubled; she may be lost in tears and pallor, but she cannot be ugly. It is only when you rise into animal nature that you find ugliness."

"True in the main only; for no lines of absolute division can be drawn in nature: I have seen ugly flowers."

"I grant it. But they are exceptional. And none of them are without beauty."

"Surely not. The ugliest soul even is not without some beauty. But I grant you that the higher you rise the more is ugliness possible, just because the greater beauty is possible. There is no ugliness to equal in its repulsiveness the ugliness of a beautiful face."

A pause followed.

"I presume," I said, "you are thinking of returning to London now. There seems so little to be gained by remaining here. When this weather begins to show itself I could wish myself in my own parish. But I am sure the change, even through the winter, will be good for my daughter."

"I must be going soon," he answered. "But it would be too bad to take offence at the old lady's first touch of temper. I mean to wait and see whether we shall not have a little bit of St Martin's summer, as Shakspere calls it; after which, hail London, queen of smoke and"——

"And what?" I asked, seeing he hesitated.

"'And soap,' I was fancying you would say. For you never will allow the worst of things, Mr Walton."

"No, surely I will not. For one thing, the worst has never been seen by anybody yet. We have no experience to justify it."

We were chatting in this loose manner, when Walter came to the door to tell me that a messenger had come from Mrs Stokes.

I went down to see him, and found her husband.

"My wife be very bad, sir," he said. "I wish you could come and see her."

"Does she want to see me?" I asked.

"She's been more uncomfortable than ever since you was there last," he said.

"But," I repeated, "has she said she would like to see me?"

"I can't say it, sir," answered the man.

"Then it is you who want me to see her?"

"Yes, sir. But I be sure she do want to see you. I know her way, you see, sir. She never would say she wanted anything in her life. She would always leave you to find it out. So I got sharp at that, sir."

"And then, would she allow she had wanted it when you got it her?"

"No, never, sir. She be peculiar—my wife. She always be."

"Does she know that you have come to ask me now?"

"No, sir."

"Have you courage to tell her?"

The man hesitated.

"If you haven't courage to tell her," I resumed, "I have nothing more to say. I can't go; or, rather, I will not go."

"I will tell her, sir."

"Then you will tell her that I refused to come until she sent for me herself."

"Ben't that rather hard on a dying woman, sir?"

"I have my reasons. Except she send for me herself, the moment I go she will take refuge in the fact that she did not send for me. I know your wife's peculiarity too, Mr Stokes."

"Well, I *will* tell her, sir. It's time to speak my own mind."

"I think so. It was time long ago. When she sends for me, if it be in the middle of the night, I shall be with her at once."

He left me and I returned to Percivale.

"I was just thinking before you came," I said, "about the relation of Nature to our inner world. You know I am quite ignorant of your art, but I often think about the truths that lie at the root of it."

"I am greatly obliged to you," he said, "for talking about these things. I assure you it is of more service to me than any professional talk. I always think the professions should not herd together so much as they do; they want to be shone upon from other quarters."

"I believe we have all to help each other, Percivale. The sun himself could give us no light that would be of any service to us but for the reflective power of the airy particles through which he shines. But anything I know I have found out merely by foraging for my own necessities."

"That is just what makes the result valuable," he replied. "Tell me what you were thinking."

"I was thinking," I answered, "how every one likes to see his own thoughts set outside of him, that he may contemplate them *objectively*, as the philosophers call it. He likes to see the other side of them, as it were."

"Yes, that is, of course, true; else I suppose, there would be no art at all."

"Surely. But that is not the aspect in which I was

considering the question. Those who can so set them forth are artists; and however they may fail of effecting such a representation of their ideas as will satisfy themselves, they yet experience satisfaction in the measure in which they have succeeded. But there are many more men who cannot yet utter their ideas in any form. Mind, I do expect that, if they will only be good, they shall have this power some day; for I do think that many things we call differences in kind, may in God's grand scale prove to be only differences in degree. And indeed the artist—by artist, I mean, of course, architect, musician, painter, poet, sculptor—in many things requires it just as much as the most helpless and dumb of his brethren, seeing in proportion to the things that he can do, he is aware of the things he cannot do, the thoughts he cannot express. Hence arises the enthusiasm with which people hail the work of an artist; they rejoice, namely, in seeing their own thoughts, or feelings, or something like them, expressed; and hence it comes that of those who have money, some hang their walls with pictures of their own choice, others"——

"I beg your pardon," said Percivale, interrupting; "but most people, I fear, hang their walls with pictures of other people's choice, for they don't buy them at all till the artist has got a name."

"That is true. And yet there is a shadow of choice even there; for they won't at least buy what they dislike. And again the growth in popularity may be only what first attracted their attention—not determined their choice."

"But there are others who only buy them for their value in the market."

"'Of such is not the talk,' as the Germans would say. In as far as your description applies, such are only tradesmen, and have no claim to be considered now."

"Then I beg your pardon for interrupting. I am punished more than I deserve, if you have lost your thread."

"I don't think I have. Let me see. Yes. I was saying that people hang their walls with pictures of their choice; or provide music, &c., of their choice. Let me keep to the pictures: their choice, consciously or un consciously, is determined by some expression that these pictures give to what is in themselves—the buyers, I mean. They like to see their own feelings outside of themselves."

"Is there not another possible motive—that the pictures teach them something?"

"That, I venture to think, shows a higher moral condition than the other, but still partakes of the other; for it is only what is in us already that makes us able to lay hold of a lesson. It is there in the germ, else nothing from without would wake it up."

"I do not quite see what all this has to do with Nature and her influences."

"One step more, and I shall arrive at it. You will admit that the pictures and objects of art of all kinds, with which a man adorns the house he has chosen or built to live in, have thenceforward not a little to do with the education of his tastes and feelings. Even when he is not aware of it, they are working upon him, for good, if he has chosen what is good, which alone shall be our supposition."

"Certainly; that is clear."

"Now I come to it. God, knowing our needs, built our house for our needs—not as one man may build for another, but as no man can build for himself. For our comfort, education, training, he has put into form for us all the otherwise hidden thoughts and feelings of our heart. Even when he speaks of the hidden things of the Spirit of God, he uses the forms or pictures ot Nature. The world is, as it were, the human, unseen world turned inside out that we may see it. On the walls of the house that he has built for us, God has hung up the pictures—ever living, ever changing pictures—of all that passes in our souls. Form and colour and motion are there,—ever modelling, ever renewing, never wearying. Without this living portraiture from within, we should have no word to utter that should represent a single act of the inner world. Metaphysics could have no existence, not to speak of poetry, not to speak of the commonest language of affection. But all is done in such spiritual suggestion, portrait and definition are so avoided, the whole is in such fluent evanescence, that the producing mind is only aided, never overwhelmed. It never amounts to representation. It affords but the material which the thinking, feeling soul can use, interpret, and apply for its own purposes of speech. It is, as it were, the forms of thought cast into a lovely chaos by the inferior laws of matter, thence to be withdrawn by what we call the creative genius that God has given to men, and moulded, and modelied, and arranged, and built up to its own shapes and its own purposes."

"Then I presume you would say that no mere transcript, if I may use the word, of nature, is the worthy work of an artist."

"It is an impossibility to make a mere transcript. No man can help seeing nature as he is himself. For she has all in her. But if he sees no meaning in especial that he wants to give, his portrait of her will represent only her dead face, not her living, impassioned countenance."

"Then artists ought to interpret nature?"

"Indubitably. But that will only be to interpret themselves—something of humanity that is theirs, whether they have discovered it already or not. If to this they can add some teaching for humanity, then indeed they may claim to belong to the higher order of art, however imperfect they may be in their powers of representing—however lowly, therefore, their position may be in that order.'

CHAPTER XXXV.

THE SORE SPOT.

E went on talking for some time. Indeed we talked so long that the dinner-hour was approaching, when one of the maids came with the message that Mr Stokes had called again, wishing to see me. I could not help smiling inwardly at the news. I went down at once, and found him smiling too.

"My wife do send me for you this time, sir," he said. "Between you and me, I cannot help thinking she have something on her mind she wants to tell you, sir."

"Why shouldn't she tell you, Mr Stokes? That would be most natural. And then if you wanted any help about it, why, of course here I am."

"She don't think well enough of my judgment for that, sir. And I daresay she be quite right. She always do make me give in before she have done talking. But she have been a right good wife to me, sir."

"Perhaps she would have been a better if you hadn't given in quite so much. It is very wrong to give in when you think you are right."

"But I never be sure of it when she talk to me awhile."

"Ah, then, I have nothing to say, except that you ought to have been surer—*sometimes;* I don't say *always*."

"But she do want you very bad now, sir. I don't think she'll behave to you as she did before. Do come, sir."

"Of course I will—instantly."

I returned to the study, and asked Percivale if he would like to go with me. He looked, I thought, as if he would rather not. I saw that it was hardly kind to ask him.

"Well, perhaps it is better not," I said, "for I do not know how long I may have to be with the poor woman. You had better wait here and take my place at the dinner-table. I promise not to depose you if I should return before the meal is over."

He thanked me very heartily. I showed him into the drawing-room, told my wife where I was going, and not to wait dinner for me—I would take my chance—and joined Mr Stokes.

"You have no idea, then," I said, after we had gone about half-way, "what makes your wife so uneasy?"

"No, I haven't," he answered. "Except it be," he resumed, "that she was too hard, as I thought, upon our Mary, when she wanted to marry beneath her, as wife thought."

"How beneath her? Who was it she wanted to marry?"

"She did marry him, sir. She has a bit of her mother's temper, you see, and she would take her own way."

"Ah! there's a lesson to mothers, is it not? If they want to have their own way, they mustn't give their own temper to their daughters."

"But how are they to help it, sir?"

"Ah! how indeed? But what is your daughter's husband?"

"A labourer, sir. He works on a farm out by Carpstone."

"But you have worked on Mr Barton's farm for many years, if I don't mistake."

"I have, sir. But I am a sort of a foreman now, you see."

"But you weren't so always, and your son-in-law, whether he work his way up or not, is, I presume, much where you were when you married Mrs Stokes."

"True as you say, sir. And it's not me that has anything to say about it. I never gave the man a nay. But you see my wife, she always do be wanting to get her head up in the world, and since she took to the shop-keeping"——

"The shop-keeping!" I said, with some surprise. "I didn't know that."

"Well, you see, sir, it's only for a quarter, or so, of

the year. You know it's a favourite walk for the folks as comes here for the bathing—past our house, to see the great cave down below. And my wife she got a bit of a sign put up, and put a few ginger-beer bottles in the window, and"——

"A bad place for the ginger-beer," I said.

"They were only empty ones with corks and strings, you know, sir. My wife she know better than put the ginger-beer its own self in the sun. But I do think she carry her head higher after that, and a farm-labourer, as they call them, was none good enough for her daughter."

"And hasn't she been kind to her since she married, then?"

"She's never done her no harm, sir."

"But she hasn't gone to see her very often, or asked her to come and see you very often, I suppose."

"There's ne'er a one o' them crossed the door of the other," he answered, with some evident feeling of his own in the matter.

"Ah! But you don't approve of that yourself, Stokes?"

"Approve of it? No, sir. I be a farm-labourer once myself. And so I do want to see my daughter now and then. But she take after her mother, she do. I don't know which of the two it is as does it, but there's no coming and going between Carpstone and this."

We were approaching the house. I told Stokes he had better let her know I was there; for that, if she had changed her mind, it was not too late for me to go home again without disturbing her. He came back saying she was still very anxious to see me.

"Well, Mrs Stokes, how do you feel to-day?" I asked, by way of opening the conversation. "I don't think you look much worse."

"I be much worse, sir. You don't know what I suffer, or you wouldn't make so little of it. I be very bad."

"I know you are very ill, but I hope you are not too ill to tell me why you are so anxious to see me. You have got something to tell me, I suppose."

With pale and death-like countenance, she appeared to be fighting more with herself than with the disease which yet had nearly overcome her. The drops stood upon her forehead, and she did not speak. Wishing to help her, if I might, I said—

"Was it about your daughter you wanted to speak to me?"

"No," she muttered. "I have nothing to say about my daughter. She was my own. I could do as I pleased with her."

I thought with myself, we must have a word about that by and by, but meantime she must relieve her heart of the one thing whose pressure she feels.

"Then," I said, "you want to tell me about something that was not your own?"

"Who said I ever took what was not my own?" she returned fiercely. "Did Stokes dare to say I took anything that wasn't my own?"

"No one has said anything of the sort. Only I can

not help thinking, from your own words and from your own behaviour, that that must be the cause of your misery."

"It is very hard that the parson should think such things," she muttered again.

"My poor woman," I said, "you sent for me because you had something to confess to me. I want to help you, if I can. But you are too proud to confess it yet, I see. There is no use in my staying here. It only does you harm. So I will bid you good morning. If you cannot confess to me, confess to God."

"God knows it, I suppose, without that."

"Yes. But that does not make it less necessary for you to confess it. How is he to forgive you, if you won't allow that you have done wrong?"

"It be not so easy that as you think. How would you like to say you had took something that wasn't your own?"

"Well, I shouldn't like it, certainly; but if I had it to do, I think I should make haste and do it, and so get rid of it."

"But that 's the worst of it; I can't get rid of it."

"But," I said, laying my hand on hers, and trying to speak as kindly as I could, although her whole behaviour would have been exceedingly repulsive but for her evidently great suffering, "you have now all but confessed taking something that did not belong to you. Why don't you summon courage and tell me all about it? I want to help you out of the trouble as easily as ever I can; but I can't if you don't tell me what you've got that isn't yours."

"I haven't got anything," she muttered.

"You had something then, whatever may have become of it now."

She was again silent.

"What did you do with it?"

"Nothing."

I rose and took up my hat. She stretched out her hand, as if to lay hold of me, with a cry.

"Stop, stop. I'll tell you all about it. I lost it again. That's the worst of it. I got no good of it."

"What was it?"

"A sovereign," she said, with a groan. "And now I'm a thief, I suppose."

"No more a thief than you were before. Rather less, I hope. But do you think it would have been any better for you if you hadn't lost it, and had got some good of it, as you say?"

She was silent yet again.

"If you hadn't lost it you would most likely have been a great deal worse for it than you are—a more wicked woman altogether."

"I'm not a wicked woman."

"It is wicked to steal, is it not?"

"I didn't steal it."

"How did you come by it, then?"

"I found it."

"Did you try to find out the owner?"

"No. I knew whose it was."

"Then it was very wicked not to return it. And, I say again, that if you had not lost the sovereign you would have been most likely a more wicked woman than you are."

"It was very hard to lose it. I could have given it back. And then I wouldn't have lost my character as I have done this day."

"Yes, you could; but I doubt if you would."

"I would."

"Now, if you had it, you are sure you would give it back?"

"Yes, that I would," she said, looking me so full in the face that I was sure she meant it.

"How would you give it back? Would you get your husband to take it?"

"No! I wouldn't trust him."

"With the story you mean? You do not wish to imply that he would not restore it."

"I don't mean that. He would do what I told him."

"How would you return it, then?"

"I should make a parcel of it, and send it."

"Without saying anything about it?"

"Yes. Where's the good? The man would have his own."

"No, he would not. He has a right to your confession, for you have wronged him. That would never do."

"You are too hard upon me," she said, beginning to weep angrily.

"Do you want to get the weight of this sin off your mind?" I said.

"Of course I do. I am going to die. Oh dear! oh dear!"

"Then that is just what I want to help you in. You must confess, or the weight of it will stick there."

"But, if I confess, I shall be expected to pay it back."

"Of course. That is only reasonable."

"But I haven't got it, I tell you. I have lost it."

"Have you not a sovereign in your possession?"

"No, not one."

"Can't you ask your husband to let you have one?"

"There! I knew it was no use. I knew you would only make matters worse. I do wish I had never seen that wicked money."

"You ought not to abuse the money. It was not wicked. You ought to wish that you had returned it. But that is no use. The thing is to return it now. Has your husband got a sovereign?"

"No. He may ha' got one since I be laid up. But I never can tell him about it. And I should be main sorry to spend one of his hard earning in that way, poor man."

"Well, I'll tell him. And we'll manage it somehow."

I thought for a few moments she would break out in opposition, but she hid her face with the sheet instead, and burst into a great weeping.

I took this as a permission to do as I had said, and went to the room-door and called her husband. He came, looking scared. His wife did not look up, but lay weeping. I hoped much for her and him too from this humiliation before him, for I had little doubt she needed it.

"Your wife, poor woman," I said, "is in great distress because—I do not know when or how—she picked up a sovereign that did not belong to her, and instead of returning, put it away somewhere, and lost it. This is what is making her so miserable."

"Deary me!" said Stokes, in the tone with which he would have spoken to a sick child; and going up to his wife he sought to draw down the sheet from her face, apparently that he might kiss her, but she kept tight hold of it, and he could not. "Deary me!" he went on. "We 'll soon put that all to rights. When was it, Jane, that you found it?"

"When we wanted so to have a pig of our own; and I thought I could soon return it," she sobbed from under the sheet.

"Deary me! Ten years ago! Where did you find it, old woman?"

"I saw Squire Tresham drop it, as he paid me for some ginger-beer he got for some ladies that was with him. I do believe I should ha' given it back at the time, but he made faces at the ginger-beer, and said it was very nasty, and I thought, well, I would punish him for it."

"You see it was your temper that made a thief of you, then," I said.

"My old man won't be so hard on me as you, sir. I wish I had told him first."

"I would wish that, too," I said, "were it not that I am afraid you might have persuaded him to be silent about it, and so have made him miserable and wicked too. But now, Stokes, what is to be done? This money must be paid. Have you got it?"

The poor man looked blank.

"She will never be at ease till this money is paid," I insisted.

"Well, sir, I 'ain't got it; but I'll borrow it of some one. I'll go to master, and ask him."

"No, my good fellow, that won't do. Your master would want to know what you were going to do with it, perhaps; and we mustn't let more people know about it than just ourselves and Squire Tresham. There is no occasion for that. I'll tell you what. I'll give you the money, and you must take it—or, if you like, I will take it to the squire, and tell him all about it. Do you authorize me to do this, Mrs Stokes?"

"Please, sir. It's very kind of you. I will work hard to pay you again, if it please God to spare me. I am very sorry I was so cross-tempered to you, sir; but I couldn't bear the disgrace of it."

She said all this from under the bed-clothes.

"Well, I'll go," I said; "and as soon as I've had my dinner, I'll get a horse and ride over to Squire Tresham's. I'll come back to-night and tell you about it. And now I hope you will be able to thank God for forgiving you this sin. But you must not hide and cover it up, but confess it clean out to him, you know."

She made me no answer, but went on sobbing.

I hastened home, and, as I entered, sent Walter to ask the loan of a horse which a gentleman, a neighbour, had placed at my disposal.

When I went into the dining-room, I found that they had not sat down to dinner. I expostulated; it was against the rule of the house, when my return was uncertain.

"But, my love," said my wife, "why should you not let us please ourselves sometimes? Dinner is so much nicer when you are with us."

"I am very glad you think so," I answered. "But there are the children: it is not good for growing creatures to be kept waiting for their meals."

"You see there are no children; they have had their dinner."

"Always in the right, wifie; but there 's Mr Percivale."

"I never dine till seven o'clock—to save daylight," he said.

"Then I am beaten on all points. Let us dine."

During dinner I could scarcely help observing how Percivale's eyes followed Wynnie, or, rather, every now and then settled down upon her face. That she was aware, almost conscious of this, I could not doubt. One glance at her satisfied me of that. But certain words of the apostle kept coming again and again into my mind, for they were winged words those, and even when they did not enter they fluttered their wings at my window: "Whatsoever is not of faith is sin." And I kept reminding myself that I must heave the load of sin off me, as I had been urging poor Mrs Stokes to do; for God was ever seeking to lift it, only he could not without my help, for that would be to do me more harm than good, by taking the one thing in which I was like him away from me—my action. Therefore I must have faith in him, and not be afraid; for, surely, all fear is sin, and one of the most oppressive sins from which the Lord came to save us.

Before dinner was over the horse was at the door. I mounted, and set out for Squire Tresham's.

I found him a rough but kind-hearted, elderly man. When I told him the story of the poor woman's misery, he was quite concerned at her suffering. When I produced the sovereign, he would not receive it at first, but requested me to take it back to her, and say she must keep it by way of an apology for his rudeness about her ginger-beer; for I took care to tell him the whole story, thinking it might be a lesson to him too. But I begged him to take it, for it would, I thought, not only relieve her mind more thoroughly, but help to keep her from coming to think lightly of the affair afterwards. Of course I could not tell him that I had advanced the money, for that would have quite prevented him from receiving it. I then got on my horse again, and rode straight to the cottage.

"Well, Mrs Stokes," I said, "it's all over now. That's one good thing done. How do you feel yourself now?"

"I feel better now, sir. I hope God will forgive me."

"God does forgive you. But there are more things you need forgiveness for. It is not enough to get rid of one sin. We must get rid of all our sins, you know. They're not nice things, are they, to keep in our hearts?

It is just like shutting up nasty corrupting things, dead carcasses, under lock and key, in our most secret drawers as if they were precious jewels."

"I wish I could be good, like some people, but I wasn't made so. There 's my husband now. I do believe he never do anything wrong in his life. But then, you see, he would let a child take him in."

"And far better too. Infinitely better to be taken in. Indeed there is no harm in being taken in; but there is awful harm in taking in."

She did not reply, and I went on—

"I think you would feel a good deal better yet, if you would send for your daughter and her husband now, and make it up with them, especially seeing you are so ill."

"I will, sir. I will directly. I 'm tired of having my own way. But I was made so."

"You weren't made to continue so, at all events. God gives us the necessary strength to resist what is bad in us. He is making at you now; only you must give in, else he cannot get on with the making of you. I think very likely he made you ill now, just that you might bethink yourself, and feel that you had done wrong."

"I have been feeling that for many a year.

"That made it the more needful to make you ill; for you had been feeling your duty, and yet not doing it; and that was worst of all. You know Jesus came to lift the weight of our sins, our very sins themselves, off our hearts, by forgiving them and helping us to cast them away from us. Everything that makes you uncomfortable must have sin in it somewhere, and he came to save you from it. Send for your daughter and her husband, and, when you have done that, you will think of something else to set right that's wrong."

"But there would be no end to that way of it, sir."

"Certainly not, till everything was put right."

"But a body might have nothing else to do, that way."

"Well, that's the very first thing that has to be done. It is our business in this world. We were not sent here to have our own way and try to enjoy ourselves."

"That is hard upon a poor woman that has to work for her bread."

"To work for your bread is not to take your own way, for it is God's way. But you have wanted many things your own way. Now, if you would just take his way, you would find that he would take care you should enjoy your life."

"I'm sure I haven't had much enjoyment in mine."

"That was just because you would not trust him with his own business, but must take it into your hands. If you will but do his will, he will take care that you have a life to be very glad of and very thankful for. And the longer you live, the more blessed you will find it. But I must leave you now, for I have talked to you long enough. You must try and get a sleep. I will come and see you again to-morrow, if you like."

"Please do, sir. I shall be very grateful."

As I rode home I thought, if the lifting of one sin off

the human heart was like a resurrection, what would it be when every sin was lifted from every heart! Every sin, then, discovered in one's own soul must be a pledge of renewed bliss in its removing. And when the thought came again of what St Paul had said somewhere—"whatsoever is not of faith is sin"—I thought what a weight of sin had to be lifted from the earth, and how blessed it might be. But what could I do for it? I could just begin with myself, and pray God for that inward light which is his spirit, that so I might see him in everything and rejoice in everything as his gift, and then all things would be holy, for whatsoever is of faith must be the opposite of sin; and that was my part towards heaving the weight of sin, which, like myriads of gravestones was pressing the life out of us men, off the whole world. Faith in God is life and righteousness—the faith that trusts so that it will obey—none other. Lord, lift the people thou hast made into holy obedience and thanksgiving, that they may be glad in this thy world.

CHAPTER XXXVI.

THE GATHERING STORM.

THE weather cleared up again the next day, and for a fortnight it was lovely. In this region we saw less of the sadness of the dying year than in our own parish, for there being so few trees in the vicinity of the ocean, the autumn had nowhere to hang out her mourning flags. But there, indeed, so mild is the air, and so equable the temperature, all the winter through, compared with the inland counties, that the bitterness of the season is almost unknown. This, however, is no guarantee against furious storms of wind and rain.

Not long after the occurrence last recorded, Turner paid us another visit. I confess I was a little surprised at his being able to get away so soon again; for of all men a country surgeon can least easily find time for a holiday; but he had managed it, and I had no doubt, from what I knew of him, had made thorough provision for his cure in his absence.

He brought us good news from home. Everything was going on well. Weir was working as hard as usual; and everybody agreed that I could not have got a man to take my place better.

He said he found Connie much improved; and, from my own observations, I was sure he was right. She was now able to turn a good way from one side to the other, and finding her health so steady besides, Turner encouraged her in making gentle and frequent use of her strength, impressing it upon her, however, that everything depended on avoiding everything like a jerk or twist of any sort. I was with them when he said this. She looked up at him with a happy smile.

"I will do all I can, Mr Turner," she said, "to get out of people's way as soon as possible."

Perhaps she saw something in our faces that made her add—

"I know you don't mind the bother I am; but I do. I want to help, and not be helped—more than other people—as soon as possible. I will therefore be as gentle as mamma and as brave as papa, and see if we don't get well, Mr Turner. I mean to have a ride on old Spry next summer.—I do," she added, nodding her pretty head up from the pillow, when she saw the glance the doctor and I exchanged. "Look here," she went on, poking the eider-down quilt up with her foot.

"Magnificent," said Turner; "but mind, you must do nothing out of bravado. That won't do at all."

"I have done," said Connie, putting on a face of mock submission.

That day we carried her out for a few minutes, but hardly laid her down, for we were afraid of the damp from the earth. A few feet nearer or farther from the soil will make a difference. It was the last time for many weeks. Any one interested in my Connie need not be alarmed; it was only because of the weather, not because of her health.

One day I was walking home from a visit I had been paying to Mrs Stokes. She was much better, in a fair way to recover indeed, and her mental health was improved as well. Her manner to me was certainly very different, and the tone of her voice, when she spoke to her husband especially, was changed: a certain roughness in it was much modified, and I had good hopes that she had begun to climb up instead of sliding down the hill of difficulty, as she had been doing hitherto.

It was a cold and gusty afternoon. The sky eastward and overhead was tolerably clear when I set out from home; but when I left the cottage to return, I could see that some change was at hand. Shaggy vapours of light gray were blowing rapidly across the sky from the west. A wind was blowing fiercely up there, although the gusts down below came from the east. The clouds it swept along with it were formless, with loose fringes—disreputable, troubled, hasty clouds they were, looking like mischief. They reminded me of Shelley's "Ode to the West Wind," in which he compares the "loose clouds" to hair, and calls them "the locks of the approaching storm." Away to the west, a great thick curtain of fog, of a luminous yellow, covered all the sea-horizon, extending north and south as far as the eye could reach. It looked ominous. A surly secret seemed to lie in its bosom. Now and then I could discern the dim ghost of a vessel through it, as tacking for north or south it came near enough to the edge of the fog to show itself for a few moments, ere it retreated again into its bosom. There was exhaustion, it seemed to me, in the air, notwithstanding the coolness of the wind, and I was glad when I found myself comfortably seated by the drawing-room fire and saw Wynnie bestirring herself to make the tea.

"It looks stormy, I think, Wynnie," I said.

Her eye lightened, as she looked out to sea from the window.

"You seem to like the idea of it," I added.

"You told me I was like you, papa; and you look as if you liked the idea of it too."

"*Per se*, certainly, a storm is pleasant to me. I should not like a world without storms any more than I should like that Frenchman's idea of the perfection of the earth, when all was to be smooth as a trim shaven lawn, rocks and mountains banished, and the sea breaking on the shore only in wavelets of ginger-beer or lemonade, I forget which. But the older you grow, the more sides of a thing will present themselves to your contemplation. The storm may be grand and exciting in itself, but you cannot help thinking of the people that are in it. Think for a moment of the multitude of

I found the whole household full of the storm. The children kept pressing their faces to the windows trying to pierce as by force of will through the darkness, and discover what the wild thing out there was doing. They could see nothing; all was one mass of blackness and dismay, with a soul in it of ceaseless roaring. I ran up to Connie's room, and found that she was left alone. She looked restless, pale, and frightened. The house quivered, and still the wind howled and whistled through the adjoining bark-hut.

"Connie, darling, have they left you alone?" I said.

"Only for a few minutes, papa. I don't mind it."

"Don't be frightened at the storm, my dear. He who could walk on the sea of Galilee, and still the storm of that little pool, can rule the Atlantic just as well. Jeremiah says 'he divideth the sea when the waves thereof roar.'"

The same moment Dora came running into the room.

"Papa!" she cried, "the spray—such a lot of it—came dashing on the windows in the dining-room. Will it break them?"

"I hope not, my dear. Just stay with Connie while I run down."

"Oh, papa! I do want to see."

"What do you want to see, Dora?"

"The storm, papa."

"It is as black as pitch. You can't see anything."

"Oh, but I want to—to—be beside it."

"Well, you shan't stay with Connie, if you are not willing. Go along. Ask Wynnie to come here."

The child was so possessed by the commotion without, that she did not seem even to see my rebuke, not to say feel it. She ran off, and Wynnie presently came. I left her with Connie, put on a long waterproof cloak, and went down to the dining-room. A door led from it immediately on to the little green in front of the house, between it and the sea. The dining-room was dark, for they had put out the lights that they might see better from the windows. The children and some of the servants were there looking out. I opened the door cautiously. It needed the strength of two of the women to shut it behind me. The moment I opened it, a great sheet of spray rushed over me. I went down the little grassy slope. The rain had ceased, and it was not quite so dark as I had expected. I could see the gleaming whiteness all before me. The next moment a wave rolled over the low wall in front of me, breaking on it, and wrapping me round in a sheet of water. Something hurt me sharply on the leg; and I found on searching that one of the large flat stones that lay for coping on the top of the wall, was on the grass beside me. If it had struck me straight, it must have broken my leg.

There came a little lull in the wind, and just as I turned to go into the house again, I thought I heard a gun. I stood and listened, but heard nothing more, and fancied I must have been mistaken. I returned and tapped at the door; but I had to knock loudly before they heard me within. When I went up to the drawing-room, I found that Percivale had joined our party. He and Turner were talking together at one of the windows.

"Did you hear a gun?" I asked them.

"No. Was there one?"

"I 'm not sure. I half fancied I heard one, but no other followed. There will be a good many fired to-night, though, along this awful coast."

"I suppose they keep the life-boat always ready," said Turner.

"No life-boat even, I fear, would live in such a sea," I said, remembering what the officer of the coastguard had told me.

"They would try, though, I suppose," said Turner.

"I do not know," said Percivale. "I don't know the people. But I have seen a life-boat out in as bad a night—whether in as bad a sea, I cannot tell: that depends on the coast, I suppose."

We went on chatting for some time, wondering how the coastguard had fared with the vessel ashore at the Goosepot. Wynnie joined us.

"How is Connie, now, my dear?"

"Very restless and excited, papa. I came down to say, that if Mr Turner didn't mind, I wish he would go up and see her."

"Of course—instantly," said Turner, and moved to follow Wynnie.

But the same moment, as if it had been beside us in the room, so clear, so shrill was it, we heard Connie's voice shrieking, "Papa! papa! There's a great ship ashore down there. Come! come!"

Turner and I rushed from the room in fear and dismay. "How? What? Where could the voice come from?" was the unformed movement of our thoughts. But the moment we left the drawing-room the thing was clear, though not the less marvellous and alarming. We forgot all about the ship, and thought only of our Connie. So much does the near hide the greater that is afar! Connie kept on calling, and her voice guided our eyes.

A little stair led immediately from this floor up to the bark-hut, so that it might be reached without passing through the bedroom. The door at the top of it was open. The door that led from Connie's room into the bark-hut was likewise open, and light shone through it into the place—enough to show a figure standing by the furthest window with face pressed against the glass. And from this figure came the cry, "Papa! papa! Quick! quick! The waves will knock her to pieces!"

In very truth, it was Connie standing there.

CHAPTER XXXVIII.

THE SHIPWRECK.

THINGS that happen altogether have to be told one after the other. Turner and I both rushed at the narrow stair. There was not room for more than one upon it. I was first, but stumbled on the lowest step and fell. Turner put his foot on my back, jumped over me, sprang up the stair, and when I reached the top of it after him, he was meeting me with Connie in his arms, carrying her back to her room. But the girl kept crying—

"Papa, papa! the ship, the ship!"

My duty woke in me. Turner could attend to Connie far better than I could. I made one spring to the window. The moon was not to be seen, but the clouds were thinner, and light enough was soaking through them to show a wave-tormented mass some little way out in the bay; and in that one moment in which I stood looking, a shriek pierced the howling of the wind, cutting through it like a knife. I rushed bare-headed from the house. When or how the resolve was born in me I do not know, but I flew straight to the sexton's, snatched the key from the wall, crying only "ship ashore!" and rushed to the church.

I remember my hand trembled so that I could hardly get the key into the lock. I made myself quieter, opened the door, and feeling my way to the tower, knelt before the keys of the bell-hammers, opened the chest, and struck them wildly, fiercely. An awful jangling, out of tune and harsh, burst into monstrous being in the storm-vexed air. Music itself was untuned, corrupted, and returning to chaos. I struck and struck at the keys. I knew nothing of their normal use. Noise, outcry, *reveillé* was all I meant.

In a few minutes I heard voices and footsteps. From some parts of the village, out of sight of the shore, men and women gathered to the summons. Through the door of the church, which I had left open, came voices in hurried question. "Ship ashore!" was all I could answer, for what was to be done I was helpless to think.

I wondered that so few appeared at the cry of the bells. After those first nobody came for what seemed a long time. I believe, however, I was beating the alarum for only a few minutes altogether, though when I look back upon the time in the dark church, it looks like half-an-hour at least. But indeed I feel so confused about all the doings of that night that in attempting to describe them in order, I feel as if I were walking in a dream.

Still, from comparing mine with the recollected impressions of others, I think I am able to give a tolerably correct result. Most of the incidents seem burnt into my memory so that nothing could destroy the depth of the impression; but the order in which they took place is none the less doubtful.

A hand was laid on my shoulder.

"Who is there?" I said, for it was far too dark to know any one.

"Percivale. What is to be done? The coastguard is away. Nobody seems to know about anything. It is of no use to go on ringing more. Everybody is out, even to the maid-servants. Come down to the shore and you will see."

"But is there not the life-boat?"

"Nobody seems to know anything about it, except that 'it's no manner of use to go trying of that with such a sea on.'"

"But there must be some one in command of it," I said.

"Yes," returned Percivale. "But there doesn't seem to be one of the crew amongst the crowd. All the sailor-like fellows are going about with their hands in their pockets."

"Let us make haste, then," I said; "perhaps we can find out. Are you sure the coastguard have nothing to do with the life-boat?"

"I believe not. They have enough to do with their rockets."

"I remember now that Roxton told me he had far

more confidence in his rockets than in anything a life-boat could do, upon this coast at least."

While we spoke, we came to the bank of the canal. This we had to cross, in order to reach that part of the shore opposite which the wreck lay. To my surprise, the canal itself was in a storm, heaving and tossing and dashing over its banks.

"Percivale!" I exclaimed, "the gates are gone! The sea has torn them away."

"Yes; I suppose so. Would God I could get half-a-dozen men to help me. I have been doing what I could; but I have no influence amongst them."

"What do you mean?" I asked. "What could you do if you had a thousand men at your command?"

He made me no answer for a few moments, during which we were hurrying on for the bridge over the canal. Then he said—

"They regard me only as a meddling stranger, I suppose, for I have been able to get no useful answer. They are all excited, but nobody is doing anything."

"They must know about it a great deal better than we," I returned; "and we must take care not to do them the injustice of supposing they are not ready to do all that can be done."

Percivale was silent yet again.

The record of our conversation looks as quiet on the paper as if we had been talking in a curtained room, but all the time the ocean was raving in my very ear, and the awful tragedy was going on in the dark behind us. The wind was almost as loud as ever, but the rain had

Page 538.

quite ceased, and when we reached the bridge the moon shone out white, as if aghast at what she had at length succeeded in pushing the clouds aside that she might see. Awe and helplessness oppressed us. Having crossed the canal, we turned to the shore. There was little of it left, for the waves had rushed up almost to the village. The sand and the roads, every garden wall, every window that looked seaward, was crowded with gazers. But it was a wonderfully quiet crowd, or seemed so at least, for the noise of the wind and the waves filled the whole vault, and what was spoken was heard only in the ear to which it was spoken. When we came amongst them we heard only a murmur as of more articulated confusion. One turn, and we saw the centre of strife and anxiety—the heart of the storm that filled heaven and earth, upon which all the blasts and the billows broke and raved.

Out there in the moonlight lay a mass of something whose place was discernible by the flashing of the waves as they burst over it. She was far above low-water mark —lay nearer the village by a furlong than the spot where we had taken our last dinner on the shore. It was strange to think that yesterday the spot lay bare to human feet, where now so many men and women were isolated in a howling waste of angry waters; for the cry of women came plainly to our ears, and we were helpless to save them. It was terrible to have to do nothing. Percivale went about hurriedly, talking to this one and that one, as if he still thought something might be done. He turned to me.

"Do try, Mr Walton, and find out for me where the aptain of the life-boat is."

I turned to a sailor-like man who stood at my elbow and asked him.

"It's no use, I assure you, sir," he answered. "No boat could live in such a sea. It would be throwing away the men's lives."

"Do you know where the captain lives?" Percivale asked.

"If I did, I tell you it is of no use."

"Are you the captain yourself?" returned Percivale.

"What is that to you?" he answered—surly now. "I know my own business."

The same moment several of the crowd nearest the edge of the water made a simultaneous rush into the surf, and laid hold of something, which, as they returned drawing it to the shore, I saw to be a human form. It was the body of a woman—alive or dead I could not tell. I could just see the long hair hanging from the head which itself hung backward helplessly as they bore her up the bank. I saw too a white face, and I can recall no more.

"Run, Percivale," I said, "and fetch Turner. She may not be dead yet."

"I can't," answered Percivale. "You had better go yourself, Mr Walton."

He spoke hurriedly. I saw he must have some reason for answering me so abruptly. He was talking to a young fellow whom I recognized as one of the most dis-

solute in the village; and just as I turned to go, they walked away together.

I sped home as fast as I could. It was easier to get along now that the moon shone. I found that Turner had given Connie a composing draught, and that he had good hopes she would at least be nothing the worse for the marvellous result of her excitement. She was asleep exhausted, and her mother was watching by her side. It seemed strange that she could sleep, but Turner said it was the safest reaction—partly, however, occasioned by what he had given her. In her sleep she kept on talking about the ship.

We hurried back to see if anything could be done for the woman. As we went up the side of the canal, we perceived a dark body meeting us. The clouds had again obscured, though not quite hidden the moon, and we could not at first make out what it was. When we came nearer it showed itself a body of men hauling something along. Yes, it was the life-boat, afloat on the troubled waves of the canal, each man seated in his own place, his hands quiet upon his oar, his cork jacket braced about him, his feet out before him, ready to pull the moment they should pass beyond the broken gates of the lock out on the awful tossing of waves. They sat very silent, and the men on the path towed them swiftly along. The moon uncovered her face for a moment, and shone upon the faces of two of the rowers.

"Percivale! Joe!" I cried.

"All right, sir!" said Joe.

"Does your wife know of it, Joe?" I almost gasped.

"To be sure," answered Joe. "It's the first chance I've had of returning thanks for her. Please God, I shall see her again to-night."

"That's good, Joe. Trust in God, my men, whether you sink or swim."

"Ay, ay, sir," they answered as one man.

"This is your doing, Percivale," I said, turning and walking alongside of the boat for a little way.

"It's more Jim Allen's," said Percivale. "If I hadn't got a hold of him I couldn't have done anything."

"God bless you, Jim Allen," I said. "You'll be a better man after this, I think."

"Donnow, sir," returned Jim, cheerily. "It's harder work than pulling an oar."

The captain himself was on board. Percivale having persuaded Jim Allen, the two had gone about in the crowd seeking proselytes. In a wonderfully short space they had found almost all the crew, each fresh one picking up another or more, till at length the captain, protesting against the folly of it, gave in, and once having yielded, was, like a true Englishman, as much in earnest as any of them. The places of two who were missing were supplied by Percivale and Joe, the latter of whom would listen to no remonstrance.

"I've nothing to lose," Percivale had said. "You have a young wife, Joe."

"I've everything to win," Joe had returned. "The only thing that makes me feel a bit faint-hearted over it, is that I'm afraid it's not my duty that drives me to it, but the praise of men, leastways of a woman. What would Aggy think of me if I was to let them drown out there and go to my bed and sleep? I must go."

"Very well, Joe," returned Percivale. "I daresay you are right. You can row, of course?"

"I can row hard, and do as I 'm told," said Joe.

"All right," said Percivale. "Come along."

This I heard afterwards. We were now hurrying against the wind towards the mouth of the canal, some twenty men hauling on the tow-rope. The critical moment would be in the clearing of the gates, I thought, some parts of which might remain swinging. But they encountered no difficulty there, as I heard afterwards. For I remembered that this was not my post, and turned again to follow the doctor.

"God bless you, my men!" I said, and left them.

They gave a great hurrah, and sped on to meet their fate. I found Turner in the little public-house whither they had carried the body. The woman was quite dead.

"I fear it is an emigrant vessel," he said.

"Why do you think so?" I asked, in some consternation.

"Come and look at the body," he said.

It was that of a woman about twenty, tall and finely formed. The face was very handsome, but it did not need the evidence of the hands to prove that she was one of our sisters who have to labour for their bread.

"What should such a girl be doing on board ship but going out to America or Australia?—to her lover, perhaps," said Turner. "You see she has a locket on her neck. I hope nobody will dare to take it off. Some of these people are not far derived from those who thought a wreck a Godsend."

A sound of many feet was at the door just as we turned to leave the house. They were bringing another body—that of an elderly woman—dead, quite dead. Turner had ceased examining her, and we were going out together, when, through all the tumult of the wind and waves, a fierce hiss, vindictive, wrathful, tore the air over our heads. Far up, seawards, something like a fiery snake shot from the high ground on the right side of the bay, over the vessel, and into the water beyond it.

"Thank God! that's the coastguard," I cried.

We rushed through the village, and up on the heights, where they had planted their apparatus. A little crowd surrounded them. How dismal the sea looked in the struggling moonlight! I felt as if I were wandering in the mazes of an evil dream. But when I approached the cliff, and saw down below the great mass of the vessel's hulk, with the waves breaking every moment upon her side, I felt the reality awful indeed. Now and then there would come a kind of lull in the wild sequence of rolling waters, and then I fancied for a moment that I saw how she rocked on the bottom. Her masts had all gone by the board, and a perfect chaos of cordage floated and swung in the waves that broke over her. But her bowsprit remained entire, and shot out into the foamy dark, crowded with human beings. The first rocket had missed. They were preparing to fire another. Roxton stood with his telescope in his hand, ready to watch the result.

"This is a terrible job, sir," he said when I approached him. "I doubt if we shall save one of them."

"There's the life-boat!" I cried, as a dark spot appeared on the waters approaching the vessel from the other side.

"The life-boat!" he returned with contempt. "You don't mean to say they've got *her* out! She'll only add to the mischief. We'll have to save her too."

She was still some way from the vessel, and in comparatively smooth water. But between her and the hull the sea raved in madness. The billows rode over each other, in pursuit, as it seemed, of some invisible prey. Another hiss, as of concentrated hatred, and the second rocket was shooting its parabola through the dusky air. Roxton raised his telescope to his eye the same moment.

"Over her starn!" he cried. "There's a fellow getting down from the cat-head to run aft.—Stop, stop!" he shouted involuntarily. "There's an awful wave on your quarter."

His voice was swallowed in the roaring of the storm. I fancied I could distinguish a dark something shoot from the bows towards the stern. But the huge wave fell upon the wreck. The same moment Roxton exclaimed—so coolly as to amaze me, forgetting how men must come to regard familiar things without discomposure—

"He's gone! I said so. The next'll have better luck, I hope."

That man came ashore alive, though.

All were forward of the foremast. The bowsprit, when I looked through Roxton's telescope, was shapeless as with a swarm of bees. Now and then a single shriek rose upon the wild air. But now my attention was fixed on the life-boat. She had got into the wildest of the broken water. At one moment she was down in a huge cleft, the next balanced like a beam on the knife edge of a wave, tossed about hither and thither as if the waves delighted in mocking the rudder. But hitherto she had shipped no water. I am here drawing upon the information I have since received; but I did see how a huge wave, following close upon the back of that on which she floated, rushed, towered up over her, toppled, and fell upon the life-boat with tons of water; the moon was shining brightly enough to show this with tolerable distinctness. The boat vanished. The next moment, there she was, floating helplessly about like a living thing stunned by the blow of the falling wave. The struggle was over. As far as I could see, every man was in his place; but the boat drifted away before the storm shorewards, and the men let her drift. Were they all killed as they sat? I thought of my Wynnie, and turned to Roxton.

"That wave has done for them," he said. "I told you it was no use. There they go."

"But what is the matter?" I asked. "The men are sitting every man in his place."

"I think so," he answered. "Two were swept overboard, but they caught the ropes and got in again. But don't you see they have no oars?"

That wave had broken every one of them off at the rowlocks, and now they were as helpless as a sponge.

I turned and ran. Before I reached the brow of the hill another rocket was fired and fell wide shorewards, partly because the wind blew with fresh fury at the very moment. I heard Roxton say, "She's breaking up. It's no use. That last did for her;" but I hurried off for the other side of the bay, to see what became of the life-boat. I heard a great cry from the vessel as I reached the brow of the hill, and turned for a parting glance. The dark mass had vanished, and the waves were rushing at will over the space. When I got to the shore the crowd was less. Many were running, like myself, towards the other side, anxious about the life-boat. I hastened after them; for Percivale and Joe filled my heart.

They led the way to the little beach in front of the parsonage. It would be well for the crew if they were driven ashore there, for it was the only spot where they could escape being dashed on rocks.

There was a crowd before the garden-wall, a bustle, and great confusion of speech. The people, men and women, boys and girls, were all gathered about the crew of the life-boat, which already lay, as if it knew of nothing but repose, on the grass within.

"Percivale!" I cried, making my way through the crowd.

There was no answer.

"Joe Harper!" I cried again, searching with eager eyes amongst the crew, to whom everybody was talking.

Still there was no answer; and from the disjointed phrases I heard, I could gather nothing. All at once I saw Wynnie looking over the wall, despair in her face, her wide eyes searching wildly through the crowd. I could not look at her till I knew the worst. The captain was talking to old Coombes. I went up to him. As soon as he saw me, he gave me his attention.

"Where is Mr Percivale?" I asked, with all the calmness I could assume.

He took me by the arm, and drew me out of the crowd, nearer to the waves, and a little nearer to the mouth of the canal. The tide had fallen considerably, else there would not have been the standing-room, narrow as it was, which the people now occupied. He pointed in the direction of the Castle-rock.

"If you mean the stranger gentleman"——

"And Joe Harper, the blacksmith," I interposed.

"They 're there, sir."

"You don't mean those two—just those two—are drowned?" I said.

"No, sir; I don't say that; but God knows they have little chance."

I could not help thinking that God might know they were not in the smallest danger. But I only begged him to tell me where they were.

"Do you see that schooner there, just between you and the Castle-rock?"

"No," I answered; "I can see nothing. Stay. I fancy I can. But I am always ready to fancy I see a thing when I am told it is there. I can't say I see it."

"I can, though. The gentleman you mean, and Joe Harper too, are, I believe, on board of that schooner."

"Is she aground?"

"Oh dear no, sir. She's a light craft, and can swim there well enough. If she d been aground, she'd ha' been ashore in pieces hours ago. But whether she'll ride it out, God only knows, as I said afore."

"How ever did they get aboard of her? I never saw her from the heights opposite."

"You were all taken up with the ship ashore, you see, sir. And she don't make much show in this light. But there she is, and they're aboard of her. And this is how it was."

He went on to give me his part of the story; but I will now give the whole of it myself, as I have gathered and pieced it together.

Two men had been swept overboard, as Roxton said—one of them was Percivale—but they had both got on board again, to drift, oarless, with the rest—now in a windless valley—now aloft on a tempest-swept hill of water—away towards a goal they knew not, neither had chosen, and which yet they could by no means avoid.

A little out of the full force of the current, and not far from the channel of the small stream, which, when the tide was out, flowed across the sands nearly from the canal-gates to the Castle-rock, lay a little schooner belonging to a neighbouring port, Boscastle, I think, which, caught in the storm, had been driven into the bay when it was almost dark, some considerable time before the great ship. The master, however, knew the ground well. The current carried him a little out of the wind, and would have thrown him upon the rocks next, but he managed to drop anchor just in time, and the cable held; and there the little schooner hung in the skirts of the storm, with the jagged teeth of the rocks within an arrow-flight. In the excitement of the great wreck, no one had observed the danger of the little coasting bird. If the cable held till the tide went down, and the anchor did not drag, she would be safe; if not, she must be dashed to pieces.

In the schooner were two men and a boy: two men had been washed overboard an hour or so before they reached the bay. When they had dropped their anchor, they lay down exhausted on the deck. Indeed they were so worn out that they had been unable to drop their sheet-anchor, and were holding on only by their best bower. Had they not been a good deal out of the wind, this would have been useless. Even if it held she was in danger of having her bottom stove in by bumping against the sands as the tide went out. But that they had not to think of yet. The moment they lay down they fell asleep in the middle of the storm. While they slept it increased in violence.

Suddenly one of them awoke, and thought he saw a vision of angels. For over his head faces looked down upon him from the air—that is, from the top of a great wave. The same moment he heard a voice, two of the angels dropped on the deck beside him, and the rest vanished. Those angels were Percivale and Joe. And angels they were, for they came just in time, as all angels do—never a moment too soon or a moment too late: the schooner *was* dragging her anchor. This was soon plain even to the less experienced eyes of the said angels.

But it did not take them many minutes now to drop their strongest anchor, and they were soon riding in perfect safety for some time to come.

One of the two men was the son of old Coombes, the sexton, who was engaged to marry the girl I have spoken of in the end of the twenty-first chapter.

Percivale's account of the matter, as far as he was concerned, was, that, as they drifted helplessly along, he suddenly saw from the top of a huge wave, the little vessel below him. They were, in fact, almost upon the rigging. The wave on which they rode swept the quarter-deck of the schooner.

Percivale says the captain of the life-boat called out "Aboard!" The captain said he remembered nothing of the sort; if he did, he must have meant it for the men on the schooner—to get on board the life-boat. Percivale, however, who had a most chivalrous—ought I not to say Christian?—notion of obedience, fancying the captain meant them to board the schooner, sprang at her fore-shrouds. Thereupon, the wave sweeping them along the schooner's side, Joe sprang on the main-shrouds; and they dropped on the deck together.

But although my reader is at ease about their fate, we who were in the affair were anything but easy at the time corresponding to this point of the narrative. It was a terrible night we passed through.

When I returned, which was almost instantly, for I could do nothing by staring out in the direction of the schooner, I found that the crowd was nearly gone. One little group alone remained behind, the centre of which was a woman. Wynnie had disappeared. The woman who remained behind was Agnes Harper.

The moon shone out clear as I approached the group. Indeed the clouds were breaking up, and drifting away off the heavens. The storm had raved out its business, and was departing into the past.

"Agnes," I said.

"Yes, sir," she answered, and looked up as if waiting for a command. There was no colour in her cheeks or in her lips—at least it seemed so in the moonlight—only in her eyes. But she was perfectly calm. She was leaning against the low wall, with her hands clasped, but hanging quietly down before her.

"The storm is breaking up, Agnes," I said.

"Yes, sir," she answered, in the same still tone. Then, after just a moment's pause, she spoke out of her heart.

"Joe's at his duty, sir?"

I have given the utterance a point of interrogattion: whether she meant that point I am not quite sure.

"Indubitably," I returned. "I have such faith in Joe, that I should be sure of that in any case. At all events, he 's not taking care of his own life. And if one is to go wrong, I would ten thousand times rather err on that side. But I am sure Joe has been doing right, and nothing else."

"Then there's nothing to be said, sir—is there?" she returned, with a sigh that sounded as of relief.

I presume some of the surrounding condolers had been giving her Job's comfort by blaming her husband.

"Do you remember, Agnes, what the Lord said to his mother when she reproached him with having left her and his father?"

"I can't remember anything at this moment, sir," was her touching answer.

"Then I will tell you. He said, 'Why did you look for me? Didn't you know that I must be about something my Father had given me to do?' Now Joe was and is about his Father's business, and you must not be anxious about him. There could be no better reason for not being anxious."

Agnes was a very quiet woman: when without a word she took my hand and kissed it, I felt what a depth there was in the feeling she could not utter. I did not withdraw my hand, for I knew that would be to rebuke her love for Joe.

"Will you come in and wait?" I said indefinitely.

"No, thank you, sir. I must go to my mother. God will look after Joe: won't he, sir?"

"As sure as there is a God, Agnes," I said; and she went away without another word.

I put my hand on the top of the wall and jumped over. I started back with terror, for I had almost alighted on the body of a woman lying there. The first insane suggestion was that it had been cast ashore; but the next moment I knew that it was my own Wynnie.

She had not even fainted. She was lying with her handkerchief stuffed into her mouth to keep her from screaming. When I uttered her name, she rose, and without looking at me, walked away towards the house. I followed. She went straight to her own room and shut the door. I went to find her mother. She was with Connie, who was now awake, lying pale and frightened. I told Ethelwyn that Percivale and Joe were on board the little schooner, which was holding on by her anchor, that Wynnie was in terror about Percivale, that I had found her lying on the wet grass, and that she must get her into a warm bath and to bed. We went together to her room.

She was standing in the middle of the floor, with her hands pressed against her temples.

"Wynnie," I said, "our friends are not drowned. I think you will see them quite safe in the morning. Pray to God for them."

She did not hear a word.

"Leave her with me," said Ethelwyn, proceeding to undress her, "and tell nurse to bring up the large bath. There is plenty of hot water in the boiler: I gave orders to that effect, not knowing what might happen."

Wynnie shuddered as her mother said this; but I waited no longer, for when Ethelwyn spoke, every one felt her authority. I obeyed her, and then went to Connie's room.

"Do you mind being left alone a little while?" I asked her.

"No, papa. Only——are they all drowned?" she said with a shudder.

"I hope not, my dear. But be sure of the mercy of God whatever you fear. You must rest in him, my love, for he is Life, and will conquer death both in the soul and in the body."

"I was not thinking of myself, papa."

"I know that, my dear. But God is thinking of you and every creature that he has made. And for our sakes you must be quiet in heart, that you may get better, and be able to help us."

"I will try, papa," she said; and, turning slowly on her side, she lay quite still.

Dora and the boys were all fast asleep, for it was very late. I cannot, however, say what hour it was.

Telling nurse to be on the watch because Connie was alone, I went again to the beach. I called first, however, to inquire after Agnes. I found her quite composed, sitting with her parents by the fire, none of them doing anything, scarcely speaking, only listening intently to the sounds of the storm now beginning to die away.

I next went to the place where I had left Turner. Five bodies lay there, and he was busy with a sixth. The surgeon of the place was with him. and they quite expected to recover this man.

I then went down to the sands. An officer of the revenue was taking charge of all that came ashore—chests and bales, and everything. For a week the sea went on casting out the fragments of that which she had destroyed. I have heard that, for years after, the shifting of the sands would now and then discover things buried that night by the waves.

All the next day the bodies kept coming ashore, some peaceful as in sleep; others broken and mutilated. Many were cast upon other parts of the coast. Some four or five only, all men, were recovered. It was strange to me how I got used to it. The first horror over, the cry that yet another body had come, awoke only a gentle pity, no more dismay or shuddering. But finding I could be of no use, I did not wait longer than just till the morning began to dawn with a pale ghastly light over the seething raging sea—for the sea raged on, although the wind had gone down. There were many strong men about, with two surgeons, and all the coastguard, who were well accustomed to similar though not such extensive destruction; the houses along the shore were at the disposal of any one who wanted aid; the parsonage was at some distance; and I confess that when I thought of the state of my daughters, as well as remembered former influences upon my wife, I was very glad to think there was no necessity for carrying thither any of those whom the waves cast on the shore.

When I reached home, and found Wynnie quieter, and Connie again asleep, I walked out along our own downs, till I came whence I could see the little schooner still safe at anchor. From her position I concluded, correctly as I found afterwards, that they had let out her cable far enough to allow her to reach the bed of the little stream, where the tide would leave her more gently. She was clearly out of all danger now, and if Percivale and Joe had got safe on board of her, we might confidently expect to see them before many hours were past. I went home with the good news.

For a few moments I doubted whether I should tell Wynnie, for I could not know with any certainty that Percivale was in the schooner. But presently I recalled former conclusions to the effect that we have no right to modify God's facts for fear of what may be to come. A little hope founded on a present appearance, even if that hope should never be realized, may be the very means of enabling a soul to bear the weight of a sorrow past the point at which it would otherwise break down. I would therefore tell Wynnie, and let her share my expectation of deliverance.

I think she had been half-asleep, for when I entered her room, she started up in a sitting posture, looking wild, and putting her hands to her head.

"I have brought you good news, Wynnie," I said. "I have been out on the downs, and there is light enough now to see that the little schooner is quite safe."

"What schooner?" she asked listlessly, and lay down again, her eyes still staring awfully unappeased.

"Why the schooner they say Percivale got on board."

"He isn't drowned then!" she cried with a choking voice, and put her hands to her face, and burst into tears and sobs.

"Wynnie," I said, "look what your faithlessness brings upon you. Everybody but you has known all night that Percivale and Joe Harper are probably quite safe. They may be ashore in a couple of hours."

"But you don't know it. He may be drowned yet."

"Of course there is room for doubt—but none for despair. See what a poor helpless creature hopelessness makes you."

"But how can I help it, papa?" she asked piteously. "I am made so."

But as she spoke, the dawn was clear upon the height of her forehead.

"You are not made yet, as I am always telling you. And God has ordained that you shall have a hand in your own making. You have to consent, to desire that what you know for a fault shall be set right by his loving will and spirit."

"I don't know God, papa."

"Ah, my dear! that is where it all lies. You do not know him, or you would never be without hope."

"But what am I to do to know him?" she asked, rising on her elbow.

The saving power of hope was already working in her. She was once more turning her face towards the Life.

"Read as you have never read before about Christ Jesus, my love. Read with the express object of finding out what God is like, that you may know him, and may trust him. And now give yourself to him, and he will give you sleep."

"What are we to do," I said to my wife, "if Percivale continue silent? For even if he be in love with her, I doubt if he will speak."

"We must leave all that, Harry," she answered.

She was turning on myself the counsel I had been giving Wynnie. It is strange how easily we can tell our brother what he ought to do, and yet, when the case comes to be our own, do precisely as we had rebuked him for doing. I lay down and fell fast asleep.

CHAPTER XXXIX.

THE FUNERAL.

T was a lovely morning when I woke once more. The sun was flashing back from the sea, which was still tossing, but no longer furiously, only as if it wanted to turn itself every way to flash the sunlight about. The madness of the night was over and gone; the light was abroad, and the world was rejoicing. When I reached the drawing-room—which afforded the best outlook over the shore, there was the schooner lying dry on the sands, her two cables and anchors stretching out yards behind her. But halfway between the two sides of the bay rose a mass of something shapeless, drifted over with sand. It was all that remained together of the great ship that had the day before swept over the waters like a live thing with wings—of all the works of man's hands the nearest to the shape and sign of life. The wind had ceased altogether, only now and then a little breeze arose which

murmured "I am very sorry," and lay down again. And I knew that in the houses on the shore dead men and women were lying.

I went down to the dining-room. The three children were busy at their breakfast, but neither wife, daughter, nor visitor had yet appeared. I made a hurried meal, and was just rising to go and inquire further into the events of the night, when the door opened, and in walked Percivale, looking very solemn, but in perfect health and well-being. I grasped his hand warmly.

"Thank God," I said, "that you are returned to us, Percivale."

"I doubt if that is much to give thanks for," he said.

"We are the judges of that," I rejoined. "Tell me all about it."

While he was narrating the events I have already communicated, Wynnie entered. She started, turned pale and then very red, and for a moment hesitated in the doorway.

"Here is another to rejoice at your safety, Percivale," I said.

Thereupon he stepped forward to meet her, and she gave him her hand with an emotion so evident that I felt a little distressed—why I could not easily have told, for she looked most charming in the act,—more lovely than I had ever seen her. Her beauty was unconsciously praising God, and her heart would soon praise him too. But Percivale was a modest man, and I think attributed her emotion to the fact that he had been in danger in the way of duty,—a fact sufficient to move the heart of any good woman.

She sat down and began to busy herself with the teapot. Her hand trembled. I requested Percivale to begin his story once more; and he evidently enjoyed recounting to her the adventures of the night.

I asked him to sit down and have a second breakfast while I went into the village, whereto he seemed nothing loath.

As I crossed the floor of the old mill to see how Joe was, the head of the sexton appeared emerging from it. He looked full of weighty solemn business. Bidding me good morning, he turned to the corner where his tools lay, and proceeded to shoulder spade and pickaxe

"Ah, Coombes! you 'll want them," I said.

"A good many o' my people be come all at once, you see, sir," he returned. "I shall have enough ado to make 'em all comfortable like."

"But you must get help, you know. You can never make them all comfortable yourself alone."

"We 'll see what I can do," he returned. "I ben't a bit willing to let no one do my work for me, I do assure you, sir."

"How many are there wanting your services?" I asked.

"There be fifteen of them now, and there be more, I don't doubt on the way."

"But you won't think of making separate graves for them all," I said. "They died together: let them lie together."

The old man set down his tools, and looked me in the face with indignation. The face was so honest and old, that without feeling I had deserved it, I yet felt the rebuke.

"How would you like, sir," he said, at length, "to be put in the same bed with a lot of people you didn't know nothing about?"

I knew the old man's way, and that any argument which denied the premiss of his peculiar fancy, was worse than thrown away upon him. I therefore ventured no farther than to say that I had heard death was a leveller.

"That be very true; and, mayhap, they mightn't think of it after they'd been down awhile—six weeks, mayhap, or so. But anyhow, it can't be comfortable for 'em, poor things. One on 'em be a baby: I daresay he'd rather lie with his mother. The doctor he say one o' the women be a mother. I don't know," he went on reflectively, "whether she be the baby's own mother, but I daresay neither o' them'll mind it if I take it for granted, and lay 'em down together. So that's one bed less."

One thing was clear, that the old man could not dig fourteen graves within the needful time. But I would not interfere with his office in the church, having no reason to doubt that he would perform its duties to perfection. He shouldered his tools again and walked out. I descended the stair, thinking to see Joe; but there was no one there but the old woman.

"Where are Joe and Agnes?"

"You see, sir, Joe had promised a little job of work to be ready to-day, and so he couldn't stop. He did say Agnes needn't go with him; but she thought she couldn't part with him so soon, you see, sir."

"She had received him from the dead—raised to life again," I said. "It was most natural. But what a fine fellow Joe is: nothing will make him neglect his work!"

"I tried to get him to stop, sir, saying he had done quite enough last night for all next day; but he told me it was his business to get the tire put on Farmer Wheatstone's cart-wheel to-day just as much as it was his business to go in the life-boat yesterday. So he would go, and Aggy wouldn't stay behind."

"Fine fellow, Joe!" I said, and took my leave.

As I drew near the village, I heard the sound of hammering and sawing, and apparently everything at once in the way of joinery: they were making the coffins in the joiners' shops, of which there were two in the place.

I do not like coffins. They seem to me relics of barbarism. If I had my way, I would have the old thing decently wound in a fair linen cloth, and so laid in the bosom of the earth whence it was taken. I would have it vanish, not merely from the world of vision, but from the world of form, as soon as may be. The embrace of the fine life-hoarding, life-giving mould, seems to me comforting, in the vague, foolish fancy that will sometimes emerge from the froth of reverie—I mean of subdued consciousness remaining in the outworn frame,

But the coffin is altogether and vilely repellent. Of this, however, enough. I hate even the shadow of sentiment, though some of my readers who may not yet have learned to distinguish between sentiment and feeling, may wonder how I dare to utter such a barbarism.

I went to the house of the county magistrate hard by, for I thought something might have to be done in which I had a share. I found that he had sent a notice of the loss of the vessel to the Liverpool papers, requesting those who might wish to identify or claim any of the bodies, to appear within four days at Kilkhaven.

This threw the last upon Saturday, and before the end of the week it was clear that they must not remain above ground over Sunday. I therefore arranged that they should be buried late on the Saturday night.

On the Friday morning, a young woman and an old man, unknown to each other, arrived by the coach from Barnstaple. They had come to see the last of their friends in this world; to look, if they might, at the shadow left behind by the departing soul. For as the shadow of any object remains a moment upon the magic curtain of the eye after the object itself has gone, so the shadow of the soul, namely, the body, lingers a moment upon the earth, after the object itself has gone to the "high countries." It was well to see with what a sober sorrow the dignified little old man bore his grief. It was as if he felt that the loss of his son was only for a moment. But the young woman had taken on the hue of the corpse she came to seek. Her eyes were sunken as if with the weight of the light she cared not for, and her cheeks had already pined away as if to be ready for the grave. A being thus emptied of its glory seized and possessed my thoughts. She never even told us whom she came seeking, and after one involuntary question, which simply received no answer, I was very careful not even to approach another. I do not think the form she sought was there; and she may have gone home with the lingering hope, to cast the grey aurora of a doubtful dawn over her coming days, that, after all, that one had escaped.

On the Friday afternoon, with tne approbation of the magistrate, I had all the bodies removed to the church. Some in their coffins, others on stretchers, they were laid in front of the communion-rail. In the evening these two went to see them. I took care to be present. The old man soon found his son. I was at his elbow as he walked between the rows of the dead. He turned to me and said quietly—

"That's him, sir. He was a good lad. God rest his soul. He's with his mother; and if I'm sorry, she's glad."

With that he smiled, or tried to smile. I could only lay my hand on his arm, to let him know that I understood him, and was with him. He walked out of the church, sat down upon a stone, and stared at the mould of a new-made grave in front of him. What was passing behind those eyes God only knew—certainly the man himself did not know. Our lightest thoughts are of more awful significance than the most serious of us can imagine.

For the young woman, I thought she left the church with a little light in her eyes; but she had said nothing. Alas! that the body was not there could no more justify her than Milton in letting her

> frail thoughts dally with false surmise.

With him, too, she might well add—

> Ay me! whilst thee the shores and sounding seas
> Wash far away.

But God had them in his teaching, and all I could do was to ask them to be my guests till the funeral and the following Sunday were over. To this they kindly consented, and I took them to my wife, who received them like herself, and had in a few minutes made them at home with her, to which no doubt their sorrow tended, for that brings out the relations of humanity and destroys its distinctions.

The next morning a Scotchman of a very decided type, originally from Aberdeen, but resident in Liverpool, appeared, seeking the form of his daughter. I had arranged that whoever came should be brought to me first. I went with him to the church. He was a tall, gaunt, bony man, with long arms and huge hands, a rugged granite-like face, and a slow ponderous utterance, which I had some difficulty in understanding. He treated the object of his visit with a certain hardness, and at the same time lightness, which also I had some difficulty in understanding.

"You want to see the"——I said, and hesitated.

"Ow ay—the boadies," he answered. "She winna

be there, I daursay, but I wad jist like to see; for I wadna like her to be beeried gin sae be 'at she was there, wi'oot biddin' her good-bye like."

When we reached the church, I opened the door and entered. An awe fell upon me fresh and new. The beautiful church had become a tomb: solemn, grand, ancient, it rose as a memorial of the dead who lay in peace before her altar-rail, as if they had fled thither for sanctuary from a sea of troubles. And I thought with myself: will the time ever come when the churches shall stand as the tombs of holy things that have passed away, when Christ shall have rendered up the kingdom to his Father, and no man shall need to teach his neighbour or his brother, saying, "Know the Lord?" The thought passed through my mind and vanished as I led my companion up to the dead.

He glanced at one and another and passed on. He had looked at ten or twelve ere he stopped, gazing on the face of the beautiful form which had first come ashore. He stooped, and stroked the white cheeks, taking the dead in his great rough hands, and smoothed the brown hair tenderly, saying, as if he had quite forgotten that she was dead—

"Eh, Maggie! hoo cam *ye* here, lass?"

Then, as if for the first time the reality had grown comprehensible, he put his hands before his face, and burst into tears. His huge frame was shaken with sobs for one long minute, while I stood looking on with awe and reverence. He ceased suddenly, pulled a blue cotton handkerchief with yellow spots on it—I see it now—from his pocket, rubbed his face with it as if drying it with a towel, put it back, turned, and said, without looking at me, "I'll awa' hame."

"Wouldn't you like a piece of her hair?" I asked.

"Gin ye please," he answered gently, as if his daughter's form had been mine now, and her hair were mine to give.

By the vestry door sat Mrs Coombes, watching the dead, with her sweet solemn smile, and her constant ministration of knitting.

"Have you got a pair of scissors there, Mrs Coombes?" I asked.

"Yes, to be sure, sir," she answered, rising, and lifting a huge pair by the string suspending them from her waist.

"Cut off a nice piece of this beautiful hair," I said.

She lifted the lovely head, chose, and cut off a long piece, and handed it respectfully to the father.

He took it without a word, sat down on the step before the communion-rail, and began to smooth out the wonderful sleave of dusky gold. It was, indeed, beautiful hair. As he drew it out, I thought it must be a yard long. He passed his big fingers through and through it, but tenderly, as if it had been still growing on the live lovely head, stopping every moment to pick out the bits of sea-weed and shells, and shake out the sand that had been wrought into its mass. He sat thus for nearly half-an-hour, and we stood looking on with something closely akin to awe. At length he folded it up, drew from his pocket an old black leather book, laid it carefully in the innermost pocket, and rose. I led the way from the church, and he followed me.

Outside the church, he laid his hand on my arm, and said, groping with his other hand in his trowsers-pocket—

"She'll hae putten ye to some expense—for the coffin an' sic like."

"We'll talk about that afterwards," I answered. "Come home with me now, and have some refreshment."

"Na, I thank ye. I hae putten ye to eneuch o' tribble already. I'll jist awa' hame."

"We are going to lay them down this evening. You won't go before the funeral. Indeed, I think you can't get away till Monday morning. My wife and I will be glad of your company till then."

"I'm no company for gentle-fowk, sir."

"Come and show me in which of these graves you would like to have her laid," I said.

He yielded and followed me.

Coombes had not dug many spadefuls before he saw what had been plain enough—that ten such men as he could not dig the graves in time. But there was plenty of help to be had from the village and the neighbouring farms. Most of them were now ready, but a good many men were still at work. The brown hillocks lay about the churchyard—the mole-heaps of burrowing Death.

The stranger looked around him. His face grew critical. He stepped a little hither and thither. At length he turned to me and said—

"I wadna like to be greedy; but gin ye wad lat her lie next the kirk there—i' that neuk—I wad tak' it kindly. And syne gin ever it cam' aboot that I cam' here again, I wad ken whaur she was. Could ye get a sma' bit heidstane putten up? I wad leave the siller wi' ye to pay for 't."

"To be sure I can. What will you have put on the stone?"

"Ow jist—lat me see—Maggie Jamieson—nae Marget, but jist Maggie. She was aye Maggie at hame. Maggie Jamieson, frae her father. It 's the last thing I can gie her. Maybe ye micht put a verse o' Scripter aneath 't, ye ken."

"What verse would you like?"

He thought for a little.

"Isna there a text that says, 'The deid shall hear his voice'?"

"Yes: 'The dead shall hear the voice of the Son of God.'"

"Ay. That 's it. Weel jist put that on.—They canna do better than hear his voice," he added, with a strange mixture of Scotch ratiocination.

I led the way home, and he accompanied me without further objection or apology. After dinner, I proposed that we should go upon the downs, for the day was warm and bright. We sat on the grass. I felt that I could not talk to them as from myself. I knew nothing of the possible gulfs of sorrow in their hearts. To me their forms seemed each like a hill in whose unseen bosom lay a cavern of dripping waters, perhaps with a subterranean torrent of anguish raving through its hollows and tumbling down hidden precipices, whose voice God only heard, and God only could still. The daughter *might*, though from her face I did not think it, have gone away against her father's will. That son *might* have been a ne'er-do-weel at home—how could I tell? The woman *might* be looking for the lover that had forsaken her—I could not divine. I would speak no words of my own. The Son of God had spoken words of comfort to his mourning friends, when he was the present God and they were the forefront of humanity: I would read some of the words he spoke. From them the human nature in each would draw what comfort it could. I took my New Testament from my pocket, and said, without any preamble,

"When our Lord was going to die, he knew that his friends loved him enough to be very wretched about it. He knew that they would be overwhelmed for a time with trouble. He knew, too, that they could not believe the glad end of it all, to which end he looked, across the awful death that awaited him—a death to which that of our friends in the wreck was ease itself. I will just read to you what he said."

I read from the fourteenth to the seventeenth chapter of St John's Gospel. I knew there were worlds of meaning in the words into which I could hardly hope any of them would enter. But I knew likewise that the best things are just those from which the humble will draw the truth they are capable of seeing. Therefore I read as for myself, and left it to them to hear for themselves. Nor did I add any word of comment, fearful of darkening counsel by words without knowledge. For the Bible is awfully set against what is not wise.

When I had finished, I closed the book, rose from the grass, and walked towards the brow of the shore. They rose likewise and followed me. I talked of slight things; the tone was all that communicated between us. But little of any sort was said. The sea lay still before us, knowing nothing of the sorrow it had caused.

We wandered a little way along the cliff. The burial-service was at seven o'clock.

"I have an invalid to visit out in this direction," I said: "would you mind walking with me? I shall not stay more than five minutes, and we shall get back just in time for tea."

They assented kindly. I walked first with one, then with another; heard a little of the story of each; was able to say a few words of sympathy, and point, as it were, a few times, towards the hills whence cometh our aid. I may just mention here, that since our return to Marshmallows, I have had two of them, the young woman and the Scotchman, to visit us there.

The bell began to toll, and we went to church. My companions placed themselves near the dead. I went into the vestry till the appointed hour. I thought, as I put on my surplice, how, in all religions but the Christian, the dead body was a pollution to the temple. Here the Church received it, as a holy thing, for a last embrace ere it went to the earth.

As the dead were already in the church, the usual form could not be carried out. I therefore stood by the communion-table, and there began to read: "I am the resurrection and the life, saith the Lord: he that believeth in me, though he were dead, yet shall he live: and whosoever liveth and believeth in me shall never die."

I advanced as I read, till I came outside the rails, and stood before the dead. There I read the Psalm, "Lord, thou hast been our refuge;" and the glorious lesson, "Now is Christ risen from the dead, and become the first-fruits of them that slept." Then the men of the neighbourhood came forward, and in long solemn procession bore the bodies out of the church, each to its grave. At the church door I stood and read, "Man that is born of a woman;" then went from one to another of the graves, and read over each, as the earth fell on the coffin-lid, "Forasmuch as it hath pleased Almighty God of his great mercy." Then, again, I went back to the church door, and read, "I heard a voice from heaven;" and so to the end of the service.

Leaving the men to fill up the graves, I hastened to lay aside my canonicals, that I might join my guests. But my wife and daughter had already prevailed on them to leave the churchyard.

A word now concerning my own family. Turner insisted on Connie's remaining in bed for two or three days. She looked worse in face—pale and worn; but it was clear from the way she moved in bed, that the fresh power called forth by the shock had not vanished with the moment.

Wynnie was quieter almost than ever. But there was

a constant *secret* light, if I may use the paradox, in her eyes. Percivale was at the house every day, always ready to make himself useful. My wife bore up wonderfully. As yet the much greater catastrophe had come far short of the impression made by the less. When quieter hours should come, however, I could not help fearing that the place would be dreadfully painful to all but the younger ones, who, of course, had the usual child-gift of forgetting. The servants, even Walter, looked thin and anxious.

That Saturday night, I found myself, as I had once or twice found myself before, entirely unprepared to preach. I did not feel anxious, because I did not feel that I was to blame: I had been so much occupied. I had again and again turned my thoughts thitherward, but nothing recommended itself to me so that I could say, "I must take that;" nothing said plainly, "This is what you have to speak of."

As often as I had sought to find fitting matter for my sermon, my mind had turned to death and the grave; but I shrunk from every suggestion, or rather, nothing had come to me that interested myself enough to justify me in giving it to my people. And I always took it as my sole justification in speaking of anything to the flock of Christ, that I cared heartily in my own soul for that thing. Without this consciousness, I was dumb. And I do think, highly as I value prophecy, that a clergyman ought to be at liberty upon occasion to say, "My friends, I cannot preach to-day." What a riddance it would be for the Church—I do not say if every priest were to speak sense, but only if every priest were to abstain from speaking of that in which, at the moment, he feels little or no interest!

I went to bed, which is often the very best thing a man can do; for sleep will bring him from God that which no effort of his own will can compass. I have read somewhere—I will verify it by present search—that Luther's translation of the verse in the psalm, "so he giveth to his beloved sleep," is, "he giveth his beloved sleeping," or while asleep. Yes, so it is—literally, in English, "It is in vain that ye rise early, and then sit long, and eat your bread with care, for to his friends he gives it sleeping." This was my experience in the present instance, for the thought of which I was first conscious when I awoke was—"Why should I talk about death? Every man's heart is now full of death. We have enough of that, even the sum that God has sent us on the wings of the tempest. What I have to do, as the minister of the new covenant, is to speak of life." It flashed in on my mind: "Death is over and gone. The resurrection comes next: I will speak of the raising of Lazarus."

The same moment I knew that I was ready to speak. Shall I or shall I not give my reader the substance of what I said? I wish I knew how many of them would like it, and how many would not. I do not want to bore them with sermons, especially seeing I have always said that no sermons ought to be printed, for in print they are but what the old alchymists would have called a *caput mortuum*, or death's head, namely, a lifeless lump of residuum at the bottom of the crucible; for they have no longer the living human utterance which gives all the power on the minds of the hearers. But I have not, either in this, or in my preceding narrative, attempted to give a sermon as I preached it. I have only sought to present the substance of it in a form fitter for being read, somewhat cleared of the unavoidable, let me say necessary—yes, I will say *valuable* repetitions and enforcements by which the various considerations are pressed upon the minds of the hearers. These are entirely wearisome in print—useless too, for the reader may ponder over every phrase till he finds out the purport of it—if indeed there be such readers now-a-days.

I rose, went down to the bath in the rocks, had a joyous physical ablution, and a swim up and down the narrow cleft, from which I emerged as if myself newly born or raised anew, and then wandered about on the downs full of hope and thankfulness, seeking all I could to plant deep in my mind the long-rooted truths of resurrection, that they might be not only ready to blossom in the warmth of the spring-tides to come, but able to send out some leaves and promissory buds even in the wintry time of the soul, when the fogs of pain steam up from the frozen clay soil of the body, and make the monarch-will totter dizzily upon his throne, to comfort the eyes of the bewildered king, reminding him that the King of kings hath conquered Death and the Grave. There is no perfect faith that cannot laugh at winters and grave-yards, and all the whole array of defiant appearances. The fresh breeze of the morning visited me. "O God!" I said in my heart, "would that when the dark day comes in which I can feel nothing, I may be able to front it with the memory of this day's strength, and so help myself to trust in the Father! I would call to mind the days of old, with David the king."

When I returned to the house, I found that one of the sailors who had been cast ashore with his leg broken, wished to see me. I obeyed, and found him very pale and worn.

"I think I am going, sir," he said; "and I wanted to see you before I die."

"Trust in Christ, and do not be afraid," I returned.

"I prayed to him to save me when I was hanging to the rigging, and if I wasn't afraid then, I 'm not going to be afraid now, dying quietly in my bed. But just look here, sir."

He took from under his pillow something wrapped up in paper, unfolded the envelope, and showed a lump of something—I could not at first tell what. He put it in my hand, and then I saw that it was part of a bible, with nearly the upper half of it worn or cut away, and the rest partly in a state of pulp.

"That 's the bible my mother gave me when I left home first," he said. "I don't know how I came to put it in my pocket, but I think the rope that cut through that when I was lashed to the shrouds would a'most have cut through my ribs if it hadn't been for it."

"Very likely," I returned. "The body of the Bible

has saved your bodily life: may the spirit of it save your spiritual life."

"I think I know what you mean, sir," he panted out. "My mother was a good woman, and I know she prayed to God for me.'

"Would you like us to pray for you in church to-day?"

"If you please, sir; me and Bob Fox. He's nearly as bad as I am."

"We won't forget you," I said. "I will come in after church and see how you are."

I knelt and offered the prayers for the sick, and then took my leave. I did not think the poor fellow was going to die.

I may as well mention here, that he has been in my service ever since. We took him with us to Marshmallows, where he works in the garden and stables, and is very useful. We have to look after him though, for his health continues delicate.

CHAPTER XI.

THE SERMON.

HEN I stood up to preach, I gave them no text, but with the eleventh chapter of the Gospel of St. John open before me, to keep me correct, I proceeded to tell the story in the words God gave me, for who can dare to say that he makes his own commonest speech?

"When Jesus Christ the son of God, and therefore our elder brother, was going about on the earth, eating and drinking with his brothers and sisters, there was one family he loved especially—a family of two sisters and a brother; for, although he loves everybody as much as they can be loved, there are some who can be loved more than others. Only God is always trying to make us such that we can be loved more and more. There are several stories—oh, such lovely stories!—about that family and Jesus. And we have to do with one of them now.

"They lived near the capital of the country, Jerusalem, in a village they called Bethany; and it must have been a great relief to our Lord, when he was worn out with the obstinacy and pride of the great men of the city, to go out to the quiet little town, and into the refuge of Lazarus's house, where every one was more glad at the sound of his feet than at any news that could come to them.

"They had at this time behaved so ill to him in Jerusalem, taking up stones to stone him even, though they dared not quite do it, mad with anger as they were—and all because he told them the truth—that he had gone away to the other side of the great river that divided the country, and taught the people in that quiet place. While he was there, his friend Lazarus was taken ill, and the two sisters, Martha and Mary, sent a messenger to him, to say to him, 'Lord, your friend is very ill.' Only they said it more beautifully than that: 'Lord, behold, he whom thou lovest is sick.' You know when any one is ill, we always want the person whom he loves most to come to him. This is very wonderful. In the worst things that can come to us, the first thought is of love. People, like the Scribes and Pharisees, might say, 'What good can that do him?' And we may not in the least suppose the person we want knows any secret that can cure his pain; yet love is the first thing we think of. And here we are more right than we know; for, at the long last, love will cure everything; which truth, indeed this story will set forth to us. No doubt the heart of Lazarus, ill as he was, longed after his friend, and, very likely, even the sight of Jesus might have given him such strength that the life in him could have driven out the death which had already got one foot across the threshold. But the sisters expected more than this. They believed that Jesus, whom they knew to have driven disease and death out of so many hearts, had only to come and touch him—nay, only to speak a word, to look at him, and their brother was saved. Do you think they presumed in thus expecting? The fact was, they did not believe enough; they had not yet learned to believe that he could cure him all the same whether he came to them or not, because he was always with them. We cannot understand this; but our understanding is never a measure of what is true.

"Whether Jesus knew exactly all that was going to take place, I cannot tell. Some people may feel certain upon points that I dare not feel certain upon. One thing I am sure of—that he did not always know everything beforehand, for he said so himself. It is infinitely more valuable to us, because more beautiful and godlike in him, that he should trust his Father than that he should foresee everything. At all events he knew that his Father did not want him to go to his friends yet. So he sent them a message to the effect that there was a particular reason for this sickness, that the end of it was not the death of Lazarus, but the glory of God. This I think he told them by the same messenger they sent to him; and then instead of going to them he remained where he was.

"But oh, my friends, what shall I say about this wonderful message? Think of being sick for the glory of God! of being shipwrecked for the glory of God! of being drowned for the glory of God! How can the sickness, the fear, the brokenheartedness of his creatures be for the glory of God? What kind of a God can that be? Why just a God so perfectly, absolutely good that the things that look least like it are only the means of clearing our eyes to let us see how good he is. For he is so good that he is not satisfied with *being* good. He loves his children so, that except he can make them good like himself, make them blessed by seeing how good he is, and desiring the same goodness in themselves, he is not satisfied. He is not like a fine, proud bene factor, who is content with doing that which will satisfy his sense of his own glory, but like a mother who puts her arm round her child, and whose heart is sore till she can make her child see the love which is her glory. The glorification of the Son of God is the glorification of the human race, for the glory of God is the glory of man, and that glory is love! Welcome sickness, welcome sorrow, welcome death, revealing that glory!

"The next two verses sound very strangely together, and yet they almost seem typical of all the perplexities of God's dealings. The old painters and poets represented Faith as a beautiful woman holding in her hand a cup of wine and water, with a serpent coiled up within. High-hearted Faith! she scruples not to drink of the life-giving wine and water: she is not repelled by the upcoiled serpent. The serpent she takes but for the type of the eternal wisdom that looks repellent because it is not understood. The wine is good, the water is good, and if the hand of the supreme Fate put that cup in her hand, the serpent itself must be good too, harmless at least to hurt the truth of the water and the wine. But let us read the verses.

"'Now Jesus loved Martha, and her sister, and Lazarus. When he had heard therefore that he was sick, he abode two days still in the same place where he was.'

"Strange! his friend was sick: he abode two days where he was! But remember what we have already heard. The glory of God was infinitely more for the final cure of a dying Lazarus,—who, give him all the life he could have, would yet, without that glory, be in death,—than the mere presence of the Son of God. I say *mere* presence, for, compared with the glory of God, the very presence of his Son, so dissociated, is nothing. He abode where he was that the glory of God, the final cure of humanity, the love that triumphs over death, might shine out and redeem the hearts of men, so that death could not touch them.

"After the two days, the hour had arrived. He said to his disciples, 'Let us go back to Judæa.' They expostulated because of the danger, saying, 'Master, the Jews of late sought to stone thee; and goest thou thither again?' The answer which he gave them I am not sure whether I can thoroughly understand, but I think, in fact I know it must bear on the same region of life—the will of God. I think what he means by walking in the day, is simply, doing the will of God. That was the sole, the all-embracing light in which Jesus ever walked.

I think he means that now he saw plainly what the Father wanted him to do. If he did not see that the Father wanted him to go back to Judæa, and yet went, that would be to go stumblingly, to walk in the darkness. There are twelve hours in the day—one time to act—a time of light and the clear call of duty; there is a night when a man, not seeing where or hearing how, must be content to rest. Something not inharmonious with this, I think, he must have intended; but I do not see the whole thought clearly enough to be sure that I am right. I do think further that it points at a clearer condition of human vision and conviction than I am good enough to understand; though I hope one day to rise into this upper stratum of light.

"Whether his scholars had heard anything of Lazarus yet I do not know. It looks a little as if Jesus had not told them the message he had had from the sisters. But he told them now that he was asleep, and that he was going to wake him. You would think they might have understood this. The idea of going so many miles to wake a man might have surely suggested death. But the disciples were sorely perplexed with many of his words. Sometimes they looked far away for the meaning when the meaning lay in their very hearts; sometimes they looked into their hands for it when it was lost in the grandeur of the ages. But he meant them to see into all that he said by and by, although they could not see into it now. When they understood him better, then they would understand what he said better. And to understand him better, they must be more lik him, and to make them more like him he must go away and give them his spirit—awful mystery which no man but himself can understand.

"Now he had to tell them plainly that Lazarus was dead. They had not thought of death as a sleep. I suppose this was altogether a new and Christian idea. Do not suppose that it applied more to Lazarus than to other dead people. He was none the less dead that Jesus meant to take a weary two days' journey to his sepulchre and wake him. If death is not a sleep, Jesus did not speak the truth when he said Lazarus slept. You may say it was a figure; but a figure that is not like the thing it figures is simply a lie.

"They set out to go back to Judæa. Here we have a glimpse of the faith of Thomas, the doubter. For a doubter is not without faith. The very fact that he doubts, shows that he has some faith. When I find any one hard upon doubters, I always doubt the *quality* of his faith. It is of little use to have a great cable, if the hemp is so poor that it breaks like the painter of a boat. I have known people whose power of believing chiefly consisted in their incapacity for seeing difficulties. Of what fine sort a faith must be that is founded in stupidity, or far worse, in indifference to the truth and the mere desire to get out of hell! That is not a grand belief in the Son of God, the radiation of the Father. Thomas's want of faith was shown in the grumbling, self-pitying way in which he said, 'Let us also go that we may die with him.' His Master had said that he was going to wake him. Thomas said, 'that we may die with him.' You may say, 'he did not understand him.' True, it may be, but his unbelief was the cause of his not understanding him. I suppose Thomas meant this as a reproach to Jesus for putting them all in danger by going back to Judæa; if not, it was only a poor piece of sentimentality. So much for Thomas's unbelief. But he had good and true faith notwithstanding; for *he went with his Master*.

"By the time they reached the neighbourhood of Bethany, Lazarus had been dead four days. Some one ran to the house and told the sisters that Jesus was coming. Martha, as soon as she heard it, rose and went to meet him. It might be interesting at another time to compare the difference of the behaviour of the two sisters upon this occasion with the difference of their behaviour upon another occasion likewise recorded; but with the man dead in his sepulchre, and the hope dead in these two hearts, we have no inclination to enter upon fine distinctions of character. Death and grief bring out the great family likenesses in the living as well as in the dead.

"When Martha came to Jesus, she showed her true though imperfect faith by almost attributing her brother's death to Jesus' absence. But even in the moment, looking in the face of the Master, a fresh hope, a new budding of faith began in her soul. She thought—'what if, after all, he were to bring him to life again!' Oh, trusting heart, how thou leavest the dull-plodding intellect behind thee! While the conceited intellect is reasoning upon the impossibility of the thing, the expectant faith beholds it accomplished. Jesus, responding instantly to her faith, granting her half-born prayer, says, 'Thy brother shall rise again;' not meaning the general truth recognized, or at least assented to by all but the Sadducees, concerning the final resurrection of the dead, but meaning, 'Be it unto thee as thou wilt. I will raise him again.' For there is no steering for a fine effect in the words of Jesus. But these words are too good for Martha to take them as he meant them. Her faith is not quite equal to the belief that he actually will do it. The thing she could hope for afar off she could hardly believe when it came to her very door. 'Oh yes,' she said, her mood falling again to the level of the commonplace, 'of course, at the last day.' Then the Lord turns away her thoughts from the dogmas of her faith to himself, the Life, saying, 'I am the resurrection and the life: he that believeth in me, though he were dead, yet shall he live. And whosoever liveth and believeth in me, shall never die. Believest thou this?' Martha, without understanding what he said more than in a very poor part, answered in words which preserved her honesty entire and yet included all he asked, and a thousandfold more than she could yet believe: 'Yea, Lord; I believe that thou art the Christ, the Son of God, which should come into the world.'

"I dare not pretend to have more than a grand glimmering of the truth of Jesus' words, 'shall never die'; but I am pretty sure that when Martha came to die, she found that there was indeed no such thing as she had meant when she used the ghastly word *death*, and said with her first new breath, 'Verily, Lord, I am not dead.'

"But look how this declaration of her confidence in the Christ operated upon herself. She instantly thought of her sister; the hope that the Lord would do something swelled within her, and, leaving Jesus, she went to find Mary. Whoever has had a true word with the elder brother, straightway will look around him to find his brother, his sister. The family feeling blossoms: he wants his friend to share the glory withal. Martha wants Mary to go to Jesus too.

"Mary heard her, forgot her visitors, rose, and went. They thought she went to the grave: she went to meet its conqueror. But when she came to him, the woman who had chosen the good part praised of Jesus, had but the same words to embody her hope and her grief that her careful and troubled sister had uttered a few minutes before. How often during those four days had not the self-same words passed between them! 'Ah, if he had been here, our brother had not died!' She said so to himself now, and wept, and her friends who had followed her wept likewise. A moment more, and the Master groaned; yet a moment, and he too wept. 'Sorrow is catching;' but this was not the mere infection of sorrow. It went deeper than mere sympathy; for he groaned in his spirit and was troubled. What made him weep? It was when he saw them weeping that he wept. But why should he weep, when he knew how soon their weeping would be turned into rejoicing? It was not for their weeping, so soon to be over, that he wept, but for the human heart everywhere swollen with tears, yea, with griefs that can find no such relief as tears; for these, and for all his brothers and sisters tormented with pain for lack of faith in his Father in heaven, Jesus wept. He saw the blessed well-being of Lazarus on the one side, and on the other the streaming eyes from whose sight he had vanished. The veil between was so thin! yet the sight of those eyes could not pierce it: their hearts must go on weeping—without cause, for his Father was so good. I think it was the helplessness he felt in the impossibility of at once sweeping away the phantasm death from their imagination that drew the tears from the eyes of Jesus. Certainly it was not for Lazarus; it could hardly be for these his friends—save as they represented the humanity which he would help, but could not help even as he was about to help them.

"The Jews saw herein proof that he loved Lazarus; but they little thought it was for them and their people, and for the Gentiles whom they despised, that his tears were now flowing—that the love which pressed the fountains of his weeping was love for every human heart, from Adam on through the ages.

"Some of them went a little further, nearly as far as the sisters, saying, 'Could he not have kept the man from dying?' But it was such a poor thing, after all, that they thought he might have done. They regarded merely this unexpected illness, this early death; for I daresay Lazarus was not much older than Jesus. They did not think that, after all, Lazarus must die some time; that the beloved could be saved, at best, only for a little while. Jesus seems to have heard the remark, for he again groaned in himself.

"Meantime they were drawing near the place where he was buried. It was a hollow in the face of a rock, with a stone laid against it. I suppose the bodies were laid on something like shelves inside the rock, as they are in many sepulchres. They were not put into coffins, but wound round and round with linen.

"When they came before the door of death, Jesus said to them, 'Take away the stone.' The nature of Martha's reply, the realism of it, as they would say now-a-days, would seem to indicate that her dawning faith had sunk again below the horizon; that in the presence of the insignia of death, her faith yielded, even as the faith of Peter failed him when he saw around him the grandeur of the high-priest, and his master bound and helpless. Jesus answered—oh, what an answer!—To meet the corruption and the stink which filled her poor human fancy, 'the glory of God' came from his lips: human fear; horror speaking from the lips of a woman in the very jaws of the devouring death; and the 'said I not unto thee?' from the mouth of him who was so soon to pass worn and bloodless through such a door! 'He stinketh,' said Martha. 'The glory of God,' said Jesus. 'Said I not unto thee, that, if thou wouldest believe, thou shouldest see the glory of God?'

"Before the open throat of the sepulchre Jesus began to speak to his Father aloud. He had prayed to him in his heart before—most likely while he groaned in his spirit. Now he thanked him that he had comforted him, and given him Lazarus as a first-fruit from the dead. But he will be true to the listening people as well as to his ever-hearing Father, therefore he tells why he said the word of thanks aloud—a thing not usual with him, for his father was always hearing him. Having spoken it for the people, he would say that it was for the people.

"The end of it all was that they might believe that God had sent him—a far grander gift than having the dearest brought back from the grave—for he is the Life of men.

"'Lazarus come forth.'"

"And Lazarus came forth, creeping helplessly, with inch-long steps of his linen-bound limbs. 'Ha! Ha! brother! sister!' cries the human heart. The Lord of Life hath taken the prey from the spoiler! he hath emptied the grave! Here comes the dead man, welcome as never was child from the womb—new-born—and in him all the human race new-born from the grave!

"'Loose him and let him go,' and the work is done. The sorrow is over, and the joy is come. Home, home, Martha, Mary, with your Lazarus! He too will go with you, the Lord of the Living. Home, and get the feast ready, Martha! Prepare the food for him who comes hungry from the grave, for him who has called him thence. Home, Mary, to help Martha! What a household yours will be! What wondrous speech will pass between the dead come to life, and the living come to die!

"But what pang is this that makes Lazarus draw hurried breath, and turns Martha's cheeks so white? Ah! at the little window of the heart, the pale eyes of the defeated Horror look in. What! is he there still?

Ah, yes, he will come for Martha, come for Mary, come yet again for Lazarus—yea, come for the Lord of Life himself, and carry all away. But look at the Lord. He knows all about it, and he smiles. Does Martha think of the words he spoke, 'He that liveth and believeth in me shall never die?' Perhaps she does, and like the moon before the sun, her face returns the smile of her Lord.

"This, my friends, is a fancy in form, but it embodies a dear truth. What is it to you and me that he raised Lazarus? We are not called upon to believe that he will raise from the tomb that joy of our hearts which lies buried there beyond our sight. Stop. Are we not? We *are* called upon to believe this. Else the whole story were for us a poor mockery. What is it to us that the Lord raised Lazarus?—Is it nothing to know that our Brother is Lord over the grave? Will the harvest be behind the first-fruits? If he tells us he cannot, for good reasons, raise up our vanished love to-day, or to-morrow, or for all the years of our life to come, shall we not mingle the smile of faithful thanks with the sorrow of present loss, and walk diligently waiting? That he called forth Lazarus showed that he was in his keeping, that he is lord of the living, and that all live to him—that he has a hold of them, and can draw them forth when he will. If this is not true, then the raising of Lazarus is false—I do not mean merely false in fact, but false in meaning. If we believe in him, then in his name, both for ourselves and for our friends, we must deny death and believe in life. Lord Christ, fill our hearts with thy life."

CHAPTER XLI.

CHANGED PLANS.

N a day or two Connie was permitted to rise and take to her couch once more. It seemed strange that she should look so much worse, and yet be so much stronger. The growth of her power of motion was wonderful. As they carried her, she begged to be allowed to put her feet to the ground. Turner yielded, though without quite ceasing to support her. He was satisfied, however, that she could have stood upright for a moment at least. He would not, of course, risk it, and made haste to lay her down.

The time of his departure was coming near, and he seemed more anxious the nearer it came. For Connie continued worn-looking and pale, and her smile, though ever ready to greet me when I entered, had lost much of its light. I noticed, too, that she had the curtain of her window constantly so arranged as to shut out the sea.

I said something to her about it once. Her reply was—

"Papa, I can't bear it. I know it is very silly; but I think I can make you understand how it is. I was so fond of the sea when I came down. It seemed to lie close to my window, with a friendly smile ready for me every morning when I looked out. I dare say it is all from want of faith, but I can't help it: it looks so far away now, like a friend that had failed me, that I would rather not see it."

I saw that the struggling life within her was grievously oppressed; that the things which surrounded her were no longer helpful. Her life had been driven as to its innermost cave, and now when it had been enticed to venture forth and look abroad, a sudden pall had descended upon Nature. I could not help thinking that the good of our visit to Kilkhaven had come, and that evil, from which I hoped we might escape, was following. I left her, and sought Turner.

"It strikes me, Turner," I said, "that the sooner we get out of this the better for Connie."

"I am quite of your opinion. I think the very prospect of leaving the place would do something to restore her. If she is so uncomfortable now, think what it will be in the many winter nights at hand."

"Do you think it would be safe to move her?"

"Far safer than to let her remain. At the worst, she is now far better than when she came. Try her. Hint at the possibility of going home, and see how she will take it."

"Well, I shan't like to be left alone, but if she goes, they must all go, except, perhaps, I might keep Wynnie. But I don't know how her mother would get on without her."

"I don't see why you should stay behind. Mr Weir would be as glad to come as you would be to go, and it can make no difference to Mr Shepherd."

It seemed a very sensible suggestion. I thought a moment. Certainly it was a desirable thing for both my sister and her husband. They had no such reasons as we had for disliking the place, and it would enable her to avoid the severity of yet another winter. I said as much to Turner, and went back to Connie's room.

The light of a lovely sunset was lying outside her window. She was sitting so that she could not see it. I would find out her feeling in the matter without any preamble.

"Would you like to go back to Marshmallows, Connie?" I asked.

Her countenance flashed into light.

"Oh! dear papa! do let us go," she said. "That would be delightful."

"Well, I think we can manage it, if you will only get a little stronger for the journey. The weather is not so good to travel in as when we came down."

"No. But I am ever so much better, you know, than I was then."

The poor girl was already stronger from the mere prospect of going home again. She moved restlessly on her couch, half mechanically put her hand to the curtain pulled it aside, looked out, faced the sun and the sea, and did not draw back. My mind was made up. I left her and went to find Ethelwyn. She heartily approved of the proposal for Connie's sake, and said that it would be scarcely less agreeable to herself. I could see a certain troubled look above her eyes, however.

"You are thinking of Wynnie," I said.

"Yes. It is hard to make one sad for the sake of the rest."

"True. But it is one of the world's recognized necessities."

"No doubt."

"Besides, you don't suppose Percivale can stay here the whole winter. They must part some time."

"Of course. Only they did not expect it so soon."

But here my wife was mistaken.

I went to my study to write to Weir. I had hardly finished my letter when Walter came to say that Mr Percivale wished to see me. I told him to show him in.

"I am just writing home to say that I want my curate to change places with me here, which I know he will be glad enough to do. I see Connie had better go home."

"You will all go then, I presume," returned Percivale.

"Yes, yes; of course."

"Then I need not so much regret that I can stay no longer. I came to tell you that I must leave to-morrow."

"Ah! Going to London?" I said interrogatively.

"Yes. I don't know how to thank you for all your kindness. You have made my summer something like a summer—very different indeed from what it would otherwise have been."

"We have had our share of advantage, and that a large one. We are all glad to have made your acquaintance, Mr Percivale."

He made no answer.

"We shall be passing through London within a week or ten days in all probability. Perhaps you will allow us the pleasure of looking at some of your pictures then?"

His face flushed. What did the flush mean? It was not one of mere pleasure. There was confusion and perplexity in it. But he answered at once:

"I will show you them with pleasure. I fear, however, you will not care for them."

Would this fear account for his embarrassment? I hardly thought it would, but I could not for a moment imagine, with his fine form and countenance before me, that he had any serious reason for shrinking from a visit.

He began to search for a card.

"Oh, I have your address. I shall be sure to pay you a visit. But you will dine with us to-day, of course?" I said.

"I shall have much pleasure," he answered, and took his leave.

I finished my letter to Weir, and went out for a walk.

I remember particularly the thoughts that moved in me and made that walk memorable. Indeed, I think I remember all outside events chiefly by virtue of the inward conditions with which they were associated. Mere outside things I am very ready to forget: moods of my own mind do not so readily pass away, and with the memory of some of them every outward circumstance returns. For a man's life is where the kingdom of heaven is—within him. There are people who, if you ask the story of their lives, have nothing to tell you but the course of the outward events that have constituted, as it were, the clothes of their history. But I know, at the same time, that some of the most important crises in my own history, by which word history I mean my growth towards the right conditions of existence, have been beyond the grasp and interpretation of my intellect: they have passed, as it were, without my consciousness being awake enough to lay hold of their phenomena; the wind had been blowing: I had heard the sound of it but knew not whence it came nor whither it went; only when it was gone, I found myself more responsible, more eager than before.

I remember this walk from the thoughts I had about the great change hanging over us all. I had now arrived at the prime of middle life, and that change which so many would escape if they could, but which will let no man pass, had begun to show itself a real fact upon the horizon of the future. Death looks so far away to the young, that while they acknowledge it unavoidable, the path stretches in such vanishing perspective before them, that they see no necessity for thinking about the end of it yet; and far would I be from saying they ought to think of it. Life is the true object of a man's care: there is no occasion to make himself think about death. But when the vision of the inevitable draws nigh, when it appears plainly on the horizon, though but as a cloud the size of a man's hand, then it is equally foolish to meet it by refusing to meet it, to answer the questions that will arise by declining to think about them. Indeed, it is a question of life then, and not of death. We want to keep fast hold of our life, and, in the strength of that, to look the threatening death in the face. But to my walk that morning.

I wandered on the downs till I came to the place where a solitary rock stands on the top of a cliff looking seaward, in the suggested shape of a monk praying. On the base on which he knelt, I seated myself, and looked out over the Atlantic. How faded the ocean appeared! It seemed as if all the sunny dyes of the summer had been diluted and washed with the fogs of the coming winter, when I thought of the splendour it wore when first from these downs I gazed on the outspread infinitude of space and colour.

"What," I said to myself, at length, "has she done since then? Where is her work visible? She has riven, and battered, and destroyed, and her destruction too has passed away. So worketh Time and its powers. The exultation of my youth is gone; my head is gray; my wife is growing old; our children are pushing us from our stools; we are yielding to the new generation; the glory for us hath departed; our life lies weary before us like that sea, and the night cometh when we can no longer work."

Something like this was passing vaguely through my mind. I sat in a mournful stupor, with a half-consciousness that my mood was false and that I ought to rouse myself and shake it off. There is such a thing as a state of moral dreaming, which closely resembles the intellectual dreaming in sleep. I went on in this false dreamful mood, pitying myself like a child tender over his hurt and nursing his own cowardice, till, all at once, "a little pipling wind," blew on my cheek. The morning was very still: what roused that little wind, I cannot tell; but what that little wind roused, I will try to tell. With that breath on my cheek, something within me began to stir. It grew and grew until the memory of a certain glorious sunset of red and green and gold and blue, which I had beheld from these same heights, dawned within me. I knew that the glory of my youth had not departed, that the very power of recalling with delight that which I had once felt in seeing, was proof enough of that; I knew that I could believe in God all the night long even if the night were long. And the next moment I thought how I had been reviling in my fancy God's servant, the sea. To how many vessels had she not opened a bounteous highway through the waters, with labour, and food, and help, and ministration, glad breezes and swelling sails, healthful struggle, cleansing fear and sorrow, yea and friendly death! Because she had been commissioned to carry this one or that one, this hundred or that thousand of his own creatures from one world to another, was I to revile the servant of a grand and gracious Master? It was blameless in Connie to feel the late trouble so deeply that she could not be glad: she had not had the experience of life, yea, of God, that I had had; she must be helped from without. But for me, it was shameful that I, who knew the heart of my Master, to whom at least he had so often shown his truth, should ever be doleful and oppressed. Yet even me he had now helped from within. The glory of existence as the child of the Infinite had again dawned upon me. The first hour of the evening of my life had, indeed, arrived; the shadows had begun to grow long, so long that I had begun to mark their length; this last little portion of my history had vanished, leaving its few grey ashes behind in the crucible of my life; and the final evening must come, when all my life would lie behind me, and all the memory of it return, with its mornings of gold and red, with its evenings of purple and green; with its dashes of storm, and its foggy glooms; with its white-winged aspirations, its dull-red passions, its creeping envies in brown and black and earthy yellow. But from all the accusations of my conscience, I would turn me to the Lord, for he was called Jesus because he should save his people from their sins. Then I thought what a grand gift it would be to give his people the power hereafter to fight the consequences of their sins. Anyhow, I would trust the Father, who loved me with a perfect love, to lead the soul he had made, had compelled to be, through the gates of the death-birth, into the light of life beyond. I would cast on him the care, humbly challenge him with the responsibility he had himself undertaken, praying only for perfect confidence in him, absolute submission to his will.

I rose from my seat beside the praying monk and walked on. The thought of seeing my own people again filled me with gladness. I would leave those I had here learned to love with regret; but I trusted I had taught them something, and they had taught me much; therefore there could be no end to our relation to each other—it could not be broken, for it was *in the Lord*, which alone can give security to any tie. I should not, therefore, sorrow as if I were to see their faces no more.

I now took my farewell of that sea and those cliffs. I should see them often ere we went, but I should not feel so near them again. Even this parting said that I must "sit loose to the world,"—an old Puritan phrase, I suppose; that I could gather up only its uses, treasure its best things, and must let all the rest go; that those things I called mine, earth, sky, and sea, home, books, the treasured gifts of friends, had all to leave me, belong to others, and help to educate them. I should not need them. I should have my people, my souls, my beloved faces tenfold more, and could well afford to part with these. Why should I mind this chain passing to my eldest boy, when it was only his mother's hair, and I should have his mother still?

So my thoughts went on thinking themselves, until at length I yielded passively to their flow.

I found Wynnie looking very grave when I went into

the drawing-room. Her mother was there too, and Mr Percivale. It seemed rather a moody party. They wakened up a little, however, after I entered, and before dinner was over, we were all chatting together merrily.

"How is Connie?" I asked Ethelwyn.

"Wonderfully better already," she answered.

"I think everybody seems better," I said. "The very idea of home seems reviving to us all."

Wynnie darted a quick glance at me, caught my eyes, which was more than she had intended, and blushed; sought refuge in a bewildered glance at Percivale, caught his eyes in turn, and blushed yet deeper. He plunged instantly into conversation, not without a certain involuntary sparkle in those eyes.

"Did you go to see Mrs Stokes this morning?" he asked.

"No," I answered. "She does not want much visiting now; she is going about her work, apparently in good health. Her husband says she is not like the same woman; and I hope he means that in more senses than one, though I do not choose to ask him any questions about his wife."

I did my best to keep up the conversation, but every now and then after this it fell like a wind that would not blow. I withdrew to my study. Percivale and Wynnie went out for a walk. The next morning he left by the coach—early. Turner went with him.

Wynnie did not seem very much dejected. I thought that perhaps the prospect of meeting him again in London kept her up.

CHAPTER XLII.

THE STUDIO.

I WILL not linger over our preparations or our leave-takings. The most ponderous of the former were those of the two boys, who, as they had wanted to bring down a chest as big as a corn-bin, full of lumber, now wanted to take home two or three boxes filled with pebbles, great oyster-shells, and sea-weed.

Weir, as I had expected, was quite pleased to make the exchange. An early day had been fixed for his arrival; for I thought it might be of service to him to be introduced to the field of his labours. Before he came, I had gone about among the people, explaining to them some of my reasons for leaving them sooner than I had intended, and telling them a little about my successor, that he might not appear among them quite as a stranger. He was much gratified by their reception of him, and had no fear of not finding himself quite at home with them. I promised, if I could comfortably manage it, to pay them a short visit the following summer, and, as the weather was now getting quite cold, hastened our preparations for departure.

I could have wished that Turner had been with us on the journey, but he had been absent from his cure to the full extent that his conscience would permit, and I had not urged him. He would be there to receive us, and we had got so used to the management of Connie, that we did not feel much anxiety about the travelling. We resolved, if she seemed strong enough as we went along, to go right through London, making a few days there the only break in the transit.

It was a bright cold morning when we started. But Connie could now bear the air so well, that we set out with the carriage open, nor had we occasion to close it. The first part of our railway journey was very pleasant. But when we drew near London, we entered a thick fog, and before we arrived, a small dense November rain was falling. Connie looked a little dispirited, partly from weariness, but no doubt from the change in the weather.

"Not very cheerful, this, Connie, my dear," I said.

"No, papa," she answered; "but we are going home, you know."

Going home. It set me thinking—as I had often been set thinking before, always with fresh discovery and a new colour on the dawning sky of hope. I lay back in the carriage and thought how the November fog this evening in London, was the valley of the shadow of death we had to go through on the way *home.* A shadow like this would fall upon me ; the world would grow dark and life grow weary; but I should know it was the last of the way home.

Then I began to question myself wherein the idea of this home consisted. I knew that my soul had ever yet felt the discomfort of strangeness, more or less, in the midst of its greatest blessedness. I knew that as the thought of water to the thirsty *soul*, for it is the soul far more than the body that thirsts even for the material water, such is the thought of home to the wanderer in a strange country. As the weary soul pines for sleep, and every heart for the cure of its own bitterness, so my heart and soul had often pined for their home. Did I know, I asked myself, where or what that home was? It could consist in no change of place or of circumstance; no mere absence of care; no accumulation of repose; no blessed communion even with those whom my soul loved: in the midst of it all I should be longing for a homelier home—one into which I might enter with a sense of infinitely more absolute peace than a conscious child could know in the arms, upon the bosom of his mother. In the closest contact of human soul with human soul, when all the atmosphere of thought was rosy with love, again and yet again on the far horizon would the dim, lurid flame of unrest shoot for a moment through the enchanted air, and Psyche would know that not yet had she reached her home. As I thought this I lifted my eyes, and saw those of my wife and Connie fixed on mine, as if they were reproaching me for saying in my soul that I could not be quite at home with them.

Then I said in my heart, "Come home with me, beloved—there is but one home for us all. When we find—in proportion as each of us finds—that home, shall we be gardens of delight to each other—little chambers of rest—galleries of pictures—wells of water."

Again, what was this home? God himself. His thoughts, his will, his love, his judgments, are man's home. To think his thoughts, to choose his will, to love his loves, to judge his judgments, and thus to know that he is in us, with us, is to be at home. And to pass through the valley of the shadow of death is the way home, but only thus, that as all changes have hitherto led us nearer to this home, the knowledge of God, so this greatest of all outward changes—for it is but an outward change—will surely usher us into a region where there will be fresh possibilities of drawing nigh in heart, soul, and mind to the Father of us. It is the father, the mother, that make for the child his home. Indeed. I doubt if the home-idea is complete to the parents of a family themselves when they remember that their fathers and mothers have vanished.

At this point something rose in me seeking utterance.

"Won't it be delightful, wife," I began, "to see our fathers and mothers such a long way back in heaven?"

But Ethelwyn's face gave so little response, that I felt at once how dreadful a thing it was not to have had a good father or mother. I do not know what would have become of me but for a good father. I wonder how anybody ever can be good that has not had a good father. How dreadful not to be a good father or good mother! Every father who is not good, every mother who is not good, just makes it as impossible to believe in God as it can be made. But he is our one good Father, and does not leave us, even should our fathers and mothers have thus forsaken us, and left him without a witness.

Here the evil odour of brick-burning invaded my nostrils, and I knew that London was about us. A few moments after, we reached the station, where a carriage was waiting to take us to our hotel.

Dreary was the change from the stillness and sunshine of Kilkhaven to the fog and noise of London; but Connie slept better that night than she had slept for a good many nights before.

After breakfast the next morning, I said to Wynnie,

"I am going to see Mr Percivale's studio, my dear: have you any objection to going with me?"

"No, papa," she answered blushing. "I have never seen an artist's studio in my life."

"Come along then. Get your bonnet at once. It rains, but we shall take a cab, and it won't matter."

She ran off, and was ready in a few minutes. We gave the driver directions, and set out. It was a long drive. At length he stopped at the door of a very common-looking house, in a very dreary-looking street, in which no man could possibly identify his own door except by the number. I knocked. A woman who looked at once dirty and cross, the former probably the cause of the latter, opened the door, gave a bare assent to my question whether Mr Percivale was at home, withdrew to her den with the words "second-floor," and left us to find our own way up the two flights of stairs. This, however, involved no great difficulty. We knocked at the door of the front-room. A well-known voice cried, "Come in," and we entered.

Percivale, in a short velvet coat, with his palette on his thumb, advanced to meet us cordially. His face wore a slight flush, which I attributed solely to pleasure, and nothing to any awkwardness in receiving us in such a poor place as he occupied. I cast my eyes round the room. Any romantic notions Wynnie might have indulged concerning the marvels of a studio, must have paled considerably at the first glance around Percivale's room—plainly the abode if not of poverty, then of self-denial, although I suspected both. A common room, with no carpet save a square in front of the fire-place; no curtains except a piece of something like drugget nailed flat across all the lower half of the window to make the light fall from upwards; two or three horse-hair chairs, nearly worn out; a table in a corner, littered with books and papers; a horrible lay-figure, at the present moment dressed apparently for a scarecrow; a large easel, on which stood a half-finished oil-painting—these constituted almost the whole furniture of the room. With his pocket-handkerchief Percivale dusted one chair for Wynnie and another for me. Then standing before us, he said:

"This is a very shabby place to receive you in, Miss Walton, but it is all I have got."

"A man's life consisteth not in the abundance of the things he possesses," I ventured to say.

"Thank you," said Percivale. "I hope not. It is well for me it should not."

"It is well for the richest man in England that it should not," I returned. "If it were not so, the man who could eat most would be the most blessed."

"There are people, even of my acquaintance, however, who seem to think it does."

"No doubt; but happily their thinking so will not make it so even for themselves."

"Have you been very busy since you left us, Mr Percivale?" asked Wynnie.

"Tolerably," he answered. "But I have not much to show for it. That on the easel is all. I hardly like to let you look at it, though."

"Why?" asked Wynnie.

"First, because the subject is painful. Next, because it is so unfinished that none but a painter could do it justice."

"But why should you paint subjects you do not like people to look at?"

"I very much want people to look at them."

"Why not us, then?" said Wynnie.

"Because you do not need to be pained."

"Are you sure it is good for you to pain anybody?" I said.

"Good is done by pain—is it not?" he asked.

"Undoubtedly. But whether *we* are wise enough to know when and where and how much is the question."

"Of course I do not make the pain my object."

"If it comes only as a necessary accompaniment, that may alter the matter greatly," I said. "But still I am not sure that anything in which the pain predominates can be useful in the best way."

"Perhaps not," he returned.—"Will you look at the daub?"

"With much pleasure," I replied, and we rose and stood before the easel. Percivale made no remark, but left us to find out what the picture meant. Nor had I long to look before I understood it—in a measure at least.

It represented a garret-room in a wretchedly ruinous condition. The plaster had come away in several places, and through between the laths in one spot hung the tail of a great rat. In a dark corner lay a man dying. A woman sat by his side, with her eyes fixed, not on his face, though she held his hand in hers, but on the open door, where in the gloom you could just see the struggles of two undertaker's men to get the coffin past the turn of the landing toward the door. Through the window there was one peep of the blue sky, whence a ray of sunlight fell on the one scarlet blossom of a geranium in a broken pot on the window-sill outside.

"I do not wonder you did not like to show it," I said. "How can you bear to paint such a dreadful picture?"

"It is a true one. It only represents a fact."

"All facts have not a right to be represented."

"Surely you would not get rid of painful things by huddling them out of sight?"

"No; nor yet by gloating upon them."

"You will believe me that it gives me anything but pleasure to paint such pictures—as far as the subject goes," he said with some discomposure.

"Of course. I know you well enough by this time to know that. But no one could hang it on his wall who would not either gloat on suffering or grow callous to it. Whence then would come the good I cannot doubt you propose to yourself as your object in painting the picture? If it had come into my possession, I would"——

"Put it in the fire," suggested Percivale, with a strange smile.

"No. Still less would I sell it. I would hang it up with a curtain before it, and only look at it now and then when I thought my heart was in danger of growing hardened to the sufferings of my fellow-men, and forgetting that they need the Saviour."

"I could not wish it a better fate. That would answer my end."

"Would it now? Is it not rather those who care little or nothing about such matters that you would like to influence? Would you be content with one solitary person like me? And, remember, I wouldn't buy it. I would rather not have it. I could hardly bear to know it was in my house. I am certain you cannot do people good by showing them *only* the painful. Make it as painful as you will, but put some hope into it, something to show that action is worth taking in the affair. From mere suffering people will turn away, and you cannot blame them. Every show of it without hinting at some door of escape, only urges them to forget it all. Why should they be pained if it can do no good?"

"For the sake of sympathy, I should say," answered Percivale.

"They would rejoin, 'It is only a picture. Come along.' No; give people hope, if you would have them act at all—in anything."

"I was almost hoping you would read the picture rather differently. You see there is a bit of blue sky up there, and a bit of sunshiny scarlet in the window."

He looked at me curiously as he spoke.

"I can read it so for myself, and have metamorphosed its meaning so. But you only put in the sky and the scarlet to heighten the perplexity and make the other look more terrible."

"Now I know that as an artist I have succeeded, however I may have failed otherwise. I did so mean it. But knowing you would dislike the picture, I almost hoped, in my cowardice, as I said, that you would read your own meaning into it."

Wynnie had not said a word. As I turned away from the picture, I saw that she was looking quite distressed, but whether by the picture, or the freedom with which I had remarked upon it, I do not know. My eyes falling on a little sketch in sepia, I began to examine it, in the hope of finding something more pleasant to say. I perceived in a moment, however, that it was nearly the same thought, only treated in a gentler and more poetic mode. A girl lay dying on her bed. A youth held her hand. A torrent of summer sunshine fell through the window, and made a lake of glory upon the floor. I turned away.

"You like that better, don't you, papa?" said Wynnie, tremulously.

"It is beautiful, certainly," I answered. "And if it were only one, I should enjoy it—as a mood. But coming after the other, it seems but the same thing more weakly embodied."

I confess I was a little vexed. For I had got much interested in Percivale, for his own sake, as well as for my daughter's, and I had expected better things from him. But I saw that I had gone too far.

"I beg your pardon, Mr Percivale," I said. "I fear I have been too free in my remarks. I know, likewise, that I am a clergyman and not a painter, and therefore incapable of giving the praise which I have little doubt your art at least deserves."

"I trust that honesty cannot offend me, however much and justly it may pain me."

"But now I have said my worst, I should much like o see what else you have at hand to show me."

"Unfortunately I have too much at hand. Let me see."

He strode to the other end of the room where several pictures were leaning against the wall with their faces turned towards it. From these he chose one, but before showing it fitted it into an empty frame that stood beside. He then brought it forward and set it on the easel. I will describe it, and then my reader will understand the admiration which broke from me after I had regarded it for a time.

A dark hill rose against the evening sky which shone through a few thin pines on its top. Along a road on the hill-side, four squires bore a dying knight—a man past the middle age. One behind carried his helm, and another led his horse, whose fine head only appeared in the picture. The head and countenance of the knight were very noble, telling of many a battle, and ever for the right. The last had doubtless been gained, for one might read victory as well as peace in the dying look. The party had just reached the edge of a steep descent, from which you saw the valley below, with the last of the harvest just being reaped, while the shocks stood all about in the fields, under the place of the sunset. The sun had been down for some little time. There was on gold left in the sky, only a little dull saffron; but plenty of that lovely liquid green of the autumn sky, divided with a few streaks of pale rose. The depth of the sky overhead, which you could not see for the arrangement of the picture, was mirrored lovelily in a piece of water that lay in the centre of the valley.

"My dear fellow!" I cried, "why did you not show me this first, and save me from saying so many unkind things? Here is a picture to my own heart. It is glorious. Look here, Wynnie," I went on. "You see it is evening. The sun's work is done, and he has set in glory, leaving his good name behind him in a lovely harmony of colour. The old knight's work is done too; his day has set in the storm of battle, and he is lying lapt in the coming peace. They are bearing him home to his couch and his grave. Look at their faces in the dusky light. They are all mourning for and honouring the life that is ebbing away. But he is gathered to his fathers like a shock of corn fully ripe; and so the harvest stands golden in the valley beneath. The picture would not be complete, however, if it did not tell us of the deep heaven overhead, the symbol of that heaven whither he who has done his work is bound: what a lovely idea to represent it by means of the water, the heaven embodying itself in the earth, as it were, that we may see it! And observe how that dusky hillside, and those tall slender mournful-looking pines, with that sorrowful sky between, lead the eye and point the heart upward towards that heaven. It is indeed a grand picture—full of feeling—a picture and a parable." *

I looked at the girl. Her eyes were full of tears—either called forth by the picture itself, or by the pleasure of finding something of Percivale's work appreciated by me who had spoken so hardly of his other pictures.

"I cannot tell you how glad I am that you like it," she said.

"Like it!" I returned. "I am simply delighted with it—more than I can express—so much delighted that if I could have this alongside of it, I should not mind

* This is a description, from memory only, of a picture painted by Arthur Hughes.

hanging that other, that hopeless garret, on the most public wall I have."

"Then," said Wynnie bravely, though in a tremulous voice, "you confess, don't you, papa, that you were *too* hard on Mr Percivale at first?"

"Not too hard on his picture, my dear; and that was all he had yet given me to judge by. No man should paint a picture like that. You are not bound to disseminate hopelessness; for where there is no hope, there can be no sense of duty."

"But surely, papa, Mr Percivale has *some* sense of duty," said Wynnie, in an almost angry tone.

"Assuredly, my love. Therefore I argue that he has some hope; and therefore again that he has no right to publish such a picture."

At the word *publish* Percivale smiled. But Wynnie went on with her defence.

"But you see, papa, that Mr Percivale does not paint such pictures only. Look at the other."

"Yes, my dear. But pictures are not like poems, lying side by side in the same book, so that the one can counteract the other. The one of these might go to the stormy Hebrides, and the other to the vale of Avalon. But even then, I should be strongly inclined to criticize the poem, whatever position it stood in, that had *nothing*, positively nothing, of the aurora in it."

Here let me interrupt the course of our conversation to illustrate it by a remark on a poem which has appeared within the last twelvemonth from the pen of the greatest living poet, and one who, if I may dare to judge, will continue the greatest for many, many years to come. It is only a little song, "I stood on a tower in the wet." I have found few men who, whether from the influence of those prints which are always on the outlook for something to ridicule, or from some other cause, did not laugh at the poem. I thought and think it a lovely poem, although I am not quite sure of the transposition of words in the last two lines. But I do not *approve* of the poem, just because there is no hope in it. It lacks that touch or hint of *red* which is as essential, I think, to every poem as to every picture—the life-blood—the one pure colour. In his hopeful moods, let a man put on his singing robes, and chant aloud the words of gladness—or of grief, I care not which—to his fellows; in his hours of hopelessness, let him utter his thoughts only to his inarticulate violin, or in the evanescent sounds of any other stringed instrument; let him commune with his own heart on his bed, and be still; let him speak to God face to face if he may—only he cannot do that and continue hopeless; but let him not sing aloud in such a mood into the hearts of his fellows, for he cannot do them much good thereby. If it were a fact that there is no hope, it would not be a *truth*. No doubt, if it were a fact, it ought to be known; but who will dare be confident that there is no hope? Therefore, I say, let the hopeless moods, at least, if not the hopeless men, be silent.

"He could refuse to let the one go without the other," said Wynnie.

"Now you are talking like a child, Wynnie, as indeed

all partisans do at the best. He might sell them together, but the owner would part them.—If you will allow me, I will come and see both the pictures again to-morrow."

Percivale assured me of welcome, and we parted, I declining to look at any more pictures that day, but not till we had arranged that he should dine with us in the evening.

CHAPTER XLIII.

HOME AGAIN.

WILL not detain my readers with the record of the few days we spent in London. In writing the account of it, as in the experience of the time itself, I feel that I am near home, and grow the more anxious to reach it. Ah! I am growing a little anxious after another home, too; for the house of my tabernacle is falling to ruins about me. What a word *home* is! To think that God has made the world so that you have only to be born in a certain place, and live long enough in it to get at the secret of it, and henceforth that place is to you a *home* with all the wonderful meaning in the word. Thus the whole earth is a home to the race; for every spot of it shares in the feeling: some one of the family loves it as *his* home. How rich the earth seems when we so regard it—crowded with the loves of home! Yet I am now getting ready to *go home*—to leave this world of homes, and go home. When I reach that home, shall I even then seek yet to go home? Even then, I believe, I shall seek a yet warmer, deeper, truer home in the deeper knowledge of God—in the truer love of my fellow-man. Eternity will be, my heart and my faith tell me, a travelling homeward, but in jubilation and confidence and the vision of the beloved.

When we had laid Connie once more in her own room, at least the room which since her illness had come to be called hers, I went up to my study. The familiar faces of my books welcomed me. I threw myself in my reading-chair, and gazed around me with pleasure. I felt it so homely here. All my old friends—whom somehow I hoped to see some day—present there in the spirit ready to talk with me any moment when I was in the mood, making no claim upon my attention when I was not! I felt as if I should like, when the hour should come, to die in that chair, and pass into the society of the witnesses in the presence of the tokens they had left behind them.

I heard shouts on the stair, and in rushed the two boys.

"Papa! papa!" they were crying together.

"What is the matter?"

"We 've found the big chest just where we left it."

"Well, did you expect it would have taken itself off?"

"But there 's everything in it just as we left it."

"Were you afraid then that, the moment you left it, it would turn itself upside down, and empty itself of all its contents on the floor?"

They laughed, but apparently with no very keen appreciation of the attempt at a joke.

"Well, papa, I did not think anything about it; but—but—but—there everything is as we left it."

With this triumphant answer, they turned and hurried a little abashed, out of the room; but not many moment elapsed before the sounds that arose from them were sufficiently reassuring as to the state of their spirits. When they were gone, I forgot my books in the attempt to penetrate and understand the condition of my boys thoughts. And I soon came to see that they were right and I was wrong. It was the movement of that undeveloped something in us which makes it possible for us in everything to give thanks. It was the wonder of the discovery of the existence of law. There was nothing that they could understand, *à priori*, to necessitate the remaining of the things where they had left them. No doubt there was a reason in the nature of God, why all things should hold together, whence springs the law of gravitation, as we call it; but as far as the boys could understand of this, all things might as well have been arranged for flying asunder, so that no one could expect to find anything where he had left it. I began to see yet further into the truth that in everything we must give thanks, and whatever is not of faith is sin. Even the laws of nature reveal the character of God, not merely as regards their ends, but as regards their kind, being of necessity fashioned after ideal facts of his own being and will.

I rose and went down to see if everybody was getting

settled, and how the place looked. I found Ethel already going about the house as if she had never left it, and as if we all had just returned from a long absence, and she had to show us home-hospitality. Wynnie had vanished, but I found her by and by in the favourite haunt of her mother before her marriage—beside the little pond called the Bishop's Basin, of which I do not think I have ever told my readers the legend. But why should I mention it, for I cannot tell it now? The frost lay thick in the hollow when I went down there to find her; the branches, lately clothed with leaves, stood bare and icy around her. Ethelwyn and I had almost forgotten that there was anything out of the common in connexion with the house; the horror of this mysterious spot had laid hold upon Wynnie. I resolved that that night I would, in her mother's presence, tell her all the legend of the place, and the whole story of how I won her mother. I did so, and I think it made her trust us more. But now I left her there, and went to Connie. She lay in her bed, for her mother had got her thither at once, a perfect picture of blessed comfort. There was no occasion to be uneasy about her. I was so pleased to be at home again with such good hopes that I could not rest, but went wandering everywhere, into places even which I had not entered for ten years at least, and found fresh interest in everything. For this was home, and here I was.

Now I fancy my readers, looking forward to the end, and seeing what a small amount of print is left, blaming me; some, that I have roused curiosity without satisfying it; others, that I have kept them so long over a dull book and a lame conclusion. But out of a life one cannot always cut complete portions, and serve them up in nice shapes. I am well aware that I have not told them the *fate*, as some of them would call it, of either of my daughters. This I cannot develop now, even as far as it is known to me; but, if it is any satisfaction to them to know this much—and it will be all that some of them mean by *fate*, I fear—I may as well tell them now that Wynnie has been Mrs Percivale for many years, with a history well worth recounting; and that Connie has had a quiet happy life for nearly as long, as Mrs Turner. She has never got strong, but has very tolerable health. Her husband watches her with the utmost care and devotion. My Ethelwyn is still with me. Harry is gone home. Charlie is a barrister of the Middle Temple. And Dora—I must not forget Dora—well, I will say nothing about her *fate*, for good reasons—it is not quite determined yet. Meantime she puts up with the society of her old father and mother, and is something else than unhappy, I fully believe.

"And Connie's baby?" asks some one out of ten thousand readers. I have no time to tell you about her now; but as you know her so little it cannot be such a trial to remain, for a time at least, unenlightened with regard to her *fate*.

The only other part of my history which could contain anything like incident enough to make it interesting in print, is a period I spent in London some few years after the time of which I have now been writing. But I am getting too old to regard the commencement of another history with composure. The labour of thinking into sequences, even the bodily labour of writing, grows more and more severe. I fancy I can think correctly still; but the effort necessary to express myself with corresponding correctness becomes, in prospect, at least, sometimes almost appalling. I must therefore take leave of my patient reader—for surely every one who has followed me through all that I have here written, well deserves the epithet—as if the probability that I shall write no more were a certainty, bidding him farewell with one word: "*Friend, hope thou in God*," and for a parting gift offering him a new, and, I think, a true rendering of the first verse of the eleventh chapter of the Epistle to the Hebrews:—

"Now faith is the essence of hopes, the trying of things unseen."

Good-bye.

www.ingramcontent.com/pod-product-compliance
Lightning Source LLC
LaVergne TN
LVHW021102110826
845150LV00001B/149

* 9 7 8 1 4 2 5 5 6 5 7 1 8 *